# FLESHING THE ARCHIVE

# FLESHING THE ARCHIVE

## *An Intimate Genealogy of Chicana Knowledge Praxis*

MARÍA EUGENIA COTERA

UNIVERSITY OF TEXAS PRESS
*Austin*

Cotera, María Eugenia, "Fleshing the Archive: Reflections on Chicana Memory Practice", *Oral History* vol 49, no. 2 (2021): 49–56 by permission of the Oral History Society (www.ohs.org.uk)


Printed in the United States of America
First edition, 2025



♾ The paper used in this book meets the minimum requirements of ANSI/NISO Z39.48-1992 (R1997) (Permanence of Paper).

Library of Congress Cataloging-in-Publication Data

Names: Cotera, María Eugenia, 1964– author
Title: Fleshing the archive : an intimate genealogy of Chicana knowledge praxis / María Eugenia Cotera.
Other titles: Intimate genealogy of Chicana knowledge praxis | Joe R. and Teresa Lozano Long series in Latin American and Latino art and culture
Description: First edition. | Austin : University of Texas Press, [2026] | Series: Latin American and Latino art and culture | Includes bibliographical references.
Identifiers: LCCN 2025012433 (print) LCCN 2025012434 (ebook)
ISBN 978-1-4773-3295-5 (hardcover)
ISBN 978-1-4773-3296-2 (paperback)
ISBN 978-1-4773-3297-9 (pdf)
ISBN 978-1-4773-3298-6 (epub)
Subjects: LCSH: Cotera, María Eugenia, 1964– | Cotera, Martha | Anzaldúa, Gloria | Mexican American women—United States—History—20th century | Feminism—United States—History—20th century | Mexican American women—Intellectual life | Mexican American women—Political activity | Women historians—United States | Archives—Social aspects—United States | Digital preservation—United States | Oral history—United States | Collective memory—United States | Autobiographical memory | Ethnohistory—United States | Mexican American women—United States—History
Classification: LCC E184.M5 C668 2026 (print) | LCC E184.M5 (ebook) | DDC 305.48/868720730904—dc23/eng/20250908
LC record available at https://lccn.loc.gov/2025012433
LC ebook record available at https://lccn.loc.gov/2025012434

doi:10.7560/332955

*The University of Texas Press gratefully acknowledges the Joe R. and Teresa Lozano Long Endowment in Latin American and Latino Art and Culture for its support of this publication.*

# CONTENTS

# ILLUSTRATIONS

# FLESHING THE ARCHIVE

# Introduction

# CHICANA KNOWLEDGE PRAXIS BEFORE AND AFTER THE DIGITAL TURN

*The master detective assumes initially there is no such thing as an innocent object or event. She stops along the way interrogating lamp-posts and dead cats, incidentally making herself ridiculous to passersby. But gradually, through great patience and a little luck, she amasses enough by way of object and event that when spread out all across her bed, or her breakfast table, or even her living room carpet they begin to group themselves into little piles of similarity. Aha, says the detective at the end of much rumination, and sends out little notes inviting the well-dressed suspects into the drawing room for a scene of revelation and finally accusation.*

SHEILA ORTIZ TAYLOR, *Southbound*

For the past fifteen years I have made a scholarly home in the Chicana archive, piecing together a story of becoming from the scattered traces of memory preserved in women's personal collections. Like Sheila Ortiz Taylor's "master detective," I have sought out these archival traces—tracking the networks and knowledge projects that they document—not only in the interests of historiographic justice, but also because I believe that the futures interrupted, the paths not taken, and the truncated possibilities to which they bear witness remain relevant to our work as Chicanx feminist scholar-activists today.[1] In *Fleshing the Archive* I offer a genealogy of Chicana feminist knowledge praxis that tracks the strategies Chicanas deployed as they moved in, through, and around sites of social, political, and institutional power in the late twentieth century.

The book draws directly from archival documents and oral histories collected by the Chicana por Mi Raza Digital Memory Collective, a post-custodial digital archive that I launched in 2009 in partnership with Linda Garcia Merchant, which currently houses hundreds of oral history video recordings with Chicanas and Latinas active in the movement years, as well as thousands of digitized items from their personal collections. I turn to this rich composite text to tell a story about the radical knowledge forms that Chicanas produced in the movement years. Charting what Emma Pérez has termed "sitios y lenguas," or the sites and discourses of these modalities of Chicana knowledge—from Martha Cotera's work as an information specialist and feminist writer in Texas, to the generation of Chicana scholar-activists who carved out a space for the study of "la mujer" in California, to the queer world making of the poet, scholar, and filmmaker Osa Hidalgo de la Riva—*Fleshing the Archive* surfaces a hidden genealogy that demonstrates how these ephemeral (and always precarious) efforts to reimagine knowledge as a collective and community-building endeavor speak to the urgencies of the present moment.[2]

In this genealogy of knowledge praxis, I move beyond simply summoning the spectral presence of Chicanas in the movement years—as stable subjects that can be "recovered" and accorded their proper place in history—to explore the epistemological and methodological implications of their persistent haunting and our equally persistent desire to revisit the utopian imaginaries of the past. Indeed, in building the archive of embodied and documentary memory from which this book draws, I have been struck time and time again by the resonances between our twenty-first-century Chicanx digital praxis and the knowledge projects that Chicanas undertook in the 1970s: the shared impulse to create collaborative sites of information exchange, to challenge the hierarchies of the university, to expand our pedagogy beyond the classroom, to imagine radical futures in the shadow of institutional precarity. These moments of startling convergence have surfaced hidden technologies of resistance that beckon us to recognize ourselves in the radical futures imagined by Chicanas in the 1970s. As José Esteban Muñoz so eloquently put it in *Cruising Utopia* (his queer countergenealogy), we must "think and feel a *then and there*," not only to uncover a history formerly hidden from view but also to challenge "the here and now's totalizing rendering of reality." Searching this landscape of truncated utopian possibilities to construct my own genealogy of praxis, I surface not only the who, what, when, and where of important Chicana knowledge formations in the 1970s but also the *how*, for it is precisely the question of praxis that links our contemporary efforts to change the world and those of the generation that preceded us, and perhaps more importantly, such a genealogy offers up, in Muñoz's words, "blueprints and schemata of a forward-dawning futurity."[3]

Indeed, a focus on praxis reveals not only the historical and continuing conditions of precarity in which Chicana knowledge is elaborated but also a long tradition of imagining otherwise: from community-based research and cultural centers to the development of Chicana bibliographies, syllabi, and curricula and collectives that would establish a foothold for Chicana feminist studies in the academy, to our current efforts to document and preserve Chicana history through digital tools.[4] In its simplest definition, "praxis" means process, but as a philosophical concept it also poses an important challenge to the mind/body, thought/action binary that often structures our understanding of knowledge and its practical applications. Praxis is at the center of Karl Marx's conceptualization of human activity and agency in that it describes the "free, universal, creative and self-creative activity through which man creates (makes, produces) and changes (shapes) his historical, human world and himself; an activity specific to man, through which he is basically differentiated from all other beings."[5] The Brazilian philosopher and educator Paolo Freire took up this humanistic strain in Marx's thinking about praxis, placing it at the center of his conceptualization of *conscientização* (*concientización*, or consciousness-raising), a horizontal and dialogic process of knowledge creation whereby individuals unmask the nature of oppression through collective reflection and action. In *Pedagogy of the Oppressed*, which was published in 1968 and read widely by movement organizers in the late 1960s and the 1970s, particularly those engaged in the struggle for Chicano studies, Freire outlined the stakes of what was an essentially "educational" process, noting that

> one of the gravest obstacles to the achievement of liberation is that oppressive reality absorbs those within it and thereby acts to submerge human beings' consciousness. Functionally, oppression is domesticating. To no longer be prey to its force, one must emerge from it and turn upon it. This can be done only by means of the praxis: reflection and action upon the world in order to transform it.[6]

This concept of praxis as "reflection and action" was central to the elaboration of movement theories of oppression as well as the development of strategies for social transformation. For example, consciousness-raising sessions—which were not exclusive to the women's movement—were essentially educational projects that engaged participants in reading, study, reflection, and what Freire called "problem-posing," with the specific aim of developing strategies for social change. Direct actions that were a result of this process of concientización would also be analyzed and evaluated (*crítica/autocrítica*), and thus they actively shaped evolving theories and practices of social change. As applied in movement contexts, praxis was the dialectical entwinement of theory/reflection and action/creation, and thus necessitated that "theory" be put in the service of social transformation and, in turn, that lived experience inform theories of oppression.

Chicana knowledge praxis in the 1970s and 1980s operated at the intersection of popular education/organizing and academic knowledge systems. While there were several institutionally based efforts to develop curricula and increase numbers of faculty who were committed to building programs of study, Chicana knowledge projects in this period were not limited to academic institutions. Instead, they engaged on all fronts of the struggle for social justice, from political organizing to writing and research, to the production of poetry, stories, and visual images that shaped the movement imaginary. Refusing to wait for institutional recognition to produce knowledge, Chicanas mostly self-published their poetry, essays, books, newspapers, and bibliographies in limited runs that were later duplicated (usually via mimeograph) and distributed widely. Examples of this independent publishing practice include *Encuentro Femenil* (1973–1974), published by Las Hijas de Cuauhtémoc; *Mama Sappho / The People's Press* (1973–1974), the first Chicana lesbian newsletter (published by Osa Hidalgo de la Riva and her sister Liz Hidalgo de la Riva); and Martha Cotera's foundational texts, *Diosa y Hembra* (1976) and *The Chicana Feminist* (1977). Chicana feminist newspapers like *Hijas de Cuauhtémoc* (1971) and collections of writing produced by students in early classes on La Chicana, including *Imágenes de la Chicana* (1974 and 1975), became a core curriculum in the first Chicana consciousness-raising sessions and classes and were central to the development of a Chicana studies curriculum in the academy. While some early publications did emerge as a result of institutional support—for example, *HEMBRA: Hermanas en Movimiento Brotando Raices de Aztlán* (1976), a single-issue journal that was edited by Inés Hernández Tovar (Ávila) and received funding from a Modern Language Association grant—their readership extended far beyond academic spaces.

In the following pages, I explore these transgressive sitios y lenguas of Chicana knowledge production in order to document the complex and heterogeneous modes through which women forged a knowledge praxis at the intersection of multiple movement spaces in the community and the academy. Tracing the various knowledge-building initiatives that Chicanas undertook inside and outside the academy—from Martha Cotera's radical information projects, to the struggle for Chicana studies in California, to Osa Hidalgo de la Riva's queer mujerista praxis—I offer not only an intellectual genealogy grounded in memory (both embodied and documentary) but also an invitation to reimagine our own work as scholar-activists through a dialogue with the past.

I set the scene for this dialogue in chapter 1, "Fleshing the Archive," by explicating the approach to archival recovery at the center of the Chicana por Mi Raza project. Building on the work of feminist and queer scholars who have themselves turned to personal collections and embodied memory to address silences about the past, I argue that our Chicanx digital praxis *fleshes* the archive of movement history, engaging it as a site of dialogue and *encuentro* (encounter) rather than as a stable "object" to be interpreted. This approach challenges the traditional relation of production between archives as objects of analysis and scholars as agents of interpretation, a relation that transforms radical memory into what Achille Mbembe terms "evidence," and thereby its traces into "remains." Our Chicanx digital praxis embraces a different set of methodological procedures, centering collaboration, reciprocity, relatedness, and a shared obligation to the past, present, and future. Lifting the veil on the philosophies, methodologies, and ethical practices of our approach to historical recovery—which have been inspired by the very knowledge projects it has uncovered—I explore how affect, haunting, and experiences of what Avery Gordon calls "transformative recognition" defamiliarize objectivist norms of history and the accounts of the past that they have produced. Like Gloria Anzaldúa's "autohistoria" (an intervention into traditional historiography and its objectivist ethos), fleshing the archive is a praxis of historical analysis that weaves together multiple strands of memory—the personal, the collective, the documentary—allowing us to write *with* the past rather than about it. In the chapters that follow, each of which is inspired by moments of transformative recognition (when the present collides with the past in particularly resonant ways), I explore examples of Chicana knowledge praxis that open up novel sites of historical inquiry and new ways of thinking about our work as scholar-activists.

Chapters 2 and 3 focus on Martha P. Cotera and her work to build new informatic futures for Chicana knowledge production. Drawing from materials in her substantial personal archive as well as multiple oral history interviews (spanning from 1973 to 2020), I examine how Cotera integrated her work as an organizer, librarian, archivist, and "information specialist" as she moved between institutional formations and activist spaces. In chapter 2, "La Tlamatini: Information as a Praxis of Freedom," I show how Cotera's information philosophy was grounded in her lived experience as a Chicana working within and against ideologies of knowledge (both movement and institutional) that sustain relations of domination and subordination. In response to these lived contradictions, Cotera developed a radical approach to information—what I call her "tlamatini information praxis"—that challenged the containment of knowledge in institutions and imagined alternative "information hubs" where knowledge by and for the community could be preserved and shared. In chapter 3, "Tlamatini Infrastructures in the Shadow of Precarity," I show how Cotera's radical tlamatini praxis was carried over into her work on autonomous information infrastructure projects in the 1970s, particularly the Chicana Research and Learning Center, which was established by Martha Cotera and Olivia "Evey" Chapa in 1973 and was the first research center dedicated entirely to Chicanas and women of color. Significantly, the center was not based in the university; instead it was imagined as a community knowledge hub that could provide the necessary resources for the development of Chicana studies within the developing fields of Chicano studies and women's studies. Flipping the conventional script for how knowledge flows (from the university to the community), Cotera and her collaborators used the Chicana Research and Learning Center to diversify the curriculum from *outside* the institution. Together, chapters 2 and 3 offer an alternative history of information science and its radical application in Chicana knowledge praxis, a history that speaks (quite intimately) to my own investments as a developer of contemporary Chicana information hubs.

In the second half of the book I pivot to California and to a generation of Chicana feminist scholar-activists who built Chicana studies in the 1970s. In chapter 4, "X Marks the Spot: Mapping the Sitios y Lenguas of Chicana Studies in California (1969–1971)," I follow the network of Chicana feminists that emerged in the wake of the 1969 Santa Barbara conference (widely regarded as a foundational moment for the field of Chicano studies), focusing on how they came together through the work of building Chicano studies across the state. Documenting the largely invisible institutional labor that these women undertook in organizations like the Chicano Council on Higher Education, a formation that has been largely ignored in historical examinations of the field, I show how they mobilized emergent institutional and organizing networks to challenge Chicano studies from within. Chapter 5, "Beyond a History of Violence: The Knowledge Modalities of Chicana Studies in the 1970s," centers on feminist pedagogy and explores the ways in which Chicanas used the classroom as an alternative site for organizing and knowledge production. Surveying the syllabi and assignments of classes in two predominant centers of Chicana feminist thought, San Diego State University and California State University, Northridge, I show how the "consciousness-raising group" organizing model of the late 1960s was carried over into the first classes on "la mujer" and how Chicanas mobilized the classroom as a "nerve center" (as Anna NietoGomez puts it) for knowledge production in the 1970s. In both chapters, I shift attention from the institutions, organizations, and individuals that have been centered in histories of the formation of Chicano studies as a field, to the mostly ignored spaces, networks, and knowledge-making modalities of the Chicana feminist scholar-activist, in order to tell the story of Chicano studies in a different voice. Centering new historical subjects and sites of inquiry, this voice gives narrative form to a Chicana knowledge praxis that moved between and within multiple sites, from institutional formations to the classroom, to communities of struggle outside the university. My analysis of these various efforts demonstrates how Chicana knowledge praxis in the early 1970s was collaborative, transgenerational, and institutionally unruly, directed not only toward building a field but also to addressing the most pressing needs of women in the community. It represented one possible future for the field of Chicano studies: a path not followed, but still redolent with possibility for us today.

The concluding chapter, "Mujerista Genealogies: Encuentros in the Queer Chicana Archive," was inspired by the startling convergences between the filmmaker Osa Hidalgo de la Riva's "mujerista theory and praxis" and our own Chicanx digital praxis. Drawing from a large collection of materials in Hidalgo de la Riva's personal archive that document three generations of queer "mujerista practitioners" in her family, I trace an intergenerational genealogy of her mujerista praxis. Both the Mujeres de la Riva Archive (as Osa Hidalgo de la Riva has named it) and their embodied intergenerational memory tell an "underground story" of lesbian sexuality in the late twentieth century that challenges what Horacio Roque Ramírez terms the "narrative exclusions" of both Chicano movement and gay and lesbian historiographies.[7] Indeed, if Chicanas are largely absent from or marginalized in accounts of the Chicano movement, lesbianas, as many scholars have argued, have been invisibilized by the silences around sexuality within movement spaces, which limited discussions of sexual politics to a heteronormative frame, including within Chicana feminism. Breaking this silence, the Mujeres de la Riva Archive provides stunning evidence of early women of color formations, like Lola de la Riva's Centro de Arte and the Mextiza Colectiva, that intersected with and departed from both Chicano movement and lesbian political and cultural formations. Following the scattered traces of queer memory in the Mujeres de la Riva Archive, I reconstruct, in the words of Liliana González and Stacy Macías, a "Chicana lesbian body politic forged at the crossroads of Chicanismo, women of color feminism, lesbian identity politics, working-class consciousness, and transnational solidarity sensibilities."[8]

Like the archival collection from which it draws, *Fleshing the Archive* explores this genealogy of Chicana feminist praxis to surface memory and heal the haunting intergenerational wound of historiographic erasure. This aim resonates with what Gloria Anzaldúa has described as the Coyolxauhqui imperative: "the impulse to write something down, the desire and urgency to communicate, to make meaning, to make sense of things, to create myself through this knowledge-producing act." For Anzaldúa the Coyolxauhqui imperative is not only the "struggle to heal oneself and heal the *sustos* resulting from woundings, traumas, racism, and other acts of violation *que hechan pedazos nuestras almas*, split us, scatter our energies, and haunt us," but also "the act of calling back those pieces of the self/soul that have been dispersed or lost." Both a scholarly impulse to record, recover, and reevaluate the past and a gesture of mourning and re-membering a "self" and potentiality that has been lost (or scattered), the Coyolxauhqui imperative is an effort to "heal and achieve integration" in the face of historical erasures and temporal fragmentation. As Anzaldúa has noted,

> When fragmentations occur you fall apart and feel as though you've been expelled from paradise. Coyolxauhqui is my symbol for the necessary process of dismemberment and fragmentation, of seeing that self or the situations you're embroiled in differently. It is also my symbol for reconstruction and reframing, one that allows for putting the pieces together in a new way. The Coyolxauhqui imperative is an ongoing process of making and unmaking. There is never any resolution, just the process of healing.[9]

In the following pages I put "the pieces together in a new way" to recover the radical traces of Chicana knowledge praxis from an alternative archive that is itself a reassemblage of documentary "evidence" and personal memory. This archival assemblage includes materials digitized by Chicana por Mi Raza, oral histories collected on our many trips, unrecorded conversations on the phone or in person where an insight was shared, documents in institutional archives, online collections like the Education Resources Information Center (ERIC), scholarly books and articles about the Chicano movement and Chicano studies (grounded in their own eclectic and idiosyncratic archives), obscure publications that transgress the boundary between primary and secondary documents, as well as unpublished manuscripts and position papers, among many other items left scattered in the dustbin of history as a result of institutional neglect. Examining this archival wreckage closely, looking for associative paths, moments of startling convergence when multiple documents begin to speak in unison, we can begin to see a different landscape emerge, with new points of interest, new sites of analysis, and new sitios y lenguas of Chicana feminist discourse.

More than simply an intellectual history, this book traces the connective tissue between the knowledge projects of an earlier generation and our own work and commitments as Chicana scholar-activists today. In telling a story of Chicana knowledge praxis that intentionally thins the temporal distance between these two sites of memory, I want to make visible how Chicana knowledge praxis has consistently moved in and through scales of power (social, cultural, and political) to create new sitios y lenguas where Chicanas can survive and thrive. Lifting the curtain on the moments of transformative recognition that arise in our encounters with the Chicana past, *Fleshing the Archive* invites readers to "reconstruct" and "reframe" our shared history—to put Coyolxauhqui back together again, piece by scattered piece.

*Chapter 1*

# FLESHING THE ARCHIVE

*The decolonial imaginary is intangible to many because it acts much like a shadow in the dark. It survives as a faint outline gliding against a wall or an object. The shadow is the figure between the subject and the object on which it is cast, moving and breathing through an in between space. . . . The historian's political project, then, is to write a history that decolonizes otherness.*

EMMA PÉREZ, *The Decolonial Imaginary*

*If haunting describes how that which appears to be not there is often a seething presence, acting on and often meddling with taken-for-granted realities, the ghost is just a sign, or the empirical evidence . . . that tells you a haunting is taking place.*

AVERY GORDON, *Ghostly Matters*

The archive in my mother's home refuses to stay in its proper place. Spreading tendrils of memory promiscuously across her office, it spills over into unexpected domestic terrains, often surprising you, like a ghost, in its sudden appearance. Indeed, on any given morning you might encounter, as I have, a yellowed movement newspaper lying inauspiciously on the breakfast table, pulled from its resting place in some repurposed box for a quick consultation about events long past. My mother did not come by this wealth of materials by accident. It was gathered over a lifetime of activism in grassroots mobilizations, feminist collecting projects, institutional initiatives, and political formations. As one of the foremost voices in the early development of Chicana feminist knowledge, Martha P. Cotera produced a substantial oeuvre of feminist writing, including two books, *Diosa y Hembra: The History and Heritage of Chicanas in the U.S.* (1976) and *The Chicana Feminist* (1977), as well as numerous bibliographies, sourcebooks, and historical essays. In addition to this literary production, she amassed a large collection of materials on Chicanas, Latinas, lesbians, and women of color through her various information projects, including the Chicana Research and Learning Center, established in Austin, Texas, in 1974.

The contents of my mother's personal archive are what you might find in any institutional collection documenting the work of a leading activist and scholar: unpublished manuscripts, business and personal correspondence, rolled-up posters, pamphlets, chapbooks, newspapers and journals, video and cassette tapes, photographs, and videos from her many presentations across the years. But some of the objects in her personal collection—poster board displays of newspaper clippings and photographs she created for small-scale community exhibits and presentations, old T-shirts, clunky awards and framed certificates, the diosas, calaveras, dried flowers, and family photos that populate her altar—might never make it into an institutional archive. All of these artifacts—the legitimately "archival" and the everyday objects of remembrance—intermingle in my mother's home, a seemingly unruly jumble of relics from the past that persistently nose into the present. On her bookshelves, rare small-press books refuse to stay in their lane, nudging up to contemporary scholarly texts, almost as if they are performing the evolution of Chicana feminist thought in bibliographic form. Sheaves of old correspondence documenting a conference, meeting, or long-disbanded Chicana organization might sit in a fresh manila folder alongside the draft of an essay she is working on, an intermingling that challenges the commonsense notion that there must be a cutoff point at which our present irreconcilably becomes the past. In my mother's home we live within the archive, but the archive lives as well, beckoning us to see the past in the context of an increasingly urgent present that ceaselessly demands our attention.

My mother's sprawling personal collection is not unique. In fact, as the archive stories in this book demonstrate, it is just one node in a stunningly rich and largely unexplored constellation of Chicana memory that haunts the official archive of multiple historiographic imaginaries (the women's movement, the Chicano movement, and gay liberation). Preserved in boxes in living rooms, basements, home offices, garages, and storage units, this submerged archive documents an archipelago of Chicana knowledge in the 1960s and 1970s that expands our current genealogy of the development of women of color discourse. We might think of the collections amassed and carefully preserved by Chicanas like my mother as a kind of composite text, an as-yet-unwritten history of intellectual and organizational labor that documents the conditions of articulation that brought us to the place we are now—a place in which we can write and speak about Chicana feminism in our classrooms, conferences, and scholarly publications.

The archival objects and memories that I draw from in *Fleshing the Archive* were gathered by the Chicana por Mi Raza Digital Memory Collective, an oral history and archive collection project I started in 2009 in partnership with Linda Garcia Merchant.[1] Since the project's official launch in 2010, we have worked with a growing collective of scholars, archivists, media makers, students, and community members to build the largest digital repository of Chicana feminism in the world, with hundreds of oral histories and over thirty thousand archival objects from the personal collections of women who were politically active in the 1960s, 1970s, and 1980s. As with any recovery project, our determination to build this online repository was, first and foremost, a response to a major gap in our collective memory of the movement years. Indeed, scholars of the women's movement, the Chicano movement, and gay liberation have demonstrated how dominant historical imaginaries have tended to frame out the contributions of Chicanas. Multiple critiques of the "wave model" of feminist historiography have brought to light the problematic nature of an analytical lens that frames *This Bridge Called My Back* as heralding the "third wave" of the women's movement.[2] This genealogical model feeds the popular notion that women of color were relative latecomers to feminism, while also, crucially, ignoring the interventions of women of color who were actively producing feminist knowledge (in both white feminist and ethnic nationalist spaces) during, and even before, the emergence of the "second wave." Likewise, Chicano movement historiography produced in the 1980s and 1990s more often than not reinforced popular understandings of the movement as a four-part harmony of land rights, farmworker rights, urban youth and educational struggles, and electoral organizing led by "a cosmology of male heroes that reifies the 'great man' narrative and interpretive structure."[3] As new historical work on Chicana feminism has demonstrated, this approach erases the myriad forms of labor and modes of leadership that contributed to the Chicano movement: the community building, networking, and political organizing, the aesthetic work, the writing and speaking, the forging of new curricula and academic programs, among many other activities. Scholars like Alma García, Vicki Ruiz, Teresa Córdova, Dolores Delgado Bernal, Dionne Espinoza, Maylei Blackwell, Marisela Chávez, and Lorena Oropeza (among many others) have recuperated this hidden labor and demonstrated that Chicanas were active political agents who shaped the key terms of struggle within both the women's movement and the Chicano movement. Focusing on the ways in which women of color articulated a form of resistance that addressed interlocking systems of power and subordination in multiple and sometimes interconnected movement spaces, this scholarship has called attention to the "multi-sited" (Blackwell's term) nature of women of color praxis.[4]

Likewise, queer of color scholars like Yolanda Retter Vargas, Deena González, Catrióna Rueda Esquibel, and Yvette Saavedra (among others) have uncovered the centrality of Chicana lesbiana thought to the development of Chicana feminism, and have challenged what Roque Ramírez calls the "narrative exclusions" in both Chicana/o and gay and lesbian historiography that have kept them in the shadows for far too long.[5] As with the Chicana por Mi Raza project, much of this new scholarship has been built from the ground up: by finding and forging relationships with the women who were active in the 1960s, 1970s, and 1980s; by interviewing them and conducting oral histories; and by collecting and interpreting their personal archives. This is risky and important field-building work that is rarely undertaken in the traditional way. As Horacio Roque Ramírez and Nan Alamilla Boyd point out about queer oral history, "Unlike researchers who choose to work with special collections of well-preserved documents, those who study women, queers . . . and other subaltern groups such as communities of color and migrant workers by and large have had to start from scratch: where no documents or acid-free folder existed, researchers set out to create them."[6] With scant institutional archives dedicated to the legacy of Chicana feminism and few secondary sources that document their history, the scholars who do this work must frequently create their own archives, genealogies, and methodologies. In doing so, they produce historical analyses that swim against the tide of the methodological and interpretive norms of traditional historiography.

The need to create such alternative archives of knowledge is made manifest by profound gaps in the historical record. Of the hundreds of women that the Chicana por Mi Raza project has interviewed since its inception, less than ten have institutional archives in their name—a structured absence that in no way reflects the importance of their contributions to movement history. For example, when the Chicana por Mi Raza team visited Enriqueta Vasquez in 2018, we were shocked to discover works of art, rare photographs, movement newspapers, correspondence with Elizabeth "Betita" Martínez, and numerous original manuscripts in her home and outbuildings in rural northern New Mexico. No institutional archive had yet collected her papers, despite the fact that she had a regular column in the newspaper *El Grito* and was at the forefront of movement activities in northern New Mexico.[7] While radical librarians like my mother (who helped establish a Mexican American papers project at the Benson Latin American Collection in 1974),

Yolanda Retter Vargas, and others have labored to build a Chicana and lesbiana presence in the "official" archive, the Chicana archive still haunts the margins of institutional knowledge production about the movement years, a palimpsest produced in the invisibilizing feedback loop between historiography and archives.[8]

Scholars like Michel-Rolph Trouillot, Michael Frisch, Antoinette Burton, Horacio Roque Ramírez, and others have observed how political and social imperatives shape archival imaginaries, and how in turn, "reliable sources" (found in institutional archives) structure historical knowledge.[9] Questions of archival value, which determine decisions regarding limited institutional resources, are often shaped by extant scholarship on a given subject, which in turn is based largely on the sources housed in institutional archives. This invisibilizing feedback loop is especially acute for queer subjects, who are doubly disappeared by these mechanics of erasure because of a pattern of "evidence tampering" in the archive with respect to sexual identity. In "On the Side of Angels," her comprehensive dissertation documenting lesbian life in Los Angeles from the 1970s to the 1990s, Yolanda Retter Vargas notes the challenges of recovering lesbian history when "large amounts of evidence have been lost or suppressed" in both personal and institutional archival collections: "Papers, photos and diaries containing lesbian evidence have too frequently been destroyed or sanitized by protective and homophobic relatives (Emily Dickinson's), researchers (Eleanor Roosevelt's biographer) and lesbians themselves. Even members of other marginalized groups hesitate to make this facet of a woman's life known." She concludes that "although the history of women and people of color has also been lost, the records of these two groups are substantial in comparison to those of lesbians, gays and other 'sexual outlaws.'"[10] Such practices of erasure are amplified in the organization of institutional archives, which are all too often shaped by "archival conditions beyond our control," as Durba Ghosh notes: "conditions such as whether the archivist or librarian is sympathetic or drawn to the project, whether the proposed topic or research is congenial to particular types of national narratives, and whether the nation-state in which we do our research is invested in preserving and protecting the records we need."[11]

To tease out the political implications of the material processes and social relations of production that shape archival knowledge, we need only return to the illustrative example of my mother's archive, where the unruliness of the living archive in her home—which refuses to keep the past in its proper place—stands in stark contrast to the collection of materials representing her life's work housed in the Benson Latin American Collection. At the Benson, my mother's collection is organized by year and category, sorted, indexed, and stored in boxes, and thus made *legible* to scholars, but only under strict surveillance. Access to her papers is carefully controlled, available to the public, but still cut off from the everyday enactment of Chicana feminism. Scholars can make knowledge from this archive, to be sure, but for whom? And what ghosts are pushed into the shadows in the archivists' first interpretive pass at meaning making? How is dominant knowledge shaped in and through this process of archival interpretation? Who chooses the stories that are allotted their place in the archive, and thus their rightful recognition in the history books? What memories count as meaningful enough to preserve?

In "The Power of the Archive and Its Limits," Achille Mbembe speaks to these questions as they relate to the preservation of radical and decolonial knowledge. He argues that institutional archives function as ordering systems of the state that contain and control the wayward traces of radical knowledge: "Archives are born from a desire to reassemble these traces rather than destroy them. The function of the archive is to thwart the dispersion of these traces and the possibility, always there, that left to themselves, they might eventually acquire a life of their own. Fundamentally, the dead should be formally prohibited from stirring up disorder in the present."[12] Continuing with this metaphor, Mbembe posits that "the best way to ensure that the dead do not stir up disorder" is to contain their traces within the archive, a "sepulchre where these remains are laid to rest."[13] What Mbembe is highlighting here is not simply how institutional archives are sites of state power but also how the archival process itself transforms radical traces into objects of inquiry, or "remains." Mbembe's decidedly pessimistic view of the institutional archive as a "sepulchre" highlights some critical questions for Chicanx archival praxis. Is it possible to document and preserve a history of struggle without transforming its radical traces into mere "evidence"? Can a different orientation to archival praxis enable these radical traces to "acquire a life of their own"?

## THE ARCHIVE IS AN ENCUENTRO—A LIVE SPACE

The Chicana por Mi Raza Digital Memory Collective has engaged these questions through a praxis of archival recovery that centers relationship building and memory keeping. In many ways this approach is an organic response to the deeply personal nature of the archive we have sought to preserve.[14] The project's cofounder Linda Garcia Merchant and I both grew up in the movement, attending conferences, meetings, and rallies with our mothers (Martha Cotera and Ruth Mojica-Hammer), who were friends and frequent coconspirators in

Chicano and women's movement organizing activities. Linda and I reconnected in 2007, when she was screening her film *Las Mujeres de la Caucus Chicana*, which documents how Chicanas in the National Women's Political Caucus organized to ensure that their issues were adequately represented on the national stage of the women's movement. At the time, I was teaching classes in Latino studies and women's studies at the University of Michigan, and was becoming increasingly frustrated by the lack of secondary sources on Chicanas in the 1970s. Responding to a shared sense that our mothers' work at the crossroads of multiple movements had been largely forgotten, we decided to collaborate on a digital recovery project that would provide scholars, teachers, and filmmakers with access to oral histories documenting Chicana activism in the movement years. The project began in 2009 when we traveled to Texas with two students from the University of Michigan (Adonia Arteaga and Carolyn Racine) to conduct a series of oral history interviews with Chicanas active in the Raza Unida Party (Martha Cotera, Rosie Castro, Alma Canales, and Linda del Toro). Using my parents' house in Austin as our home base, Linda and I soon discovered that my mother's personal archive had a profound impact on the students who were working with us. Indeed, they spent long hours going through old newspapers and other artifacts in her collection, seemingly possessed by what Derrida has called an "archive fever," which drove them deeper and deeper into the Chicana past. At the end of our trip, the students commemorated their journey with tattoos inspired by the imagery in the radical publications they had encountered in my family home. Reflecting on this experience, I began to think of the archive as a live space, an active *encuentro* (encounter) with memory, where the present and the past were in dialogue.[15]

In some ways, the Chicana por Mi Raza project looks like any other post-custodial digital archive. Its collection is organized in a login-protected digital repository that contains hundreds of oral histories and thousands of artifacts, a Chicana memory "mothership" accessible to project collaborators and members of our "memory collective," which includes scholars, students, community members, and the women we interview. While access to the repository is limited to our collective, brief biographies, oral history clips, selected documents, and visualizations are shared through a public website (www.chicanapormiraza.org) that offers a peek into the repository to users outside the collective. Almost all of this material is produced by students working on the project. Deploying state-of-the-art digital infrastructure to manage, secure, and preserve our repository, as well as public-facing projects like our website, community exhibits, classes, and field schools, we seek not only to encourage scholarship and teaching on Chicanas but also to stage the archive as a "live" space of encuentro with the past where a broad community of practitioners can come together to build a field of knowledge. The first and most essential premise of our work is that what we are building in and through our praxis of oral history, archival collection, digitization, pedagogy, and historical interpretation is not only a collection but also a collective: a structure of feeling nurtured through acts of transgenerational memory exchange. This approach to archival development pushes us to reimagine the archive as a shared intergenerational knowledge space and a set of living relationships (which do not end once the collection of data is done), rather than as a static repository waiting to be mined by properly credentialed scholars.

Our acts of historical recuperation are thus envisioned as a collective process whereby multiple collaborators—scholars, teachers, students, technologists, the women we interview, and even those who stumble across our site when searching for information about Chicanas—have a shared responsibility for preserving and activating Chicana memory. Community-based archival and oral history projects like Chicana por Mi Raza respond to absences in the historical record, even as they also seek to reformat individualistic modes of scholarly production that reinforce existing hierarchies of knowledge and expertise. In her discussion of community-based oral history projects, Rina Benmayor has noted that the acknowledgment of a "common objective of moving forward as a community" helps to create relations of trust and reciprocity among project participants who occupy very different positionalities.[16] This collective vision of knowledge production opens up a space for individuals who do not consider themselves experts (students) or historically important (a common assertion of the women we interview) to contribute to the project, because "even the most modest effort of documentation is deemed important to a community that has traditionally been denied a dignified public voice and historical recognition."[17] Given the precarity of Chicana memory, our collective is animated by a shared sense of urgency that with each passing year, Chicana stories and documents are in grave danger of disappearing entirely. Through practices of oral history and archival recovery, the Chicana por Mi Raza Digital Memory Collective preserves the radical traces of this history, even as it builds intergenerational relationships between memory keepers.

While we have followed established scholarly protocols in our oral history work (from release forms to sharing transcriptions with participants), we also understand that there are other "protocols" that make the project accountable to the Chicana knowledge it seeks to surface. Therefore, in our praxis we foreground horizontal relationships of knowledge production and *respeto* (respect) for the women we interview, as coproducers of knowledge. Our practices of scanning archives in place, of showing women how to access their materials in our online collection, of encouraging them to use it to produce knowledge on their own, and of collaborating with them on writing projects and public exhibitions are all examples of how the Chicana por Mi Raza Digital Memory Collective revisions the archive as an active site of exchange where participants work together to coproduce knowledge.[18] The women we interview are more than resources to be mined for information about the past; they are *collaborators* in our intimate acts of memory keeping. We record our oral histories in their homes and in other spaces in which they are at home, and we very rarely take personal items out of their homes. This commitment to post-custodial practice is not simply an expedient solution to archival collection and dissemination; it is a direct response to the sense of betrayal that many of the women we interview feel as a result of their past interactions with archivists who have taken their materials and never accessioned them (citing funding limitations), or scholars who have recorded their stories and left them to languish in archives that the community (and the women themselves) do not have access to. As a result of these extractive knowledge practices, those who have offered their insights and archives to institutions and scholarly projects are profoundly mistrustful of scholars bearing gifts, and they often express feelings of being used and still left out of the historical record.

Our commitment to building a living archive of memory, as opposed to producing yet another individually authored book, essay, or documentary film, is as much a response to this unequal knowledge relationship as it is an effort to honor the modes of knowledge we have surfaced in the process of memory exchange.[19] For this reason, when we introduce the Chicana por Mi Raza project to the women we interview, we always foreground its collectivist ethos. We walk them through how to access and use our digital platform and show them objects and stories in the archive (a process that often surfaces distant memories for them). We highlight our students' work on the archive and show the women our public website, which includes the biographies and curations the students have created. We tell them the project's origin story, how it emerged from our commitment to preserving our mothers' memories, and how it has become a transgenerational labor of love. We make explicit the project's aims to build a shared repository of memory, and we draw connections between the aims of Chicana por Mi Raza and the collective intellectual ethos that birthed Chicana feminism. Thus, the women we interview (many of whom have become active collaborators on the project) often recognize themselves in the aims of our project—which has, after all, been inspired by their own examples of collective knowledge production, a point of connection that has drawn even reluctant participants into the project.

Our memory keeping is not isolated to data gathering and the "scene" of research; it also happens in those more intimate encounters that go unrecorded and are thus left out of published historical accounts: In the stories of past and present struggles that emerge as we sit with them and leaf through photo albums and scan countless letters, proposals, and periodicals. In the hours spent idly chatting as we poke around in spare rooms, attics, basements, garages, and outbuildings, finding long-forgotten items shoved into the corners of offices and under beds. It extends over countless meals, cafecitos—and the occasional gin and tonic—where we experience the archive as a live space of encuentro and a collective effort to build a future that includes Chicanas in its memoryscape. In the process, we inhabit their stories (as they inhabit us)—an exchange that produces new ways of understanding the past and new technologies of resistance for the future.

Because the primary aim of our memory keeping is not to record or document history, but to open up a space for relationality between the present and the past, we see our interviews as opportunities for learning through intergenerational story sharing, rather than data gathering. Whereas dominant scholarly discourse values interpretation—the act of applying one's theoretical expertise to the "evidence" of history—our praxis privileges the *process* of collection (typically the province of feminized labor) as a critical site of transformative knowledge. I have written elsewhere about how students who work with Chicana por Mi Raza are affected by their role as critical witnesses, and how their memory work (reflective writing, short biographies, timelines, and other curations) is a form of "theorizing from the flesh" that often leads to a "deeper understanding of the connections between theory, experience, and political action."[20] Indeed, our interviews are explicitly framed as an intimate, even familial, process of transgenerational Chicana memory exchange in which students act not as documenters (who record the scene and capture the knowledge) but as critical witnesses who are essential participants in storytelling.

This approach resonates with the work of Indigenous women and women of color oral historians who are attentive to the intersubjective, affective, and transformational dimensions of story sharing. For example, Sue Anderson, Jaimee Hamilton, and Lorina L. Barker have described their oral history methodology as "yarning," a mode of storytelling grounded in Indigenous traditions of intergenerational knowledge transmission.[21] They insist that the ultimate purpose of yarning is not to preserve history but to enact a decolonizing encounter between the present and the past through a "lived experience of the story . . . whereby the listener is tasked with the responsibility of transferring the knowledge onto the next generation."[22] Pushing against objectivist models of research that rely on a distanced observer, yarning demands that participants mutually inhabit stories, extracting a "truth" from them that is not *only* historical. Instead, yarning is a process of re-memory in which "to know 'the truth' is to experience a narrator's knowledge, to feel the emotions of the story, to envision the story, and to become one with the story."[23] In this sense, yarning is geared toward a different futurity than the one imagined by archivists and historians: "For some Indigenous Australian communities," they note, "making an enduring record is not a priority. The stories themselves are, after all, the recording."[24]

Echoing this attention to the intersubjective and affective dimensions of oral history in her essay "Emotion and Pedagogy," Rina Benmayor discusses the digital storytelling projects that students in her Latina Life Stories class created in response to reading various autobiographical texts—from testimonio to oral history—as potent examples of how "personal narrative," when linked to "bodily emotion," can become a source of critical knowledge. As with yarning, a sense of relatedness and accountability between storyteller and listener/reader grounds both the intersubjective process of story sharing and its epistemological stakes. For Benmayor's students, this relationship is not forged through traditional familial or kinship ties; rather, it is grounded in a shared set of historical and cultural experiences that "[stir] feelings that are deeply rooted in [her students'] memories," feelings that can be "empowering both personally and politically." Indeed, Benmayor insists that emotion is the engine of this process of "critical reflection" in that it catalyzes the "move from the individual to the social," enabling a "theorizing from the flesh" (to use Cherríe Moraga's phrase) that leads to transformational knowledge.[25]

Like the intergenerational participants in yarning, and the students who are moved to critical reflection by the testimonios they encounter in Benmayor's class, the student researchers who work with the Chicana por Mi Raza project often "become one with the story," a process that pushes them to imagine different stories for the future. Drawn into a familial relationship to the project, they feel accountable for producing knowledge about that past that will honor the memory of the women whose stories they have witnessed. But as critical witnesses, they also see themselves embedded in the story and thus develop new insights about the workings of power and the long tradition of noninstitutional knowledge making hiding in plain sight. For Latina students who rarely see the lives of their mothers, grandmothers, and aunties in history books, this process of intergenerational story sharing takes on particular significance. More than simply revealing a "hidden history" of Chicana feminism, our scenes of encuentro often stir memories of the "pláticas [conversations] with grandmas, parents, and other adults" that they have experienced in their own households. In their article "Vamos a Platicar," Cindy Fierros and Dolores Delgado Bernal describe how such organic scenes of knowledge exchange constitute their own epistemological tradition. Delgado Bernal notes that it was through these pláticas that she received crucial cultural knowledge when she was growing up: information about who she was, where she "came from, and how to be with others." She writes, "I learned to respect my elders and those who had few material possessions. I learned always to look for a bargain, never to pay full price for anything, and to share what I had with others. From my grandmothers and my mother, I learned women could be strong and independent." For Fierros and Delgado Bernal, pláticas are not just casual conversations around the kitchen table; they are an epistemology from below that allows participants to "witness shared memories, experience, stories, ambiguities, and interpretations," giving them "a knowledge connected to personal, familial, and cultural history."[26] Likewise, our Chicanx digital praxis is not only a methodology for collecting and preserving history; it is an epistemology from below that has deep roots in Chicana ways of knowing.[27]

A reflection essay written by one of our research assistants beautifully illustrates this epistemological process. In the summer of 2018, I traveled from Ann Arbor, Michigan, to Milwaukee, Wisconsin, with two undergraduate research interns, Aneliza Ruíz and Sonia Olmos. We visited Milwaukee to conduct interviews with several women who had been active in the Latina Task Force, a group formed in the mid-1980s as a response to the continued marginalization of Latina issues in both Latina/o-led organizations and (white) women's organizations. In a reflection essay that Sonia wrote about the experience, she recognized something deeply personal in our interviews with the women of the Latina Task Force. Shifting between the "distant" past (the early 1980s) to a somewhat more proximal and intimate time/space, Sonia recalls how when she was a child,

> The señoras [women elders] in my family would gather around in a circle during family events as a way of claiming territory in a public space donde ellas mandan [where they ruled]. If children were given access to enter into their space, their role was to listen and observe while they led the discussions. Interruptions from outsiders were prohibited and viewed as disrespectful. Las señoras collectively created a space of healing, support, and empowerment because, allí todas eran hermanas y comadres

> (pero también unas chismosas) [in that space all were sisters and comrades, but also gossips]. For me, hearing the stories of the Latina Task Force was like listening attentively to las señoras from my family because they showed how "chismear" [to gossip] can be a feminista praxis to create social change. Por andar de chismosas [as a result of their gossiping] mujeres who were mostly in their twenties and thirties and identified as first generation, low-income, or children of migrants would voluntarily get together after work in the South Side of Milwaukee during the early 1980s to recreate a ritual of circle gathering like the one las señoras would practice.[28]

Examining the Latina Task Force through the prism of the "circles of gathering" in her mother's kitchen, Sonia transforms two pasts simultaneously and thus is able to see the "chisme" of las señoras as something more than mere gossip, and the consciousness-raising work of the Latina Task Force as part of a long tradition of women creating spaces of freedom within the constraints of heteropatriarchal culture, spaces where "they could flourish into mujeres chingonas [badass women]."[29] But another, more personal kind of transformation is implied in this encuentro with the past—one that illuminates the intersubjective memory praxis at the heart of the Chicana por Mi Raza project—for in merging the time/space of her mother's kitchen and that of the Latina Task Force, Sonia also makes an important connection between her role as a critical witness in our interviews and her childhood memories of listening quietly to las señoras as they swapped stories and chismes. She reveals, in other words, how the act of transgenerational memory exchange can help us see the interconnected nature of the past, present, and future. These affective dimensions of memory keeping are the ties that bind members of the intergenerational "circle of gathering" that is the Chicana por Mi Raza Digital Memory Collective.

Indeed, for many of the women we interview, our students' presence as critical witnesses in the encuentro not only highlights the urgency of the project but also surfaces long-standing traditions of memory exchange. In their presence, women share sometimes painful memories, stories of loss and vulnerability, but also stories of strategic maneuvering, and sometimes even chisme (usually spoken off camera) that bring new insights about struggles past and present. They understand that our students are not just empty vessels to be filled with memories of the past; rather, through such scenes of encuentro they inhabit stories and make new knowledge with them. Refracting and remixing the past through their own embodied memory work, students come to understand that theory making and knowledge production are not confined to the academy, that they take place in far more quotidian and familiar spaces, like our mothers' kitchens. This is the embodied memory produced when we refigure the archive as an encuentro: an approach that moves beyond simply documenting the past, and demands that we inhabit each other's stories, making new knowledge in the process. It is what allows Sonia to see chisme as a key feminista praxis, and to develop her own version of Anzaldúa's autohistoria-teoría that interweaves her experience as a critical witness with the story of the Latina Task Force and the stories shared in the circles of gathering in her mother's kitchen. It is what transforms this digital collection of documents and oral history recordings into a collective praxis, a circle of gathering where veteranas, scholars, students, and community members come together not only to create new histories but also to imagine new ways of knowing that interrupt dominant scripts about our past, present, and future. Pushing against extractive modes of knowledge production that reduce lived memory and carefully preserved documents to their use value as historical "evidence," our Chicanx digital praxis reveals that the Chicana archive is not a place, or even a collection—it is us.

## THE ARCHIVE IS A HAUNTING—THAT BECKONS

When we haunt the Chicana archive—snooping in its basement and closet corners, getting lost in intimate collections of artifacts for hours that seem to pass like minutes, listening for whispered secrets (which have not been so quietly kept, after all)—we are inevitably haunted in return. Much more than merely the product of an overactive scholarly imagination (a willingness to be possessed by the past), archival hauntings beckon us to see beyond the "cold knowledge" of objectivist research and to imagine a different mode of investigation grounded in a sense of relationality and mutual recognition. In *Ghostly Matters: Haunting and the Sociological Imagination*, Avery Gordon explores the epistemological implications of such hauntings and the "trouble" they cause to the boundaries of official narratives and traditional methodological practices. For Gordon, the ghost summoned in the archival traces of a disappeared or forgotten social world represents both a silenced or marginalized figure and a "symptom of what is missing" or what has been lost, "sometimes a life, sometimes a path not taken."[30] Because such specters make their appearance when "the trouble they represent and symptomize is no longer being contained or repressed or blocked from view," haunting is a sign that "what's been concealed is very much alive and present, interfering precisely with those always incomplete forms of containment and repression ceaselessly directed toward us."[31] Indeed, we are haunted by the silences in the historical record precisely at the moment when we are confronted with "evidence" of social worlds previously hidden from view, an experience that defamiliarizes taken-for-granted reality and pushes us to imagine the present we might have inhabited had the ghosts never become ghosts in the first place.

Both noun and verb, the apparition is at once a "seething presence" and an uncanny *experience* in "which something lost, or barely visible, or seemingly not there to our supposedly well-trained eyes, makes itself known or apparent to us."[32] When the ghost makes her presence known, saying to the investigator, *Look . . . I am not here*, she signals a truncated possibility, a "path not taken," a buried potentiality that defamiliarizes the historical trajectory that leads to the present. Thinning the distance between the present and the past, haunting transforms one's "experience of being in time, the way we separate the past, the present, and the future," opening up a third space (an encuentro)—across time—that challenges the temporal sense making of historiographic logics.[33]

For Gordon, apprehending the significance of the apparition's interruption of business as usual, "seeing" it and "reading" its message properly, requires a different orientation to scholarly inquiry: "a particular way of knowing what has happened or is happening" that draws us "affectively, sometimes against our will and always a bit magically, into the structure of feeling of a reality we come to experience, not as cold knowledge, but as a transformative recognition."[34] Animated by a sensibility to the message of the apparition (or as Gloria Anzaldúa might put it, "la facultad") and a willingness to follow its scattered traces wherever they may lead, transformative recognition centers associative processes and uncanny temporal convergences where the defamiliarization of taken-for-granted reality coalesces

> into a moment of connection, a configuration. Through this door a certain kind of search is established, one that often leads along an associative path of correspondences. This path of correspondences is not like the causality associated with social science or related modes that share its basic epistemology: it blasts through the rational, linearly temporal, and discrete spatiality of our conventional notions of cause and effect, past and present, conscious and unconscious.[35]

By scrambling our sense of space and time, and by extension, the conceptual boundaries that subtend empiricism and its will to know the material world, the process of transformative recognition—of seeing ourselves in the past—reorients both the nature of our historical investigations and its intentions. To read the message of the ghost, to apprehend the meaning of its haunting, requires a "different sort of receptiveness and welcome," one that, like our Chicanx digital praxis, centers on relatedness, intersubjectivity, and a "will to heal."[36]

Indeed, as the stories I've shared about our students' work on the Chicana por Mi Raza project suggest, our process of gathering the radical traces of Chicana memory inevitably surfaces haunting moments of transformative recognition where we/they feel an uncanny sense of kinship with the past and its radical futures. The stories of Chicana knowledge praxis that I have gathered in this book reflect this process of recognition, where the utopian imaginaries of Chicanas in the 1970s speak to, and transform, not only my understanding of the past, but also the ways I imagine my own praxis as a scholar. In pointing to the Chicana futures that were cut off, structurally invisibilized, made unavailable to us as technologies of resistance, these transformative hauntings beckon us to enter through a different door, "the door of the uncanny, the door of the fragment, the door of the shocking parallel," to explore the utopian imaginaries that haunt the margins of the historiographic record and its sense making technologies, not just as relics of the past that allow us to correct the historical record and provide the ghost its final justice but as blueprints for a future that we can create together.[37]

## THE ARCHIVE IS A RELATION—A SPACE TO CREATE KNOWLEDGE TOGETHER

In this book I offer a "different sort of receptiveness and welcome" to the specter of Chicana knowledge praxis, one that is grounded in the praxis that has shaped the archive from which it draws. Thus my approach to tracing the networks and projects of Chicana knowledge in the 1970s centers a process of encuentro with the past that fleshes the archive through a process of intergenerational memory exchange. This approach is as much a rejection of a false objectivism (structuring traditional modes of social scientific inquiry) that imagines distance to be the *only* guarantor of "truth" as it is an effort to actively re-member a Chicana body of knowledge through a dialogue with the women I write about. Such a dialogic process necessarily raises methodological as well as epistemological questions. Indeed, when the archive "talks back," memory, enlivened, moves from object of inquiry to participant, and narratives about the past become more fluid and subject to critical reinterpretation. In the process of encuentro, our stories inevitably fold into one another—theirs in moments of backward reflection and sudden remembering, mine as I sift through personal and institutional archives and ask follow-up questions in emails and phone calls, incessantly prodding the gears of memory—a mutual enfolding that somehow feels both natural and transgressive.

In her essay "Memory Work," Anna NietoGomez describes this intersubjective process as a dialogue between "scholar" and "subject."

> Scholars like yourselves help me with my dig, the telling, and retelling process. You call for an interview. I ask for questions. The questions are limited to what the scholar knows. Therefore, they limit my search. I prepare for your visit, I go to my files, to conduct the dig. It is a manual data search. Then I assemble, dis-assemble, and reorganize my files. The next phase is a collaborative process. Together, the scholar and I engage in collaborative telling and retelling. The telling is dependent on your insightful feedback and additional questions. The more you know, the more I can tell you. Consequently, together, we work as a team trying to understand more with each telling. It is through the telling and retelling that I can uncover more of the memory site, link it together, analyze, interpret, and reinterpret what I remember.[38]

Anna's formulation of research as a profoundly dialogical and embodied process—an iterative telling and retelling between scholar and subject—challenges boundaries that underwrite objectivist norms of inquiry: between present and past, emotion and reason, investigator and object of knowledge. This understanding of historical inquiry as a process of cocreation between the scholar and the subject has pushed me to think more deeply about methodology and the profoundly dialogic nature of meaning making about a proximal past that can still be accessed through lived memory. This is especially important with respect to the subjugated Chicana archive, which, more often than not, exists at the margins of the official record because it is constituted in countermemory and personal collections rather than institutional archives. Just as the encuentro with lived memory transforms the Chicana archive from a static repository to a live space, the process of storytelling that emerges from that space fleshes the archive as a site of active knowledge production and ongoing interpretation.

Fleshing the archive means abandoning the guise of objective observer and "becom[ing] one with the story," sorting through the past with collaborators who bring their lived experience to the dialogue, an iterative process of interpretation and re-memory that allows us to arrive at meaning together.[39] It means following the "breadcrumbs," as Anna puts it, cross-checking personal memory with archival documents and secondary sources, returning to inconsistencies or contradictions, and remembering again. Because it involves the shaping and reshaping of sometimes traumatic memories of institutional violence and marginalization, fleshing the archive also exposes the radical uncertainties and porousness of memory, and the ways in which even archival documents have been misread or misremembered. In *An Archive of Feelings*, Ann Cvetkovich notes that "trauma challenges common understandings of what constitutes an archive. Because trauma can be unspeakable and unrepresentable and because it is marked by forgetting and dissociation, it often seems to leave behind no records at all."[40] Moreover, trauma makes the recuperation of one's own story all the more difficult, as Anna observes: "Remembering is similar to conducting an archeological dig of the mind and body[.] The problem is, I am part of the ruin."[41] Walking through the "ruin" together in a dialogical process of intergenerational memory exchange, we multiply the number of possible interpreters of the past, so that "we might be able to understand more with each telling." In centering our relatedness, fleshing the archive disrupts the temporal divides between the past and the present (a central feature of empiricist history) and undermines the hierarchies of scholarly production that define some interlocutors as "interpreters" and others as "data."[42] Indeed, when we flesh the archive, we give up the ghost of narrative authority and reveal ourselves as only one interlocutor of an ongoing dialogue. Fleshing the archive allows us to write *with* the past rather than about it, inviting us to see in a "shadow in the dark" the "faint outline" of our own radical imaginaries.[43]

## Chapter 2

# LA TLAMATINI: INFORMATION AS A PRAXIS OF FREEDOM

*It cannot be denied that the university is a place of refuge, and it cannot be accepted that the university is a place of enlightenment. In the face of these conditions one can only sneak into the university and steal what one can. To abuse its hospitality, to spite its mission, to join its refugee colony, its gypsy encampment, to be in but not of—this is the path of the subversive intellectual in the modern university. . . .*

*. . . After all, the subversive intellectual came under false pretenses, with bad documents, out of love. Her labor is as necessary as it is unwelcome. The university needs what she bears but cannot bear what she brings. And on top of all that, she disappears. She disappears into the underground, the downlow lowdown maroon community of the university, into the Undercommons of Enlightenment, where the work gets done, where the work gets subverted, where the revolution is still black, still strong.*

STEFANO HARNEY AND FRED MOTEN, *The Undercommons*

*I am always amazed that an insignificant purveyor of information and knowledge, a* Tlamatini *(Knowledge Keeper) can actually help transform communities.*

MARTHA COTERA, EMAIL COMMUNICATION

Leafing through the soft pages of an old Chicano newspaper in my mother's collection, a blurry photo suddenly catches me off guard. A young woman in a Mexican dress looks piercingly into the camera as she holds a child close to her, the trace of a smile softening her stern beauty. My eyes shift to the little girl at her side. Noticing the messy hair and poncho slightly askew, I suddenly recognize her, or rather, me, or rather, *us*. We are standing in front of the Crystal City library in Texas, a place of learning that was like a second home to me in the early 1970s. It is a mise-en-scène that summons a flood of memories. I spent many hours with my mother in that library as she built its Chicano collection, dutifully participating in community events and children's programs that she organized, witnessing her efforts, both large and small, to realize her vision of what a library for the people could be. In the process of building that library for the "total community" of Cristal, my mother articulated a tlamatini praxis of information that would shape her approach not only to feminist *concientización* (consciousness-raising) but also to the knowledge projects she pursued into the 1970s.

Looking at this photograph, I am haunted by the echoes of the radical information futures my mother imagined as she stood with me in front of the Crystal City library. More than the symptom of a nostalgic desire for a Chicana future long past, this haunting summons me affectively, against my will, a bit magically even, into a structure of feeling of a reality that I cannot help but experience as a kind of recognition, not just of my younger self but of the person I have somehow fallen into.[1] Like my mother, I too have built collections from scratch, "stealing" the resources that my proximity to power has made available in order to elaborate a Chicana information praxis that is "in but not of" the institution, as Fred Moten and Stefano Harney so eloquently put it.[2] I recognize myself in her struggle to carve out this fugitive ground, to create an autonomous knowledge space, to elaborate a praxis of information in collaboration with the community. Seeing myself reflected in her, I recognize, too, the familiar erasures that exile the ghosts of that Chicana information praxis to the margins of institutional knowledge systems and their archives. Indeed, a close reading of this archival object illuminates the gendered mechanics of this erasure.

"La Biblioteca," the brief article that accompanies our photo, is one of several in the newspaper intended to offer a snapshot of life in Crystal City after the "Chicano takeover" of the town. Even as the photo and its accompanying article provide precious evidence of my mother's contributions to this historic effort, it also enacts a symbolic restructuring of her labor. Referring respectfully to my mother by the patriarchal honorific "Martha Piña de Cotera," the article describes her as an experienced librarian with strong movement credentials, "volunteering her time and talents in an effort to develop expanded community library facilities in Cristal."[3] The absence of my mother's name in the title of the article—or perhaps more tellingly, its replacement with the physical space of "la biblioteca"—coupled with her domestication as a wife and mother in both the article's reference to her married name (in the possessive "*de* Cotera") and the image of maternal protection that illustrates it, tells a familiar story of how Chicana contributions to movement activities were, more often than not, framed as supportive "labors of love." Thinking about this maternalization of my mother's labor reminded me of something Anna NietoGomez once wrote about the predominant image

Page 14 September, 1971 Cristal

# La Biblioteca

The library facilities in Cristal have always been inadequate. Limited staff, scarcity of materials, and an insensitivity to Chicano culture and Spanish-readers account for much of the community's indifference. Now, with the increase in program administrators, bilingual teachers, and college-oriented students, the need for quality facilities is accentuated. So the school and city of Cristal are coordinating efforts to centralize and expand community library services. This may eventually mean a new, larger library building but current efforts will concentrate on expanding collections.

An exchange service, hopefully to include a mobile unit, will begin for Spanish-readers. Classics will be included but the emphasis will be on novelas which are very popular in the community. Material written on and by Chicanos about our history and culture and on other ethnic groups such as Blacks and Native Americans needs to be compiled. Bilingual, basic adult education and economic development materials must be collected. And finally, a collection of city, county, state, and federal documents that might be relevant to the community will be made available.

Marta Piña de Cotera, a naturalized citizen from Nuevo Casas Grandes, Chihuahua, Mexico, is presently working on a Master's degree in Education from Antioch College. She has been the senior library assistant at the Bexar County Spanish Archives in 1963, and was in charge of U.S. Documents at the Texas State Library in Austin from 1964 to 1968. She and her husband, Juan Cotera, have long been active en el movimiento. Their most recent contribution was at the Colegio Jacinto Treviño in Mercedes, Texas, where Marta took on the task of assembling all bilingual materials for use in the all-Chicano college.

She has now volunteered her time and talents as a consultant and coordinator in the efforts to develop expanded community library facilities in Cristal. Assisting her is a committee of COP students attending Southwest Texas Junior College in Uvalde, and a committee of MAYO and other high school students. They are preparing a list of necessary academic resource materials and thinking of ways students can help in the fund-raising. Already they are organizing special files on Bilingualism, Chicano Studies, and the Social Sciences. Ciudadanos Unidos will assist in planning and financing collections and subscriptions for adult Spanish-speaking programs. TEAM (Texans for the Educational advancement of the Mexican American) is interested in promoting local education programs. This fall volunteers will keep the library open evenings for students who need a place to study or residents who work during the day.

LIBRARY CONSULTANT MARTA COTERA AND DAUGHTER, MARUCA

The University of Texas is donating several hundred volumes to augment the academic collection and many free periodical subscriptions are being donated. Any organization or individual desiring to donate library materials please contact Marta Cotera, Drawer 310, Crystal City, Texas 78839 (tel. 512 374 3229).

LAS ESCUELAS (cont. from p. 9) ...

To augment this program another free night school, known as La Universidad Libre de Cristal, was organized in the fall of 1970 by Erasmo Andrade. Twelve teachers volunteered their services and facilities were donated by the school district. A survey was taken to determine how best teachers could match their talents to community needs. The Spanish class had several Anglo enrollees, and for a class project students began to tape the Spanish oral history of Cristal from several senior citizens. The largest class was in citizenship with 90 enrollees. In all, 225 Cristaleños took advantage of this program. In June, a graduation ceremony complete with diplomas and speeches was held and all involved felt La Universidad Libre was a great success.

In coordination with the new school programs additional school facilities are being planned. CCISD has traditionally been the third poorest district in Texas and its physical plant reflects this rating. New showers and a parking lot are only interim measures until a new high school plant can be built. The present high school was built for 200 students and now serves 700. The cafeteria that can seat only 96 students must serve 600. Office space, library, science labs, and gym are out-dated and inadequate. The lower grades also need a new physical plant. A cheaply constructed WW II Japanese detention camp now serves as a junior high and elementary school. Other parts of the camp are being used as teacher housing.

The school board has promised Cristal a new high school by 1973. Plans for an elementary school and teacher housing are also being pursued. Alan Y. Tenaguchi, whose family was detained in Cristal during WW II and who is presently dean of the School of Architecture at the U. of Texas, has offered his services in designing the schools. When the blueprints are complete the school will hire local Chicano construction firms, employing many Cristaleños and training others.

The scope of these changes has gone beyond even the student walkout demands. An advisory committee with student, parent, and teacher members is elected annually to assist the school board in selecting those policies it will implement.

An example of Cristal's new school policy is its ban on military recruiting in the schools. The Crystal City school board is one of the first in the nation to take an official stand against the war. In Texas, Chicanos constitute 14.8% of the population but they make up 23.4% of the Texas Viet Nam war dead. This statistic is enough to explain our position. And the board has taken the positive step of providing draft counseling services for male students.

SCHOOL BOARD MEMBERS: ED MAYER, RODOLFO PALOMO, JOSE ANGEL GUTIERREZ (PRESIDENT), ARTURO GONZALES, MIGUEL PEREZ AND EDUARDO TREVINO. WAYNE HAMILTON WAS NOT PRESENT FOR THIS PICTURE.

FIGURE 2.1. *Article featuring a photograph of Martha and María Cotera in front of the Crystal City library. "La Biblioteca,"* Cristal, *special issue of* La Verdad, *September 1971. Martha Cotera personal collection.*

of Chicanas in the mid-1970s. She notes that while there were many examples of "Chicana leaders in the community, people did not see them outside of their role as mothers, grandmothers, or daughters. It was as if there was a cultural hysterical blindness. There was a great sense of denial that Chicanas were separate independent thinking human beings." For this reason, Chicana community leaders had to "walk on eggshells as they endeavored the daily sociopolitical psychological process to labor and negotiate within the family and in the community just to speak out much less to organize."[4] In this sense, like so many pieces of evidence uncovered in the Chicana archive, the article "La Biblioteca" documents not only how Chicanas navigated the conflicting demands of community gender norms and movimiento agendas, but also how the discursive framing of Chicana technologies of freedom as supportive labors of love has shaped our understanding of their work within the Chicano movement.[5] While there can be little doubt that my mother's efforts to build library collections and information systems to serve the community were based in a practice of care—and love—this love was animated not by a maternal instinct but by a belief that *information* was a critical infrastructure for liberation.

Indeed, my mother's radical vision of information was the beating heart of her work as a librarian, information specialist, organizer, and writer. In an email she sent me after many conversations about her information praxis, she reflected on why knowledge preservation and dissemination were such important aspects of her movement work.

> My libraries and other information efforts have been my armories; for fighting power structures, for educating communities AND convincing communities that they have a right to their tax dollars (by showing them the economics); and by connecting communities with directories [and other resources]. . . . I am always amazed that an insignificant purveyor of information and knowledge, a *Tlamatini* (Knowledge Keeper) can actually help transform communities.[6]

A few days later she followed up with another email, explaining the significance of the tlamatini in "the knowledge base of Nahuatl Culture." The email included a transcription she had made from a translated Nahuatl passage in Miguel León-Portilla's 1963 book *La Filosofía Náhuatl: Estudiada en Sus Fuentes*, which describes the tlamatini in the following way:

> The wise one: a light, a torch, a thick torch that does not smoke.
> A pierced mirror, a mirror pierced on both sides.
> Theirs is the black and red ink, theirs are the codices.

> They are writing and wisdom (Tlilli Tlapalli).
> It is the way, a true guide for others.
> They lead people and things, they are a guide in human affairs.
> The true sage is careful (like a physician) and preserves tradition.
> Theirs is the handed-down wisdom, they teach it, they follow the path of truth.
> Teacher of truth, they never cease to admonish.
> They make wise countenances of others, to them they give a face (a personality), leading them to develop it.
> They open the ears, and enlighten.
> They are the teacher of guides, they give them their way, one depends on them.
> They put a mirror before others, make them wise, careful; the tlamatini makes a face (a personality) appear in them.
> They look at things, regulate their path, arrange and order.
> Apply their light on the world.
> They know (what is) above us (and), the region of the dead.
> Everyone is comforted by them, corrected, taught.
> Thanks to the tlamatini, the people humanize their will and receive strict education.
> It comforts the heart, it comforts people, it helps, it remedies, it cures everyone.[7]

León-Portilla's gloss of the original Nahuatl (put in writing by Fray Bernardino de Sahagún, who himself drew from elder Indigenous "informants" in Tepepulco and Tlatelolco) paints an expansive picture of the tlamatini as teacher, reader, writer, historian (keeper of memory), guide, observer of the natural world, psychologist, and moralist orienting the will of the people toward a clearer understanding of their place in the world. Thus, León-Portilla concludes, "It seems quite proper to attribute to the wise man—anachronously and by analogy, to be sure—the qualities of those men we designate today as teachers, psychologists, moralists, cosmologists, metaphysicians, and humanists."[8] While my mother drew on León-Portilla's remediation of Sahagún's text on the tlamatini (itself a remediation of the oral knowledge passed on to him by elders in Tepepulco and Tlatelolco), she revised his gendered assumptions, pointedly titling her transcription "TLAMATINI (male and female)."

In this chapter I follow the tracks of my mother's radical information work, picking through the archives, personal recollections, and scattered secondary sources that document her development as a librarian, information specialist, archivist, and, later, feminist writer in the late 1960s and early 1970s. In and through these projects, she sought to humanize information, to expand its flows and publics, and to produce new sitios y lenguas for the articulation of Chicana identity. Tracing her emergence as an early developer of archival collections and networked information systems sheds new light on the importance of radical librarianship and information dissemination projects to the elaboration of Chicana/o movement goals, particularly with respect to the development of Chicana/o studies, as Brenda Sendejo has noted.[9] Moreover, it offers an important context for the publication projects my mother pursued in the late 1970s, *Diosa y Hembra* (1976) and *The Chicana Feminist* (1977), as knowledge projects that were a strategic extension of her commitment to democratizing information in the service of liberation.[10] Moving in and through the variety of projects she pursued in the 1960s, 1970s, and 1980s—from organizing collections, to envisioning radical community-based knowledge centers, to publishing and disseminating Chicana feminist materials—Martha Cotera elaborated a tlamatini praxis of information as a vehicle for autonomy and self-determination, as a knowledge resource that could be recaptured by the community (from the university) and put to use (sometimes against the university), and as a critical form of memory and re-memory that allowed women and men to see radical futures in the reflection of their shared past.

## "IF WE DON'T MAKE THE INFORMATION, NO ONE IS GOING TO MAKE IT FOR US"

Martha Cotera's entrance into the profession as a librarian and information specialist in the early 1960s could not have come at a more propitious time. The civil rights movement was in full swing, bringing greater public awareness of the systematic marginalization of Black and brown communities, both urban and rural. Multiple scholars have documented the ways in which President Lyndon B. Johnson's War on Poverty programs of the mid-1960s, including the Model Cities Program, Volunteers in Service to America (VISTA), and TRIO, supported a variety of Chicano movement initiatives.[11] Fewer have explored how federal funding for education information initiatives and library services supported Chicano movement knowledge projects like those pursued by my mother and other librarians and educators in the 1960s and 1970s.[12]

With the passage of a constellation of new domestic programs designed to address systemic inequality in education, including the Library Services and Construction Act of 1964, the Elementary and Secondary Education

Act of 1965, and the Bilingual Education Act of 1968, new federal funding became available to address the education and information needs of underserved communities.[13] This new federal money would give rise to a plethora of Chicano movement initiatives designed to address the pressing information needs of the Mexican American community. Chicana/o librarians and information specialists like Roberto Haro, Arnulfo Trejo, Elizabeth Martinez, Nelly Fernandez, Martha Cotera, and many others were at the forefront of this information revolution. They established independent community libraries, outreach programs, and bookmobiles in underserved communities. They produced lists of resources for Chicano studies departments and programs, developed library guides to Mexican American materials, and compiled countless bibliographies and databases to support a burgeoning scholarly field. They established libraries and built archival collections within research centers and community spaces. They worked with new federally funded information networks like the Educational Research Information Clearinghouse (now called the Education Resource Information Center) and the National Clearinghouse for Bilingual Education, developing specialized databases to assist Chicano educators, researchers, and community organizers. They demanded institutional change in libraries and graduate programs in information science, calling for the hiring of bilingual/bicultural librarians in Spanish-speaking communities, affirmative action programs, and hard funding lines for outreach programs. They started Latina/o caucuses and organizations (e.g., REFORMA) within professional associations like the American Library Association and the Society of American Archivists to push for institutional change, and they wrote reports and articles that documented this labor for the federal agencies that funded them and for library journals. While these efforts to increase information access for both scholars and the community are rarely featured in accounts of the Chicano movement, they were nevertheless instrumental to its goals.[14] Martha Cotera's professional trajectory as a librarian and an information specialist, and later as a feminist writer (she wrote her first article on Chicana feminist history in 1973), offers an embodied history of Chicana/o information praxis that illuminates the ways in which she, and others in the field, worked to further the goals of the Chicano movement from within a knowledge system designed to sustain hierarchies of power.

By her own account, Martha first came to understand the power of information through her childhood experience in the El Paso Public Library. She recalls how her mother, Altagracia Castaños—who was raising two daughters on her own and working multiple jobs to sustain the family—would drop her and her sister, Velia, off at the public library to spend the day whenever she had to work double shifts. Martha flourished in the space of the library, which was like a second home to her, developing as a reader and thinker under the watchful eyes of the mostly progressively minded white women who worked there and who clearly recognized a budding bibliophile in the young girl. She remembers that it was Elizabeth Kelly, the children's librarian when Velia and she (ages six and nine) first moved to El Paso, who taught them both how to read. Kelly became a "life-long mentor" to Martha: She hired her as a library aide, found scholarship money for her to go to Texas Western College (now the University of Texas at El Paso), and introduced her to Marcelle Hamer, head of the Southwest collection at the library, who would become another instrumental mentor.[15] Indeed, in 1958, when Kelly decided to organize uncatalogued materials in the library's basement and to create a new department for federal, international, and state documents and periodicals, Hamer encouraged Martha, by that time a college student, to apply for the job of senior library aide, which in actual practice turned out to be the position of acting director of the department.[16] According to Martha, Hamer recognized her as an "independent sort" who would thrive in the semiautonomous world of the archives: "She said, 'If you want to do anything in this library alone, autonomous, you yourself, do it in documents. So you just ask to be in charge of that. Just do it.'"[17]

Martha was let loose in the "wild region in the public library which is documents, federal documents, . . . state documents, local documents, oral history, a lot of things that had not been touched."[18] Because the El Paso library was part of the Federal Depository Library Program that made US federal government publications available to the public, the job of organizing its collection of government documents gave Martha access to "privileged" information, including up-to-the-minute reports on civil rights hearings and federal archives documenting how the House Un-American Activities Committee had targeted civil rights leaders across the Southwest.[19] Martha became intimately familiar with this archive of power as she worked to organize and index the sprawling collection—which also included Southwestern archives, genealogies, periodicals, and rare books—learning not only about the different ways the state responds to challenges to its hegemony but also about how archival silences sustain relations of domination and subordination. She noticed, for example, that while the library had numerous collections documenting Anglo settlement of the border, it had very few materials on Mexican settlement in the region, and she wondered how this lack of archival sources influenced the kinds of political claims that Mexican Americans might make on the state.[20] Through this arduous cataloging project, Martha not only acquired the basic skills of organizing collections but also developed a deeper understanding of the importance of information: how it could be used to connect people to their own history, how it could reveal disparities in resource allocation, and how it could lay bare the networks of power that structurally marginalized her community. For Martha, this new role as a collections specialist was a "step beyond being a librarian" because it involved organizing information into an "identifiable form so that teachers, scholars and others can get their hands on it."[21] From this moment on, she considered herself "an information specialist and a bibliographer more than anything else."[22]

Reflecting on this period of her life, Martha recalls how she came to the realization that being a librarian was potentially "very very radical, because you've got information that is almost privileged—because it is esoteric—that you can feed to the community for their use."[23] Indeed, her access to the city planning documents in the El Paso library's collection revealed how the Mexican American community had been systematically underserved by the library commission. In what was surely her first act of public advocacy, Martha exposed these disparities and, working with the community, pushed for the next library branch (the Armijo branch) to be built in El Paso's Segundo Barrio.[24] From this first experience with conducting research to change public policy (what she would later come to understand as "power structure research"), Martha learned that information could be a "powerful tool for community development."[25] Indeed, it was in the collection room of the El Paso Public Library that Martha came to understand how the library could be both a site for the preservation of "esoteric" knowledge (the very infrastructure of power) and also, potentially, a resource for challenging structural inequality.

This lesson was cemented by the contradictions she faced working as a document librarian for the Texas State Library in Austin.[26] According to Martha, she got the State Library job as a result of Marcelle Hamer's powerful professional network: "Ms. Hamer had been J. Frank Dobie's research assistant and was well connected in Austin with all the librarians, and she connected me with Dr. [Nettie Lee] Benson and Dr. Dorman Winfrey," who was then head of the State Library. Winfrey hired Martha as director of federal documents "before the job even opened up in 1964 because of my five years of experience in El Paso."[27] At the State Library (in a position that was third from the top within the library's staff hierarchy), Martha was tasked with managing federal depositories across the state, organizing the sprawling collection of documents housed in the library's archive, and assisting the Texas legislature in research for the development of public policy. She recalls that the library had seemingly countless "documents piled up for a hundred and some-odd years and they had never had a document librarian to get them in order and index them, put them up, service, anything." Martha set up the department, organized and indexed the books, and got a patron service up and running in just four years. As Hamer had predicted earlier, she labored alone at first, but in a few years' time she was running a huge department with a staff of seven. "We had over 600,000 items and we serviced all the state agencies and we coordinated services for about twenty-eight [federal] Depositories throughout a certain part of the state."[28]

Martha's elevated position at the State Library was by any measure a coup for a young Mexican American librarian in 1964, especially in Texas, where relations between Anglos and Mexican Americans were historically fraught. David Montejano has documented the antagonisms and compromises that characterized Mexican and Anglo relations in the "making of Texas" in the nineteenth and early twentieth centuries.[29] By the mid-1960s, when Martha and her husband, Juan, arrived in Austin, a rising Mexican American civil rights movement was actively challenging the Anglo power structure in Texas and drawing national attention to the racial and economic marginalization of Mexicans in rural agricultural communities like the Lower Rio Grande Valley and Crystal City, as well as urban spaces like Austin and San Antonio (just seventy-five miles from Crystal City).[30] During her time at the State Library, Martha and Juan became increasingly more involved with the Chicano movement in Austin, building important connections to an earlier generation of Mexican American activists at the University of Texas, including Professors George Sánchez and Américo Paredes, as well as a network of progressive Anglos and Mexican Americans who were working to improve conditions for Mexican Americans throughout Texas. Through her work at the State Library, Martha also forged important professional connections to a growing network of progressive educators, librarians, and researchers who were finding creative ways to capitalize on newly available federal funding to service the education and information needs of the Mexican American community.[31]

As she had done in El Paso, and as she would continue to do in the years that followed, Martha used her access to state and federal information systems and documents to conduct power structure research in the service of various Chicano mobilizations. "There were too many things happening in Austin," she recalls. "There were problems with the police, problems with the school, problems with elections, problems with everything and we were more and more involved. . . . We were involved with a lot of planning, social services kind of things in Austin."[32] She and Juan worked on numerous projects during this intense period. They helped establish community-controlled clinics, fought "urban renewal" projects that affected Black and brown communities, assisted in legal battles over educational equity, and demanded a livable infrastructure (paved and lighted streets) in long-ignored East Austin barrios.

Shadowing these exciting new political and professional convergences were the contradictions of working within the documentary apparatus of the state, an archive of power that upheld the very unequal relations that Martha was increasingly working to undo in her off-hours. These contradictions were highlighted when in the midst of an extended legal battle to repeal the poll tax (a legal mechanism designed to suppress Mexican American and African American voting in Texas), she was asked by Governor John Connally to find evidence in the state archive to prove that the poll tax was not a regressive tax.[33] Martha recalls that it was this experience that made her realize how research could impact policy. Indeed, it was within this archive of power—preserved in the local, state, and federal documents that she was organizing and that were being put to use in the service of repressive policies—that she would develop her considerable power structure research skills.[34] While her boss, State Librarian Dorman Winfrey, had always been sympathetic to her political commitments and supportive of her professionally, Martha sensed that her rising visibility within the Chicano movement would only undermine her status as a department head, and quite possibly damage the reputation of the institution itself. Tasked with doing the research work of the state against the needs of the community—at a time when she was being increasingly drawn into the legal and political battles precipitated by Chicano movement demands for equal justice—Martha felt she had to choose between the path of activism and her professional career. She decided to quit her job at the State Library in 1968: "I just wanted to cut out when it became obvious that I might create an embarrassing situation for them."[35]

She would temporarily resolve these professional contradictions by taking a job as library director and information specialist at the Southwest Educational Development Laboratory (SEDL), a nonprofit educational research center focused on bilingual and migrant education. Funded by a development grant from the US Office of Education, SEDL was one of twenty regional educational laboratories that were established from February to September of 1966, in an effort to develop "validated" instructional and curricular innovations that could be adopted at the local level to address "educational problems of national significance."[36] Each laboratory pursued distinct strategic program areas and operated as an autonomous (though mostly federally funded) nonprofit agency. Their mission was to bring together "individuals from state departments of education, public and private schools, colleges and universities, schools of education, and industrial and cultural organizations" who were familiar with the "educational problems of an area," were "competent to design and direct programs" to address those problems, and "who would have the experience and authority to operate in the jurisdictions affected by such programs."[37] A major programmatic focus of SEDL, where Martha worked, was bilingual/bicultural education, which encompassed educational materials for bilingual and migrant children, as well as in-service training for teachers.[38]

Martha was well familiar with the "educational problems" of the children who were at the center of SEDL's mission, and she also had the "experience and authority" to effectively implement the laboratory's mission to address the educational needs of underserved Mexican American communities. Indeed, during her four years at the State Library, she had become increasingly involved in educational reform initiatives, particularly in the area of bilingual/bicultural education. She also had access to the newest bilingual/bicultural education research as a result of her work with emergent networked information resources like the Educational Research Information Clearinghouse (ERIC), a massive database of research studies, reports, and other educational resources made available to the public through a network of regional clearinghouses (she was one of the consultants who assisted in the development of ERIC's first thesaurus of search terms in 1966).[39] Moreover, she had several years of experience as an information consultant for education researchers in various federally funded clearinghouses and research centers, among them SEDL.

She also had on-the-ground experience (and credibility) with teachers, parents, and students who, by the late 1960s, were actively challenging an apartheid-like educational system in Texas. In her off-hours, Martha worked with Texans for the Educational Advancement of Mexican Americans (TEAM), an organization of educational advocates started in the early 1960s to address inequality in Texas schools by conducting assessments of the unequal distribution of resources across the Austin Independent School District and documenting instances of racism within schools across the state.[40] She was also actively involved with University of Texas students in the Mexican American Student Organization (MASO), and later the Mexican American Youth Organization (MAYO), as they demanded increased numbers of Chicana/o students, faculty, and staff on campus; a more relevant curriculum; and the establishment of a Center for Mexican American Studies.

SEDL seemed like the perfect place for Martha to merge her professional aspirations as an information specialist and librarian with her desire to support the struggle for educational equity in Texas.[41] Several colleagues in her network of educational activists had committed to working with the lab, including Josué González, the president of TEAM; José Cárdenas, who would become the first Chicano superintendent of San Antonio's Edgewood School District in 1969; Blandina "Bambi" Cardenas, who would eventually pursue a doctorate in education and become the president of the University of Texas–Pan American; Mario Benitez, a University of Texas professor and a noted expert in bilingual/bicultural education; and Andre Guerrero, an expert on migrant student curricula. Moreover, the "laboratory" model seemed to offer a perfect opportunity for researchers, educators, policy experts, and community activists to work together on substantive change in educational services for Mexican American children, particularly migrant and Spanish-dominant learners. Martha envisioned her work at the lab as an ideal way to channel her knowledge and skills while also contributing to the pressing educational needs of her community: "I felt that bilingual, bicultural programs were needed. And maybe I could put in my eight hours of work there, or longer, and still do something positive."[42]

By 1968, when Martha joined SEDL, her educational advocacy work was being elaborated in an increasingly radical context with the eruption of Chicano student walkouts—many of them orchestrated by MAYO—in high schools across Texas.[43] Martha recalls that "TEAM was a lot of the energy behind school walkouts in Texas," and Chicanas/os at the lab "were all educational activists" who supported the student walkouts: "They were developing the materials, I was doing the information. We were all members of TEAM. We would do surveys of the schools and show where there were inequities." Describing the "underhanded" way that Chicanas/os at SEDL funneled resources to the community, she notes,

> The powers that be at the Southwest Lab didn't realize that we were developing materials at the Lab and with St. Edward's University activists, the priests there . . . to help the school walkouts. A lot of the work we did was kind of underhanded and using the resources of the "master's house" to help the community. And so all of us were developing curriculum to be used at the walkouts . . . the walkout at Weslaco, the walkout in Houston, the walkouts in Dallas, the walkouts in Del Rio, the walkout in El Paso, and then the walkout in Crystal City, but there were many other student walkouts.[44]

Indeed, when MAYO helped organize a massive student walkout in Crystal City, Texas, in December of 1969, Josué González, then president of TEAM (and a SEDL staff member), mobilized Chicana/o staff at the lab to assist in the effort. Martha recalls how Chicanas/os at SEDL collectively sprang into action, using their access to cutting-edge research on bilingual/bicultural education—and even office supplies—to support the students who had walked out: "That's the only good thing [SEDL] ever did, was provide resources. They didn't know it. *We took it* [my emphasis]. Through those resources, I would help communities in trouble with communication lines, curriculum material, pencils, papers—anything we could get together in Austin."[45] When TEAM members from across the state traveled to Crystal City in mid-December to set up a "liberation school" during the Christmas holidays, Martha helped to develop a curriculum with Blandina Cardenas, one of her colleagues at SEDL, and worked with other TEAM members and the community to coordinate the effort. Martha recalls that the TEAM chapter in Austin recruited more than twenty-seven volunteers to tutor in Crystal City, and provided $200 to $300 worth of materials for the effort.[46]

> What we would do is get local volunteers and volunteers from Austin and different cities . . . and we would find a church or auditorium or some place. The parents would do the cooking and help with the general logistics, putting up the people that went to volunteer. And we would have curriculum to give to the teachers that would do a teach-in. . . . And they would negotiate—the walkout leaders—with TEA, the Texas Education Agency, so the children wouldn't lose credit. And then that way the kids wouldn't get behind in school, you know, and they would continue with their semester. But the District would lose money. And so the District had to negotiate because every day they were losing money from the State. And so this was a very good strategy to get the school districts to reform services for Latino students. So, without the Lab knowing, we would develop these curriculums.[47]

But even while Chicana/o staff at SEDL were able to capitalize on their access to resources and federal funding to support direct action efforts like the walkouts in Crystal City and elsewhere, they were also frustrated by the institutional barriers that seemingly made structural change impossible. What good was it to demand more Chicana/o teachers and administrators when schools of education, like the one at the University of Texas, refused to recruit and train Chicana/o educators, and universities were resisting demands for the establishment of Chicano studies departments that could provide the crucial research infrastructure for a new curriculum? Where would educational professionals come from if Chicanas/os were facing institutional barriers at every stage of their educational journeys from elementary school to higher education?[48] Indeed, these very institutional barriers were reflected in the staffing patterns at SEDL, an irony that did not escape the attention of Chicana/o staff. While the organizational mission of the regional educational laboratories promoted a vision of working with the community to address educational inequality, in reality SEDL's administrative structure rarely included Mexican Americans, much less nonprofessionals, in substantive decision-making processes.[49] For Martha and other Chicanas/os associated with the lab, this racialized division of labor reflected the racism at the heart of the "white liberal" approach to incremental social change.[50]

While SEDL's focus on developing bilingual/bicultural programs undoubtedly spoke to Martha's need to do "information work" that mattered, her role within the lab's Anglo-dominant structure raised new contradictions as the Chicano movement, like other ethnic movements in the late 1960s, shifted toward a more radical vision of self-determination and autonomy. Martha admits that she "went to work with [SEDL] very idealistically" but left "very disillusioned. But on the other hand this was good, because I figured out that . . . it's very difficult to grow and develop as a Chicano within an Anglo institution." For Martha, the experience at SEDL was "eye-opening for working, or not working with the white liberal establishment. . . . I realized that you just cannot do it . . . the two systems cannot grow . . . within each other. . . . They can grow side by side; they can interact. But interaction is not developing within." While the ideals behind the lab's organizational structure—which brought researchers, educators, and community members together to develop projects that would be implemented in underserved communities—spoke to her growing understanding of how information could be put to liberatory ends, she came to realize that a group led by Anglos, however well-intentioned in its efforts, "was incapable of structuring the education curriculum and philosophy that we need."[51] In order to develop new educational approaches from within, Chicanas/os would have to build their own institutions, free from Anglo control.

Martha's disillusionment with SEDL reflected a "growing discontent and distrust of Anglo-controlled institutions" within the Chicano movement in the late 1960s.[52] The historian Carlos L. Cantú has noted how this shift from liberal demands for inclusion to calls for "educational self-determination" signaled an increasing sense among educational activists that "in order to disrupt the foundations of institutionalized discrimination in Texas schools they needed to gain control of the means of educational production."[53] Like Martha, many Chicano educational activists in Texas were frustrated at the slow pace of educational reforms, and especially with the haphazard implementation of new policies around bilingual and migrant education. But they were also galvanized by their involvement in direct action efforts like the school walkouts, an experience that not only highlighted the pressing issues affecting Chicano youth but also exposed them to a radical praxis of education in the liberation schools that were coordinated by TEAM. Indeed, while volunteers were tasked with teaching students from their textbooks so they could keep up with the standard curriculum, they also developed early prototypes of ethnic studies courses that exposed students to Chicano history, arts, and culture, as well as power structure research. In his political memoir, *The Making of a Chicano Militant*, José Ángel Gutiérrez recalls that TEAM's liberation classes were a huge success in the community, drawing not just students but also "parents in large numbers" to the various churches and even outdoor spaces that had become a new classroom for the people.[54]

Martha recalls that it was during the Crystal City walkouts that she and other TEAM members, including Aurelio Montemayor and Andre Guerrero, first discussed the idea of expanding their pedagogical efforts and forming an independent college to train Chicano educators.[55] The idea for an independent college was formally proposed by Narciso Alemán at the first national MAYO meeting on December 19, 1969 (held at La Lomita mission in Mission, Texas). After some debate, the plan was endorsed by MAYO, and the first independent Chicano college, Colegio Jacinto Treviño, was born.[56] Tasked with developing the "intellectual impetus" for the new independent college, the educator and activist Aurelio Montemayor drew together fellow TEAM members, including Martha and Juan Cotera, to write a series of position papers for Colegio Jacinto Treviño that, in the words of Andre Guerrero, offered a "blueprint for educational change in the Southwest."[57] For the next ten months Martha worked on two position papers. Her position paper "Bicultural Education in a Humanistic Setting" proposed a pedagogical approach that drew from Mexican cultural values to develop both knowledge and concientización among members of the Mexican American community.[58] Her position paper "The Library and Information Functions as Meaningful Activities in a Chicano Graduate Program" outlined an ambitious plan for a library that would make Colegio Jacinto Treviño an "intelligence unit / information hub for the entire community."[59] Determined to take an active role in making the colegio dream a reality, Martha submitted her resignation to SEDL in January of 1970 and moved to Mercedes, Texas, with her husband and their preschool-aged daughter (me). Juan would teach urban planning at Colegio Jacinto Treviño, and she would "set up the library and also teach information." She took with her the tools of her trade and little else: "We went totally on a volunteer basis. We did not have a salary. And . . . they gave us an apartment and we had contributions from the community. . . . They gave us a lot of food . . . USDA food."[60]

Upon arriving in Mercedes, Martha began building Colegio Jacinto Treviño's "information hub," starting with a base of resources that she had brought with her from SEDL and Andre Guerrero's collection of materials from his work with Teacher Corps (about ten to fifteen boxes in total). Drawing on her long-standing connections to the University of Texas, Martha was also able to get curricular support for the colegio from senior scholars like George Sánchez and Américo Paredes (who visited Jacinto Treviño in its first few months of existence and gave a public lecture).[61] Yet, despite this promising start, the original collective that brought Colegio Jacinto Treviño into being would be undone within the year, a victim—like so many other visionary projects in the late 1960s—of unrealistic demands for ideological purity and differences of vision regarding how to best serve the community.[62] Some, like Andre Guerrero and Leonard Mestas (the only member of the collective who held a PhD), would move on to form another autonomous education project, Juárez–Lincoln University, while others, like Martha and Juan, would put their talents and expertise to work in the service of other Chicano movement self-determination efforts.[63] Notwithstanding this disappointment, the process of designing an autonomous "intelligence unit / information hub for the entire community" undoubtedly shaped Martha's understanding of the importance of information to the struggle for Chicana/o self-determination. As Carlos Cantú notes, the rise of autonomous knowledge projects like Colegio Jacinto Treviño reflected the desire of Chicanas/os "to claim control of influential institutions, to work collectively as historical agents, and to transform their own realities."[64] These would be the signature aims of Martha's information praxis in the 1970s.

There is a photo of my parents packing to leave for Mercedes in 1970. Surrounded, as always, by her library, my mother is smiling broadly as my father hands her two books from the shelf, ostensibly to pack them in the box at her side. I cannot help but see in this image an act of revolutionary love that captures the joy and the promise of that critical juncture in my mother's trajectory as a tlamatini. Indeed, her decampment in 1970 from the institution to its peripheries marked an important refusal: a final, irrevocable theft that was the logical extension of her practice of stealing the "master's tools" that began with that first moment she was allowed access to them in the El Paso Public Library. My mother had used her access to powerful information infrastructures and "esoteric" knowledges to feed the community over and over again, until she refused to continue to be a resource of the state and stole herself away, taking with her the experience, the connections, and the skills she had developed working within the master's house and putting them into service for an autonomous project that she believed would allow a new

FIGURE 2.2. *Martha and Juan Cotera pack to leave Austin for Mercedes, Texas, in 1970. [AS-70-76114-003], Photograph by Larry Murphy.* Austin American-Statesman *Photographic Morgue (AR.2014.039). Austin History Center, Austin Public Library.*

generation of Chicana/o educators to develop a knowledge base from within. But this joyous photo, and the leave-taking it documents, is also shadowed by institutional erasure, leaving me to wonder about what it meant for her to betray the institution at this juncture in her professional life. She had landed the Texas State Library job as a result of Marcelle Hamer's powerful connections. Her boss, State Librarian Dorman Winfrey, was supportive of her professionally and would have no doubt promoted her career, perhaps even encouraging her to get a degree in library science, a credential that would have secured her status as one of the leading Chicana librarians of the decade. Indeed, had she chosen the credentialed path—the "path of professionalization," as Stefano Harney and Fred Moten put it—she would have certainly been granted visibility in historical accounts of Chicana/o librarianship. But she refused that future when she embraced fugitivity, disappearing "into the underground, the downlow lowdown maroon community of the university, into the Undercommons of Enlightenment, where the work gets done, where the work gets subverted."[65] It was a decision that would seal her fate as both an intellectual and a librarian. Though she would emerge as a leading voice in Chicana feminism, her work as a librarian would become a palimpsest in historical accounts of Chicana/o librarianship.

My mother once told me a story about an exchange she had with her boss at SEDL shortly after submitting her resignation. When he asked her how much Colegio Jacinto Treviño was paying her, she replied, "'Nothing, I'm just going to do it for them for free.' And he said, 'Well, you're going to do it for them for free, why don't you do it for us for $10,700?' I said, 'Because I don't want to do it for you, not even for $12,000.'"[66] There is an absurdist humor in this haggling over a salary that she knew would never be paid. A rebelliousness, too, in the way she marks the value of her labor. In refusing to be undersold, but also refusing the idea that her labor could be bought and sold in the first place, my mother lifted the veil that hid her "underhanded" activities within the archive of power and revealed herself, finally, as a "subversive intellectual" who had come "under false pretenses, with bad documents, out of love."[67] But my mother's shift from "stealing" to "fugitivity" was not simply an escape from the contradictions of working within an Anglo institution during a historical moment characterized by calls for greater self-determination; it was an embrace of a different kind of "unsettled" information praxis, a "being in motion that has learned that 'organizations are obstacles to organizing ourselves' (The Invisible Committee in The Coming Insurrection) and that there are spaces and modalities that exist separate from the logical, logistical, the housed and the positioned."[68] My mother's escape to these "spaces and modalities" radically transformed her information praxis. For the next decade she would follow the path of the tlamatini, building libraries and collections, creating data infrastructures and knowledge projects, raising consciousness, and putting the resources of the state and its institutions to work for the community.

## LA BIBLIOTECA: THE LIBRARY REIMAGINED

While the political turmoil at Colegio Jacinto Treviño prevented Martha from fully realizing her concept for an information/research hub for the total community, the idea would provide an animating vision for the development of comprehensive library services for Chicanas/os in Crystal City, Texas. When she and Juan left Mercedes, Texas, for Crystal City in June of 1971, the small town had become ground zero for MAYO's Winter Garden Project, a political plan coordinated by José Ángel Gutiérrez to gain community control of the city councils, school boards, and county governments of Zavala, La Salle, and Dimmit Counties (where Chicanas/os were the demographic majority).[69] Capitalizing on the successful mobilization of the Chicana/o community around the 1969 student walkouts, the Raza Unida Party—the local political mechanism of the Winter Garden Project—won important positions in Crystal City's 1970 municipal elections, gaining Chicano majorities on the city council and the school board. Chicano control of these bodies was further consolidated when Anglos resigned their positions in protest, or were forced out.[70] These electoral victories, and the ones that followed, created sweeping economic, political, and social changes in Crystal City. As Armando Navarro notes in his analysis of the "quiet revolution" launched by the Winter Garden Project, the Crystal City takeover offered a new cadre of Chicana/o professionals from across the state (and the Southwest) the opportunity to contribute their knowledge and skills to a radical experiment in Chicana/o self-determination and community control.[71] Like Martha and Juan, they answered José Ángel Gutiérrez's call for Chicanas/os to "take power" over the key political, economic, and educational infrastructures that had for too long systematically marginalized working-class Chicanas/os, and to envision new infrastructures that would serve "the poor, the working class, the migrant."[72] Juan became the director of the urban renewal office and would lead the effort to extend basic services to long-ignored barrios, from upgraded housing and public facilities, to fundamental infrastructure like sewage, water, and electrification. Martha worked with the new city government to develop culturally relevant library and information services for the Chicana/o community of Cristal.

During her first six months in Crystal City, she worked (on a voluntary basis) to rebuild the library at the city's high school, which had suffered years of neglect under the haphazard supervision of a school librarian who, like many Anglo teachers and staff, had resigned in the wake of the walkouts.[73] As Martha recalls, the high school library program was "a mess." The reference materials were stored in a closet, students were not taught how to use indexes, none of the periodicals were cataloged or organized, and most of the library's subscriptions were for industry magazines that weren't even housed in the library (which suggested that school library funds were being used to purchase professional publications for the agriculture industry).[74] Martha set to work at the high school immediately, pulling students out of detention to serve as her aides. Together they organized and indexed the materials, and in the process she trained them to become "experts" in information services and research, just as she herself had been trained at the El Paso Public Library. The students she worked with later served as peer library aides. She also offered the students informal training in power structure research, teaching them how information shaped public policy and how it could be mobilized as a critical tool in struggles for community self-determination. In just six months she transformed the Crystal City High School library into a site for the development of critical consciousness among the young people of Cristal through information literacy.[75]

She carried this praxis into her work at the Crystal City Public Library. While the city library was in somewhat better shape than the high school library, it had very few Spanish-language materials and only one Chicana/o movement periodical, *El Grito*.[76] Reimagining the public library as a knowledge center for the community, Martha developed programs, services, and collections designed to help Chicanas/os in Crystal City feel that they had ownership over the institution—its books and games, and even its archives—just as they had come to feel about their schools.[77] Working with a budget of just $10,500 (which covered her salary and the salary of one assistant, books, supplies, and programming), Martha expanded the library's collection, acquiring Chicana/o literary and scholarly works, movement periodicals, and, through a donation from the Mexican government, a collection of about two thousand books in Spanish, covering a basic undergraduate curriculum, including volumes on "pre-Columbian history, colonial history, art aesthetics, revolutionary period history and contemporary history."[78] In order to get a better sense of the information needs in Crystal City, she and her volunteer staff attended community meetings and neighborhood events, went to churches, and even walked door-to-door to meet potential library patrons. According to Martha, "Staff explored grocery stores, barber shops and beauty parlors" to see what people were reading in order to shape the collection. They connected with the local Spanish-language press and sought out "hidden scholars" in the area (many of whom were farmworkers) "to encourage them to use the library and to help identify materials of interest to the community."[79] Based on this survey of the community, she developed innovative approaches to creating a true library of the people, including a "novelas exchange program" (where patrons could bring in fotonovelas that they had already read and exchange them for others), puppet shows based on Mexican and Chicana/o history, learning circles where elders shared their historical knowledge and skills in arts and crafts with children, and a migrant book service that provided reading material to children on the migrant stream.[80] The library also became a site for the preservation of community knowledge through oral history and archive development projects, "so that the community could understand how [Cristal] had developed into such a radical town."[81] Most importantly, she implemented policies that opened access to the library as a physical space, extending its hours of operation to accommodate those who worked until late in the evening, launching a bookmobile in a refurbished van purchased with funds from the US Department of Labor, and even handing over the keys to the building to Teacher Corps students who were studying to become bilingual/bicultural educators. "They could study all night long in the library if they wanted to. And it was wonderful, finally, as a librarian, to have the kind of freedom where you could offer library services that were totally community oriented, where people had ownership of a library. To me, it was a dream come true."[82]

Martha's outreach efforts at the Crystal City library were in step with a general trend in radical librarianship in the early 1970s, which increasingly focused on innovative ways to service communities that had been largely ignored by traditional library programs.[83] But she also pushed against the conceptual boundaries of the "outreach" model of service provision to Chicana/o communities. For Martha, the library shouldn't just be about providing services to patrons; rather, it should be reimagined as a collectively owned space of information exchange where people could contribute their resources (time, money, documents, books, knowledge) for everyone to share: "a place for people to have materials that they can use; but to *have* them, not a place where there are materials for people to read and use. But . . . a place for them to *have*."[84] In a statement titled "Library Services to Mexican-Americans," presented to the US Commission on Libraries and Information Science on April 24, 1974, Martha insisted that the library was "one institution in the community that might serve as a Survival center for powerless persons in the community because of the information and knowledge which can be gathered there. The library is also the keeper of a community's history, recorded and unrecorded through special collections; the library is also a place for recreation and life enjoyment." Surveying the state of library services in 1974, she concluded that "the library and the materials now held by libraries in Texas means none of these things to the Chicano community. Archives and historical societies, as they now exist in local history files in the libraries, neither reflect nor represent the Chicano community. . . . 'no sirven, de nada, para nada' for the Chicano community."[85]

To address this issue, she argued, librarians would have to do more than simply expand their collections and seek out new patrons; they would have to radically reconceptualize their understanding of information itself, which, Martha contended, had been shaped by a "dehumanized way of interpreting information and knowledge" as an "end product" that

> only has validity if contained within the computer sciences, library books, magnetic tapes, and documentary films. What has happened to those carriers of data, either raw or highly digested, people? Look at the elderly who are considered solely as carriers of "outdated" data and who are shelved oftentimes in their prime when their usefulness to society could be realized? Similarly there are the poor, the "uneducated" members of our communities, who are looked down on by the gatherers of information and librarians. In relying solely on "end product" information, yet another potential avenue for humanizing one's life—contact with the experienced person, the aged, the disease-ridden, the drop out, and the unemployed is cut off.[86]

Such subjects ("the aged, the disease-ridden, the drop out, and the unemployed") were not just potential patrons, or objects of study (abstracted as empirical data); in their collective "accumulation of facts and transmitted experiences, coupled with personal experiences," they constituted "rich banks of knowledge from which each individual draws for living." Martha imagined these "rich banks of knowledge" as a kind of Chicana/o information undercommons that could be mobilized for the benefit of the "total community."[87]

In a beautiful essay on her philosophy of information services (based on her work in Crystal City), Martha outlined a "humanistic" theory of information that could surface these "rich banks of knowledge" for the benefit of the communities from which they emerged. "Information," she asserted, is "everything and everywhere," but it is manifested, first and foremost, in "human beings, by the information they accumulate through all their senses and by the transmittal of information through voice, gesture, brain waves and conscious communication by articulation or other means." While it is also found in print culture, audio and visual recordings, and even "transmitted by the physical environment," according to Martha, it is through human-to-human exchange that information has its most common transit.[88] Decentering the library as the only site for the preservation and exchange of information—and literacy as the only technology for its transmittal—Martha observed that "not one form of communication of information is the sole form. Not one motive or purpose for communicating information is the sole motive, and not one structure or service for compiling/collecting information is the sole structure for doing this."[89] Martha's "humanistic" vision of information as "everything and everywhere" challenged hierarchies of knowledge not only by explicitly identifying the people themselves as holders of "privileged" information but also by insisting that informal information networks *already existed* in "underserved" communities in the form of personal archives and family histories, shared book collections, oral traditions, storytelling, and even gossip. Compared to these human resources and networks, she contended, "traditional means of information preservation and exchange are, indeed, unimaginative and sometimes useless."[90] In embracing the Chicana/o community as both an "information bank" and a noninstitutional infrastructure for knowledge exchange, Martha exposed the limitations of the top-down infrastructural imaginary of traditional libraries and archives, an imaginary with which she had become intimately familiar in her professional transit from the Texas State Library to the Southwest Educational Development Lab, and finally to her work with Chicana/o self-determination projects like Colegio Jacinto Treviño and the "Cristal experiment." But while her work with Chicana/o self-determination projects satisfied the desire to build information infrastructures to benefit the "total community," her deep involvement in the Raza Unida Party also exposed new contradictions, particularly with respect to the gendered politics of the Chicana/o movement. These contradictions would shape new tlamatini information projects that were focused on the concientización of mujeres.

## TOWARD A CHICANA FEMINIST INFORMATION PRAXIS

At the heart of the Raza Unida Party's electoral successes in Crystal City and other Mexican American towns in South Texas was its strategy of incorporating the entire family in the political organizing process. In an interview conducted by Martha Cotera in the 1990s, José Ángel Gutiérrez described the Raza Unida Party as

> a family movement, a network of families. Instead of organizing just the men or just the kids, organize the total family and give each one of them a role . . . politicize all those group activities so that they become not only the passing of ritual, the practice of culture, but adding a political dimension as to why it's important for us to manifest ourselves as a complete person.[91]

This vision of the Chicana/o family as *the* central organizing unit for political mobilization—what Martha and others have termed "political familism"—opened up a space for women to play an expanded role in the Raza Unida Party.[92] For Martha, this strategy was about much more than recruiting more individuals to do the hard work of developing the party. As she noted in 1974, "By involving women we gain at least 50% more persons; we gain the ability to educate the total family; we gain the input/perspective that a female point of view will provide. It may not be better than a man's but it's crucial to have in order to plan policies which will be effective for the entire family and community."[93]

In her analysis of women in the Raza Unida Party, Dionne Espinoza has described how women's "work was vital to building and sustaining the infrastructure of the party in several key counties and at the statewide level." Women "ensured the smooth functioning of party headquarters, engaged in the door-to-door work of voter registration and campaigning, documented party correspondence, and organized rallies for candidates." Espinoza notes that while the party was organized hierarchically (with men, more often than not, occupying key leadership positions), its "rationalized formal structures" created many opportunities for women to take on instrumental roles at several levels in that hierarchy, "from precinct chairs, who were responsible for their designated voter areas, to county chairs, who convened meetings of the precinct chairs, to county-level executive committees just below the State Executive Committee."[94] For Chicanas, the dual experience of working within (if sometimes against) the party structure and mobilizing women to become active political agents raised new questions about the ideology of political familism and the "proper" role that women should play in the movement. Indeed, while the party had undoubtedly elevated La Chicana from an idealized "Adelita" figure, her role in the movement was nevertheless conditioned by a heteropatriarchal vision of the Chicano family that placed women in a distinctly supportive, or "logistical," role.[95]

While Martha notes that questions around the nature and degree of women's involvement had haunted the peripheries of the Chicana/o movement in Texas since at least the mid-1960s, they became particularly acute during the formation of the Raza Unida Party, when a series of movement conferences were organized across the state in order to develop a coordinated political platform for the party in advance of its first convention.[96] She recalls that it was at one of these meetings—the Raza Unida Conference in Houston in 1970—that a group of Chicanas and their male allies decided to caucus and demand workshops dealing with bread-and-butter issues relevant to the community (housing, health, childcare, education, cultural arts). Interrupting the scheduled proceedings, a group of eight women rushed the podium and pushed Martha to the microphone to voice their concerns. "Fortunately," she recalls, "I was able to articulate what we wanted. But I have to say that that did not endear me to . . . the guys. And somebody, a young man from the audience, screamed at me and said, 'You go back home and do the dishes where you belong!'" This moment of heteropatriarchal regulation and boundary keeping marked a turning point for Martha:

> I realized . . . I'm an information person, a librarian, a researcher, an archivist. I had worked archives in [the University of Texas] and worked archives in El Paso. And . . . all of a sudden I realized that all of these men, all they understood about women and everything that they thought about women was that—oh, and . . . because [the young man] also said . . . "Where you belong . . ." or something in reference to our culture, you know, like as our culture . . . dictates, or something like that. . . . You know, and then I thought to myself . . . these men, and a lot of women, don't have a clue. . . . They think that culture is defined . . . as who does the dishes around the house? That's their definition of culture, literally. And I thought . . . who needs a movement like this? [If] we cannot define culture . . . as something that is positive for all of us beyond logistics? . . . Culture is not who does the dishes around the house. Culture is not . . . a question of logistics. What you're talking about is logistics, not values, not culture, not anything. You know, you're talking logistics. That was . . . a real big moment for me. . . . That's when it all started, in a way.[97]

Although watching a cadre of male leaders consistently control the agenda for the future of the Chicano movement was undoubtedly frustrating, it was the experience of being publicly dismissed by a "young man" (Martha was thirty at the time) simply because she was a woman that cracked open the patriarchal ideology behind Chicano movement definitions of community, *carnalismo* (brotherhood), and political familism, revealing some of the fissures that would destabilize those concepts moving forward, as she, and many other Chicanas across the Southwest, experienced similar aha moments.[98]

This moment of public regulation also revealed that a very particular definition of culture was being mobilized in the ideology of cultural nationalism: "These men really defined culture as . . . who can dance Folklorico . . . who can make nice ceramics," or worse, "who does the dishes . . . who takes care of the babies." Moreover, demands for fealty to "traditional culture" were all too often grounded in a limited understanding of women's roles in the family and community, one that "defined [our] role logistically . . . as homemakers, defined us as mothers, you know, as wives, as lovers, you know, but not really as leaders or as decision-makers . . . within our own families and our own communities."[99] Martha understood that these limited definitions of culture and women's roles within the family structured the hierarchies of value of Chicano movement labor. Indeed, while the men were happy to accept "women that did the hard work of the [Raza Unida] party," women who "had an agenda that went beyond helping them logistically" were often ostracized and accused of not aligning with "Chicana/o cultural norms."[100] According to Martha, this dynamic was complicated by the increasing visibility of the women's liberation movement in left circles and in popular media in the late 1960s. When "the Women's Movement [came] along, all of a sudden, you know, these men kind of start looking around and saying, 'Wait a minute. We've got *feminism* here. You know, what are we going to do? We've got feminism here.' And they say, 'Ah, you're a feminist.' And we say, 'What? Who's a feminist? We're just doing what we've always done.'"[101]

Indeed, there were many examples of empowered women (who might be defined as feminists) within the Chicana/o movement in Texas. María L. de Hernández of San Antonio (who joined the Raza Unida Party in 1970) had engaged in political, educational, and labor struggles since at least the 1930s. Her keynote address at the first statewide Raza Unida Conference in Austin, Texas, in 1970 was an implicit recognition of this long history of activism. Moreover, the Crystal City native Virginia Múzquiz had played a key role in organizing the first Mexicano electoral takeover in Crystal City in 1963, when five Mexican American candidates (known as Los Cinco) won places on the city council. She had even run for the Texas legislature in 1964, and José Ángel Gutiérrez himself had served as her campaign manager.[102] It was his experience working with Múzquiz that taught Gutiérrez how to mobilize family networks for political organizing. Indeed, as Martha Cotera has suggested in her writing and speeches, Virginia Múzquiz is the true mother of political familism and had continued to play a key role as a mentor and political organizer in Crystal City after the electoral victories that swept Chicanas/os and the Raza Unida Party into power in 1970.[103] There was a deeper history too. Martha recalls that as a child, the elder women in her family would regale her with stories of "Doña Josefa Ortiz de Dominguez, Leona Vicario, Sor Juana [Inés de la Cruz], Doña Marina (La Malinche) and La Monja Alferez," accounts that were "full of analysis about why men were purposeful in portraying these women as silly, crazy, or insubordinate."[104] That many Chicanos, and even some Chicanas, in the Raza Unida Party viewed feminism as a "foreign" and divisive ideology, as opposed to something organic to Chicana/o communities, was symptomatic of this intentional erasure.

For Martha, the negative vision of feminism among the ranks of both men and women in the movement was essentially an *information* problem. As she noted in a 1973 oral history interview,

> If the guys are concerned now and confused, I think, more than anything else it's because we don't know. Once we know that [women are] part of our background, our history and that we cannot castigate women, say, for following in this tradition, then we won't say, well, this woman was strong because she's copying, or emulating the gringo. . . . If they feel that she is strong because she is emulating Chicano models, we'll be free again . . . because Chicano women have been very free in the movement to activate and to move and everything. It's just very recently that we've had a lot of suspicion cast upon us and we've had a lot of problems. . . . We've got to show that it is part of our tradition to have women involved and that we're acting in the proper historical context [*laughter*].[105]

As Martha frequently pointed out in the many speeches, essays, and workshops that document her work in the early 1970s, the "logistical" definition of women's proper roles as supporters and nurturers of the movement—but not partners and leaders in the development of ideology and political strategy—was not a reflection of traditional values; in fact, it had cut off a long tradition of "Mexicano feminism" (the title of her first published essay in 1973) that was essential to actualizing the goals of the Chicano movement in Texas and beyond. This gendered division of labor also ignored an important source of experiential information that was critical to the development of an effective party platform that could address the needs of the total community. If women were to be a key force in building a national political movement for Chicana/o self-determination, then they would have to become active political agents: to see themselves reflected in Chicana/o history, to develop the skills to organize rallies and political campaigns, to educate Chicana/o children, and to speak on behalf of Chicana/o communities.

From 1971 to 1978 (when the Raza Unida Party dissolved), Martha and other Chicanas in Texas—including Evey Chapa, Ino Alvarez, Consuelo

"Chelo" Avila, Lydia Espinosa, Rosie Castro, and Virginia Múzquiz—would work to fill this information gap and reclaim feminism from both Chicano nationalists, who saw it as a foreign threat to community solidarity, and Anglo feminists, who saw only themselves in its history, through an organized process of concientización. As Martha notes, the challenge of the "emergent Anglo feminist movement and the doubts it cast on Chicana commitment actually produced some positive results. More than ever women found themselves working on mutual development, on values clarification and on development of female leadership."[106] Martha recounts that for her, this process of feminist development and concientización began informally with the walkouts in Crystal City, when TEAM teachers (many of whom were women) requested educational materials that could be used to train high school walkout leaders: "I was always directing women who seemed to have an interest in women's issues towards feminist materials. . . . We had to develop these materials because a lot of the leaders of the walkouts were young women, so we needed to find materials to help them develop as leaders."[107] Building on this early work, and on the work of Chicana caucuses at local and statewide conferences, Martha Cotera, Ino Alvarez, and Evey Chapa launched a statewide initiative in 1973, Mujeres Pro Raza Unida (also known as Mujeres por la Raza), to bring more women into the party and train them to be effective leaders.

Evey Chapa recalls how the 1972 Raza Unida statewide campaign precipitated an "awakening" among women in the party:

> We went, ooh, goodness. If we can break through these barriers and bring everybody together with the issues that we think are important to the community, then we will be more successful, and more people will have power, self-empowerment. . . . If you educate one man, you educate one man. You educate a woman, you educate a whole bunch of living things in your household. And that's where we went with it.[108]

Chapa notes that their organizing began as an effort to mobilize a critical, yet underrecognized, constituency of the Raza Unida Party. At one of their earliest meetings, she recalls asking the women in attendance,

> "Look in this room and see who is doing all the work." And we all raised our hand, "We're doing all the work." So, if we bring five, times five, times five of us into the fold, into the working situation, then it'll be a more powerful situation for what we're trying to accomplish. And that was the birth of Mujeres por la Raza Unida.[109]

The first Mujeres Pro Raza Unida Conference was held in San Antonio on August 4, 1973. Over 160 women from across the state, including 30 from Crystal City, came together in sessions on the history and structure of the Raza Unida Party, political organizing, and education. They also engaged in consciousness-raising sessions focused on their Chicana identity. According to Cynthia Orozco, Martha Cotera prepared "A Reading List for Chicanas" to help guide the discussion. In an account of the San Antonio conference that she wrote for *La Verdad* (Crystal City's Spanish-language newspaper), Martha stated that "the purpose of this and other Mujeres Pro Raza Unida conferences is to teach women political techniques to use in their community, precinct, county, and state."[110] Martha noted that Chicanas at the conference enthusiastically embraced the opportunity to think seriously about their roles and responsibilities in the movimiento—from the perspective of women—and called for more opportunities to develop their consciousness as political agents. They also produced a number of resolutions to be incorporated into the Raza Unida Party platform, including a resolution in support of the striking Farah apparel company workers (who were 90 percent women), a resolution against police brutality, and a resolution against the construction of a Texas Ranger Hall of Fame in Waco, Texas.

After the first statewide meeting of Mujeres Pro Raza Unida, "eight regional Mujeres por la Raza Unida conferences were organized throughout the state," and numerous local chapters were established, including in San Antonio, Crystal City, Houston, Fort Worth, Austin, Kingsville, and Temple. According to Martha, a typical program for Mujeres Pro Raza Unida conferences included an overview of the Raza Unida Party's history, "concientización and Chicana history, political organizing, Party structure, special sessions for young women, and social and economic issues such as labor organizing, child care, education, sex discrimination, and employment." In addition to these sessions, organizers usually conducted preconference assessments of participants "to determine their level of awareness on women's issues and also on community issues."[111] This process of concientización was not isolated to the Raza Unida Party, or even the Chicano movement as a whole; it also reached into emerging feminist formations outside the movement. In order to ensure that Raza Unida Party women, and Chicanas outside the party, were included in national discussions of women in politics, Mujeres Pro Raza Unida established a powerful caucus within the National Women's Political Caucus. From this position they demanded recognition not only for the Raza Unida Party (as a registered political party) but also for a separate Chicana caucus that included Raza Unida Party women, Democrats, and Republicans from across the nation.[112]

The process of concientización mobilized by Mujeres Pro Raza Unida "established a consciousness of egalitarian values" among Raza Unida Party women, but even more importantly, it produced a "voluminous literature" as well as a Chicana model for "political training" that was the basis for a critical knowledge infrastructure for Chicanas in the early 1970s.[113] This voluminous literature included reading lists, resource books, teaching guides, bibliographies, and historical materials that were distributed, exchanged, and reproduced at Mujeres Pro Raza Unida conferences, caucus meetings, and workshops. It also included essays, poems, and articles in movement journals and newspapers, written by Martha Cotera, Evey Chapa, Inés Hernández Tovar (Ávila), and many others, to raise consciousness about Chicanas as political agents. Martha's training as a librarian and information specialist, her access to federal research databases like the Educational Research Information Clearinghouse (ERIC), and her connections to a growing network of Chicana feminists across the Southwest and Midwest (she was in regular correspondence with Anna NietoGomez, Betita Martínez, Cecilia Burciaga, Beverly Sánchez-Padilla, Julie Ruiz, Ruth Mojica-Hammer, and Olga Villa, among many others) placed her in an ideal position to collect and produce feminist materials that could be used to develop Chicanas as leaders in the movement in Texas and beyond.

Wearing multiple hats in the movement—librarian, archivist, information specialist, workshop leader, organizer, speaker, political candidate (she ran for the Texas State Board of Education on the 1972 Raza Unida Party ticket), and, increasingly, writer—Martha put her access to information to work in the early 1970s in the interest of creating a field of knowledge for and by Chicanas. By her own account, she turned to writing because she felt that there was a need to reach a much broader audience of women in order to combat the developing narrative of feminism (within both the Chicano movement and the women's movement) as exclusively white and middle-class. She pushed back against this narrative in her first published feminist essay, "Mexicano Feminism," which appeared in *Magazín* in September of 1973.[114] Part of a special section on "la mujer mexicana" that included essays by Chelo Avila and Evey Chapa, "Mexicano Feminism" drew from historical research and other materials that Martha had developed for her concientización workshops to challenge claims that feminism was "an ideology of an alien culture" and to demonstrate the "rich legacy of heroines and activists in social movements, and armed rebellions from which we can draw models to emulate."[115]

At first, Martha had resisted the urge to write. In an oral history interview conducted in the spring of 1973, shortly before her essay appeared in print, Martha noted that she had turned to writing as a last resort, to get the information out more quickly and to a broader swath of people. "I've never had time for writing," she insisted at the time. "Even in my field I don't write. I lecture a lot, but I've never written. But I'm going to have to write, because we're going to have to take the lead."[116] Ironically, this essay that she did *not* want to write was the nucleus for her comprehensive, federally funded study, *Profile on the Mexican American Woman* (1976), which she later published as *Diosa y Hembra: The History and Heritage of Chicanas in the U.S.* (1976), a book that would be read, photocopied, and shared by Chicanas across the country, cementing her reputation as a leading Chicana feminist public intellectual. But even as she was emerging as a strong Chicana feminist voice in print, Martha, a librarian at heart, was also thinking about ways to institutionalize and preserve the work she and others were doing to promote concientización among Chicanas. Working in collaboration with Chicanas across the country (in Texas, California, Washington, DC, and the Midwest), she conceptualized a plan for the Chicana Research and Learning Center, a multivalent information hub that would draw from the workshops and materials they had already developed and generate new resources and knowledge by and about Chicanas and women of color. Part grassroots research center, part educational collective, and part information clearinghouse, the Chicana Research and Learning Center was in many ways a feminist articulation of Martha's earlier vision for an intelligence unit and information hub at Colegio Jacinto Treviño that could serve as a resource for the development of the total community. Before long, the Chicana Research and Learning Center would become a key knowledge infrastructure for Chicana feminist concientización in Texas and beyond.

Chapter 3

# TLAMATINI INFRASTRUCTURES IN THE SHADOW OF PRECARITY

*I've always been a strong believer in alternative institutions. You know, if the regular institutions don't work . . . get out there and do something, even today . . . get out there and do something, because it's never gonna happen if you wait until people decide out of the goodness of their heart that it's time to provide the resources.*

MARTHA COTERA, ORAL HISTORY INTERVIEW, 2018

*I think that a lot of research that we started was followed up. I think we were the pioneers. I think we were the foremothers . . . of the Chicana academic movement. And . . . I believe that in that, you have all your careers because of us [*laughs*]. We're going to demand royalties very soon [*laughs*]. Ah, but that you're there, that you're there, that you're following up . . . that you figured out who your foremothers were, which is what we did when we [uncovered] Jovita Idar and the Magones, and all of those people. We did the same thing. And I never . . . dreamed back then that I would be here doing the same thing, . . . that maybe I'm your Jovita.*

EVEY CHAPA, ORAL HISTORY INTERVIEW, 2011

In the summer of 2020, my mother sent me an email with a cryptic message: "For my own sake. Thank you for forcing this issue, love you, Mom." Attached was a document with a series of reflections incited by our many pláticas about her information praxis in the 1970s. In the document, she recalled how her faith in the power of information was first ignited by informal pláticas with the elder women in her family:

> When I took in my grandmother's and my mother's lectures on Doña Josefa Ortiz de Domínguez, Leona Vicario, Sor Juana, Doña Marina (La Malinche) and La Monja Alférez, they were full of analysis about why men were purposeful in portraying these women as silly, crazy, or insubordinate. As in the case of Leona Vicario, when men said that the

> reason she melted her jewelry down for armaments to help in the war for independence, and went into battle, they said she only did it to be with her fiancée Andrés de Quintana Roo. Same way they defended the other heroines and gave me information on why and how they took action, and why their actions were justified. They always pointed to Sor Juana's story of cutting off her beautiful hair when she was frustrated that she was learning Latin too slowly, and that she did not deserve such beauty if she was so dumb.
>
> Their favorite saying was that information and knowledge was "tumba burros," meaning that when people became informed, they were no longer "burros" (ignorant).

Whenever she felt "insulted, diminished and marginalized as a young immigrant in El Paso," my mother simply followed her grandmother's and mother's model and "reached out to history, and learned that El Paso was our Indigenous space, and that all borders were artificial to our Indian ancestors. From birth, I never strayed far from books, as a girl, and always, they have been my safety-net, my 'just in case.'" That is why, she explained, information and analysis continue to be her "weapon of choice in our liberation."

> My "libraries" and other information efforts have been my armories; for fighting power structures, for educating communities AND convincing communities that they have a right to their tax dollars (by showing them the economics); connecting communities with directories, I moved from provider of information to producer of information and MORE UNCOMFORTABLY, to INFLUENCER, using information to drive policy and social change. I never intended to be an influencer or leader of any type. [But] I can be very effective in the role when I need to be because I can frame an entire campaign, all based on information; where people live, how people connect to each other, who are the most invested people in the issue, and who are the best campaigners on an issue, then I put a plan together and determine how long the campaign will last, how much it will cost, and what the results will be. This is how we built lasting social programs in Austin [Texas], created change, and built lasting institutions. I am always amazed that an insignificant purveyor of information and knowledge, a *Tlamatini* (Knowledge Keeper) can actually help transform communities.[1]

In this chapter I draw from my mother's comprehensive personal collection, which is currently being digitized by the Chicana por Mi Raza project, as well as a series of interviews, pláticas, and email exchanges about her information praxis, to trace her radical tlamatini knowledge praxis in the information projects she pursued in the mid-1970s.

Though Martha Cotera is generally known for her important early writings on Chicana feminism—which, along with the work of Enriqueta Vazquez, Betita Martínez, Anna NietoGomez, and others, laid the groundwork for the development of an intersectional analytic grounded in the lived experience of working-class Chicanas—she thought of herself, first and foremost, as an "information specialist."[2] Indeed, the expansive vision of information justice that shaped much of the work she undertook in both the Chicano movement and the women's movement in the 1970s was carried over into the projects she pursued after returning to Austin in 1973, from her contributions to the Mexican American Papers project at the Benson Latin American Collection at the University of Texas to a series of independent information projects she pursued into the 1980s, including the National Migrant Information Clearinghouse, the Chicana Research and Learning Center, and her publishing firm, Information Systems Development. Across these varied spaces and projects, Martha Cotera used her access to infrastructures of power—databases, federal grants, libraries, and institutions—not just to transform institutions from within but also to move resources into the community.

Yet, even as I recover these radical traces of the information infrastructures she built during this fruitful period, I am also haunted by their precarity. Because of the ephemeral nature of much of this information work, my mother is largely absent in histories of Chicano/Latino librarianship, even as her tlamatini information praxis is mostly invisible in the canon of Chicana feminist thought. On the one hand, my mother's refusal to conform her tlamatini vision to the accepted flows of knowledge from institutions to communities, and her insistence on information self-determination—reflected in her practice of creating knowledge hubs outside traditional institutions—meant that projects like the National Migrant Information Clearinghouse and the Chicana Research and Learning Center were quite vulnerable to fluctuating funding streams, sometimes hostile administrative bureaucracies, and shifting policy priorities. Indeed, if longevity is the measure of success, then it is not surprising that her various information projects, all of which pretty much ended by the late 1980s, have mostly been forgotten in accounts of Chicano/Latino librarianship in the 1970s. On the other hand, the recuperation of my mother's writing, particularly *Diosa y Hembra*, as her primary contribution to Chicana feminism has overshadowed the revolutionary information work she undertook during the same period, and consequently has reinforced a genealogical framework for Chicana feminist thought that privileges texts over resources. This framework, I have argued, reflects prevailing hierarchies in the academy, where recovery projects like the Chicana por Mi Raza archive are often seen as "labors of love," a form of community engagement, or simply as resources to be used by scholars, instead of forms of knowledge production in their own right.[3] And yet, as I will demonstrate, the information infrastructures Martha developed in the 1970s were as instrumental to the production of Chicana feminist thought as were her published essays, speeches, and books; in fact, the two were inextricably linked in her tlamatini praxis.

Speaking of the importance of infrastructure in a 2018 interview, my mother noted, "Without infrastructure, you don't get policy written, you don't get changes done, and also, without knowledge of that infrastructure, how do you pass that information from one generation to the next, so that the next generation doesn't have to start the process all over again?"[4] For her, projects like the National Migrant Information Clearinghouse and the Chicana Research and Learning Center offered alternative infrastructures for marginalized communities to navigate existing scales of power and radically transform information and its flows. In exploring the information infrastructures my mother developed in the 1970s, I aim to surface a genealogy of Chicana knowledge praxis that examines process (infrastructure) as well as product (texts), and thus illuminates how the two are mutually constituted.

## KNOWLEDGE WITHOUT WALLS: THE NATIONAL MIGRANT INFORMATION CLEARINGHOUSE

Martha and her husband, Juan, spent just two years in Crystal City (1971–1973) before returning to Austin. According to Martha, they had always planned on a limited time frame for their work in Crystal City so that residents themselves could take on leadership positions within the city's new Chicano-controlled administration.[5] Anticipating her return to Austin, she began working with Andre Guerrero and Leonard Mestas on a new federally funded information project, the National Migrant Information Clearinghouse. The three had been among the founding faculty at Colegio Jacinto Trevino in 1970 and 1971 and had stayed in close communication after the political purges that pushed them out of the colegio. While Martha and Juan had moved on to Crystal City, Mestas and Guerrero had secured jobs in Fort Worth, with the National Clearinghouse for Bilingual Education, where they continued to develop plans for an independent Chicano university.[6]

In 1972, Mestas and Guerrero left their jobs at the National Clearinghouse for Bilingual Education to establish the Juárez–Lincoln Center (later

University) in Austin, Texas. As Jaime Puente notes in his master's thesis on Juárez–Lincoln, the move to Austin was the "cornerstone of the political project Guerrero and Mestas carried forward from Mercedes [Colegio Jacinto Treviño], and the tactical prowess of the decision helped establish Juárez–Lincoln as the leading source of knowledge and information for the Chicana/o Movement in Texas."[7] Following the model of Jacinto Treviño, Juárez–Lincoln was conceived as both an alternative educational center—where graduate students could pursue master's degrees through applied research—and a "training ground for activist educators who would be armed with the knowledge, consciousness, and pedagogical tools to radicalize the public school system in the state and nation."[8] The organization also aspired to be a leading center of research and information on Chicano issues that could provide direct services to the community, influence public policy, and work with emerging Chicano studies programs to forward scholarship and curriculum development within academia. The decision to establish Juárez–Lincoln in Austin made sense on multiple levels. First, St. Edward's University, a Catholic institution that was one of the first universities to host the College Assistance Migrant Program in 1972, offered to provide an institutional home for Juárez–Lincoln, with free office space and access to its libraries, which would enable the independent university to launch without having to build up its academic infrastructure.[9] The move to Austin also meant proximity to important research hubs and educational networks like the Southwest Educational Development Laboratory, Texans for the Educational Advancement of Mexican Americans, and the new Center for Mexican American Studies at the University of Texas.[10] Puente notes that the move to Austin "solved several practical problems while advancing the school's political agenda of developing a sustainable model of bilingual education to serve one of the nation's poorest and most underserved populations."[11]

As their strategy of relying on existing institutional infrastructures suggests, sustained funding for Juárez–Lincoln was scarce during this period of transition. Nevertheless, in 1972 Mestas and Guerrero were able to secure federal funding for their university from an unlikely source, the US Department of Labor, by submitting a grant for the development of a National Migrant Information Clearinghouse (NMIC). This major multiyear grant would secure Juárez–Lincoln's economic stability as it developed its curricular and research agenda in Austin.[12] Puente attributes the NMIC grant to Leonard Mestas, Juárez–Lincoln's codirector—a reasonable conclusion, given that Martha Cotera's name does not appear in the first annual report on the NMIC that Juárez–Lincoln submitted to the Department of Labor in 1973.[13] But Martha remembers it differently, pointing out that it was she and Andre Guerrero (a longtime collaborator since their days at the Southwest Educational Development Lab) who initially wrote the grant. In an interview in 2018, she described the origin story of the NMIC in this way:

> I suggested to them [Mestas and Guerrero] while I was in Crystal City, that I develop a Migrant Information Clearinghouse. . . . I knew that I could not run it out of Crystal City because . . . we were leaving Crystal City after two years. So I developed that and I made a deal with Juárez–Lincoln University, because I also stayed in touch with the people that were running it in Fort Worth, and knew that they were moving back to Austin, and so I said, I will write this proposal, and I will get it funded. If I can have a job as director or assistant director, when I return to Austin.[14]

The disjuncture between what the archive tells us and Martha's account of the origins of the NMIC highlights larger methodological dilemmas that haunt the edges of historiographic interpretation, particularly in regard to Chicanas in the 1970s, who often contributed their time and ideas to movement initiatives but seldom occupied highly visible leadership positions.[15] If the document is the ultimate "objective" source—the material evidence that something has happened—and personal memory is a necessarily "subjective" account of the thing that happened, then how might the epistemic power of the document (within an interpretive framework grounded in objectivism) silence, or even erase, alternative narratives that are more often than not "undocumented"? In *Silencing the Past*, Michel-Rolph Trouillot has cogently described how such "silences" enter the process of historical production at four crucial moments: "the moment of fact creation (the making of sources); the moment of fact assembly (the making of archives); the moment of fact retrieval (the making of narratives); and the moment of retrospective significance (the making of history in the final instance)."[16] Applying this insight to the question of the NMIC's origins pushes us to think critically about the silences that are reproduced when we privilege "reliable" documentary sources over lived memory.

Certainly, regardless of whether or not Martha's contributions were mentioned in the 1973 report of the NMIC, the project's focus on information as a platform to address the needs of migrant communities was a logical continuation of the work she had dedicated herself to since the late 1960s. Indeed, in our 2018 interview, she recalled that the NMIC's focus on migrant farmworkers stemmed from her experiences working in Mercedes and Crystal City, both of which were "sending" communities in the migrant stream. Some of the programs she developed at the Crystal City library, like book giveaways for children on the migrant stream, directly responded to the needs of youth who experienced educational disenfranchisement on multiple levels because of their migrant status.[17] She had also cultivated strong relations with the US Department of Labor through her work as a librarian in Crystal City. Martha remembers that the Department of Labor "had a big training center in Crystal City," so she enlisted the local office of the Manpower Administration (now the Employment and Training Administration) in her efforts to bring library services to rural communities. "The Manpower office donated a van, [so] we even had a van bookmobile service in a [Department of Labor] van that we converted into a . . . mobile library."[18] According to Martha, these connections helped her to determine that their best chance at receiving federal funding was to propose a grant "through the Labor Department, not through the Education Department."[19]

At the time, Martha was a leading consultant for several federally funded clearinghouses and research centers, many of them focused on migrant issues. She had collected migrant education materials at the Southwest Educational Development Lab and had helped establish the ERIC clearinghouse on Migrant and Rural Education in New Mexico (even serving on its executive board). Given this extensive experience, she understood that information data banks were critically important to the production of equitable policy initiatives. She also knew that free access to such information was precarious and subject to the shifting ideological currents of federal policy. Indeed, Martha noted in our 2018 interview that she "saw the writing on the wall" with the advent of the Nixon administration (1969–1974): "I saw that some of these information sources were going to go away. And that ERIC information clearinghouse in New Mexico, which was providing information for migrant education, was going to go away."[20] Thus, she believed that developing a central clearinghouse for these materials through Juárez–Lincoln, an independent research center focused on bilingual/bicultural education, could ensure that this vital information would be preserved for ongoing educational equity projects. Moreover, by focusing on issues of labor and economic opportunity, Juárez–Lincoln could tap into a funding stream that seemed more stable than grants from the US Department of Education, especially given the importance of migrant services to the ongoing viability of agribusiness. By all accounts, this strategy was successful. The grant from the US Department of Labor supplied the NMIC with the funds it needed to support both the clearinghouse and the development of academic research projects for the Juárez–Lincoln Center.[21]

According to Martha, the NMIC was conceived as a way to address a major issue in the provision of services to migrating farmworkers. While there were numerous federally funded, state-funded, and nonprofit agencies that provided health, education, and social services to families on the migrant stream, there was very little intrastate communication among these agencies. Moreover, although federally funded research was being conducted on migrant communities, particularly in the areas of health and education, the extent to which this research was accessible to the public was not at all clear. In response to these problems, the NMIC project proposed to "establish an information resource and data bank for migrant programs and to assist with and/or develop information resources for migrant programs. Its primary functions are to collect, analyze, compare, and disseminate information concerning migrant farm workers."[22] In providing a central clearinghouse of information that was "already available, but . . . scattered into many forms and agencies," the NMIC could help social service agencies coordinate their activities and better serve populations in need.[23] Moreover, by creating a central access point for information on migrant communities, the clearinghouse could provide programmatic models of both federally funded and nonprofit projects that could then be used by other migrant-serving nonprofits and state agencies to implement new, or improved, services to these communities. While the clearinghouse would provide a central "information hub" for research and policy, the information gathered in NMIC's data collection process, which involved on-the-ground field researchers, would also be published in regional and state sourcebooks that could then be disseminated to migrant agencies.

By November of 1973, when Martha joined the project as its deputy director, the NMIC and the Juárez–Lincoln Center had completed a successful first year of activities, mostly related to establishing the clearinghouse and developing and implementing a plan for data collection. The NMIC had moved into its offices at St. Edward's University in Austin and had hired a small staff of field researchers and data specialists. Data researchers working for the project had requested relevant materials from existing information clearinghouses and built a library of over 1,800 items. The NMIC library also included educational materials from the Southwest Educational Development Lab and Teacher Corps that Martha Cotera and Andre Guerrero had originally collected for the Jacinto Treviño library.[24] In addition to building this data bank, the NMIC had begun the arduous process of data collection in three states, California, Texas, and Florida, through its field operations section. In the NMIC's 1973 annual report, Field Data Supervisor William Manzanares provides an illuminating picture of what this data collection process involved. Using the NMIC's existing library of resources, field researchers would identify migrant programs in their target state and then determine which counties should be surveyed, based on demographic concentration and the location of regional migrant services. Next, they would conduct on-site visits with state and federal agencies dealing with labor, agriculture, and migrant affairs; regional centers for migrant education and health services; and local support programs. The NMIC disseminated the information gathered through this comprehensive scan of services in "migrant program books"—essentially directories of available services and resources—that were distributed to agencies in the state. "Such information," Manzanares noted, "will serve to inform people in any locality of exactly what resources or facilities are available to migrant farm workers. Moreover, it's our intention that these books shall prompt communications between agencies. Hopefully, the result will be better coordination and delivery of services."[25]

According to Jaime Puente, as deputy director of the NMIC, Martha developed the "research group into a highly productive organization that would serve as a bridge between academia and Chicana/o communities as well as a link between the federal government and historically disenfranchised migrant farmworkers."[26] Indeed, the NMIC's library / data bank brought together formerly scattered information that, in aggregate, presented a comprehensive picture of the state of migrant affairs in the mid-1970s. The data collection process, which was undertaken in states across the nation, added to this comprehensive picture of migrant services, even as the regional program books and directories that were produced as a result of this data collection provided a critical resource to local agencies serving farmworkers on the migrant stream. Beyond their clear utility to service providers, Martha also envisioned these directories as tools for migrants themselves, in that they provided critical information about services that were available to them and thus, as Jaime Puente observes, reduced "the miscellaneous labor costs associated with migrant work. Anything that could be done to minimize the time it took for migrants to adjust to their host communities meant time that could be used to educate themselves and their children."[27]

As in the other places she had worked and organized, Martha's approach to infrastructure development at the NMIC was grounded in her strong belief in the power of "information to drive policy and social change."[28] In an interview with Puente, she detailed how this belief was articulated through her work at the NMIC:

> We . . . developed printed directories so that the receiving communities and the migrants could have these directories when they went to Michigan, or wherever. . . . So you send them to the receiving communities who have the directories and they can hand them to the migrants or the

migrants could take the directories with them. And, they would know the schools that were receiving migrants, the health systems, the social services . . . all the resources for migrants in that community. So that it wouldn't take them years of going back, and going back, and going back because sometimes they changed. Instead of going to one city they would

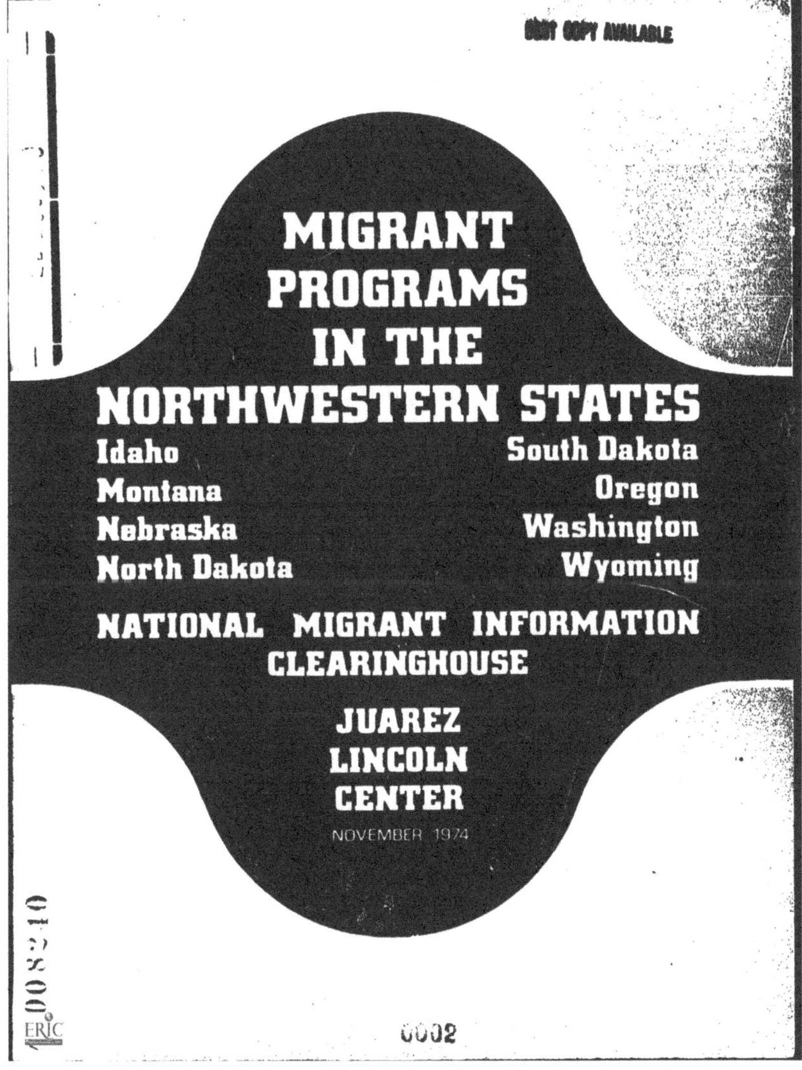


FIGURE 3.1. *Cover,* Migrant Programs in the Northwestern States *(National Migrant Information Clearinghouse / Juárez–Lincoln Center, 1974). Education Resources Information Center (ERIC) online.*

> go to another one. Instead of going to one state they might go to another state. A long learning curve that there was no time for [was shortened because] they would have the information instantaneously in their hands when they got there.[29]

Implementing this model during her tenure as NMIC's deputy director at Juárez–Lincoln, Martha oversaw the data collection process for over two dozen states and published a series of comprehensive regional directories that compiled this information for use by agencies, nonprofits, and, most importantly, migrants themselves.

Puente credits Martha Cotera with designing the "operating structure that made the clearinghouse an effective research arm for both the Chicana/o community and the Department of Labor."[30] Notwithstanding this strong record of success, Martha's tenure at the Juárez–Lincoln Center was also troubled. Although Leonard Mestas and Andre Guerrero were codirectors of the center, Mestas's "authoritarian" leadership style drowned out other voices at the NMIC. Moreover, his aversion to staff and students engaging in community work through the center inevitably clashed with Martha's commitment to community advocacy.[31] According to Puente, Mestas was exceedingly reluctant to use the resources of the NMIC and Juárez–Lincoln for direct advocacy and community work, but others on his staff, particularly Martha, envisioned the center as the ideal place where learning and research could support grassroots initiatives that emerged from within the community. Indeed, during her short tenure at Juárez–Lincoln, Martha repeatedly used the infrastructure that the center provided to launch community-based projects, including a women's advocacy project, the Mexican American Business and Professional Women's Association, the Mexican American Cultural Center, and the Chicana Research and Learning Center.[32] While Mestas's position on advocacy adhered to a traditional vision of the university as a site for "objective" research and analysis, the "university without walls" concept of Juárez–Lincoln, like that of its progenitor, Colegio Jacinto Treviño, was grounded in a different understanding of education. In her interview with Puente, Martha called Mestas's insistence that NMIC and Juárez–Lincoln maintain their distance from community advocacy "hypocritical," noting that "while he wanted employees to do his work, . . . he did not want the resources of Juárez–Lincoln . . . to be used for . . . grassroots community work"; indeed, as she recalls, Mestas "didn't even want us to have files on the community work that we were doing" that was not directly related to the center.[33] To Martha and others, this stance seemed especially problematic, since students at Juárez–Lincoln were deeply

FIGURE 3.2. *Martha Cotera at her desk in the National Migrant Information Clearinghouse at the Juárez–Lincoln Center, St. Edward's University, 1974. Martha Cotera personal collection.*

involved in educational justice initiatives and were encouraged to "become the standard bearers for political, social and economic change."[34]

Problems with gender equity at Juárez–Lincoln and the NMIC also created serious conflicts between Martha and Mestas. According to Roberto Villareal, who was hired at Juárez–Lincoln in 1974 while he was pursuing a doctoral degree at the University of Texas, Mestas "would discriminate against women; that's all there is to it."[35] Villareal recalls that his professional relationship with Mestas deteriorated as a result of his refusal to endorse such gender discrimination at the center:

> The thing that started the division between us had to do with Martha Cotera. Somebody wrote a complaint to the EEOC [US Equal Employment Opportunity Commission] that Juárez–Lincoln was discriminating against women. This was from Chicanas—Hispanic females. He had got it in his mind that Martha sent it. Now, I had to defend five of those [EEOC] things, and we lost each one. . . . Sometimes he would ask me to fire . . . women there . . . and I said "Put it in writing. I won't fire them on my own because they're doing a good job. You put it in writing, and I'll fire them." He would never put it in writing. So I never did fire anyone.[36]

While Martha's ideological differences with Leonard Mestas and the pervasive culture of gender discrimination under his leadership at Juárez–Lincoln likely influenced her decision to resign from the NMIC, her final departure was precipitated by a dispute over how the NMIC budget should be used. Juárez–Lincoln's establishment as a graduate research center had been funded in large part by the NMIC's grant with the US Department of Labor. As the center developed its graduate curriculum and began to recruit students, questions arose regarding the use of NMIC grant monies to support Juárez–Lincoln's curricular activities. Puente notes that Martha "repeatedly refused the directives of Mestas to pay for academic expenses with money designated only for [NMIC] research purposes."[37] When Mestas insisted that she sign off on hiring someone with NMIC funds to conduct Juárez–Lincoln business, Martha resigned in protest, consulting a lawyer and reporting the misappropriation of NMIC funds directly to the granting agency (the Department of Labor) and St. Edward's University.[38]

As difficult as it was, Martha's departure from the NMIC was not a complete break with Juárez–Lincoln. Indeed, she continued to work with researchers and students associated with the center on a series of library and information projects that would come to define her professional, political, and intellectual life for the next decade. These relationships had been solidified upon her return to Austin in 1973, when she reconnected with faculty and students associated with the new Center for Mexican American Studies at the University of Texas, many of whom, including Américo Paredes and Emilio Zamora (at the time a doctoral student in history at the university), had worked with her on the Colegio Jacinto Treviño effort and at the Juárez–Lincoln Center.[39] Students and faculty associated with the Center for Mexican American Studies had been advocating for the development of archival collections and library resources to serve the research needs of the new center. In the summer of 1974, a group of faculty, students, and community members like Martha Cotera formed a library committee and submitted a proposal for a "Chicano Collections Development Program" to Harold Billings, the university's associate director of general libraries and head of collection development.[40] Their demand that the university "develop Chicano or Mexican American holdings to the same level of comprehensiveness as that generally ascribed to the Latin American Collection and the Barker Texas History Center" would result in the establishment of the Mexican American Library Program (MALP), a collecting project launched in 1974 under the aegis of the Benson Latin American Collection. The MALP project had three primary objectives: (1) to organize and consolidate the university's existing manuscript collections, which included "substantial holdings of the testimony of Indigenous, Spanish Colonial and Mexican histories of the Southwest"; (2) to collect "the personal papers and archives of individuals and organizations involved in the Chicano Movement"; and (3) "to support the research of Chicanos and Chicanas" and the newly established Center for Mexican American Studies.[41]

The MALP project seemed ideally suited to Martha's skills as a librarian, especially since she could draw on the political and professional networks she had built as an information specialist in the Chicano movement to help build the collection. Indeed, she had a history with the Barker Texas History Center and the Benson Latin American Collection that stretched into the early 1960s, when she first arrived in Austin. Before she began her job at the Texas State Library in 1964, she held a temporary position at the Barker Texas History Center from 1963 to 1964, working with head librarian Chester Kielman to organize the Bexar Archives of Spanish documents. She had also developed close professional relationships with library staff, particularly Nettie Lee Benson, who had built an expansive collection of Latin American and Southwest materials for the archive that would later bear her name.[42] In addition to these strong professional relationships with staff at the University of Texas Libraries, Martha's connections to Chicano movement educational and organizing initiatives like Colegio Jacinto Treviño and the Raza Unida Party placed her in an ideal position to acquire materials from some of the most important individuals and organizations in the Southwest.

In a letter dated September 20, 1974, the interim chair of the Center for Mexican American Studies, Santos Reyes, encouraged Martha to apply for the position of "top librarian" for the MALP project, noting that Harold Billings spoke "most highly" of her.[43] Martha submitted her résumé, with letters of recommendation from José Ángel Gutiérrez (founder of the Mexican American Youth Organization and leader of the Raza Unida Party in Texas) and José A. Cárdenas (founding director of the Intercultural Development Research Association), who praised her as "the most qualified librarian in Mexican American educational materials in this country."[44] Despite their enthusiastic support, in December of 1974 another candidate for the job, Angie del Cueto Quirós—at the time a master's student in the School of Library Science and a member of the Center for Mexican American Studies Library Committee—was appointed as the first director of the MALP.[45] While the decision was undoubtedly disappointing, especially given Martha's precarious position at Juárez–Lincoln and NMIC at the time, it was not entirely surprising. As she recalls,

> I was a perfect candidate for the position of Mexican American bibliographer since there were few librarians with my eighteen years of library experience, and eight of those with Latino materials, bilingual education sources, and migrant education sources, as well as archival work experience; I had also been founding member of the National REFORMA, the organization for librarians working with the Spanish speaking. Also important were the deep and close ties I had with scholars and activists nationally. Unfortunately, those same connections virtually prohibited the approval of my employment by the top echelons of the university, primarily because of my close ties as candidate and founding member of the Raza Unida Party in Texas. I understood the situation as explained to me, and I accepted a thirteen-hour-a-week appointment as professional librarian, working externally in archives acquisitions.[46]

For nearly four decades, Martha worked at the Benson Latin American Collection as a "consultant under contract to the General Libraries" (or, as she puts it, "a librarian for hire"), establishing the "geographical, chronological, language, and format guidelines" for what would become one of the most important collections of Chicana/o archival materials in the nation. In her brief history of the MALP project, Maria Gonzalez notes that while Martha's collecting and cataloging guidelines "were not incorporated into formal policies," they were frequently "outlined in her written communications to library staff and administrators" and shaped the program's collecting approach for decades.[47] Indeed, Martha recalls that for the first fifteen years of the MALP project,

"I practically worked full time with [a] thirteen-hours-a-week salary, because some of our less experienced bibliographers needed extensive assistance with identification and ordering primary and secondary source materials."[48]

According to Maria Gonzalez, the collecting guidelines Martha established for the MALP "focused archival attention on documenting the activities of Chicanos, Mexican Americans, and Mexican immigrants in Texas and the U.S. Southwest during the period of 1910 to the present." In addition to setting the scope of archival collection, Martha also acted as a field agent for the program's collecting initiative. Capitalizing on her existing networks, she acquired important papers from a "diverse group of people including political figures, artists, writers, and educators," collecting materials from individuals involved in the Raza Unida Party, the Economy Furniture Company strike, and the Juárez–Lincoln Center, among a host of other community initiatives. Moreover, the connections she had cultivated with a growing network of Chicana feminists across the Southwest ensured that women would be included in the Benson Latin American Collection's holdings. As Gonzalez notes, "Due to her contacts and influence, the MALP archives now include a small but unique set of women's papers. Among these papers are those of Chicanas and Mexican American women who were, or remain, active as labor organizers, community activists, educators, artists, and writers."[49] While these largely behind-the-scenes activities as a contract laborer and field agent helped to establish the Benson Collection as a premier resource for the study of Mexican American history and culture, Martha is rarely acknowledged in accounts of the MALP project.[50]

I am struck by the paradoxes of my mother's engagements with these radically different institutional formations—both of which were a result of the Chicano movement's struggle for educational equity—and how they index the limits of an "institutional" approach to knowledge production that inevitably shapes its flows and rewards. Indeed, her professional experiences with Juárez–Lincoln University and the Mexican American Library Program at the University of Texas were distinct, and yet similarly marginalizing. As the deputy director for the National Migrant Information Clearinghouse, she applied Juárez–Lincoln's stated pedagogical and research vision of a "university without walls" to her work on the migrant directories and her commitment to capacity building in communities that had been largely ignored and/or actively discriminated against, only to contend with an entrenched culture of gender discrimination and an entrenched resistance from leadership to using the results of this research for direct advocacy. At the University of Texas, on the other hand, the political connections that made her a successful bibliographer and field agent for the Mexican American Library Program's collecting initiatives also aroused suspicion from university leadership when it came to offering her direct control over the project. These gendered, political, and professional contradictions no doubt highlighted the need for a different infrastructural imaginary, one that could mobilize the information infrastructures of the state—its databases, resources, and funding structures—to more radical ends.

## BRINGING TLAMATINI INFORMATION INFRASTRUCTURES INTO BEING: THE CHICANA RESEARCH AND LEARNING CENTER

The Chicana Research and Learning Center (CRLC) was established on April 17, 1973, a few months before Martha and her husband, Juan, returned to Austin to pursue new professional opportunities.[51] At the time, Martha Cotera and Evey Chapa (who would become the CRLC's first executive director) were managing the transitions endemic to movement life. Like Martha, Evey had played an instrumental role in the Raza Unida Party. As the state chair of the party in 1972, Evey ensured that the party's platform took a strong stand on women's issues. She also ran the party's state campaign, fronted by gubernatorial candidate Ramsey Muñiz and a young Chicana, Alma Canales, who ran for lieutenant governor. At the time, Martha and Evey were actively collaborating on Mujeres Pro Raza Unida, a consciousness-raising group aimed at bringing more women into political life.[52] Evey recalls that when Martha approached her with the idea of creating a "place for Chicanas," Evey was looking for a job, having just finished her campaign work with the Raza Unida Party: "I think that's when Martha went, 'Ah-ha!' Because I was so used to running without money, she said, "Let's just move her over to Austin and let her do it there [*chuckles*]." Evey was attracted to the idea of a research and learning center because her focus had always been on education. Martha told her,

> "We're going to educate. We're going to research." The books . . . said nothing about us. No history book where there was [anything] about us. Nothing, nothing, nothing. There was nothing. So I said, "This sounds great." You know, this was something that I really wanted to be involved with. She said, "Well, we need to find some money." And I said, "Okay."[53]

Evey, a graduate student at the time, recalls that she wrote a proposal to the Ford Foundation and received a Ford Fellowship. Her proposed research project was to survey the field of Chicano studies and document the extent to which Chicana studies had been incorporated into the curriculum, with the aim of producing a concept paper on the need for a Chicana Research and Learning Center. As with the researchers at the National Migrant Information Clearinghouse, Evey's scan of the field involved a lot of "letter writing and phone calls," as well as several trips to gather information on what institutions were doing to serve the academic, social, and policy needs of Chicanas. As she recalls, "It wasn't very much money but it was enough . . . to start the [Chicana Research and Learning] Center."[54]

While Evey scanned the field and searched for additional startup monies to fund her work with the CRLC, Martha found a home for the fledgling nonprofit at Juárez–Lincoln. From their office in the Juárez–Lincoln Center, Martha, Evey, and Lydia Espinosa, who joined the project in 1973 as its first research director, could access the educational resources that would help them to define the objectives of the CRLC. This affiliation with Juárez–Lincoln and, by extension, its host institution, St. Edward's University, also provided critical institutional legitimacy to the CRLC when they applied for federal grants to establish operations. The concept paper for the CRLC, written in 1974 by Martha and Evey, bears the archival traces of this institutional relationship, listing the CRLC's address as 3001 South Congress, the same as Juárez–Lincoln's.

As a registered nonprofit, the CRLC could apply for newly available Women's Educational Equity grants to fund its research and curriculum development. While the CRLC operated independently (funded through a combination of grants, paid consultancies, and publishing profits), it nevertheless drew upon the research infrastructure of state and federal institutions (libraries, archives, and information distribution systems) to produce and disseminate information on Chicanas for scholars, policymakers, teachers, and communities. Imagined as a resource for the total community, the CRLC aimed to develop "curriculum for the public schools, booklets for Chicano studies and women's studies courses, and information packets for community groups to meet their organizing needs." It would respond to the glaring need for more, and better, information on Chicanas, to inform public policy, education, and community organizing. But it would also respond to the information needs of Chicanas themselves, whose development was hampered by "cultural stereotypes held by outsiders, confusion of 'culture' with 'societal condition' [and] confusion of 'cultural heritage' with 'culture.'"[55] In keeping with Martha's conception of information as "everything and everywhere," the CRLC drew its knowledge base not only from the expertise of scholars at universities but also from grassroots organizers who were actively developing concientización projects in the community, as well as a growing national network of Chicana feminist academics,

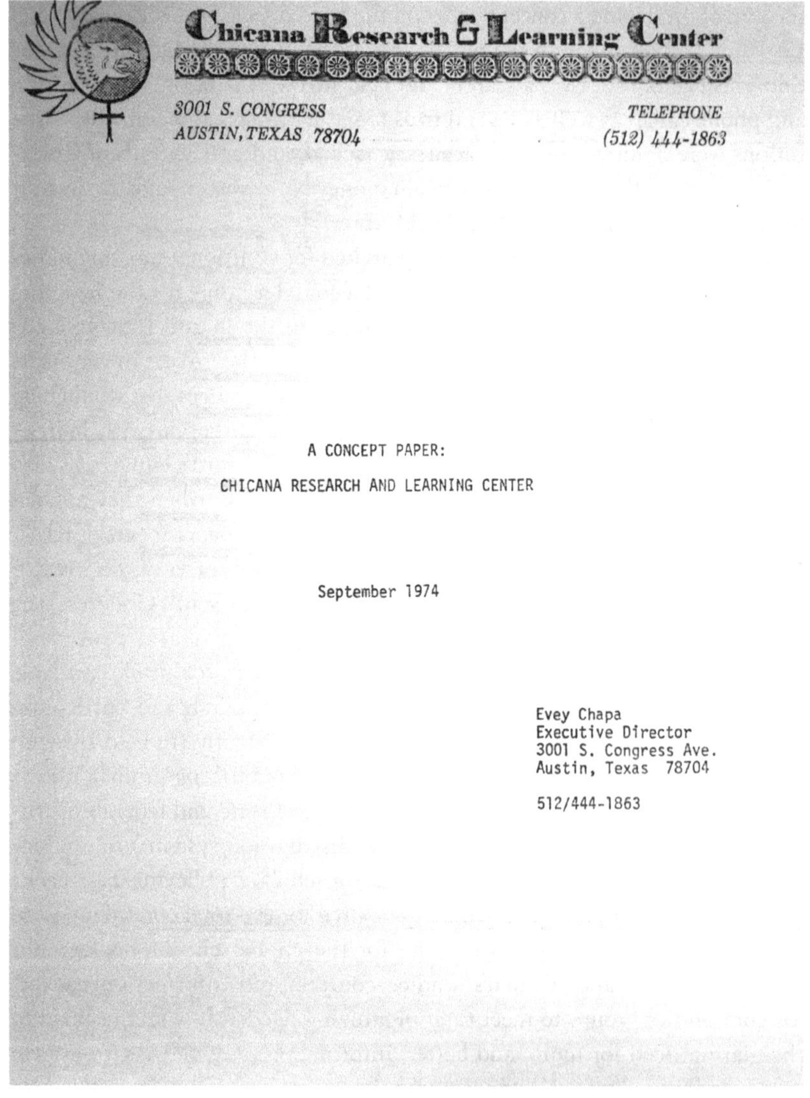
Chicana Research & Learning Center

3001 S. CONGRESS
AUSTIN, TEXAS 78704

TELEPHONE
(512) 444-1863

A CONCEPT PAPER:

CHICANA RESEARCH AND LEARNING CENTER

September 1974

Evey Chapa
Executive Director
3001 S. Congress Ave.
Austin, Texas 78704

512/444-1863

FIGURE 3.3. *Concept paper, Chicana Research and Learning Center, 1974. Martha Cotera personal collection.*

organizers, and public policy specialists, including Anna NietoGomez, Julie Ruiz, and Carmen Tafolla, among many others.[56] These institutional and community connections provided access to the critical infrastructures necessary for a fully operational Chicana information center that was, to borrow from Stefano Harney and Fred Moten, "in but not of" the institution.[57]

This ambiguous institutional positioning allowed the CRLC to focus on the production of knowledge by and for Chicanas, while also providing critical resources for the development of public policy, educational research, and a growing number of classes on La Chicana in universities. Indeed, as Brenda Sendejo has noted, the CRLC functioned as a kind of "bridge" between the community and the university, informing on-the-ground feminist concientización and capacity building, while also building Chicana feminist knowledge within the academy. Sendejo notes that the CRLC

> involved both learning about *and* conducting research on the development of women. Its founders and volunteers worked to provide a space where early, secondary sources on Chicana history could be researched, utilized, and disseminated—not just within universities, but also in the community. . . . The CRLC implemented this model through its focus on collaboration and sharing resources that epitomized the work of the Center.[58]

These resources included workshop models for assertiveness training "Chicana style," bibliographies and sourcebooks on Chicanas and women of color, curriculum and teaching guides for the public schools, "booklets for Chicano studies and women's studies courses, [and] information packets for community groups to meet their organizing needs," all of which were made available through federal information dissemination systems (like ERIC and the Women's Educational Equity Act of 1974) or published by Information Systems Development, a for-profit information consulting firm and publishing house that Martha established in 1975 to support the work of the CRLC.[59]

The infrastructural imaginary behind the Chicana Research and Learning Center (captured in its titular linkage of research and learning) was shaped by both the urgent need to produce relevant knowledge about Chicanas and their history and a desire to put that knowledge to work for Chicanas inside and outside the academy. For the organizers of the CRLC, it was

> imperative that knowledge and clarification of Chicanas' cultural values be considered in program planning by those institutions which seek to alleviate the problems of Chicanos. This information is essential to the Chicano community; to federal, state, and local agencies who are providing social services to Chicanos; as well as to the educational system which thus far has failed to fully meet the needs of the Chicano community. The Chicana Research and Learning Center seeks to provide the knowledge and expertise, encompassing the total experience of Chicanas, needed to alleviate many of the problems faced by Chicanas.[60]

Envisioning Chicana information praxis as a technology of intellectual self-determination, the CRLC was essentially an infrastructural articulation of the call to arms that Martha issued in her keynote address to the 1975 Chicana Identity Conference in Houston: "What we are is what we decide we are. And what we do with our identity is also our decision, not the decision of men, the universities, 'herstories,' 'his-stories,' or anyone else."[61] While the ultimate goal of the CRLC was to recapture knowledge making from the "universities, 'herstories,' 'his-stories,' or anyone else" and to center it within Chicana communities, the center nonetheless took hold of the means of institutional information production to articulate a "space and modality"—a "space in between" (as Sendejo puts it)—that was "separate from the logical, logistical, the housed and the positioned."[62]

Martha's tlamatini information praxis, as embodied in the mobile and unboundaried infrastructural imaginary of the CRLC, refused the romance of autonomy in favor of a stunning example of Chicana fugitivity in action. When asked in a questionnaire (developed for a Chicana workshop in 1975) whether it was better to work within the system or outside of it, Martha responded, "Work with the system, it's faster, longer lasting, economical and one can survive. *In some cases we can take the entire system and make it work for us*" (my emphasis).[63] She, Evey Chapa (who became the CRLC's unpaid executive director in 1973), and volunteers across the country put this approach into practice, using their access to both institutional and community networks to gather relevant information on Chicanas and build a clearinghouse of information—a central goal of the project because of the lack of a networked system of information exchange. The CRLC concept paper—which was produced to introduce the project to both the community and potential funders—outlines this imperative, noting that the clearinghouse would help organize existing information for Chicanas, who "have had a limited access to, or an uncoordinated supply of, information because there has been no centralized clearinghouse for the collection and dissemination of available information."[64]

To build this clearinghouse of information, Martha, Evey, and other volunteers (including Lydia Espinosa at Notre Dame University, who was research director of the CRLC) mobilized their connections to federally funded research databases and regional labs like the Bilingual Educational Lab in New Mexico and the Southwest Educational Development Lab in Austin (where Evey Chapa had also worked), an information infrastructure created in the mid-1960s and early 1970s to advance the educational goals of President Johnson's Great Society programs. According to Martha, it was

> the best network of educational information that we have ever had in this country. . . . We had labs all over the country, teacher training programs . . . focused on improving education. We had clearinghouses all over the country, [and] I was on the board of the clearinghouse in New Mexico that was for migrant education—they are the ones that published the *Profile on the Mexican American Woman*. We had a bilingual clearinghouse in Austin and another in DC. We had a women's education clearinghouse for women's studies, and we had the Women's Educational Equity Act, which published materials on women.[65]

But even during this high point of information dissemination, Martha sensed that these infrastructures would not be around for long, and she saw this moment as an opportunity that would come only "once in a lifetime, because the minute they realize how empowering education is and information is, they are going to shut the whole thing down, and that is exactly what they did. . . . In a FLASH it was gone."[66]

Cognizant of the precarity of this federal infrastructure, Martha and others at the CRLC embarked on a massive information rescue operation. They requested copies of publicly available research papers, educational models, and other resources on Chicanas and women of color from regional educational research labs and information dissemination systems like the ERIC clearinghouse. They also rescued information from more ephemeral sources like Chicano newspapers, journals, and pamphlets that were exchanged or purchased at conferences, many of which had been collected by Martha as she built libraries and information centers across Texas. These materials, along with the booklets and resource guides they had developed for Chicana workshops and training sessions, formed the base of the information clearinghouse at the CRLC. They used this knowledge base to conduct workshops, to produce bibliographies and resource guides, and to consult with educators on new curricular initiatives that would shape the development of Chicano studies and women's studies.

They also took advantage of federally funded programs like the Women's Educational Equity Act Publishing Center to produce and disseminate new information on Chicanas.[67] Because the program provided support at all stages of a research project, from development to publication, Martha saw it as the perfect mechanism to produce a large body of research on Chicanas in a very short time. Critically, reports and final manuscripts submitted to the publishing center would be published and added to the ERIC clearinghouse for dissemination purposes, but authors maintained copyright over their written material. Martha used this federally funded knowledge production model to great effect, establishing Information Systems Development, a for-profit clearinghouse and consulting service, as a vehicle to publish resources developed with the support of federally funded grant programs. Information Systems Development would make these resources available to teachers, policymakers, and organizers through its publications list, and its consulting and publishing revenues (however meager) were used to support the work of the CRLC.

The sheer number and variety of materials listed in the Information Systems Development publication list from 1984 demonstrate the utility of this model of Chicana information dissemination. It includes bibliographies and resource lists, conference and workshop models, copies of special issues of Chicana magazines and newspapers, photocopied articles and speeches, action plans, and self-published books authored by Martha and other women doing research for the CRLC, including Evey Chapa and Nella Cunningham. Information Systems Development also provided a menu of information services, from access to a large database on women of color, to "computerized and manual research assistance," to a talent bank of Chicana expertise in the community. Fusing institutional infrastructure and community knowledge in an undercommons information project that made the *entire system* work for Chicanas, Martha and the other women who worked with the CRLC furthered the goals of the Chicano movement, even as they expanded its vision of political, legal, and educational self-determination to include women.

*Diosa y Hembra: The History and Heritage of Chicanas in the U.S.*, a book that is often framed as a foundational text in the articulation of a Chicana feminist discourse, was a product of this praxis of information exchange. In 1975, Martha received $1,000 from the National Institute of Education (the research and publishing arm of the Department of Health, Education, and Welfare) to write a "profile of the Mexican American woman" that would offer an overview of "the Chicana's historical legacy," from pre-Columbian times to the present, and document Chicana "achievements in education, literature and journalism, political activities, and labor; Chicanas in the feminist movement; and the Chicana and the future."[68] Importantly, the publication would also include numerous additional materials, including an extensive bibliography, information on Chicana organizations (with addresses and contact information), and a comprehensive list of Chicana conferences and various resolutions passed from 1970 to 1975. Indeed, Martha envisioned *Profile on the Mexican American Woman* as something more than just a historical monograph:

I told them, I want to do a resource book. I want to do an outline. I'm not a writer, but I can do an outline of Mexicana history that somebody can use to write a book or books, you know, on the history and culture of Mexicanas and Chicanas. . . . I want the purpose of this book to be . . . to address the issue of what Mexicanas and . . . Chicanas have [done] of value to add to the community, . . . where have their contributions taken the community . . . as far as I could tell, from earliest of times to contemporary times. . . . This was a propaganda piece. This was so other people, like Adelaida Del Castillo or . . . [people] that were emerging in the universities, could take this . . . bibliography as a resource.[69]

**PUBLICATIONS**

**Information Systems Development of Austin, Texas distributes special publications which have been developed in-house or by federal agencies and nonprofit groups.**

**WOMEN**

**Adelante, Mujer Hispana:**
**A Conference Model for Hispanic Women**
Alicia V. Cuaron, et. al.

I3DN. 0-931730-09
A step by step guide to conference and workshop planning for Hispanic women; fundraising, organizing, budgeting, outreach, agenda setting; complete scheduling plan, poster ideas, news releases; workshop program examples, conference evaluation. 39 pages. $9.00.

**Arriba Newspaper,**
**"Chicana and Latin Artists," Special Issue, October 1983**
Photographs, features on Chicana artists of Texas; also, potter Marsha Gomez, Santa Barraza, Gloria Anzaldua; Sarita Rodriguez, Carmen Tafolla etc.; home altars and other feature articles, 16 pages, newsprint. $5.00.

**Bibliography on La Mujer Chicana. Lewis Arnold Gutierrez**
Prepared for the Center for the Study of Human Resources and the Minority Women's Employment Program; includes some obscure 1960's and 1970's journal articles and bibliographies on Chicanas. 15 pages, xerographic print, 1975. $4.75.

**La Chicana:**
**Building for the Future, An Action Plan for the 80's.**
Essays by prominent Chicana leaders on: Chicana population, employment, politics, international relations, undocumented Hispanas, leadership, education, health, media and law. Writers include Hon. Polly Baca Barragan, Esther Estrada, Ambassador Mari-Luci Jaramillo, Luz Gutierrez, Yolanda Nava and others. 1981. 8½ x 11 typescript, glossy covers. $14.95.

**Chicana Feminist.**
Martha P. Cotera.
The feminist heritage and the stereotypes surrounding the chicana's struggle

FIGURE 3.4. *Section on publications about women*, Publications List *(Information Systems Development, 1984). Martha Cotera personal collection.*

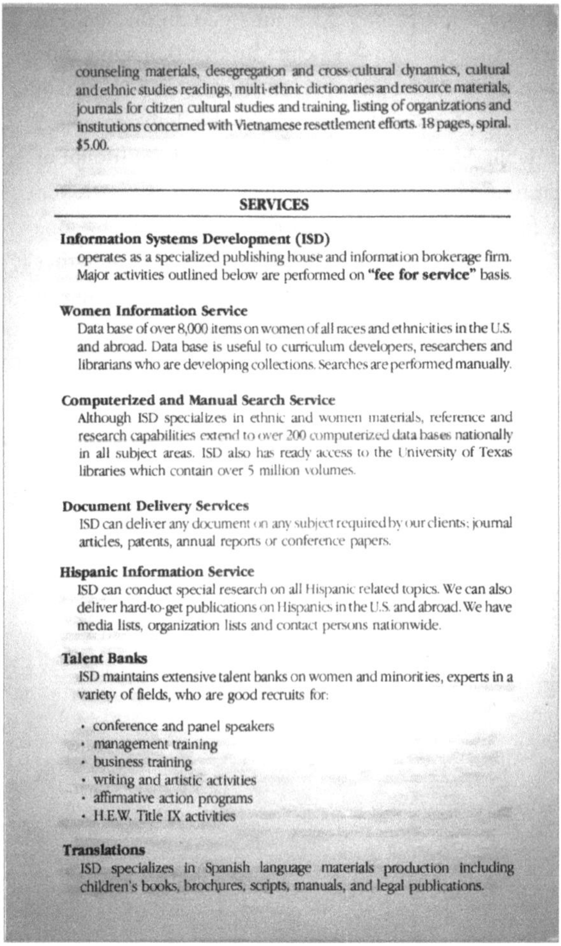

counseling materials, desegregation and cross-cultural dynamics, cultural and ethnic studies readings, multi-ethnic dictionaries and resource materials, journals for citizen cultural studies and training, listing of organizations and institutions concerned with Vietnamese resettlement efforts. 18 pages, spiral. $5.00.

**SERVICES**

**Information Systems Development (ISD)**
operates as a specialized publishing house and information brokerage firm. Major activities outlined below are performed on **"fee for service"** basis.

**Women Information Service**
Data base of over 8,000 items on women of all races and ethnicities in the U.S. and abroad. Data base is useful to curriculum developers, researchers and librarians who are developing collections. Searches are performed manually.

**Computerized and Manual Search Service**
Although ISD specializes in ethnic and women materials, reference and research capabilities extend to over 200 computerized data bases nationally in all subject areas. ISD also has ready access to the University of Texas libraries which contain over 5 million volumes.

**Document Delivery Services**
ISD can deliver any document on any subject required by our clients; journal articles, patents, annual reports or conference papers.

**Hispanic Information Service**
ISD can conduct special research on all Hispanic related topics. We can also deliver hard-to-get publications on Hispanics in the U.S. and abroad. We have media lists, organization lists and contact persons nationwide.

**Talent Banks**
ISD maintains extensive talent banks on women and minorities, experts in a variety of fields, who are good recruits for:

- conference and panel speakers
- management training
- business training
- writing and artistic activities
- affirmative action programs
- H.E.W. Title IX activities

**Translations**
ISD specializes in Spanish language materials production including children's books, brochures, scripts, manuals, and legal publications.

FIGURE 3.5. *Section on services,* Publications List *(Information Systems Development, 1984). Martha Cotera personal collection.*

In essence, *Profile on the Mexican American Woman* offered an aggregation of relevant historical and contemporary information on Chicanas in print form. Martha imagined that after it was duly filed in the information banks of the state, the publication could be used to develop Chicana policy recommendations, spur the nascent field of Chicana studies, and function as an avenue for concientización. After *Profile* was published by the National Institute of Education and disseminated through the ERIC clearinghouse in March of 1976, Martha began the process of transforming the resource book into *Diosa y Hembra: The History and Heritage of Chicanas in the U.S.*, which she then self-published through Information Systems Development in May of 1976.

While this rapid turnaround responded to the sense of urgency that drove Martha to develop multiple resources during this period, the subversive undercommons production model that brought *Diosa y Hembra* into being also had its limits. In an interview conducted in 2009, Martha lamented that for *Diosa y Hembra*, she had to leave out the resources that had appeared in *Profile on the Mexican American Woman* because she couldn't afford the

FIGURE 3.6. *Cover, Martha P. Cotera,* Profile on the Mexican American Woman *(National Educational Laboratory, 1976). Martha Cotera personal collection.*

FIGURE 3.7. *Cover, Martha P. Cotera,* Diosa y Hembra: The History and Heritage of Chicanas in the U.S. *(Information Systems Development, 1976). Martha Cotera personal collection.*

printing costs of a longer book. The result was a truncated version of *Profile* that did not include its extensive bibliography and the appendices on Chicana conferences, resolutions, and organizations. Indeed, for *Diosa y Hembra*, she removed half of the material from *Profile*, resulting in a publication that was less a comprehensive sourcebook on (and for) Chicana organizing than a broad overview of Chicana history that stretched from pre-Columbian times to the present day. As the first book-length account of this history, *Diosa y Hembra* became a critical resource for Chicana classes in the late 1970s, but Martha never intended it to be a scholarly book. In fact, she was deeply uneasy about writing a book.

> It was a difficult transition for me in the sense that I love reading, always have, I love writing, I love literature and all, but I always saw myself as a provider, and not a producer. And so . . . I had to get used to the idea. I never wanted to appropriate that other skill. . . . I always wanted to be the background person, I always wanted to be the one that set the base, kind of like a chef, you know, I never wanted to be the one to actually eat . . . you know, be on the other side of the table. And so it was really hard for me to assume that role. Now, I did not mind producing lists, because that was kind of like part of my job. And I've always done that. I've always produced bibliographies always, always. . . . I considered that part of my job. But to actually take that and then go that other step . . . and produce something for others to read . . . other than a bibliography, which is a tool, you know, was difficult. I didn't want to assume another role. . . . I felt that there were people that were better skilled, you know, and more capable of doing. So I was very uneasy writing the *Diosa y Hembra*.[70]

Martha jokes that academics saw *Diosa y Hembra* as a "prehistoric" example of Chicana history, an assessment of its reception that is illustrated in Cordelia Candelaria's 1980 review (published in *Frontiers*), which dismisses the interpretive value of the book as a historiographic contribution:

> By training and experience, Cotera is a librarian. She does not go beyond cataloging the material to offer a theoretical overview of it which would explain precisely how the data relate to each other and to the course of Chicana history. Nor does her study evince the kind of conceptual grasp of historiography to posit conclusions, however tentative, about the major periods of Chicana history.[71]

Damning the book with faint praise, Candelaria concluded that while *Diosa y Hembra* was valuable as a "spur to the reader to additional thought and further research," it was more attuned to "middle and secondary school levels where it could, in fact, serve a useful function."[72] Indeed, *Diosa y Hembra*, like *Profile on the Mexican American Woman*, the resource book that preceded it, was never intended for an exclusively academic audience. Instead, it was conceived as a consciousness-raising tool that could be used in a wide array of political spaces to demonstrate that Mexican women and Chicanas had a long history of leadership and organizing.

Notwithstanding Candelaria's ambivalent assessment of the scholarly value of *Diosa y Hembra*, the crucial resources missing from its pages—"all the bibliographical references," as well as the "appendix that had all the resolutions, all the conference minutes," published in *Profile on the Mexican American Woman*—would be photostated and preserved within the information infrastructure of the state until another tlamatini could come along and recover them. Indeed, Martha notes with pleasure that when Alma García published *Chicana Feminist Thought: The Basic Historical Writings*—her own compendium of Chicana knowledge from the 1960s and 1970s—she reprinted "the whole appendix that came out of that original ERIC document." Which was exactly what Martha had hoped for: "The whole purpose was to do the appendix so these things wouldn't get lost forever, and ever, and ever, and there'd be some place in microfiche form, or in printed form" that would preserve them.[73] In moving from an archive/compendium/sourcebook to a monograph, *Profile on the Mexican American Woman* passed into the annals of Chicana feminist knowledge as "the first attempt by a Chicana to document Chicana history."[74] But the rich source materials excised from the original text nevertheless shadow *Diosa y Hembra* in ghostly form. Cut off, but not entirely gone—a palimpsest of Martha's vision of information as a technology of freedom—the exiled sections from *Profile on the Mexican American Woman* haunt *Diosa y Hembra*, calling us to see it as something more than a history book offering what Avery Gordon terms "cold knowledge" of the past. Part historical excavation, part resource, part future archive, *Profile on the Mexican American Woman* was envisioned both as a sourcebook for Chicana concientización and as printed evidence of the efforts of Chicanas to articulate a "space in between."

The Chicana Research and Learning Center ceased active operations in 1977, when funding for Evey Chapa's position as executive director dried up. In a dispiriting memo sent to the advisory board on February 10 of that year, Evey assured them,

> All programmatic and reporting responsibilities to funding sources and all financial and reporting obligations to IRS were fulfilled before we reached this juncture. All monies received have been spent and properly

> recorded. However, there is no money to continue up keep of the Chicana Center, i.e., supplies, personnel and especially rent. Since there is no money, I had to relinquish the office at the Student Methodist Center. The documents have been placed in storage.[75]

After the departure of her trusted collaborator and executive director, Martha maintained the nonprofit status of the CRLC and continued to produce resources from the comprehensive collection of materials they had acquired. These new publications and resources included *Doña Doormat No Está Aquí / Doña Doormat Isn't Home* (1982), an assertiveness-training manual for Latinas; the *Multicultural Women's Sourcebook: Materials Guide for Use in Women's Studies and Bilingual/Multicultural Programs* (1982); and the *Latina Sourcebook: Bibliography of Mexican American, Cuban, Puerto Rican, and Other Hispanic Women Materials in the U.S.* (1982), among many other titles offered for purchase through Information Systems Development. Martha also received a Women's Educational Equity Act grant to develop Mujeres Célebres, a database and encyclopedia documenting the history of Hispanic women across the Americas, a project she continued well into the 1980s.[76] Some of the CRLC documents that Evey had placed in storage were eventually preserved at the Benson Latin American Collection (acquired by Martha as part of her work as a field agent), but a good many of these materials remain in my mother's home; indeed, she still consults them for her research, speeches, and community advocacy—a living archive that documents the unruly infrastructural imaginaries of the space in between.

## "INVISIBILITY IS AN UNNATURAL DISASTER": THE LOST FUTURES OF CHICANA INFORMATION PRAXIS

Reflecting on the ultimate demise of the Chicana Research and Learning Center and Cordelia Candelaria's dismissal of *Diosa y Hembra* as a book that "does not go beyond cataloging the material" of Chicana history, I am left to conclude that as liberating as the space in between promised to be, it was also a precarious nonspace—a "wild beyond" to institutional imaginaries that relied on the containment of knowledge/power within the institutions' walls and collections. Put into action in the aims of the CRLC and its publications and services, Martha's tlamatini information praxis redirected information and its flows to and from spaces of knowledge that were outside the extractive grasp of universities and libraries. Given its challenge to the discursive authority of these institutional repositories of knowledge, it is not surprising, then, that the story of Martha Cotera's tlamatini information praxis has been largely erased in dominant accounts of both Chicana/o librarianship and Chicana/o studies. Indeed, her invisibility in these institutional imaginaries is, to borrow from Mitsuye Yamada, an "unnatural disaster."[77]

Notwithstanding her numerous publications on library services to Spanish-speaking populations, her instrumental role in the development of regional information clearinghouses serving Mexican American communities, her involvement in the establishment of key organizations like REFORMA (the National Association to Promote Library Services to the Spanish Speaking) and GLISSA (which trained a new generation of Chicana/o and Latina/o library professionals), and her efforts to establish and sustain the Mexican American Library Program as one of the leading Mexican American archival collections in the nation, Martha Cotera is almost entirely absent from the few historical accounts of the field of library science that have been published.[78] Ironically, her absence in the history of Chicana/o librarianship might be attributed to the very efforts that she and others of her generation undertook to train a new generation of Latinx library professionals. Martha observes that although Chicana/o librarians in the 1970s "spoke of being democratic, and community-friendly . . . there was a great deal of marginalization of professionals and paraprofessionals in the field who had served for decades as librarians championing Spanish speakers, who did not have library degrees. And I pretty much accepted this, since I did not have the degree."[79]

The marginalization of paraprofessionals and those without degrees in the advent of a more "disciplined" approach to information and library services has inevitably resulted in the erasure of community-based information projects like the Chicana Research and Learning Center and the National Migrant Information Clearinghouse in historical accounts of Chicano librarianship in the 1970s and 1980s. For example, in their article "Latinos and Librarianship," Salvador Güereña (one of Martha's former colleagues at the Benson Latin American Collection) and Edward Erazo offer a comprehensive survey of the "development of library services to Latinos" since the 1960s. Calling attention to the "paucity that prevails in the professional literature that addresses this large and growing population," Güereña and Erazo promise to "identify, analyze, and discuss the relevance of major studies, reports, and other publications," as well as "key leaders in the profession" and "their seminal contributions." They also offer a survey of major professional events, special institutes, conferences, "notable grant-funded initiatives and special library projects," and the development of "special collections and archival centers," all of which, they argue, helped to propel the discussion about how best to serve the information needs of Latina/o populations.[80]

When I first encountered Güereña and Erazo's account, my admiration for its comprehensiveness was shadowed by a growing sense of disappointment at the absence of any mention of my mother's radical information work. And as I read their account, I couldn't help but feel that she was haunting the text somehow, disrupting the frequency of its seamless narrative of "Latino librarianship" with an insistent, low-key murmur: *I was there, I wrote that, I helped establish that organization, I imagined that future.* Or perhaps it is more accurate to say—and this is the ultimate irony—that my mother's archive haunts their account, offering documentary evidence of her ubiquitous presence in the countless reports and newspaper articles she collected, her correspondence with "key figures," her collection of REFORMA newsletters and meeting agendas, the riot of bibliographies and resource lists scattered throughout her office, and the vast collection of materials she accumulated in and through her radical library development projects. Her archive, and the embodied memory that gives it life, offers an important counterhistory from the margins to Güereña and Erazo's account of the starts and stops, short-lived successes, interrupted utopian imaginaries, and "persistent challenges" of the history of Latina/o librarianship.[81] My mother's exile from this history is not accidental, nor is it merely due to her lack of professional credentials; in fact, it signals the limits of inclusion in the profession, revealing the "desperate business" of professionalization—"nothing less than to convert the social individual. Except perhaps, something more, the ultimate goal of counterinsurgency everywhere: to turn the insurgents into state agents."[82] Martha's professional life tracked an opposite trajectory: from state agent to insurgent. Her tlamatini praxis—a radical philosophy of information and its flows—and her willingness to put the entire system to work for the interests of marginalized communities rejected the institutional logics that structure "organized" and "disciplined" visions of information access, with predictable consequences.

In 2010 my mother was informed that her services at the Benson Latin American Collection were no longer needed. Since helping to establish the Mexican American Library Program in 1974, she had worked as a part-time field agent for the project, sniffing out community archives ranging across a broad historical, geographic, and thematic scope. In addition to the materials she developed over a lifetime of information work, she also collected archives from key Chicana feminists, Raza Unida Party activists, poets, writers, artists, and important figures in the local Mexican American community. While she was paid for thirteen hours of work per week, the time she devoted to this work—which was, after all, motivated by her own seemingly incurable case of "archive fever"—often surpassed the hours she was paid for. Through home visits, pláticas, long work sessions devoted to organizing papeles, and all of the relational work such archival encuentros require, she brought numerous collections to the Benson. She described this community-centered archival praxis as

> a perfect cycle; the closer you are to the source of archive production, the more likely you are to collect the present and to discover treasures from the past, and the more likely it will be that archives' donors will trust you with their treasures. Also, the more likely it will be that you will connect with the users of the archives who are most likely to benefit from your work. Archive collecting is not done "behind a desk." It is hands-on, hard work.[83]

While this kind of hands-on, hard work had been indispensable in the development of the Mexican American Library Program, by 2010 such intimate labor was all but invisible to the library administrators who determined that Martha's services were no longer necessary. Her position as field agent was eliminated, and she was told that she could stay on as a "Cataloger I" at the main library if she needed the money.[84]

The summer before her departure from the Benson Latin American Collection, Linda Garcia Merchant and I, along with a couple of students, had spent several days with my mother in the library's reading room. Acting as our trusty archival guide, she helped us sort through the Raza Unida Party collection in preparation for our interviews with party women. Our time at the Benson, though brief, was particularly generative precisely because she was a part-time archivist there and thus had relatively free access to the collection. Moreover, her deep contextual knowledge of the archive—as both a participant in the Raza Unida Party and a collections specialist—helped us to understand not only the provenance but also the political context of the materials. Filling in the gaps with her personal accounts of the activities documented in the correspondence, leaflets, and programs we examined, she fleshed the archive into a story about the past that was made richer by her embodied memory. Her stories transformed the cold institutional space of the library's reading room into a lively site of encuentro and intergenerational memory exchange. There were times when I felt self-conscious about how we flouted the rules of engagement in the archive, especially when I sensed the eyes of other archivists register a glint of cool disapproval at our unruly presence in a space typically marked by a strict division between archivists and patrons. In some ways, this archival scene was an exact embodiment of the liberatory vision of information exchange that my mother imagined as one possible future for the Benson Collection: a "perfect cycle" in which communities, archives, and scholars make knowledge together.

So when my mother told me about her demotion, I couldn't help but feel that our presence in the archives had somehow brought on this regulation of her labor, reviving a troublesome ghost of the liberatory information futures she had imagined in the early 1970s. Indeed, the grimly comic symbolism of her demotion to "Cataloger I" suggests that one way to tame such specters of the past is to transform them into a vision of abstracted clerical labor, not unlike the way her name was replaced by "La Biblioteca" in the title of the *Cristal* newspaper article some forty years earlier. The erasure of my mother's legacy at the Benson Latin American Collection highlights the continuing precarity of Chicana intellectual labor, particularly when it is elaborated collectively and directed toward resource development. Often devalued as "women's work," such intellectual labor continues to be seen as primarily "quantitative" (doing) rather than theoretically sophisticated (thinking)—to draw from Adelaida Del Castillo's incisive observation about gender relations in Chicano movement organizations.[85] These gendered hierarchies of value are endemic to the academy and continue to structure a rewards system that is grounded in an individualist, product-oriented vision of knowledge production in which certain kinds of scholarly labor are privileged and others are seen as expendable labors of love. Texts are the coin of the realm in the marketplace of ideas; they get circulated, assigned to students, added to reading lists, canonized. Labors of love, on the other hand, all too often disappear.[86]

Indeed, while scholars have acknowledged the importance of texts like *Diosa y Hembra* and *The Chicana Feminist* to the development of Chicana feminist thought, Martha Cotera's radical information projects—the beating heart of her writing and organizing—leave only traces in the archive. And yet no text, however radical, could match the liberatory potential of a collective praxis that wrests the means of knowledge production from the clutches of the institution and its bourgeois individualist ethos, as Martha Cotera's information projects did, and as the Chicana por Mi Raza Digital Memory Collective (following in her footsteps) aspires to do. Indeed, as Brenda Sendejo has observed, the Chicana Research and Learning Center is "emblematic" of an alternative genealogy of Chicana feminist knowledge praxis that centers collaboration and resource development over "individualist" knowledge forms, an important "historical legacy" that continues today in radical information projects like the Chicana por Mi Raza Digital Memory Collective.[87]

Chapter 4

# X MARKS THE SPOT: MAPPING THE SITIOS Y LENGUAS OF CHICANA STUDIES IN CALIFORNIA (1969–1971)

*The goal for Chicano Studies is to develop a new man.*

CHICANO STUDIES WORKSHOP, CHICANO COUNCIL ON HIGHER EDUCATION, 1971

*Through Chicano Studies the Chicana has become involved in the issues facing the Chicano in education and the community. Through this involvement we find that the Chicana faces unique problems as a woman in this society. As a result, we find that we must also develop the identity of the Chicana, in order that she may set forth her direction and goals.*

PROPOSAL FOR A CHICANA CURRICULUM, CHICANA AD HOC COMMITTEE, CHICANO COUNCIL ON HIGHER EDUCATION, 1971

*You turn the established narrative on its head, seeing through, resisting, and subverting its assumptions. Again, it's not enough to denounce the culture's old account—you must provide new narratives embodying alternative potentials.*

GLORIA ANZALDÚA, *Light in the Dark / Luz en lo Oscuro*

At first glance they seem like a relatively quotidian example of the type of meeting notes that are a regular feature in the Chicana archive from the 1970s. Tucked away in a folder labeled "Chicana Caucus" in the Enriqueta Chavez Papers at San Diego State University, the documents include a list of the women in attendance, a summary of their agreed-upon goals, and a hand-drawn map of California, reminiscent of a battle plan, with encircled territories and strategic sites marked with an X. And then I see the date—March 21, 1971—which corresponds to the second statewide conference of the Chicano Council on Higher Education (CCHE), hosted in San Diego, where, according to a report published a month later in the first issue of

*Hijas de Cuauhtémoc* (April 1971), Chicanas convened a formal caucus to discuss their experiences in higher education. The next day, members of the caucus (which would become the Chicana Ad Hoc Committee of CCHE) presented a set of resolutions that brought attention to the problem of male supremacy in Chicano studies. This brief report in the first issue of *Hijas de Cuauhtémoc*, which offered only the barest outlines of what happened at the CCHE conference in San Diego, had intrigued me ever since I first encountered it in Anna NietoGomez's personal collection. I had long wondered about the Chicana Ad Hoc Committee—how it formed, who participated, what happened to it—and now, suddenly, I found myself staring at a set of documents that offered a wealth of important information about this early Chicana studies formation, including a long list of women from colleges and universities across California, with detailed contact information for each of them, along with notations that corresponded to the symbols on the accompanying map, indicating "educational coordinators" who were responsible for putting the Ad Hoc Committee's plan into action. The plan itself laid out a strategy for accomplishing both immediate and long-term goals for Chicanas in the community and the academy, and the map identified areas of Chicana student activity across the state—the Bay Area, Los Angeles, and San Diego—even including a helpful legend that indicated those in the California State College system, the University of California system, private universities, and two-year colleges. Together, the list of participants, the notes on the goals of the Chicana caucus, and the hand-drawn battle map trace the circuits and networks of Chicana scholar-activists in the spring of 1971, providing a tantalizing treasure map of the *sitios y lenguas* (sites and discourses) of early Chicana feminist studies.[1]

As both a strategic guide for movement building and a call for intellectual self-development, these modest mimeographed pages, along with other key documents that share space with them in Enriqueta "Henri" Chavez's substantial collection at San Diego State, offer an archival trace that—in Gloria Anzaldúa's words—turns the "established narrative on its head," inviting us to see through, resist, and subvert its assumptions and imagine "new narratives embodying alternative potentials."[2] Calling forth both an obscured past and a future imagined, if not fully realized, this apparition invites us to think not only about the past of Chicano studies—what has been left out or forgotten—but also about the future that Chicanas envisioned and enacted as they worked to build a place for themselves within the field. In this chapter and the one that follows, I trace the hidden labor and organizing networks of a generation of Chicana scholar-activists (as Anna NietoGomez has termed this cohort) in California who worked to transform Chicano studies at a moment when it was still being conceptualized as a field of inquiry. In doing so, I chart an alternative map of the field that allows women to take center stage in the "trenches of academe."[3]

Given Chicanas' relative absence in extant accounts of Chicano studies and the paucity of institutional collections that might document their activities, reconstructing the early landscape of Chicana feminist studies requires that we flesh the archive, piecing together the scattered traces of their archival presence in both institutional and personal collections and putting this documentary evidence into dialogue with personal recollections of Chicana conferences, consciousness-raising collectives, classes, and publishing projects. This dialogue between archives and embodied memory allows us to read between the lines of existing narratives and challenge frameworks that write Chicanas out of the story of Chicano studies. Feminist scholars have long noted how conceptual frameworks for understanding the past have produced absences and erasures in historical accounts of the women's movement and the Chicano movement, both of which have largely figured Chicana feminist thought as ancillary, or even divisive, to the genesis of these social movements. Such limiting conceptual frameworks are also evident in existing accounts of the genesis of Chicano studies as a discipline.

While these studies often acknowledge women's participation, they tend to conceptually bracket this activity to separate caucuses, organizations, and print networks operating at the discursive edges of the field. As in accounts of the Chicano movement more generally, foundational scholarship on the development of Chicano studies has mostly focused on leading academic figures and departments, student mobilizations (United Mexican American Students [UMAS] and Movimiento Estudiantil Chicano de Aztlán [MEChA]), scholarly journals (*Aztlán* and *El Grito*), and academic organizations (the National Association for Chicano Studies), all of which were spaces dominated by men in which Chicanas were often limited to supportive roles.[4] Moreover, whether Chicanas are referenced in footnotes, cursory acknowledgments, discrete paragraphs, or, in the best-case scenario, separate chapters, they are, more often than not, invoked through their experiences of marginalization. While such studies have provided important accounts of the field's birth in the student movement, its key conferences, scholarly organizations, publications, and journals, they have also interpolated Chicana feminist participation in the educational arm of the Chicano movement as an exception, an approach that reinforces, rather than disrupts, a male-dominated vision of the history of Chicano studies.[5] Shadowed by violence—the terms of her inclusion in the history of Chicano studies paradoxically shaped by a narrative of marginalization and exclusion—the Chicana feminist scholar-activist haunts the footnotes and marginalia of the field's narrative of becoming.

Interrupting this discursive marginalization, feminist scholarship on the Chicano movement has shifted the focus from heroic leaders and male-dominated organizations to the spaces and modalities through which Chicanas made social change. For example, in her analysis of the 1968 Los Angeles blowouts, Dolores Delgado Bernal pushes us to reconceptualize traditional paradigms of leadership that implicitly equate "public speakers and negotiators with leaders" (and thus tend to privilege male subjects) by shifting the center of analysis to dimensions of activism often considered "women's work."[6] Placing women's voices at the center of her narrative, Delgado Bernal excavates modalities of leadership that are typically ignored in conventional accounts of the movement—"networking, organizing, developing consciousness"—and shows how Chicanas shifted in and through these modalities and more traditional forms of leadership ("holding an elected or appointed office" or "acting as an official or unofficial spokesperson") to advance the struggle for educational justice.[7] Likewise, scholars like Naomi Quiñonez, Vicki Ruiz, Marisela Chávez, Dionne Espinoza, and Maylei Blackwell have challenged us to look beyond the accepted narratives—of leaders, organizations, and mobilizations—that have shaped both Chicano movement and women's movement historiography to explore the complexities of gender, race, and sexuality in organizing and identity formation, an approach that, as Blackwell has noted, "tells more intimate and nuanced stories of gender, race, and sexuality and the ways these forms of power were negotiated in the local spaces of the movement and in the dominant society."[8] Collectively these scholars have demonstrated how centering the experience of Chicanas who worked within and against the discourses, institutional formations, and political modalities of the movement years can produce "broader histories of social movement genealogies" that reveal the "hidden insurgencies" of women's organizing and leadership.[9]

Building on these frames of analysis, I turn to a network of Chicanas in California who were active—if frequently critical—participants in the revolutionary knowledge project of Chicano studies from 1968 to 1976. Unlike their male counterparts (some of whom would go on to write foundational historical accounts of Chicano studies), very few of these women would ever achieve professional status in the field they helped to build.

Indeed, this period of development for Chicana studies was, in many ways, truncated by the painful and high-profile tenure struggle of Anna NietoGomez at California State University, Northridge, in 1976. And yet women like NietoGomez, Sonia Lopez, Rita Sanchez, Dorinda Moreno, Henri Chavez, Corinne Sánchez, and a host of others in California (and beyond) were instrumental to the development of Chicano studies in its early years. They played key roles as recruiters and counselors in Educational Opportunity Programs across the Southwest, they held leadership positions in Chicano higher education organizations, and they directed federally funded grants. In addition to this critical labor in the service of Chicano studies, they also advocated for Chicanas in higher education and built an entire area of study focused on gender and sexuality within the field, often in the face of great hostility and open resistance from administrators, colleagues, and students. They formed women's caucuses in key organizations like MEChA and CCHE, using these scholarly networks to challenge the male supremacy of Chicano studies from within. They implemented independent recruitment initiatives and community-based research projects to open up the university to more Chicanas. They taught the first classes on La Chicana in fledgling programs and shared their syllabi, bibliographies, and other resources to support a small network of women teaching in this area. They published newspapers, anthologies, and journals to challenge the claim that there was not enough literature out there to justify courses on La Chicana. These modalities of scholarship and struggle are at the center of this story of Chicano studies.

In shifting our attention from the institutions, organizations, and individuals that have been centered in the field's imaginary, to the mostly ignored spaces, networks, and knowledge-making modalities of the Chicana feminist scholar-activist, I want to tell the story of Chicano studies in a different voice, one that not only engages new historical subjects and sites of inquiry but also gives narrative form to a Chicana knowledge praxis that—like Martha Cotera's tlamatini information praxis—moved between and within multiple sites, from institutional formations, to the classroom, to communities of struggle outside the university. Collaborative, transgenerational, and institutionally unruly, directed not only toward building a field but also toward addressing the most pressing needs of the community, Chicana knowledge praxis in the 1970s represented one possible future for the field of Chicano studies; a path not taken, but still redolent with possibility for us today. It is to this radical modality of knowledge—regulated, though not entirely eradicated, in the object lesson of Anna NietoGomez's tenure battle—that I now turn.

## X MARKS THE SPOT(S): TRACING THE ACTIVIST GEOGRAPHIES OF EARLY CHICANA STUDIES

In both scholarly accounts and popular memory, the movement for Chicano studies is most often narrated in a timeline that begins in the postwar years, which witnessed increased Chicano (male) college enrollment as a result of the GI Bill, and then turns to the youth insurgencies of the late 1960s, the emergence and radicalization of student organizations in colleges and universities across the Southwest (MAYO, UMAS, MAYA, MASA, and MASC, among others),[10] and the articulation of a plan for Chicano educational liberation at the 1969 Santa Barbara conference, which plays a particularly significant role in these accounts. As a threshold historical event in which the "blueprint" for Chicano studies, *El Plan de Santa Bárbara*, was conceived, the conference offers both text and context for the birth of the field, grounding it in a historical moment and an educational philosophy that lends coherence to the widely divergent organizing projects that composed the movement for Chicano studies in the early 1970s.

Yet staging the 1969 Santa Barbara conference as the establishing shot for the triumphant entrance of Chicano studies into the academy—and *El Plan de Santa Bárbara* as its script—inevitably enlists Chicanas as always already marginalized within the field's origin story, a status that is the price of their inclusion in our collective memory of Chicano studies. Only five of the thirty-three members of the steering committee that organized the conference were women, and all but one of them, Gracia Molina de Pick (a professor at Mesa College in San Diego), were students at the time. These women included Maria Diaz (de Krofcheck) of California State College at Los Angeles; Anna NietoGomez, an Educational Opportunity Program counselor and a member of UMAS at California State College at Long Beach; Rosalinda Mendez, who had participated in the blowouts as a high school student and was at the time a member of UMAS at the University of California, Irvine; and Ludi Tapia, a student at California State College at Hayward and a member of MASC (an organization associated with the Third World Liberation Front at both San Francisco State College and the University of California, Berkeley).[11] In an interview with Marisol Moreno, Luis Arroyo (a member of the steering committee) described the Santa Barbara conference as "a good example of women in secondary roles," recalling that

> the registration was handled by women. . . . In the campus organization workshop I don't recall a woman being actively involved in the discussion

> of the dialogue. I hope I'm not overstating the case but . . . I don't remember any women taking on a major role, not even Olivia Velásquez [of the East Los Angeles College organization La Vida Nueva]. . . . And Olivia never held back. . . . I can only remember one female who was active . . . Gracia Molina de Pick from [Mesa College] in the San Diego area."[12]

Unlike the Chicano Youth Liberation Conference in Denver, which had taken place just a month earlier, there was no workshop devoted to Chicanas. As Carlos Muñoz succinctly observes, "Gender inequality was not included on the agenda of the Santa Barbara conference."[13] Moreover, *El Plan de Santa Bárbara*, a publication intended to disseminate information from the workshops, resources, and position papers that were exchanged at the conference, proved to be a divisive document from the start. Indeed, its publication some six months after the Santa Barbara conference catalyzed a growing critique among Chicanas of the male-centered and nationalist vision of "Chicanismo" presented in its pages.

When we shift the frame of analysis from this origin story and its "*manifesto*" (as Cynthia Orozco wryly puts it) to the sitios y lenguas through which Chicanas built feminist studies, a startlingly different map of the field emerges.[14] Indeed, although Chicana feminists often encountered serious resistance in student organizations, scholarly formations, and newly formed departments (the prototypical sites of analysis in histories of the field), they nevertheless played significant leadership roles in other institutional spaces that have received less scholarly attention, including CCHE, which organized the Santa Barbara conference and the many meetings and conferences that followed it; Montal Educational Associates, a federally funded nonprofit that convened a series of Chicano Studies Mobile Institutes across the Southwest; and community-based research centers like the Chicana Service Action Center and Concilio Mujeres, which, like the Chicana Research and Learning Center in Texas (a subject of chapter 3), became important sites of Chicana knowledge production in the 1970s.[15] These spaces provided women with both a growing network of like-minded scholars and an alternative infrastructure that nurtured Chicana leadership and intellectual growth. Anna NietoGomez, who was involved in the State College Caucus of CCHE, the Chicana Service Action Center, and a variety of educational projects funded by Montal, speculates that because these institutional formations were essentially "communication centers" whose success relied on the "ability to bring people together and document what they were doing," they nurtured collaborative and nonhierarchical modes of organizing and leadership that favored the feminized labor of communicating, organizing, grant writing, connecting people and ideas, and consensus building. In contrast, she notes, Chicano student organizations and Chicano studies departments often adopted a more "centralized," "unilateral," and "authoritarian" vision of leadership, as well as a hierarchical model of organization that favored movement "heavies."[16] Historical accounts of the struggle for Chicano studies that focus on male-dominated organizing spaces—like academic departments, student mobilizations, and scholarly organizations—all too often replicate masculinist leadership frameworks, even as they overlook or underplay key sites in which Chicanas made instrumental contributions to the field. Mapping these understudied sitios of feminist discourse within Chicano studies reveals how women navigated institutional formations and mobilized emerging networks in higher education to share information, build a feminist curriculum and pedagogical praxis, and conduct direct action research that connected their scholarly pursuits to community needs. Moving in and between these sitios of knowledge, they developed the lenguas that wove together their multiple commitments as Chicana feminist scholar-activists.

These sitios y lenguas began to take shape at the birth of the field, in the wake of the Denver Youth Conference (March 1969) and CCHE's first statewide meeting in Santa Barbara (April 1969), which followed only a month later. According to Anna NietoGomez, women attended the Santa Barbara conference in significant numbers, and there were many strong activists among them. Nevertheless, there was no Chicana workshop on the schedule and few, if any, avenues to insert the "women's question" into the process of envisioning Chicano studies. Christina Vega, then chair of UMAS (later MEChA) at the University of California, Irvine, recalls that

> men were in large part in control of the [Santa Barbara] conference. . . . It was usually a man who was up there talking. I started to get offended at one point by what I realized was a macho or male-chauvinist perception of women's role. . . . When I interacted with male participants, they saw me not as a chairperson of MEChA, but as a female. That was bothersome to me.[17]

This marginalization was replicated on the editorial committee for *El Plan de Santa Bárbara*, the "blueprint" for Chicano studies, which was composed entirely of male scholars, including Fernando de Necochea, Juan Gómez-Quiñones, Rene Nuñez, Paul Sanchez, and Armando Valdez.[18] As several

Chicana scholars have since noted, not once in its 150 pages did *El Plan de Santa Bárbara* reference women—let alone feminism or Chicana studies—and none of the curricular models it documented included classes on La Chicana. Maylei Blackwell observes that *El Plan de Santa Bárbara* reinforced a decidedly male-centered vision for higher education by and for the Chicano that was "articulated through culturally mediated concepts of masculinity such as brotherhood, familism, and carnalismo" and either ignored entirely or, in the most generous interpretation, subsumed the educational needs and aspirations of Chicanas under the sign of a universalizing male subject.[19]

Moreover, the language and visual rhetoric of *El Plan de Santa Bárbara* mirrored the patriarchal discourse of "la familia de la raza" in *El Plan Espiritual de Aztlán*, drafted just a month earlier, in which, as Denise Segura observes, "women do not exist apart from membership in 'the Raza,' whose unity of interests is assumed to be absolute and essential. . . . Both plans assert that emulating la familia is the most effective organizing strategy for the Chicano movement, an assumption critiqued by numerous Chicanas."[20] Indeed, the *Plan de Santa Bárbara* publication included several illustrations that drew from the image vocabulary of movement newspapers and early texts like *I Am Joaquin* (1967), depicting lionized male figures as the universal subjects of the Chicano struggle for equity in higher education, and thus visually underscoring the absence of women in the vision it outlined for Chicanos in higher education.[21] Anna NietoGomez recalls that Chicanas who had participated in the Santa Barbara conference felt blindsided as they surveyed the pages of *El Plan de Santa Bárbara*: "We were aghast, we were angry." Two illustrations in particular drew their attention: "One was a graphic of scholars and leaders. We all knew who these characters were, they were the 'mero meros,' the leaders . . . and they were all men." The other graphic—one of the few that depicted women—reinforced the stereotypical image of the Mexican woman as barefoot and pregnant. "It was clear this was saying higher education isn't for women. We don't expect women to graduate. We don't see them making a difference. . . . We thought that was a very negative message, to us, and to the women coming after us."[22]

This stereotypical vision of La Chicana reverberated in the curricular models presented in *El Plan de Santa Bárbara*, which included courses on "the Chicano family" (reinforcing the idea that Chicana experience could be subsumed within la familia de la raza) but no courses that focused on the history and contemporary realities of Chicanas. Carlos Muñoz Jr., who was on the steering committee of CCHE and helped organize the Santa Barbara

FIGURE 4.1. *José Montoya, illustration of Chicano men, in Chicano Coordinating Council on Higher Education,* El Plan de Santa Bárbara: A Chicano Plan for Higher Education *(La Causa, 1969).*

conference, notes that none of the curricular proposals that were presented and discussed at the conference

> touched on the need to integrate the experience of Mexican-American women into the Chicano Studies Curriculum. The proposals were all developed by men. One explanation is that whereas Chicanos with PhDs were practically invisible, Chicanas with PhDs were actually invisible. Unfortunately none of the scholars involved in developing the proposals recognized the importance of gender at that time.[23]

The Chicano studies curricula implemented at various departments in the wake of the Santa Barbara conference largely followed this precedent of exclusion, offering classes on Chicano literature, history, and politics that rarely included women. Anna NietoGomez recalls that Chicanas at California State College (later University) at Long Beach were

> disheartened to find that the department failed to incorporate the study of women and reinforced traditional and negative stereotypes about Mexican American women. We read novels written by famous Mexican and

FIGURE 4.2. *Esteban Villa, illustration of Chicana woman, in Chicano Coordinating Council on Higher Education,* El Plan de Santa Bárbara: A Chicano Plan for Higher Education *(La Causa, 1969).*

> Chicano authors but the literature was very male centered, and the female characters were seen but not heard, were very stereotypical, and often female characters were missing through most of the book.[24]

Almost immediately after the publication of *El Plan de Santa Bárbara*, Chicana students across California began calling attention to the discursive erasure of women within its pages, an erasure that painfully illustrated their marginalization in the developing field.

In the spring of 1970, Elena H. García, a contributor to Stanford University's student newspaper *Chicanismo*, articulated this Chicana critique in a short essay entitled "Chicana Consciousness: A New Perspective, a New Hope," which was later republished in Dorinda Moreno's anthology *La Mujer: En Pie de Lucha* (1973). Identifying herself as a member of the "Chicana Caucus of *El Plan de Santa Bárbara*," García put men in Chicano studies on notice:

> Times are changing. You are coping with a new Chicana, a Chicana working within the college system. A Chicana who is seeing that her place need not only be in the home, with her husband and family. She is sensing her ability beyond that, yet not excluding it. She will go through the college system to get her degree and then she realizes she must go on, not stop the cycle at being [a] housewife. She must utilize her degree, her capacity as a Chicana woman and continue the cycle of enlightenment.[25]

Over the next few years, García's cycle of enlightenment would result in a profound shift across the landscape of Chicano studies—articulated in position papers, reading groups, new organizations, and writing published in student newspapers that collectively challenged the universalist male discourse presented in *El Plan de Santa Bárbara* and opened a space for "la nueva chicana" within the field.

From 1969 to 1971—when they caucused at CCHE's second statewide meeting in San Diego and formed the Chicana Ad Hoc Committee—Chicanas working and studying in Chicano studies departments laid the groundwork for the emergence of Chicana studies at universities and colleges across California. Informed by a growing feminist critique of the gendered contradictions of movement work, third-worldist perspectives that challenged the ideological limits of cultural nationalism, and a living tradition of Mexican women's activism, Chicana students established study groups and new organizations, conducted independent research into the historical and contemporary realities of Mexican American women to challenge the male-centered curriculum, and staked out feminist positions in articles and creative work published (usually anonymously) in movement newspapers like *La Raza*, *La Verdad*, *La Voz de Aztlán*, and *El Popo*.

In the Department of Mexican American Studies at San Diego State College (now University), a powerhouse for Chicano studies in Southern California during this period, Chicanas began organizing in 1969, immediately after attending the first Chicano Youth Liberation Conference in Denver.[26] Henri Chavez—who would later serve as steering committee chair for the State College Caucus of CCHE—remembers attending the Denver conference with a group of Chicana students from San Diego and identifies it as a "major turning point" for them.

> We saw that the only people in the kitchen were the women. [They] were the ones taking care of the kids in the childcare center. The women were the ones taking notes in all the workshops. And when you looked at the workshops, they were all being run by men. It was the Chicano man that was the keynote speaker and speaking up there in the front and, you know, putting out the ideas, and the women were just sitting back, we're just kinda, you know, taking it. And so, a group of us said, "No. We're gonna boycott this conference until you change it." And so we had a Chicana Caucus. We called it right there, got into a room and we said, "No. We are not gonna take care of the kids, we're not gonna be cooking, until you give us equal power." They said, "Men have children, too. They need to be out there." And, so, until they granted us that equality and accepted, you know, what we were proposing, you know, we were not gonna participate.[27]

The impromptu Chicana caucus at the Denver Youth Conference offered women from Texas, New Mexico, California, and many other places outside the Southwest a critical space to share stories about their experiences in the Chicano movement and, in 1970, to produce the first national statement about the role of women in the struggle. Contrary to some reports on the conference—which suggested that Chicanas in the workshop did little more than pledge allegiance to the movimiento—the discussion at the impromptu Chicana workshop in 1969 laid the groundwork for a set of radical resolutions calling for the full incorporation of women in the Chicano movement, which were later refined and presented by the Chicana workshop at the second Denver Youth Conference in 1970. Published by Henri Chavez in the San Diego student movement paper *La Verdad* (June 1970), the Chicana workshop resolutions cleverly reworked the rhetoric of Aztlán, self-determination, and la familia de la raza to directly challenge the subjugation of women within the Chicano movement.

With the grave responsibility of the re-birth and forming of our Nation of Aztlán the women have come to realize that they must begin to develop and function as complete human beings. We have reached a point in our struggle for the liberation of La Raza where the growth of our women is repressed as a great potential for strength and knowledge. *We must through education develop a full consciousness and awareness of the woman to the revolution and of the revolution to the woman.* This is the beginning for women to free themselves psychologically of thinking of themselves as inferior beings and to *educate themselves so that they too can implement the Plan de Aztlán.* In order to implement the Plan, we must understand all the things that it calls for.

With the preceding things kept in mind, we RESOLVE the following:

1. All women must participate according to their capabilities in all levels of the struggle.
2. We encourage all Chicanas to meet in their own groups for the purpose of education and discussion.
3. Self-determination of the women in terms of how they will implement their goal of becoming full human beings and of participation.
4. We must change the concept of the alienated family where the woman assumes total responsibility for the care of the home and the raising of the children to the concept of La Raza as the united family with the basis being brotherhood. La Raza, both men and women, young and old, must assume the responsibility for the love, care, education, and orientation of all the children of Aztlán. When we speak of community control we are speaking of self-determination of La Raza to decide how it wants to live. The changing concept of the family must run through all our action in the area of community control.
5. All of the preceding ideas must be included in the ideology of the La Raza Independent Political Party so that everyone, men and women, all work consciously towards the goal of the total liberation of our people. For the purpose of unity and direction, two women of La Raza have set up communication in the form of a newsletter to be shared by all women active in the struggle for the liberation of our people.
6. WE RESOLVE not to separate but to strengthen and free our nation of Aztlán, women, men, and children.[28]

The demands outlined in these resolutions—for Chicana education and self-determination, for reimagining the traditional family, and for a vision of the "total liberation" of La Raza, women, men, children—would be carried over into future interventions, particularly by Chicana students involved in CCHE who pushed for *El Plan de Santa Bárbara* to address the needs of the total community, not just male students. Indeed, Henri Chavez remembers that she and other San Diego Chicanas returned from Denver "all fired up" and ready to organize reading groups and workshops to develop Chicana identity.[29] Shortly thereafter, they formed Las Chicanas de San Diego, a study group that held weekly meetings to discuss political texts and talk about their issues. These reading groups would eventually evolve into the first classes on La Chicana at San Diego State. Carlos Vélez-Ibáñez, who was at San Diego State in the formative years of the Chicano studies department, recalls that "what gave the San Diego process its character and its intensity was the emergence of an extremely strong and persistent core of Chicana feminists" who directly challenged the limited political frameworks of the Chicano movement for educational justice: "While it had been simple to be critical of 'Anglos,' 'the system,' the 'power structure,' racism and ethnocentrism, most of us Mexican males suffered deeply from our own highly internalized sexism that had been learned early and often."[30]

Following a similar trajectory, Anna NietoGomez and Corinne Sánchez, students at California State College at Long Beach, another center of Chicano studies in California, began organizing feminist consciousness-raising sessions in the fall of 1969. The group started off as a "political education" committee for incoming women students in UMAS (which became a MEChA chapter after 1969). In an unpublished essay on the genesis of the Long Beach State Chicana group, NietoGomez recalls that while male UMAS/MEChA leaders encouraged *all* students to join the organizations (in keeping with the directives for student organizing in *El Plan de Santa Bárbara*), "they became annoyed when Chicanas interrupted 'the men's meetings' to ask questions and voice their ideas. . . . It did not occur to us to question why Chicanas needed a separate orientation committee when there wasn't a comparable one for men. Instead, we dutifully took on the task and called it the Chicanas de Aztlán Committee." As NietoGomez recalls, however, the political education committee soon strayed from its original intent as a "forum to discuss civil rights issues confronting Mexican Americans" and turned to "consciousness-raising discussions" about women's experiences of "gender inequality, male appropriation of women's ideas, and unwelcome sexual advances and other verbal or physical harassment of a sexual nature." By 1970, Las Chicanas de Aztlán had "evolved into a women's self-help support and study group" that "examined such issues as retention of Chicanas in higher education . . . human sexuality . . . and Chicanas in the prison[s]," themes that would become central to Chicana feminist scholarship and activism in the early 1970s.[31] The group would eventually publish what is widely considered to be the first Chicana newspaper, *Hijas de Cuauhtémoc*, a title inspired by their study of women in the Mexican Revolution, which they also adopted as the name of their collective. In 1971, shortly after the publication of *Hijas de Cuauhtémoc* (and as a direct result of the Chicana Ad Hoc Committee's advocacy in CCHE), Anna NietoGomez would become one of the first Chicanas in California to be hired into the tenure track to teach classes on La Chicana.[32]

By 1970 Corinne Sánchez, a cofounder of Las Hijas de Cuauhtémoc, would begin her work with Montal Educational Associates, eventually moving to Washington, DC, where she would play an instrumental role in developing curriculum and research on Chicanas/os in higher education across the Southwest. Montal was a key player in the proliferation and support of Chicano studies departments as well as bilingual/bicultural educational initiatives, hosting a number of Chicano Studies Mobile Institutes that brought together educators, students, and staff from across the Southwest to discuss curriculum, retention, and the future of the field. Notwithstanding this important effort on behalf of Chicano studies, Montal Educational Associates is often dismissed (or ignored outright) in histories of the field; indeed, Juan Gómez-Quiñones describes the establishment of the nonprofit and the students associated with it as "a blatantly disrupting, co-opting process . . . which served as the conduit to the student movement and Chicano Studies programs for a strategy emanating from an office of the Department of Health, Education and Welfare."[33] But Montal provided a critical space where women's leadership abilities could be developed beyond the limited purview of male-led student organizations and nascent departments. Indeed, as a result of her work organizing the mobile institutes, Sánchez wrote one of the earliest examinations of the emergent field, "A Challenge for Colleges and Universities: Chicano Studies," published in the fall 1970 issue of *Civil Rights Digest*.[34] She also leveraged her position as a grants coordinator and program manager at Montal to advance Chicana studies within the academy, launching several administrative and curricular training workshops in Los Angeles and Washington, DC, that focused on developing women's leadership skills in the early 1970s. Through her connections with Montal Educational Associates, Sánchez was able to fund a Chicana curriculum project that resulted in the first Chicana curriculum guide (compiled and edited by Anna NietoGomez), *New Directions in Education: Estudios Femeniles de la Chicana* (1973). Sánchez returned to Los Angeles in 1973 when Montal opened an office in the San Fernando Valley, and later that year she left the nonprofit to take a job with the Chicana Service Action Center, established by Francisca Flores, a longtime activist in Southern California.

As Corinne Sánchez's work with Francisca Flores suggests, efforts to build consciousness among women in colleges and universities were often aided by the mentorship of an older generation of activist women who shared critical insights on political strategy, connected Chicana students to long-standing social movement and civil rights networks, and supported the burgeoning Chicana print culture of the early 1970s. For example, Gracia Molina de Pick, one of the very few Chicanas who held faculty positions in this early period, was a key mentor to Chicana students at San Diego State College (later University).[35] A teacher at Mesa College in San Diego in the late 1960s, Molina de Pick had cultivated important connections to the United Farm Workers and the broader women's liberation movement and was instrumental in connecting Chicana students in San Diego to an international network of activist women.

Another example of this intergenerational leadership was Francisca Flores, who had been a fixture in the Mexican American civil rights landscape of Southern California since the 1940s. As a member of the Communist Party in San Diego and later Los Angeles, she pushed the US Communist Party to incorporate gender and race into its analysis of the working class, and she actively engaged Mexican American communities through reading groups and public lectures.[36] She was a member of the Sleepy Lagoon Defense Committee and the Asociación Nacional México Americana (founded in 1949). In the 1960s she was active with the Community Service Organization and the Mexican American Political Association, where she worked to amplify the political contributions of women by establishing the League of Mexican American Women. Through her editorial work with *Carta Editorial* (a bimonthly opinion and informational newsletter published in the 1960s) and later *Regeneración*, Flores provided opportunities for budding Chicana writers, artists, and activists to disseminate news about the Mexican American / Chicano civil rights movement and to share their creative work and opinions. With her long experience in editing and publishing, Flores would become a major resource in the development of Chicana print culture, offering many Chicanas opportunities to publish their work in *Regeneración* and supporting their efforts to publish their own newspapers and journals.

Flores's organizing efforts on behalf of Mexican American women also laid the groundwork for the Comisión Femenil Mexicana Nacional, a critical point of connection between Chicanas on college campuses and activist women in the community. Formed at a women's workshop that Francisca Flores and Simmie Romero Goldsmith organized at the Mexican American

National Issues Conference in Sacramento (October 10–11, 1970), the Comisión Femenil Mexicana Nacional was established to address women's needs and promote women's leadership "within the Chicano movement and in community life." Its aim was to investigate issues affecting Mexican American women (like employment, health care, education, and family life) and to promote programs that offered real solutions.[37] Young women who participated in the Chicana workshop at the National Issues Conference—including Francis Bojórquez, Diana Holguin, and Linda Apodaca—would eventually work with Flores to establish the first chapter of the Comisión Femenil at California State College at Los Angeles in January 1971.[38] The California State Los Angeles chapter of the Comisión Femenil staked out a strong feminist position within the developing field, resolving to defend "women's right to self-determination over her body, to establish links with other women's organizations working on the same issues nationally and internationally, to organize local, regional and national meetings and conferences, to support and promote Chicana leadership, and to place pressure on the newly-established Commission on the Status of Women (at both the state and federal level) to attend to the needs of Mexican American women."[39]

Working with an older generation of women leaders through the Comisión Femenil, Chicana students in colleges and universities across Los Angeles began to craft a research and organizing agenda for Chicana studies, as well as a scholarly praxis oriented toward community action and self-determination. This praxis would be elaborated through their work with the Chicana Service Action Center, a project launched by the Comisión Femenil in 1972 that became a hub for Chicana organizing and research in the mid-1970s. Based in Los Angeles, the Chicana Service Action Center provided direct services to women in the community, from job training to leadership development. By the mid-1970s the center would also become an important site for applied research that focused on the socioeconomic barriers (race, class, and gender) that affected the development of Chicanas in all sectors of society. Indeed, Anna NietoGomez describes the Chicana Service Action Center as a "research hub" for her class on La Chicana at California State University, Northridge. Using federal grants obtained by the center, she and her students would conduct quantitative and qualitative research to inform public policy on education, work, welfare, and other issues.[40]

In the Bay Area, Chicana students like Dorinda Moreno (San Francisco State College) and Yolanda Lopez (who would a few years later pursue a bachelor's degree in fine arts at San Diego State and join the Chicana group there) were profoundly shaped by the political reverberations of the Third World Liberation Front, a coalition of Black, Asian American, Raza

(Latina/o), and Native American student organizations (and their white allies) that shut down San Francisco State College from November 6, 1968, to March 20, 1969, demanding the recruitment of more students of color and the establishment of a School of Ethnic Studies.[41] A twice-married mother of three who was older than most of the students in the Third World Liberation Front, Moreno joined in the struggle when she returned to San Francisco from a brief sojourn in Los Angeles in 1969. She was later recruited to the newly formed La Raza Studies Department at San Francisco State by Educational Opportunity Program officer Tony Salamanca. Like Chicana students in San Diego and Los Angeles, Moreno had been mentored by a woman who was connected to the Mexican American civil rights movements of a generation before: Margaret Cruz. A founding member of the Mexican American Political Association, Cruz had been a fixture in Latina/o politics in the Bay Area since the 1950s.[42] Inspired by the Third World Liberation Front's ethos of community action and Cruz's example of community service, as well as her own lived experience as a working mother struggling to find a political and economic footing in Northern California, Moreno established Concilio Mujeres in 1970 as a special project in La Raza studies at San Francisco State. An outreach center that connected La Raza studies to the community, Concilio Mujeres was initially conceived as a "task force to encourage Spanish-speaking women to enter nontraditional professions, [to pursue] higher educational levels, and to offer psychological and sociological support to one another," but it soon became a key site for the development of Chicana feminist studies in the Bay Area, launching a Chicana teatro group (Las Cucarachas), a newspaper (*La Razón Mestiza*) and other publication projects, and an "informational clearinghouse" that distributed "materials specifically relating to Raza women."[43] In 1971 Dorinda Moreno would travel to San Diego for the second statewide CCHE conference, where she was one of the conveners of the Chicana caucus, which became the Chicana Ad Hoc Committee of CCHE.

Traversing community and university spaces from the Bay Area to Southern California, these early sitios of Chicana feminist thought (and there are surely many more yet to be uncovered) birthed a knowledge praxis centered on the contemporary realities of Mexican American women, one that shaped the interwoven scholarly, political, and pedagogical interventions of Chicana studies in its formative years. Far from isolated interventions, these sitios found common connection in a growing network related to the movement for Chicano studies. The members of this network read each other's writing in student newspapers; they connected through MEChA, which held regular regional and statewide meetings after 1969; and perhaps most significantly for the history of Chicano studies, they participated widely in CCHE, which convened a series of directional meetings following the 1969 Santa Barbara conference. In her 1974 article "La Feminista," Anna NietoGomez notes that such "conventions and conferences would bring large numbers of Chicanas together to form an effective 'temporary' Chicana caucus pressure group."[44] Mobilizing the organizing networks that had emerged post-1969, Chicanas used the caucus strategy to help define their goals, share strategy, and put pressure on organizations from within.

## NETWORKING MOVIDAS: THE CHICANO COUNCIL ON HIGHER EDUCATION AND THE STRUGGLE FOR CHICANA STUDIES IN CALIFORNIA

In most historical accounts of Chicano studies, the organization that came to be known as the Chicano Council on Higher Education is credited with hosting the Santa Barbara conference and little else.[45] Yet for several years after the Santa Barbara conference, CCHE played a prominent role in shaping the field. Its frequent regional and statewide meetings nurtured a powerful network of knowledge exchange, bringing together students, faculty, and staff in postsecondary institutions across California (including junior colleges, the California State College system, the University of California system, and private universities) to share curricula, political strategies, and resources for the development of Chicano studies. Formed by Rene Nuñez in 1968, shortly after the Los Angeles blowouts, CCHE was conceived as a way to bring strategic coherence to a number of ongoing educational justice initiatives, including those developed by activists working on improving K–12 education for Chicanas/os, university students (many of whom had been actively involved in organizing the blowouts), and a small group of faculty and staff who were administering recruitment and retention programs, or who sat on committees tasked with developing Chicano studies programs and curricula at their institutions.[46] Similar to the rationale for the establishment of independent educational institutions like Colegio Jacinto Treviño (1969) and Juárez–Lincoln (1972), CCHE organizers saw colleges and universities as a critical front for the Chicana/o struggle for equitable education and self-determination. In order to link the issues in secondary education that had precipitated the Los Angeles blowouts (tracking, curriculum, and disproportionate disciplinary action) to the rising movement for Chicano studies, CCHE called for a "statewide network of community and campus activists" that could put institutional and political pressure on campus administrators and governmental agencies "to expand equal opportunity programs to get proper attention to the needs of Mexican American youth, and to ensure that Chicano studies programs developed directly under activists' control."[47]

While the archival record of CCHE largely reflects the disproportionately male leadership structure of the movement for Chicano studies more broadly, lived memory fleshes this archive to tell a different story. Indeed, interviews with Sonia Lopez, Henri Chavez (who became the chair of the CCHE State College Caucus Steering Committee in 1971), Anna NietoGomez, and Dorinda Moreno—all active members of CCHE's California State College network—reveal that women (mostly students) played a much larger role in the development of Chicano studies in California than has been previously acknowledged. While their names may not have appeared on published programs for CCHE conferences and meetings, women were nevertheless central to keeping the organization administratively afloat from 1969 until 1973, when its influence declined. Henri Chavez recalls that some of the women who would later develop Chicana studies curricula in departments across California first came together at the regional and state meetings that CCHE organized to coordinate the implementation of academic programs and student services for Chicanas/os in higher educational institutions:

> That's how we started meeting other people. . . . So we were meeting, "Ay, have you heard of this person?" "Have you heard of that person?" You know, "They have some good ideas." And, so, we started borrowing ideas from each other and building on them, and knowing that we had support somewhere else, too. You know? That we weren't acting alone, not only as women and as Chicanas, but as Chicanos in the development of Mexican American Studies into Chicano Studies.[48]

According to Anna NietoGomez, she, Sylvia Castillo (a member of Las Hijas de Cuauhtémoc), Dorinda Moreno, Henri Chavez, and Sonia Lopez spent "more time going to CCHE meetings than going to class!"—an impression also shared by Henri and Sonia.[49] Indeed, in the early 1970s CCHE became a central site for organizing around Chicanas in higher education, providing women with important opportunities to network and build skills. They organized local and regional meetings for CCHE, took minutes, wrote position papers, developed curricular and recruitment initiatives, and ensured that newly established Chicano studies programs across California stayed in communication with one another. The largely invisible labor of bringing CCHE into being as a statewide network also helped Chicanas develop the critical leadership, writing, speaking, and organizational skills they would need to build Chicana studies.

While Chicanas in CCHE committed their time and labor to the building of Chicano studies, they also challenged the insurgent field's overwhelmingly heteropatriarchical ethos from within.[50] Regional and statewide CCHE meetings offered an important space for consciousness-raising and strategizing for Chicanas in the "trenches of academe," with the critical distinction that for them, this institutional theater of war (extending Rodolfo Acuña's military analogy) was a far more complex space to maneuver. Often, Chicanas would use the opportunity provided by regional meetings to swap stories about the silencing they were experiencing in classrooms and student meetings, and to share resources and strategies for addressing and contesting it. NietoGomez recalls the urgency of this issue among women in CCHE: "[We] were not listened to. . . . We were leaders, we were there from the beginning. Our fingerprints were on every product that was produced in Chicano Studies and in the movement, but we were still fighting to be recognized."[51] Henri Chavez remembers that regional and state meetings of CCHE helped her connect with other women and share ideas and strategies for challenging this silencing within the field:

> We were in a different location and we had . . . different types of situations but it was like, "Have you gone through this?" And some of it was . . . philosophical, . . . ideas and stuff like that. But some of it was, How do you deal with situations? . . . How do you move from here to here . . . with men or with the system, or . . . whatever you were dealing with?[52]

In the absence of their own statewide organization that could tackle these issues directly, women in CCHE often gathered in informal caucuses to define their issues and develop a collective agenda. Indeed, as NietoGomez has observed, the caucus strategy was essential for Chicanas to gain a political foothold in spaces that often defined oppression through a "monolithic" lens (of either race or gender).[53]

A malleable political form that was used frequently by activists in the 1960s and 1970s to develop distinct platforms within existing organizations, the caucus could be an informal meeting/workshop or a more structured formation aimed at gaining, and leveraging, representational power. For example, Mujeres Pro Raza Unida in Texas (NietoGomez's case study of Chicana organizing in her foundational essay "La Feminista") used the structure of the National Women's Political Caucus, where both interest groups and formal political parties could petition to be recognized as caucuses, to demand *two* caucuses—one for Raza Unida Party women and a separate Chicana caucus (which notably included women from all three political parties)—thus potentially increasing their representation to leverage power in the decision-making activities of the national women's organization.[54] In contrast, the Chicana caucus within CCHE was a much more ephemeral and temporary formation, with a shifting roster of women informally coming together at meetings and conferences. This limited its effectiveness as a pressure group within CCHE, and as Anna notes, "their diffused return to each individual organization brought few results, where numbers as well as morale were weak. This prevented any whole-hearted action to internalize the Chicana platform into Chicano organizations."[55] Nevertheless, caucusing at CCHE meetings (and also within MEChA) did help women to understand that their experiences in the nascent field were not isolated, even as it built a strong network of like-minded Chicana feminists across California, including Elena García of Stanford University, who in an essay published in 1970 identified herself as a member of the "Chicana Caucus of *El Plan de Santa Barbara*."[56] By the spring of 1971, when CCHE organized its follow-up to the Santa Barbara conference, this mostly informal Chicana caucus would host a workshop for Chicana students, faculty, and staff to concretize a master plan for their full incorporation into Chicano studies. At this workshop, they formed the Chicana Ad Hoc Committee as a regular standing committee in CCHE.

## "EL PLAN DE SANTA Y BÁRBARA"

Notwithstanding its singular status in histories of the field, the organizers of the 1969 Santa Barbara conference had envisioned it as only the first in a series of yearly CCHE conferences through which the direction and political thrust of the movement for Chicano studies would be collectively developed. However, according to a brief historical sketch of CCHE written by Henri Chavez and presented at a CCHE joint faculty retreat in October 1971, a follow-up conference had been delayed by the work of implementing new programs, which had kept the attention of CCHE members focused primarily on organizing at their own campuses. More critically for the future of CCHE, the process of establishing new programs, departments, and research centers had been undertaken in sometimes widely divergent academic settings, exacerbating existing differences in approach between those working in state colleges, the University of California system, private universities, and community colleges. These differences highlighted political, ideological, and class fissures within the CCHE network. Faculty and students in the University of California system, for example, decided to organize a separate caucus to better address their particular needs, an action that, according to Chavez's historical sketch, resulted in "misunderstandings and distrust between regions and between the State Colleges and University of California campuses."[57] The historical sketch only hints at the implications of this split, noting that it led to a period of demoralization and "dormancy that lasted through the summer and fall of 1970."[58] In truth, it was a major blow to the ideals of the Santa Barbara conference, where the discourse of "Chicanismo" and "hermandad" (brotherhood) had sought to forge a united front between faculty, students, and staff in institutions that had very different levels of access to resources. Indeed, as Chavez notes in her historical sketch, while the "original ideas" discussed in Santa Barbara "continued to be used to implement programs, and the [University of California] Caucus continued to operate and to grow in strength," by late 1970 "many of the originators felt that CCHE, having served a good purpose, was dead." Nevertheless, "some key campuses, including community colleges," remained committed to the concept of a statewide organization for Chicano studies and "began encouraging the revival of CCHE," calling for a statewide conference to reinvigorate the council and to revisit the programmatic and curricular "outlines" in El Plan de Santa Bárbara that "were obsolete or in need of updating."[59] While Chavez's historical sketch does not explicitly identify the elements of the plan that were obsolete and in need of updating, Chicanas had voiced strong criticisms of its illustrations, its omission of women in the curriculum, and the fact that it had been published without review from CCHE's membership.

Both a much-needed follow-up to the Santa Barbara conference and an effort to improve communication and coherence across the rapidly proliferating landscape of Chicano studies educational initiatives, the second statewide meeting of CCHE in San Diego (March 19–21, 1971) was, in many ways, an attempt to salvage the dream, first conceived in Santa Barbara, of a network of educators and programs that could direct the development of the field across broadly divergent institutional settings.

In recognition of the real differences between institutions in California's four-tiered higher education system, organizers of the San Diego conference proposed a unique tripartite model for the gathering, with three concurrent subconferences (to be held on Saturday, March 20), in which CCHE representatives from state colleges, private institutions, and community colleges could meet and determine their own goals and strategies for developing Chicano studies statewide. On the afternoon of the second day of the conference (Sunday, March 21), the general body would come together, with representatives from each interest group in CCHE, for a series of concurrent meetings to undertake three organizational tasks: (1) to assess the plans developed the day before and "prepare a rough draft of proposals and findings of the workshops"; (2) to establish a "working statewide organization of institutions"; and (3) to select a statewide steering committee for CCHE that could "plan a future conference." Under this new confederated model for CCHE, separate caucuses would represent the interests of state colleges, the University of California system, private universities, and community colleges, and would maintain lines of communication with one another through a statewide steering committee. This reorganization, the conference organizers hoped, would allow CCHE to realize its potential as a network of educators that could advocate for Chicano studies "politically and legislatively in State and National education movidas, that will have the strength to come to the support of threatened programs and that will be capable of continued communication and information dissemination."[60]

When Chicanas from across California gathered for the San Diego conference in March of 1971, they were poised to play a much more instrumental role in the proceedings than they had done at the first CCHE conference in Santa Barbara in 1969. Among them were self-identified feminists who had established reading groups, collectives, and organizations linked to their campuses, including Las Chicanas de San Diego, Las Hijas de Cuauhtémoc, Comisión Femenil Mexicana Nacional (Los Angeles), Concilio Mujeres (San Francisco), and Las Adelitas de Aztlán (Fresno). Many were active members, and even leaders, of UMAS, MAYA, MEChA, and other community and university organizations, and thus had firsthand experience with the gendered contradictions of social movement work, particularly the ways that leadership was assumed to be the exclusive province of men.[61] They shared the experience of being silenced or ridiculed in the Chicano studies classroom and in student meetings. Some, like Isabel Hernandez from Sacramento State, worked in Educational Opportunity Program offices and had seen how women's needs were consistently ignored in recruitment and retention programs.[62] Determined to address these and other issues at the conference in San Diego, they organized a Sunday morning workshop for women—one of the few to engage participants across the four-tier system—and formed the Chicana Ad Hoc Committee of CCHE (sometimes referred to as the Chicana caucus). Olivia Reynolds de Medina (San Diego State College) and Regina Contreras (University of California, Berkeley) documented the workshop, leaving us a trace of this historic event in a detailed list of participants, meeting notes, and a hand-drawn map. These materials, along with a proposal for a Chicana curriculum, give evidence to Chicanas' early, and coordinated, intervention in the nascent field of Chicano studies.

Thirty-five women attended the Chicana workshop on March 21, 1971. The vast majority of participants were from the California State College system, with particularly large numbers from the San Diego and Los Angeles areas (including state colleges in Los Angeles, the San Fernando Valley, and Long Beach), as well as women from Fresno, Sacramento State, and the Bay Area (Dorinda Moreno of San Francisco State was one of the conveners of the workshop). A page of meeting notes written in neat, sloping cursive outlines both short-term and longer-range goals for the group. They agreed to coordinate efforts to raise money for a contingent of Chicanas from California to attend La Conferencia de Mujeres por la Raza, the first National Chicana Conference, to be held in Houston May 28–30, 1971. They would work to establish a statewide education communication network to collect and distribute literature on Chicanas, focusing on "her role today," and develop a curriculum on "women's and men's historical role . . . in capitalistic societies." They also agreed that they should encourage Chicana students in their consciousness-raising groups and classes to write down their own "feelings and thoughts" about their role today, in "stories, poetry, essays" that could be disseminated through movement publications and used in classes. Finally, they would actively organize and support Chicanas "on all levels," from mothers and grandmothers to students in colleges, high schools, and junior high schools.[63]

To organize these varied activities, they divided the state into five different areas assigned to "regional educational coordinators" (drawn from volunteers in attendance at the workshop), who would be responsible for contacting women's groups at colleges and universities in their area and recruiting others to act as coordinators for specific campuses.[64] The Northern California region would be organized by Maria Franco at Sacramento State; Regina Contreras of the University of California, Berkeley, would coordinate activities in the Bay Area; Olivia Chumacero of Fresno State would organize Chicanas at institutions in the San Joaquin Valley and the central coast; and in the greater Los Angeles area (which had the largest concentration of Chicano studies departments), Blanca Olivares would take the lead. The regional coordinator for San Diego would be chosen at a later date. In addition to coming up with this strategic plan for the development of Chicana studies, members of the Chicana Ad Hoc Committee drafted a set of resolutions and amendments that addressed the marginalization of women in Chicano studies, which they then presented to the voting body of CCHE. According to a report on the CCHE conference that appeared in the first issue of *Hijas de Cuauhtémoc* (April 1971), Chicanas from Long Beach were behind a motion (which was passed by the general body) that *El Plan de Santa Bárbara* would "be revised to include the Chicana and her vital role in el movimiento." Building on this motion, the Chicana Ad Hoc Committee successfully lobbied for a series of

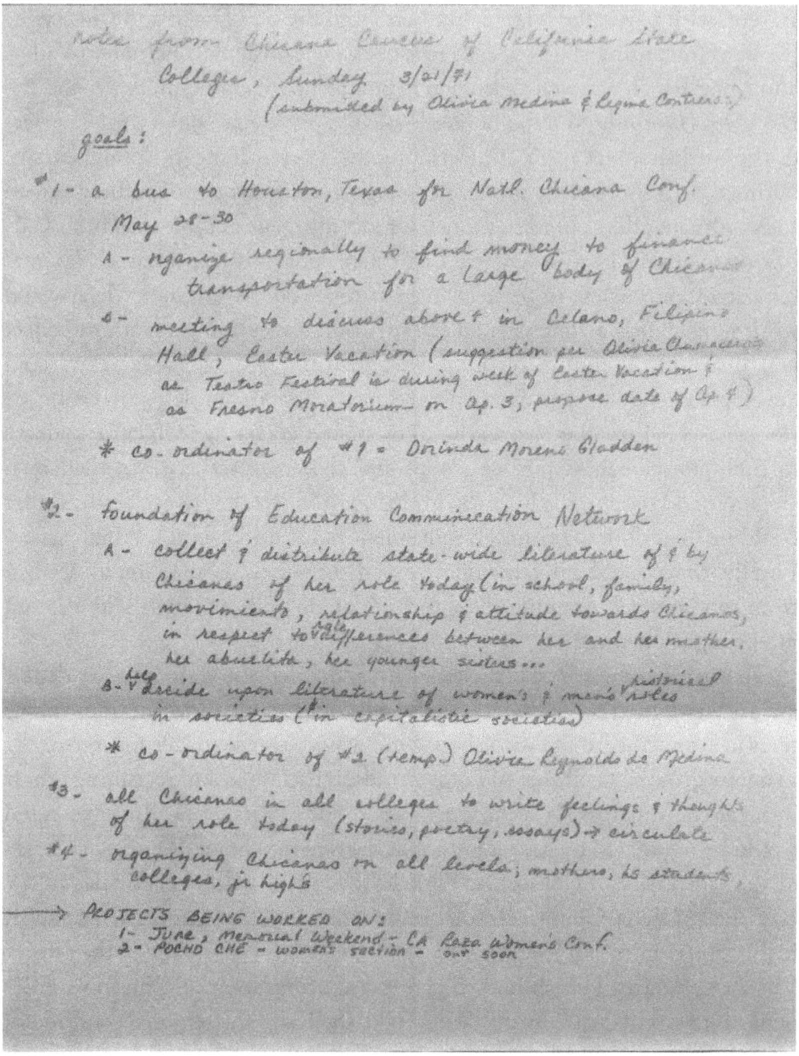

Notes from Chicana Caucus of California State Colleges, Sunday 3/21/71
(submitted by Olivia Medina & Regina Contreras)

goals:

#1 - a bus to Houston, Texas for Natl. Chicana Conf. May 28-30

A - organize regionally to find money to finance transportation for a large body of Chicanas

B - meeting to discuss above + in Delano, Filipino Hall, Easter Vacation (suggestion per Olivia Camarena as Teatro Festival is during week of Easter Vacation & as Fresno Moratorium on Ap. 3, propose date of Ap. 4)

* co-ordinator of #1 = Dorinda Moreno Gladden

#2 - foundation of Education Communication Network

A - collect & distribute state-wide literature of & by Chicanas of her role today (in school, family, movimiento, relationship & attitude towards Chicanos, in respect to role differences between her and her mother, her abuelita, her younger sisters...

B - help decide upon literature of women's & men's historical roles in societies (in capitalistic societies)

* co-ordinator of #2 (temp.) Olivia Reynoldo de Medina

#3 - all Chicanas in all colleges to write feelings & thoughts of her role today (stories, poetry, essays) → circulate

#4 - organizing Chicanas on all levels; mothers, hs students, colleges, jr highs

→ PROJECTS BEING WORKED ON:
1 - June, Memorial Weekend - CA Raza Women's Conf.
2 - POCHO CHE - WOMEN'S SECTION - OUT SOON

FIGURE 4.3. *Goals of the Chicana caucus, listed in the notes from a meeting of Chicanas from the California State Colleges, March 21, 1971. Enriqueta Chavez Papers, San Diego State University.*

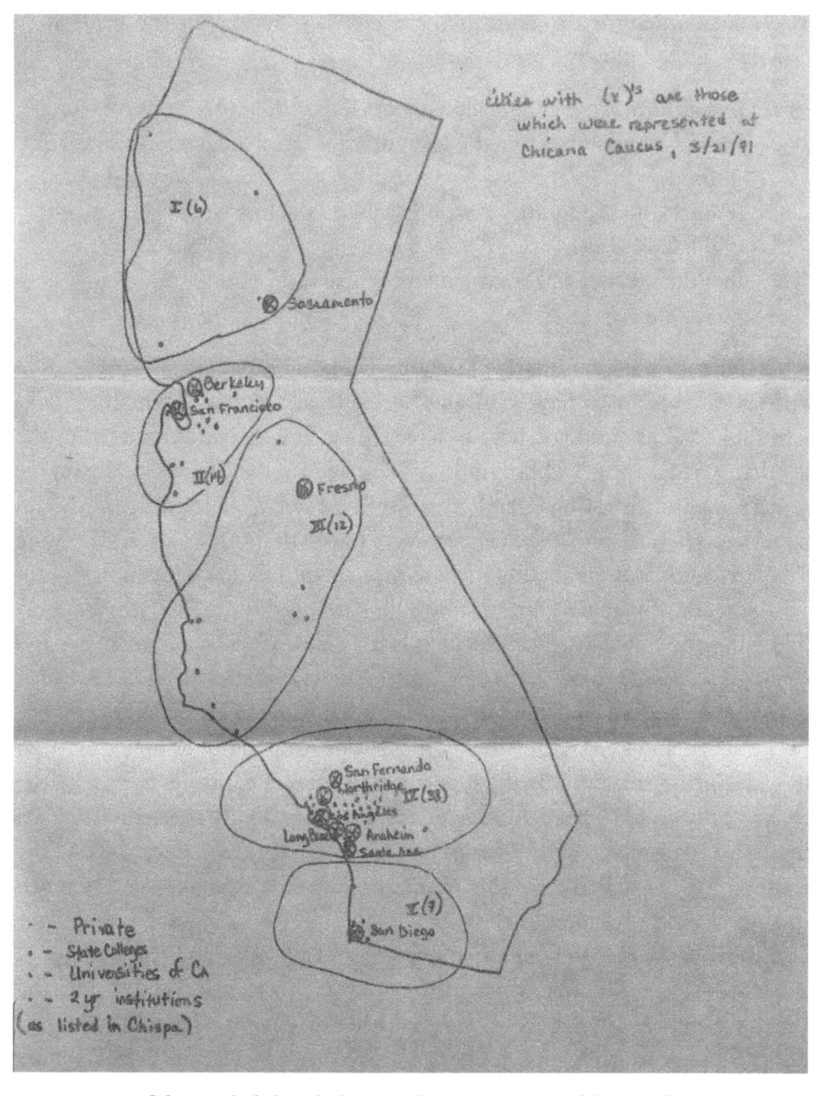


FIGURE 4.4. *Map, included with the notes from a meeting of Chicanas from the California State Colleges, March 21, 1971. Enriqueta Chavez Papers, San Diego State University.*

amendments designed to address the needs of Chicanas in the field. They established the following resolutions:

1. That no form of policy be made without adequate Chicana representation;
2. That Chicanas be recruited into significant faculty and administrative positions;
3. That all Chicano Studies Programs initiate and implement coursework on the Chicana;
4. That the cover of *El Plan* should recognize the Chicana and her movimiento input.[65]

Anna NietoGomez summarized the intervention in the following way: "We said . . . you've got to have Chicanas at all levels of decision making, and Chicano Studies. And you have to have Chicanas equally represented in the faculty, in the hiring and promotion. You have to have them equally represented in administration." And, critically, *El Plan de Santa Bárbara* should be revised so that it included women and showed that they too could become scholars: "This was all about getting Chicanas into higher education."[66]

The work of getting Chicanas into higher education began immediately following the San Diego conference. Just a week after successfully passing the CCHE resolutions, the women of the newly formed Chicana Ad Hoc Committee drafted a curriculum proposal that offers documentary evidence of the speed and skill with which Chicanas developed policy and curricular models during this period. The report is written on California State College at Long Beach letterhead and includes a brief opening statement articulating how involvement in the "issues facing the Chicano in education and the community" has underscored the "unique problems" Chicanas "face as women in this society." To address these issues, the Chicana Ad Hoc Committee argued, it was necessary for the movement to "also develop the identity of the Chicana in order that she may set forth her direction and goals."[67] Citing the low numbers of women among the academic faculty and administrative ranks, "which in itself represents the lack of attention given in developing the vast resources of the Chicana," they framed their proposed curriculum as a way to encourage more Chicanas to enter the field.[68] The model curriculum for Chicana studies, which was "to be implemented in the Fall of 1971," proposed nine "pilot courses" covering a wide array of topics and disciplines, including history, sociology, social psychology, and gender studies (third world women and sexual division of labor), as well as courses in leadership development (establishing programs, proposal writing, and volunteer work), community organizing, and applied research.[69] This document, written in 1971 and preserved in Enriqueta Chavez's papers at the San Diego State

University Library, is perhaps the first example of a Chicana studies curriculum in the field.

The intervention of Chicanas in CCHE yielded another important first for Chicana studies. As a result of their resolutions, Anna NietoGomez would be hired as a full-time faculty member at San Fernando Valley State (now California State University, Northridge) by Carlos Arce, then chair of the Chicano Studies Department, to teach classes explicitly focused on La Chicana. That fall, she offered the first class on La Chicana in Chicano studies at San Fernando Valley State, a preeminent department in the field. Indeed, as a direct result of the work of the Chicana Ad Hoc Committee, opportunities would open up for others to begin teaching the first official classes on La Chicana at state colleges across California. At San Diego State, classes on La Chicana were taught through the Mexican American Lifestyles course (a requirement for graduation), and following the CCHE conference, Dorinda Moreno would develop her own class on La Mujer in women's studies at San Francisco State.

Ironically, while the organizers of the second statewide CCHE meeting in San Diego envisioned it as a way to revive the sense of "hermandad" and collective purpose that had characterized the Santa Barbara conference in 1969, the meeting's historical significance lies less with its relatively minor impact on the development of the field (CCHE would effectively last only a few more years) than with the fact that it marked a critical turning point for the development of Chicana feminist studies. Indeed, the Chicana workshop concretized the growing sense of "hermanidad" (sisterhood) among women and a new mission to work together to develop a strong curriculum on La Chicana within Chicano studies. The article on the CCHE conference that appeared in the first issue of *Hijas de Cuauhtémoc* notes that the Chicana Ad Hoc Committee was "derived with the objectives of setting up intrastate communications of las Chicanas del movimiento through a newsletter, exchange of papers and research projects on la Chicana, the publication of journals and an anthology on women, propose classes on the Chicana and start community groups to aid in bringing la 'mujer' into the forefront of involvement in determining our destinies."[70] Together, these objectives encouraged a florecimiento of Chicana knowledge production inside and outside the academy, including an explosion of creative and analytical writing that would become essential reading material (alongside Marx, Engels, Freire, and key women's liberation texts like *Our Bodies, Ourselves*) in the first classes on La Chicana, and an innovative research and pedagogical agenda grounded in the lived experience of Chicanas.

The notes from the Chicana caucus and the proposed Chicana curriculum that followed a week later amount to less than twenty pages, and they include none of the heroic rhetorical flourishes of *El Plan de Santa Bárbara*, yet, I would argue, they give evidence of a master plan for Chicana studies in California: a Chicana "Plan de Santa y Bárbara."[71] This is not to say that the Chicana Ad Hoc Committee's master plan *determined* what would follow; rather, like *El Plan de Santa Bárbara*, it drew from an existing landscape of ideas and organizing activities to consolidate both a new philosophy (hermanidad) and a roadmap (quite literally) for the development of Chicana self-identity in colleges and barrios across California.[72] Mapping a collective vision for Chicana feminist studies across the state through networking, consciousness-raising, organizing, recruitment, teaching, and the production of knowledge, the master plan that emerged from the Chicana workshop in San Diego offers a revealing archival index to the multiple sites, inside and outside the academy, that together constituted a Chicana renaissance in California from 1971 to 1976.

Indeed, the network of Chicana scholar-activists that came together through the Chicano Council on Higher Education worked collectively to build a knowledge ecosystem long after the organization declined in relevance. They collaborated on anthologies and journals, cited each other in their scholarship, and invited each other to lecture in their classes and at the conferences they organized. While their research on education, history, sexuality, women's health, labor, and welfare rights and their creative writing rarely appeared in emergent academic journals like *Aztlán* and *El Grito*—leaving few archival traces in the mainstream publication currents of the Chicano studies field imaginary—Chicanas nevertheless developed alternative print cultures, publishing their scholarly and creative writing in short-lived women's newspapers and journals, including *Hijas de Cuauhtémoc* (three issues, 1971), *El Popo Femenil* (1973), *Encuentro Femenil* (two issues, 1973), and *Women Struggle* (1976), or in the special issues of *Regeneración* that Francisca Flores would periodically put together beginning in June 1971.[73] Chicana research and analysis appeared on a regular basis in the *Chicana Service Action Center Newsletter* (also published by Francisca Flores), which included many contributions from Anna NietoGomez, who was at the time an assistant professor at San Fernando Valley State. The Chicana classes that emerged in the wake of the San Diego conference became a key site for this knowledge production, where new research and writing could be developed and disseminated. In and through these alternative sitios of knowledge production, a growing network of Chicana feminist thinkers steadily built a field of study in the early 1970s, making the case for the analysis of gender, race, class, and sexuality in a mostly hostile institutional terrain.

# BEYOND A HISTORY OF VIOLENCE: THE KNOWLEDGE MODALITIES OF CHICANA STUDIES IN THE 1970S

*Chapter 5*

> *From the social movements of the fifties and sixties until the present day, networks of power have attempted to work through and with minority difference in culture, trying to redirect originally insurgent formations and deliver them to the normative ideals and protocols of state, capital, and academy. In this new strategic situation, hegemonic power denotes the disembodied and abstract promotion of minority representation without fully satisfying the material and social redistribution of minoritized subjects, particularly where people of color are concerned.*
>
> RODERICK A. FERGUSON, *The Reorder of Things*

> *History will reflect how the study of the Chicana created a political controversy because it mirrored the contradiction between the rhetoric of liberation and the practice of continued oppression. If you condone the oppression of women, who else is on the list? The development of Chicana Studies at [California State University, Northridge] created controversy because it analyzed sexism and its role to perpetuate this system. The study of the Chicana brought many to the conclusion that if one supports sexism, he supports Capitalism.*
>
> ANNA NIETOGOMEZ, RESIGNATION LETTER

I am sitting in Anna NietoGomez's living room surrounded by open folders and old newspapers as we ease into a plática that I know will be both illuminating and deeply painful. It is the fall of 2018, and I have come to Anna's home to learn about the early years of Chicana studies, when she and other women in California labored to build an archive of knowledge and a field of study centered on "bringing la 'mujer' into the forefront of involvement in determining our destinies."[1] I knew of this history tangentially, from other sources, some of them quite personal. My mother, Martha Cotera, had corresponded with Anna and other women in California in the early 1970s, and they frequently encountered each other at the many conferences that followed the first National Chicana Conference in Houston, Texas, which brought them together in 1971 for the first time. Indeed, several of her essays in *The Chicana Feminist* (1976) speak to the importance of Anna's thinking in the development of Chicana feminist analyses.

Not surprisingly, Anna appears frequently in my mother's archive, in her correspondence, and in her collection of print media (which includes the periodicals *Hijas de Cuauhtémoc*, *Encuentro Femenil*, and the *Chicana Service Action Center Newsletter*), giving evidence to a growing network of knowledge exchange in the 1970s that included Corinne Sánchez in Washington, DC, Beverly Sánchez-Padilla in New Mexico, Marcella Trujillo in Colorado, Julie Ruiz in Arizona, and many women across California and Texas. It was in my mother's collection that I first came across *Women Struggle*, a single-issue newspaper published in 1976 to bring attention to Anna's tenure battle at California State University, Northridge. Later, Maylei Blackwell would flesh out this archival trace in her book *¡Chicana Power!* (2011), which drew from oral histories with Chicanas and their personal archives to illuminate the institutional violence that Chicana feminists encountered in their struggle to develop an analytic on La Mujer. Our own interview with Anna, conducted by the Chicana por Mi Raza team in 2010, further fleshed this archival trace with Anna's vivid firsthand testimony about the joys of researching and teaching, and the regulation that she and others faced when they tried to address the "women's question" within the emergent field of Chicano studies.

Like my mother, Anna NietoGomez has amassed her own substantial collection of materials, fastidiously organized in folders and filing cabinets in her living room. Anna's vast personal collection (like those of Enriqueta Chavez and Sonia Lopez) documents the instrumental role she played in the development of Chicana/o studies, from her work on recruitment projects as an Educational Opportunity Program instructor at Long Beach, to her leadership in field-building organizations like the Chicano Council on Higher Education and student formations like UMAS (United Mexican American Students) and MEChA (Movimiento Estudiantil Chicano de Aztlán), to her efforts—both pedagogical and political—to push the field to include Chicanas in its disciplinary and institutional frameworks. It also documents her departure from the field, a leave-taking that would have profound implications for the development of Chicana feminist thought. Much of this archive has been preserved from her years as a student at Long Beach State and later as the first professor of Chicana studies at California State University, Northridge. But a fair portion of Anna's personal collection has itself been collected from other women's personal archives as well as the various institutional archives she has visited as part of an effort to sift through memories, embodied and archival, of a shared past. Anna is writing a book about the development of Chicana feminist thought in the 1970s, narrated through her own experience, but deeply informed by her interviews with other women and her archival research in both institutional and personal collections. She has carefully rebuilt a field of knowledge through this process of personal and collective remembrance, and on this fall day in 2018, as I sit in her living room surrounded by this stunning collection of materials, it strikes me suddenly that Anna has constructed her own counterarchive of absent presences to narrate a different origin story for Chicano studies—an understory haunted by violence.

This haunting had made itself vividly present in 2010, when Linda Garcia Merchant and I were scanning materials in Anna's collection late into the night for Chicana por Mi Raza. I remember my excitement after coming across a slide carousel that contained Anna's fabled slideshow on La Chicana, which she created in 1976 to use in her classes. Much like Martha Cotera's *Diosa y Hembra,* which appeared in print that same year, Anna's slideshow weaves a story of Chicana futures from the past, offering a sweeping visual narrative of women's agency and self-development through a series of remediated images of Aztec codices, colonial paintings, and women in the Mexican Revolution and labor organizers, mixed in with photographs of contemporary Chicanas. While Anna was never able to use the Chicana slideshow in her classes as she had originally intended, she presented it widely in both community and academic settings, reading aloud from its script as the slides flashed forward. After encountering Anna's slideshow performance at one of these events, Sylvia Morales was so taken with it that she approached her about making a short film, and together they produced the groundbreaking narrative documentary "Chicana" (1979), a work that, as Rosa Linda Fregoso has observed, counters the nationalist male-centered heroics of Luis Valdez's 1969 film "I Am Joaquin."[2]

But this archival trace of Chicana becoming was shadowed by a darker story. Indeed, there were other slides in the carousel that documented the harassment Anna faced as a result of her tenure battle at Northridge: images of her name defaced on the building's public directory, of "puta" scrawled onto her office door, of cartoonish drawings of Chicana feminists on the department's walls. Along with these startling images, there were slides documenting the organizing meetings, teach-ins, and protests of the Support Anna Nieto-Gomez committee, the collective of women and men who published *Women Struggle*. If finding Anna NietoGomez's fabled slideshow in its natural habitat momentarily thinned the boundaries between the present and the past, it was an archival encuentro that was haunted by the visual evidence of the institutional violence she faced in that moment of regulation: a ghost in the Chicana counterarchive that reminded me, once again, of all that had been lost. Eight years after this initial encuentro with Anna's personal archive, I have returned to her home—an archival site of possibility shadowed by violence—to dig up these ghosts in order to understand more deeply what it meant to discuss and apply the "women's question" in Chicano studies in the 1970s. I have returned, at least in part, to exorcise these troubling spirits from my imagining of the past, to see beyond the narrative of violence that is so often the historical framework through which we understand the early history of Chicana studies.

As Anna's mother washes dishes in the kitchen, filling the room with the reassuring thrum of domestic activity, we ease into a plática about Chicana feminist studies in the early 1970s. Anna tells me of her first classes on La Chicana at Northridge, and how she navigated the multiple sites of knowledge making that constituted the intellectual milieu of early Chicana studies. As she recounts the history of these *movidas* (modalities), I cannot help but make connections to our own Chicanx digital praxis, which seems uncannily reflected in her narrative, a strange convergence of time and space that is not uncommon in our archival encuentros. As if sensing these interior reflections, Anna shifts from her narrative about the past to talk about the immediate present, and she asks me about an essay I had shared with her a few nights before, "Unpacking Our Mothers' Libraries," in which I reflect on these convergences. As I brace myself for Anna's always incisive analysis, she unexpectedly affirms the transgenerational connections I traced in that essay: "I'm very taken by your whole modality," she begins, "because that was mine."

> First . . . you had to build a body of knowledge, and that's what you're doing. [In] building the body of knowledge first you have to collect it. A bibliography doesn't exist so you have to build it. And then you have to see it and read it. And then you have to talk about it, make it real. You have to touch it, incorporate it. But also you have to interpret it, discard, add, and search, identify what you discard, why you discarded it, and what you need to replace. And then you have to talk about the here and now. Why is this important now? If it was the present, why is it important to their community, to their lives?—you have to apply it. Or if it is about the past,

> how is it similar to what is going on now? If you learn from it, how is it applicable to the here and now? Ideally, we looked to the future, but often we didn't get there, it was too broad a scope, but in [my] Chicana class, the Chicana contemporary class, [students] always had to do a project, to give back, because it's part of that collective.[3]

Anna's textured description of Chicana knowledge production as it flows back and forth across multiple modalities—collecting, analyzing, compiling, researching, sharing, putting into action—resonates in critical ways with my mother's tlamatini information praxis (as discussed in chapters 2 and 3), and also with the Chicanx digital praxis at the center of the Chicana por Mi Raza Digital Memory Collective (as discussed in chapter 1). In "Unpacking Our Mothers' Libraries," I argued that such convergences suggested an alternative genealogy of Chicana knowledge praxis that could be traced in and through acts of "memory keeping" that are not always discernible to archivists or historians because they do not always result in published or widely circulated documents. I had suggested in the essay that such acts of story sharing, collecting and preservation, interpreting, and disseminating, whether they take place across the kitchen table or in more recognizable scholarly settings, constitute a collective effort of self-definition and identity formation, a Chicana knowledge praxis produced at the margins of multiple and intersecting spaces of domination.

While Anna's recognition of the convergences between our modalities was deeply affirming, I could not help but feel as if I had broken an essential rule of historiography. In sharing my essay with her, had I not failed to keep myself out of the story? Indeed, such encuentros with the Chicana memory, both embodied and archival, inevitably raise questions about the nature of historical inquiry, especially with respect to epistemological and methodological frameworks that are grounded in empiricist, and by extension objectivist, logics. Indeed, her recognition of the linkages between our modalities of knowledge production was also a refusal to consign the past to its proper place as a stable object of analysis. It was a moment in which the archive talked back, dramatically shifting the grounds of historical interpretation. In drawing these connections between the knowledge forms of our two temporalities, Anna fleshed the archive, transforming it from an object to be interpreted to a subject in active dialogue. In a poetic reflection on her "memory work," Anna describes the process of historical excavation as an ongoing dialogue between "scholar" and "subject" who together "engage in collaborative telling and retelling. The telling is dependent on your insightful feedback and additional questions. The more you know, the more I can tell you. Consequently, together, we might be able to understand more with each telling."[14] Anna's vision of research as a profoundly dialogical and embodied process challenges the implicit divides between present and past as well as those between investigator and object of knowledge; it pushes us to consider what it means to think and write *with* the past rather than about it. Moreover, in seeing the reflection of her modalities of knowledge in our Chicanx digital praxis, Anna illuminates a hidden thread between two distinct temporalities—envisioning a genealogy of Chicana knowledge as a dialogue between the "then and there" and the "here and now." Just as the encuentro with lived memory transforms the Chicana archive from static repository to live space, the process of storytelling that emerges from that space *fleshes the archive* as a site of active knowledge production and ongoing interpretation.

In this chapter I think *with* a generation of Chicana scholar-activists—in particular Anna NietoGomez, who is currently writing her own reflections on the period—to reconstruct an intellectual milieu and a history of praxis that can be rescued from the shadow of institutional violence. Admittedly, as with my recovery of my mother's information work, I am invested in tracing these wayward Chicana knowledge modalities to conjure an insurgent field imaginary that speaks provocatively—across the lacuna of time—to my own subversive sensibilities. In my travels with Chicanas across the vast archival archipelago of classes, pedagogies, workshops, seminars and conferences, organizations, networks, and publication projects, I have come to a deeper understanding of the subversive aims of the Chicana praxis behind the body of work that has come to be associated with the early years of Chicana feminist thought (so amply documented in Alma García's collection). I have tracked the way it challenges social logics that keep the spaces of home, community, and university neatly divided and cordoned off from one another; the way it navigates and undermines multiple institutional hierarchies, from those structuring relations of knowledge production in the classroom to the field of Chicano studies itself. Working within and against an institutional setting structured by multiple contradictions and erasures, Chicanas produced a vibrant print culture that fed early classes on La Mujer; they developed a curriculum for the careful analysis of Chicanas' historical and contemporary conditions; and they collectively crafted an approach to pedagogy that actively built a field of knowledge where there had only been silence. To be sure, the alternative modalities/movidas that they mobilized to build this archive of knowledge in the early 1970s challenged the central male subject of Chicano studies, generating a groundbreaking intersectional analysis. But in and through this feminist praxis, they also developed the critical infrastructures of care in which Chicana knowledge could be nurtured and grow, creating an alternative sitio y lengua within the field of Chicano studies. In this way, their knowledge movidas offer a provocative blueprint for how we might challenge scales of power within neoliberal institutions that, in the words of Roderick Ferguson, endeavor to "redirect originally insurgent formations and deliver them to the normative ideals and protocols of state, capital, and academy."[5]

Is it possible to rescue this story of becoming, this insurgent praxis, from the history of violence that has for so long overshadowed it? As I noted in chapter 4, while Chicanas have been nominally included in canonical accounts of the development of Chicano studies, they have been represented as operating largely in the margins of the field, a positionality that is reinforced by their appearances in the marginalia of the text: in footnotes, brief mentions, or, in the best-case scenario (as in Soldatenko's intellectual history of the field), in a separate chapter. This discursive marginalization—what Blackwell has termed the "add and stir" framework of inclusion—cements the impression that men built the field, with women alongside them as largely unacknowledged helpmeets, and, alternatively, that Chicana feminist studies arose *after* the institutionalization of Chicano studies, as opposed to alongside it. And yet, as Anna NietoGomez notes in her own account of the birth of Chicano studies, Chicanas "were leaders, we were there from the beginning, our fingerprints were on every product that was produced for Chicano studies, but we were ignored, not even acknowledged."[6]

Not surprisingly, historical accounts of Chicano studies that place Chicanas outside of the frame tend to focus on institutional formations that survive today—student organizations like MEChA, academic departments at major universities, publication outlets like *Aztlán: A Journal of Chicano Studies*, and scholarly formations like the National Association for Chicana and Chicano Studies (previously the National Association for Chicano Studies)—which, in their early years, were notoriously difficult, if not outright hostile, spaces for Chicanas who identified as feminists. Institutional violence and marginalization have thus become a central scholarly framework for understanding the development of Chicana feminist thought within Chicano studies, discursively replicating the silencing mechanisms that Chicanas faced in the 1970s in our current historical memory. While this framework correctly situates the emergence of intersectional analytics within the gendered, racial, and sexual contradictions of field formations like Chicano studies and women's studies (and their attendant political projects), it leaves largely unexplored the innovative modalities of knowledge that Anna describes, as well as the theoretical and institutional movidas that Chicanas developed to navigate and disrupt this terrain in formation. These modalities of knowledge constitute an alternative field imaginary, a provocative path not taken that continues to haunt the historical memory of Chicano studies today. In this chapter I endeavor to rebuild the habitus of this early Chicana feminist field imaginary to surface the mobile modalities of knowledge that it nurtured and to reclaim the potentialities of that lost future from a history of violence.

## MAPPING CHICANA KNOWLEDGE MODALITIES

In most historical accounts of Chicano studies, the years 1971 to 1974 stand as the high point of the institutionalization of the field as an intellectual formation.[7] Not surprisingly, given Chicanas' instrumental involvement in the institutional and organizing activities of the movement for Chicano studies, these were also watershed years for the development of Chicana feminist studies in California (and beyond). Indeed, many of the texts that we now consider canonical to early Chicana feminist thought were produced during this intellectually fertile period: the three issues of *Hijas de Cuauhtémoc* (all published in 1971), the two issues of *Encuentro Femenil* (1973–1974), and Dorinda Moreno's *La Mujer: En Pie de Lucha* (1973), all of which were independent publishing projects produced by Chicanas with ties to Chicano studies programs. In addition to these influential collections of Chicana thought, movement newspapers and magazines like *Regeneración* (published by Francisca Flores), *La Verdad*, and *La Raza* produced special issues on "la mujer" featuring Chicana poetry, essays, and artwork. Adding to this textual florecimiento, a number of anthologies of student writing were produced as part of Chicana classes during this early period, including *Imágenes de la Chicana* (Stanford University, 1974 and 1975) and *Visión* (San Diego State University, 1976), which were developed in classes taught by Rita Sanchez.

This period also witnessed a number of conferences that helped to define Chicana feminist thought. On May 8, 1971, Chicanas from across California attended the Chicana Regional Conference in Los Angeles in order to prepare a platform of issues for the upcoming National Chicana Conference in Houston. Organized by Las Hijas de Cuauhtémoc, Comisión Femenil at California State College at Los Angeles, and Chicanas in MEChA at Los Angeles City College, the Chicana Regional Conference included workshops on gender roles, the family, political education, and media and communication. For Anna NietoGomez and others who attended, the first National Chicana Conference in Houston (May 28–30, 1971) crystallized a rising consciousness among Chicanas, even as it exposed the ideological fault lines among women.[8] This feminist momentum continued in both the community and higher education. The Chicana Service Action Center, launched by Comisión Femenil in 1972, became a key site for applied research on Chicanas (Anna was an educational consultant for the center), much of which appeared in the *Chicana Service Action Center Newsletter* and in *Encuentro Femenil*, the first Chicana journal. By 1973, the same year that *Encuentro Femenil* appeared in print, Stanford University hosted the first major academic conference focused on the history and analysis of Chicana and Latin American feminisms, La Mujer Latinoamericana y la Chicana: Liberación; Teoría y Práctica.[9]

A mere two years after forming the Chicana Ad Hoc Committee at the 1971 Chicano Council on Higher Education conference in San Diego and calling for structural change within Chicano studies, Chicanas had made great strides toward their goal of creating a curriculum for the self-development of women as political agents. Classes on La Chicana were being taught in Chicano studies programs across California, and there were multiple publication projects in the works, as well as a new journal, *Encuentro Femenil*, and a published curriculum, *New Directions in Education: Estudios Femeniles de la Chicana*.[10] Indeed, the publication of *Estudios Femeniles* in 1973 marked the crystallization of a collective effort, launched at the 1971 San Diego conference (but initiated years before), to develop both a theoretical framework for understanding the intersectional nature of oppression and the institutional and community infrastructures necessary for the full development of Chicanas on and off campus.

When contemplating this immensely productive period in the development of Chicana feminist studies, one cannot help but wonder how these young women, many of whom were still students, were able to accomplish so much while also navigating the tricky ideological and institutional politics of Chicano studies as a field. The now familiar quip about Ginger Rogers, that she did everything Fred Astaire did, but "backwards and in high heels," inevitably comes to mind—especially since, as Michael Soldatenko notes, Chicanas faced daily challenges as working-class women of color within predominantly white institutions, and even within spaces of educational liberation like Chicano studies, where faculty, staff, and students frequently pushed back on their efforts to address the "women's question" as a central analytic.[11] Indeed, for all their success from 1971 to 1973, Chicanas were often valued for their labor but were marginalized from leadership roles and professional opportunities in the developing field. By 1975 Evey Chapa (at the time a doctoral student and the executive director of the Chicana Research and Learning Center in Austin, Texas) and Armando Gutierrez (an assistant professor of political science at the University of Texas at Austin) noted that Chicanas had already developed a distinct "area of study concerning la mujer Chicana" in conjunction with "Chicano Studies programs being implemented on the campuses of this nation."[12] And yet, they observed,

> Chicanas are almost totally excluded from the curricula in many textbooks used at the university level. Two examples in which this occurs are *Introduction to Chicano Studies* edited by Livie Isauro Duran and H. Russell Bernard and *Chicano Politics* edited by F. Chris Garcia. Chicanas are also virtually excluded in *Occupied America: The Chicano's Struggle Toward Liberation* by Rodolfo Acuña and in *North from Mexico* by Carey McWilliams. These four documents are among those utilized by the academic community to fill the historical void concerning Chicanos. There is, however, a void within these efforts—la mujer Chicana.[13]

The structured absence of Chicanas in the Chicano studies curriculum reflected a profound institutional disparity. By 1976 (the year of Anna NietoGomez's tenure battle at Northridge), just 96 of 473 Chicano faculty (roughly 20 percent) included in the "National List of Chicano Contacts in Higher Education" compiled by Cecilia Preciado Burciaga at Stanford University were women.[14] Of those individuals, only 24 were in Chicano studies or ethnic studies departments, and only a small handful of them were PhDs on the tenure track.[15] These statistics suggest, with numerical precision, the institutional headwinds that Chicanas faced in terms of becoming tenure-track faculty in Chicano studies departments in the 1970s.

Chicana scholars also struggled to gain a foothold in the field's primary organizational formations and publication outlets throughout the 1970s. In his study of gender representation within the National Association for Chicano Studies, the predominant scholarly association in the field, Gilberto García notes that at the organization's 1975 conference, male scholars "accounted for as much as 94.9 percent" of presenters.[16] Women scholars raised the issue of "fair and equal participation of women on panels as chairpersons, commentators, and presenters" at the business meeting of the 1975 conference, demanding that a special session focused on La Chicana be added to the program. Notwithstanding this important intervention, two years later, in 1977, male scholars still predominated at the National Association for Chicano Studies conference, comprising 82.8 percent of the presentations. A survey of the publications appearing in *Aztlán* during this period reflects the dismal representation of Chicana scholars in the field imaginary of Chicano studies. Of the 191 scholarly articles, research notes, and book reviews that *Aztlán* published from 1970 to 1980, only 32 articles were written by women (16 percent); of these, only 6 articles focused on gendered experience (3 percent), and only 2—Adaljiza Sosa-Riddell's foundational essay "Chicanas en el Movimiento" (1974) and Maxine Baca Zinn's foundational "Political Familism: Toward Sex Role Equality in Chicano Families" (1975)—directly engaged Chicana feminist frameworks. While their male colleagues assumed leadership positions in the field and published their work in scholarly journals like *Aztlán* (University of California, Los Angeles) and *El Grito* (University of California, Berkeley), Chicanas were largely excluded from these institutional avenues for professional development. Instead, they mobilized nontraditional sitios of knowledge production that built on and expanded their "repertoires of struggle."[17] Turning to their classrooms, to community research centers like the Chicana Service Action Center, and to national funding agencies like Montal Educational Associates (all spaces that have been largely ignored in histories of the field), Chicanas in California carved out sitios y lenguas to think collectively about the past, present, and future of "la mujer en el movimiento."

In many ways, the Chicana classroom functioned as a nerve center for these varied scholarly and organizing activities. Just as Martha Cotera reimagined the library as an information hub for the entire community (see chapter 2), Chicanas in California reenvisioned the classroom as a horizontal space of knowledge production that extended far beyond the walls of the institution. Because early classes on La Chicana were grounded in movement models of consciousness-raising, they embraced the Freirian ideals and strong commitment to praxis that shaped the pedagogical discourse of Chicano studies in its early years. Chicanas' teaching philosophies, action research projects, and work in the community reflected *El Plan de Santa Bárbara*'s directive for Chicano studies (borrowed from José Vasconcelos): "At this moment we do not come to work for the university, but to demand that the university work for our people."[18] In keeping with this edict, students in Chicana classes were encouraged to apply their theoretical analyses and skills to address real-world issues in applied research projects, service to the community, and publication projects that would contribute to the development of a robust Chicana studies curriculum.

The first classes on La Chicana had their origins in the workshops and reading groups initiated on and off campus to spur the political development of women and to more substantially integrate their analysis of the "women's question" into the agenda of the Chicano movement. At San Diego State, which in 1970 had launched a robust selection of lower- and upper-division courses to service its new Chicano studies major and minor, the Chicana Study Group held meetings every Wednesday from 7:00 to 9:00 p.m. to work on "research projects on various topics dealing with chicanas," including history, child-rearing and family structures, "health, social institutions, and welfare," and "Chicanas in economics" (focused on labor movements).[19] Reflecting the decidedly left ideological tenor of both Chicano studies and women's studies at San Diego State, the Chicana Study Group reading list focused on Marxist philosophy, political economy, and "revolutionary theory," but it also included Shulamith Firestone's *The Dialectic of Sex*, Ward Morton's *Woman Suffrage in Mexico*, and "selected writings done by Chicanas; Essays, Speeches, Poems, etc."[20]

The Chicana Study Group continued their consciousness-raising praxis in the classroom, first through an upper-division course already on the books, Mexican-American Life Styles (MAS 105)—which, according to the course catalog, focused on the "Mexican-American family in the past, present, and future," "the traditional and evolving roles of the man and the woman," and "the new alternatives in the twentieth century"—and later through a series of courses that included an advanced Chicana senior survey (MAS 197), a Chicana field course (MAS 99), and a Chicano-Chicana course (MAS 197) that brought men and women together to discuss the intersection of racism, classism, and sexism.[21] Like the Chicana Study Group, these classes provided relatively safe spaces within the institution where mujeres could come together to build their speaking, writing, and organizing skills, as well as to develop a political and historical analysis of power. Usually led by a teaching collective that included several members of the Chicana Study Group (Enriqueta "Henri" Chavez, Clarisa Torres, and Sonia Lopez), these courses introduced women—and, in the case of MAS 197, the Chicano-Chicana course, male students—to a critical and historical analysis of how "the cultural influences" of "family, religion, community, and economic status" have shaped the "lifestyle, attitudes and values, held by Chicanas."[22] In blending self-reflection (assignments included writing an autobiography) with historical study and discussion of contemporary issues—an application of autohistoria-teoría in the classroom—the Chicana curriculum at San Diego State University encouraged students not only to learn about their history but also (in Anna's words) "to talk about the here and now."[23]

These classes were essential to preparing young women to take leadership roles in movement formations on and off campus. Indeed, Henri Chavez, Sonia Lopez, Clarisa Torres, and others in the Chicana Study Group well understood, from their personal experience in the Chicano movement, that women had to master the discourse of theory in order to actively engage with the political heavies and to shape organizing on the ground.[24] In "Chicanas in Higher Education," a position paper written in the early 1970s, Sonia Lopez and Henri Chavez point out how political discussions "were constantly monopolized by men." When women "tried to get ideas across, the men kept silent but did not listen," but when the same idea was "repeated by a man a few minutes later . . . it was taken up and moved on."[25] Thus, developing Chicana students' comfort with political theory—particularly Marxist, feminist, and third world theories of liberation—was essential to their full participation in movement politics in the early 1970s.

Given this pedagogical aim, the curriculum Chicanas developed at San Diego State University was deeply informed by ongoing theoretical debates over Marxism and its relevance to the Chicano struggle. But it was also informed by a socialist feminist framework—the ideological position of the Women's Studies Group at San Diego State (who had founded the first women's studies department in the nation in 1972)—that explored how the gendered division of labor had historically sustained a capitalist and imperialist world order. Readings in the Chicana classes at San Diego State reflected this analytic approach. In addition to selections of writing by Chicanas from *Hijas de Cuauhtémoc*, *Regeneración*, and *Encuentro Femenil*, these courses regularly included "The Woman Question" (1886) by Edward Aveling and Eleanor Marx Aveling and a pamphlet outlining the socialist feminist position produced by the Women's Studies Group at the university.[26] Course schedules and lecture notes illustrate how Chicana instructors walked students through a Marxist analysis of the history of the family and the gendered division of labor in the home and helped them make connections between the logics of patriarchal capitalism and the issues they faced in their everyday lives. This process of concientización, which was effectively a pedagogical application of Anzaldúa's autohistoria-teoría (avant la lettre), opened space for an intersectional analysis of power that illuminated the gendered contradictions of the Chicano movement as well as the ways in which these contradictions undermined true liberation and sustained the relations of rule that had oppressed marginalized communities worldwide.

Critically, this consciousness-raising was not confined to women. Indeed, the Chicano-Chicana course (MAS 197) was specifically designed to bring men and women together to examine the "historical development of la familia . . . through an economic, political and social perspective." Applying this analysis to the "various developments within the Chicano-Chicana movement," including the rise of nationalism in the late 1960s, the course sought to address contemporary issues "such as the roles and relationships between Chicanos and Chicanas" through cross-gender dialogue. This dialogue between men and women, instructors hoped, would create an expanded political "awareness of our oppression in relation to the existing socio-economic system."[27] The section of this class taught in 1973 by an instructional team that included Clarisa Torres, Henri Chavez, Rene Lopez, and

Samuel Salazar featured assigned readings geared toward a socialist feminist analysis of power, including the Women's Studies Group pamphlet, Evelyn Reed's *Problems of Women's Liberation: A Marxist Approach*, and Leo Huberman and Paul M. Sweezy's *Introduction to Socialism*. The syllabus also included an early text from a men's consciousness-raising group, *Unbecoming Men* (1971), which featured deeply personal, and sometimes harrowing, narratives of coming into masculinity. Thus the course encouraged men (as well as women) to examine and deconstruct the gender roles that undergirded nationalist conceptualizations of identity and "la familia de la raza." MAS 197 covered a broad range of topics—including the "evolution of La Familia," the socialist feminist critique of women's liberation, child-rearing, women on welfare, Chicanos and Chicanas in prison, "men and women's bodies" (which included a reading of Anne Koedt's "The Myth of the Vaginal Orgasm"), and "lesbianism and homosexuality"—and also featured a panel on community organizing and the development of "alternative institutions." The readings, lectures, and assignments in MAS 197 were grounded in a consciousness-raising process designed to open up an honest dialogue between men and women about the nature of oppression and how patriarchy—and, importantly, heteronormativity—had affected the participants' self-development as revolutionary subjects, albeit in different ways. Indeed, the inclusion of lesbianism and homosexuality as topics for discussion and analysis in a mixed-gender Chicano studies class is notable, especially given the context of lesbian baiting that was endemic to the Chicano student movement (an issue I will explore more deeply in chapter 6).[28]

In and through this curriculum, Chicanas created an important intellectual space for the development of an intersectional analysis of race, gender, and class within the Chicano Studies Department at San Diego State University, as is evident in a position paper Sonia Lopez wrote in the early 1970s, likely for a MEChA or Chicano Council on Higher Education conference. In the paper, she noted how the process of "collective dialogue" encouraged in courses like MAS 197 had helped the department to "recognize our sexist situation through an understanding of the origin and historical development of sexism and male supremacy."[29] Having become conscious of the "negative male-female roles imposed upon it," Lopez wrote, the Department of Chicano Studies had decided to devote "part of its energies to demystifying the false reality that U.S. Media puts out and to debunking the American Dream by exposing the inherent contradictions within U.S. society of sexism, racism, and class." Moreover, she noted, as a result of this process of collective curricular and extracurricular concientización, the Chicano Studies Department at San Diego State had "developed its organization with the goal of incorporating women students into its processes."[30] The Chicana studies curriculum at San Diego State thus became a critical site for the articulation of an intersectional analysis of power, one that instrumentally shaped both the political positioning and the institutional practice of the Chicano Studies Department at the university. Indeed, as this example suggests, the Chicana classroom was not just a site for the development of an intersectional analysis but also a locus of organizing.

Not surprisingly, the projects and assignments in Chicana classes in the early 1970s were multifaceted and broad ranging, in many cases outlasting the semester and evolving into organizing, curricular, and publication projects that contributed to the development of Chicana feminist studies. The Chicana classroom was, in other words, not just a place for top-down knowledge delivery but an important hub for knowledge production that moved across multiple organizing and institutional spaces. As both a safe space where students could explore and define key social, historical, and cultural issues that affected women in the community—from more personal issues like the structure of the family, reproductive justice, and sexuality, to more political issues like women on welfare and in prisons—and a space of self-development, the classroom provided Chicana students with the knowledge, theoretical framework, and skills to become active members of the movimiento. In her unpublished essay "Production of Knowledge in the Classroom and Through Student Activism," Anna NietoGomez describes Chicana classes as a "safe training ground" for women

> to practice critical thinking, public speaking, advocacy for civil rights, organizing, and development of theories and practice. An extensive curriculum on La Chicana would study how the law, economics, and culture affect the choices she has in society. Chicana classes would raise awareness that Chicanas are leaders, professionals and change agents and they too have the ability to make a difference and contribute to the community and improve the lives of other Chicanas and their families.[31]

In addition to this self-development process, Chicana classes could also contribute to the collective effort to build a body of knowledge on La Mujer outside the institutional spaces that in the 1970s were still largely dominated by men.

In part, this approach to pedagogy was a strategic response to the material and social conditions that structured Chicano studies in the late 1960s and early 1970s. *El Plan de Santa Bárbara* did not include classes on La Chicana in any of its curricular models, and Chicano studies syllabi rarely included information on women. As Anna notes in an unpublished essay on Las Hijas de Cuauhtémoc, "We read novels written by famous Mexican and Chicano authors but the literature was very male centered, and the female characters were seen but not heard, were very stereotypical, and often female characters were missing through most of the book."[32] To address this gap in the field, students in Chicana classes (who were, after all, not much younger than their recently graduated Chicana professors) were often tasked with contributing to the field-development process, from conducting original research that could be used in other Chicana classes, to compiling specialized bibliographies and reading lists for the Chicana curriculum, to organizing recruitment efforts, conferences, and publication projects, all of which fed the project of Chicana studies. This approach to the classroom as an alternative knowledge hub—a site of research, writing, and action in the service of Chicana studies—resulted in some of the key Chicana feminist publications of the period, including *Imágenes* 1 and 2 (1974 and 1975), *El Popo Femenil* (1973), Dorinda Moreno's *La Razón Mestiza* special issue (1975), and *Visión* (1976), among many other examples, both published and unpublished.[33] Such modalities of knowledge production are beautifully illustrated in a series of pedagogical projects that Anna NietoGomez undertook during her time as a Chicana studies professor at California State University, Northridge.

## MODALITIES OF KNOWLEDGE IN THE CHICANA CLASSROOM

Anna NietoGomez joined the Chicano studies faculty at Northridge in the fall of 1971, riding a wave of Chicana organizing and consciousness-raising that seemed to surge ever more powerfully as the year progressed—from the establishment of the Chicana Ad Hoc Committee at the statewide Chicano Council on Higher Education conference in March 1971, to the Chicana Regional Conference in Los Angeles a few months later, and the National Chicana Conference in Houston in May of that year. A new Chicana newspaper, *Hijas de Cuauhtémoc*, covered many of these events, building consciousness and a print community in the process. Like Anna, Chicanas at Northridge were part of this collective effort to carve out a space for women in the liberated zone of Chicano studies. Indeed, the notes from the Chicana Ad Hoc Committee meeting list four participants from San Fernando Valley State College (now California State University, Northridge)—Irene Tovar, Martha Curiel, Maria Teran, and Irma Pendave—the second-largest contingent of representatives at the meeting.[34] In his analysis of women's organizing at Northridge, Gustavo Licón notes that Chicanas had been active in MEChA "from the start." Though not all of them agreed with the feminist position, they had all faced some degree of sexism within the organization and had "made a conscious effort to increase their presence in [MEChA's] leadership and activities."[35] Rodolfo Acuña corroborates this observation in his own account of the early years of Chicano studies at Northridge, noting that the first wave of Chicana students at the university had been advocating for more faculty committed to their educational needs as women. As a former president of MEChA in Long Beach and a member of Las Hijas de Cuauhtémoc, Anna's arrival on campus promised to answer this need. Acuña notes that Chicana students "had high expectations and supported Nieto-Gomez's agenda and classes."[36]

Having been a key participant in the networks and events that were voicing the triple oppression of La Chicana, Anna was well positioned to continue her work building Chicana studies at one of the most powerful Chicano studies departments in California. At Northridge she brought an organizing framework to her work as an instructor and scholar, teaching classes on contemporary Chicana issues and Chicana history as well as core courses in the curriculum, including Speech, Barrio Field Studies, and Urbanization of the Chicano.[37] Anna recalls that her approach to the classroom drew heavily from what she had learned working with Las Hijas de Cuauhtémoc at Long Beach, particularly the idea of knowledge building as a collective process of concientización that moved beyond research and analysis to reflection and application. Thus, she used the classroom to expose her students to the political analyses and intersectional frameworks emerging from centers of Chicana thought across California (San Diego, Los Angeles, and the Bay Area) and beyond, encouraging them to identify problems in their own lives and to apply what they had learned in the classroom to make positive change in their communities. In the absence of a fully developed Chicana curriculum at Northridge, she built her own, working closely with librarian Maria Tarango (to whom she would dedicate her foundational essay "La Feminista") to create a collection of materials, mostly gathered from movement newspapers, that she could use in her classes to familiarize students with contemporary Chicana feminist thought. Anna recalls that working with Tarango made her "ability to do research and . . . develop curriculum so much easier. She would say, 'Anna, these are all these things coming up on the woman, the Mexican woman, Chicana authors.' She would help make these mini bibliographies that . . . created a 'Chicana Section' in the library."[38]

In addition to introducing students to the critical analyses emerging in Chicana print culture, Anna developed an approach to class projects that "encouraged student activism and curriculum development" through research, work in the community, and organizing on campus.

> All students enrolled in the Chicana history and the contemporary issues classes were required to do one of the following class projects: (1) conduct academic research or oral history project; or (2) organize a Chicana conference; or (3) organize and publish a newspaper to report the issues and findings of the conference; or (4) develop a curriculum proposal for a new Chicana studies class. Each year, a group of students chose to organize an educational forum to discuss Chicana issues or create a curriculum for Chicana courses. The projects' themes included defining the problems of Chicanas, the need for Chicana studies curriculum, and organizing a Chicana student organization.[39]

Empowered by what they were learning and doing, the students in Anna's Chicana studies courses were transformed into what she calls "Chicana feminist student scholar-activists" who did not confine their intellectual labors to the classroom. Not surprisingly, her classes became a center of organizing for Chicana students at Northridge.

Starting in the fall of 1971, women in Anna's Chicana class began meeting weekly with other Chicanas on campus in an effort to identify and define the problems they faced as women. Like Chicanas at San Diego State University and California State University, Long Beach, they identified access to reproductive services and childcare as critical issues affecting their experience as students, and they organized a daylong Chicana seminar outlining these issues at the end of the fall semester, on December 12, 1971.[40] In May of 1972, as a final project for Anna's class on La Chicana, they organized Chicana Day as part of MEChA's Cinco de Mayo activities. The daylong workshop featured an afternoon discussion on racism and sexism in education led by Carmen Duran and Mercedes Gonzales of Mujeres Unidas, a community organization in the San Fernando Valley. According to Anna, women at the workshop "discussed the obstacles preventing Chicanas from excelling in higher education," including: "(1) myths and unrealistic cultural expectations of Chicanas; (2) racist, sexist attitudes of educators, counselors, and administrators in secondary schools and higher education; and (3) racist, sexist practices of Chicano special admission and regular graduate admissions programs."[41]

Building on these interventions, Chicanas at California State University, Northridge, presented an agenda for structural change at a statewide Chicano studies and MEChA conference, hosted at Northridge in May of 1972. In "Rhetoric Is Not Productive," a position paper most likely presented at the Chicana workshop for that conference, they outlined the multiple challenges women faced in the "college environment" and demanded "a more relevant curriculum on the Chicana," as well as "special services specifically for Chicanas such as day care centers, family planning and counseling . . . staffed by Chicanas."[42] The Chicana workshop at the conference put forward several resolutions to the general body that echoed those presented the year before at the Chicano Council on Higher Education conference: "(1) That all MEChA organizations have Chicana and Chicano co-chairs; (2) the establishment of a Chicana organization on each campus; and (3) a class for the development of Expressions and Ideas of the Chicana."[43] Though there was no real mechanism to guarantee that these resolutions would be enacted across MEChA chapters in California, according to Gustavo Licón, their successful passage provided some cover for "Chicanas who critiqued sexism in the movement, and it opened up more space for them to discuss gender roles and problems in the organization."[44]

In a brief history of Hermanas Unidas, a feminist organization established at Northridge in 1975 as a result of these organizing activities, Anna notes that the initial goal of the weekly meetings was simply to build "hermanidad" (sisterhood) among Chicanas, but in the process of concientización, women soon "discovered how little they knew about the Chicana," and thus their activities in 1972 and 1973 "reflect an effort to educate the general Chicano campus community about the socio-economic issues of the Chicana" and to develop "women's leadership on campus."[45] Anna's classes were an ideal space to accomplish these linked goals, as she provided her students with ample opportunities for them to study the "women's question" as it pertained to Chicanas and to apply their ideas outside of the classroom, in workshops, seminars, and conferences. A particularly illuminating example of this activist pedagogical praxis is Semana de la Mujer (Week of the Woman), "the first week-long forum devoted to the Chicana," which was conceived in Anna's La Chicana Today class (fall 1972) and carried out through several "individual studies" classes that she taught the following semester.[46]

Equal parts scholarly conference, feminist workshop, and recruitment/retention effort, Semana de la Mujer focused on "issues related specifically to the Chicana in areas of education, history, law, and sex," with the goal of encouraging "more Chicanas to continue their education through gaining a better understanding of how society affects them as women of a particular race."[47] In organizing the events related to Semana de la Mujer, Chicana students at Northridge would be exposed to some of the leading Chicana feminist thinkers and organizers in Southern California. Moreover, they would themselves contribute to this growing body of Chicana feminist thought by documenting the event, from videotaping the speakers in order to use their speeches as presentations in future Chicana and Chicano studies classes, to producing articles on speaker presentations and other activities for publication in *El Popo Femenil* (1973), a special edition of Northridge's Chicano student newspaper, *El Popo*.[48]

Semana de la Mujer and the newspaper that documented it, *El Popo Femenil*, were not simply class projects; they evolved from and contributed to an ongoing organizing agenda at Northridge that was focused on raising awareness (particularly within MEChA, Chicano studies, and the student newspaper *El Popo*) about the specific issues affecting Chicanas. This work was carried out by a strong network of Chicana student scholar-activists—many of whom had taken, or were taking, Anna's classes—women like Linda Arrequin, who had recently been elected president of the Associated Women Students at Northridge and was an outspoken advocate for Chicana students. Leveraging her new position in student government, Arrequin established an organizing committee for Semana de la Mujer within the Associated Women Students and allocated $200 in student funds to support the project (the Chicano Studies Department contributed $100 toward the effort). Audrey Camarillo, director of special programs in the Educational Participation in Communities office, worked closely with Anna as a student and an organizer during this period. Camarillo's office provided equipment and staff support for Semana de la Mujer. Paula Muñoz, coeditor of *El Popo*, was also one of Anna's students and volunteered to spearhead the production of *El Popo Femenil*, a special women's issue of the student newspaper, to document the weeklong event. The publication was also an effort to address Chicana criticisms of the paper, which, as Gustavo Licón has observed, tended toward condescension or outright hostility when covering Chicana issues.[49] Anna served as faculty advisor to both the Associated Women Students committee for Semana de la Mujer and the staff of *El Popo Femenil*.

Together, these women and the students enrolled in Anna's independent studies class developed a weeklong schedule for Semana de la Mujer (April 23–27, 1973) that included recruitment events, teatro performances, art and book exhibits, and a series of afternoon seminars that addressed issues related specifically to La Chicana in areas of education, history, law, and sex.[50] The theme of the opening day (Monday), New Horizons in Education, focused on encouraging young women to pursue college. High school students from three area schools in the San Fernando Valley, Los Angeles, and Ventura were bused to campus for a full day of activities. In the morning, they toured the university, visited classes, spoke to recruitment officers, and watched a performance by Teatro Aztlán on Chicanas in college. In the afternoon, they participated in a series workshops with leading Chicana organizers, including Maria Gaitán of CASA (Centro de Acción

Social Autónomo), who talked about the need for more Chicanas in education; Gloria Gutiérrez, editor of the recently launched *Chicana Service Action Newsletter*, who spoke to them about "Chicana self-image and adjustment to college"; and Diana Holguin, coordinator of the Chicana Service Action Center, who presented on the dismal employment conditions of Chicanas and how they could use their college education to help the community. The day's events closed with a teatro performance by Carnalas Unidas, the Lincoln Heights High School teatro. In addition to this day of recruitment activities, on Wednesday the organizers hosted a community night at the Pacoima Congregational Church for high school students and their parents. The event was designed to ease parents' fears about their daughters going off to college, a challenge that many of the week's organizers had experienced firsthand. At the evening forum on Chicanas and education, Maria Diaz de Krofcheck, an Educational Opportunity Program counselor from California State University, Los Angeles, and Gloria Gutiérrez "spoke to parents and high school students about the value of Chicanas completing high school and proceeding on to college."[51]

Tuesday's afternoon workshops, which focused on "the role of the Chicana throughout history," included presentations by Adelaida Del Castillo, who discussed Malintzin Tenepal (work that she would later publish in the second issue of *Encuentro Femenil*); and Audrey Camarillo, an undergraduate who had taken Anna's first Chicana history class and would later help organize her support committee, who presented her research on women's struggles in Mexico. Mariana Hernandez, a member of the Socialist Workers Party from Texas who ran for a US Senate seat in that state in 1972, spoke about the "triple oppression of Chicanas and the role of Chicanas in the Chicano movement."[52] Reassuring Chicana students that "they were doing the right thing" in organizing around feminist issues, Hernandez encouraged them not to be "taken aback at name-calling strategies" and "efforts to label the Chicana movement a 'white women's movement,'" which were merely tactics "to discredit and stop the people who were organizing a new movement." As Hernandez pointed out, "One of the tasks of a new movement is to explain itself and that organizing Chicana conferences and publishing new ideas was an important way for the Chicana movement to do this."[53]

Thursday's workshops focused on Chicanas and the law. Peggy Salazar, accompanied by three representatives of the Mexican American Research Association who had been incarcerated at the California Institution for Women in Corona, presented a workshop titled "La Chicana en la Pinta [Prison]." Nora Martinez Rolfe led a discussion on immigration, which was followed by a workshop titled "Chicana versus Welfare," led by Alicia

Escalante and Jessie Corona from the East Los Angeles Welfare Rights Organization.[54]

Semana de la Mujer ended on Friday, April 27, with a series of workshops and presentations that delved into questions of sexuality and identity. Enriqueta "Henri" Chavez and María Gracia from Las Chicanas at San Diego State University led a workshop on reproductive health. Sylvia Delgado, a Northridge undergraduate student who was also a counselor for the East Los Angeles Free Clinic (and the author of several frank essays in *Regeneración* that broke the silence around sexuality and drug use in the community), talked to students about human sexuality.[55] The two final events of the conference created a controversy that reverberated beyond the Northridge campus. Isabel Navar, an instructor at the University of California, Los Angeles (and one of the few speakers at the weeklong event who held a PhD), was scheduled to lead a workshop on Chicana identity. At the time, she was teaching a course called "Chicana: Breaking the Stereotype," which, according to Anna, drew the attention of "a group of Chicano Nationalists from UCLA" who "protested and blocked her entry into the forum and passed out leaflets accusing her of being irrelevant to the movement because she was 'agringada.' I threw their leaflets into the trash can and then escorted her into the room. Isabel's speech was not provocative; we never understood why these men were so militant."[56] The final panel, "Machismo and the Chicana," elicited a negative response much closer to home. In a letter to the Chicano Studies Department chair, sent a week after the closing events of Semana de la Mujer, a "concerned Chicana" echoed the discourse that Mariana Hernandez had warned conference participants about just a few days earlier:

> I am concerned with the direction that the Chicanas are taking in the movement. The final discussion of the day was on the machismo and the Chicana. Words such as liberation, sexism, male chauvinism, etc., were prevalent throughout the discussion. The role of male vs. female, the role of individuals was constantly stressed. Not once did I hear mention of the role of the familia in this struggle for chicana recognition. The terms mentioned above plus the theme of individualism is a concept of Anglo society: terms prevalent in the Anglo woman's movement. The familia has always been our strength in our culture. But, it seems evident from that discussion that the women at CSU Northridge are not concerned with the familia, but are influenced by the Anglo Women's movement.[57]

Focusing her critique on "Isabelle [*sic*]" Navar's workshop on identity, the author questioned both her credentials—"just because she has a Ph.D. doesn't qualify her to speak as a Chicana"—and the workshop's focus on identity: "I personally felt it was a worthless discussion. . . . And since when does a Chicana need identity? If you are a real Chicana then no one regardless of the degrees needs to tell you about it. The only ones who need identity are the vendidas, the falsas, and the opportunists."[58]

Interestingly, the editors of *El Popo Femenil* chose to reprint this letter in the newspaper, along with a response that spoke directly to the author's critique of the identity workshop: "It is unfortunate, but a typical reaction to overlook a whole week of 17 events just because one or two of those events were not in agreement with your ideas." Equating the letter writer's focus on "terms prevalent in the Anglo woman's movement," like "liberation, sexism, [and] male chauvinism," to the red-baiting that had been used to demonize Chicano activists, the editors noted that this tactic tries "to scare people into ignoring the concepts which many people believe are affecting La Raza and the movement. It is because of these 'Taboos' that people have avoided coming to grips with these issues, learning about them," and then deciding for themselves what they believe.[59]

Published in May of 1973, just a month after the events of Semana de la Mujer, *El Popo Femenil* brought these "taboo issues" to the forefront of the conversation. The special issue of *El Popo* was conceived to serve multiple functions. First, it would provide important documentation of the ideas and conversations that had circulated at Semana de la Mujer, extending its reach beyond the time/space of the event itself. It was also envisioned as a pedagogical tool, both for the students who worked on the newspaper and for those who wished to pursue research on La Chicana. While *El Popo Femenil*'s limited format, a relatively scant fifteen pages, could only give an overview of the topics discussed at Semana de la Mujer, including women in higher education, prisons, welfare rights, sexism in the movement, and Chicana history—all of which would be explored more thoroughly in the first and second issues of *Encuentro Femenil*—it could nevertheless leave critical "breadcrumbs" (as Anna often puts it) for emerging scholars to follow. Indeed, on the paper's last page was a reading list of materials on the contemporary Chicana, drawn directly from Anna's syllabus, that included examples of Chicana print culture like *Regeneración* and *Hijas de Cuauhtémoc*, *Encuentro Femenil* (the journal published that same summer), and Dorinda Moreno's *La Mujer: En Pie de Lucha*. Also on the list were materials that provided a critical political and historical context for understanding La Mujer, including Third World Communications' *Third World Women*, Ward Morton's *Woman Suffrage in Mexico*, and selections from Frederick Turner's *The Dynamic of Mexican Nationalism*, as well as a section on human sexuality, with *The Birth Control Handbook* and *Our Bodies, Ourselves* listed as recommended readings.

More than simply offering important historical documentation of Semana de la Mujer, *El Popo Femenil* would provide young Chicana scholar-activists with a resource that could be used in both consciousness-raising groups and classrooms.

As a broader consciousness-raising tool, *El Popo Femenil* had the potential to reach Chicanas across California (and beyond), providing an accessible forum for the discussion of the issues they faced in their own communities. In her analysis of print culture and the formation of Chicana counterpublics, Maylei Blackwell notes that "the practice of publishing conference proceedings and continuing debates in print" was vital as both a mode of circulating information on movement activities and a "mode of contestation." In this way, "movement print culture functioned as a mediating space where new ideas, theories, and political claims were constructed, negotiated, and contested."[60] For Chicanas, many of whom worked on Chicano student movement newspapers—including *El Popo* at California State University, Northridge; *El Alacrán* at California State University, Long Beach; and *La Verdad* at San Diego State University—publishing their ideas in print allowed them "to move in and through, and sometimes outside of, nationalist discourse and created a space where sexism within the movement could be challenged."[61] Indeed, Anna's experience working at *La Raza* (Los Angeles) and publishing the three issues of *Hijas de Cuauhtémoc* reinforced the importance of print culture to the development of Chicana feminist thought inside and outside the academy. Reflecting on this period in 2003, she noted that reporting on feminist activities "produced a collective knowledge that created a sense of collective feminist leadership for cultural social change."[62] Thus, Chicana newspapers like *El Popo Femenil* "became a pedagogical tool to identify, discuss, and develop Chicana feminist values, Chicana feminist issues, and Chicana Studies."[63]

Following the model of *Hijas de Cuauhtémoc*, *El Popo Femenil* not only documented the events and debates surrounding Semana de la Mujer but also included stories about sex discrimination in Chicano organizations (reprinted from the *Chicana Service Action Center Newsletter*), original research on cross-racial relationships ("A Cause of Tension Between the Chicano and the Chicana, the Relationship Between the Chicano and the Anglo Woman"), a critique of Octavio Paz, announcements for a Chicana summer study group and a course on women's health at the Self-Help Clinic on Crenshaw, and poetry by Chicana students, including a poem by Angelina de la Torre that captured what it felt like to be trapped in "a world of contradictions" in which

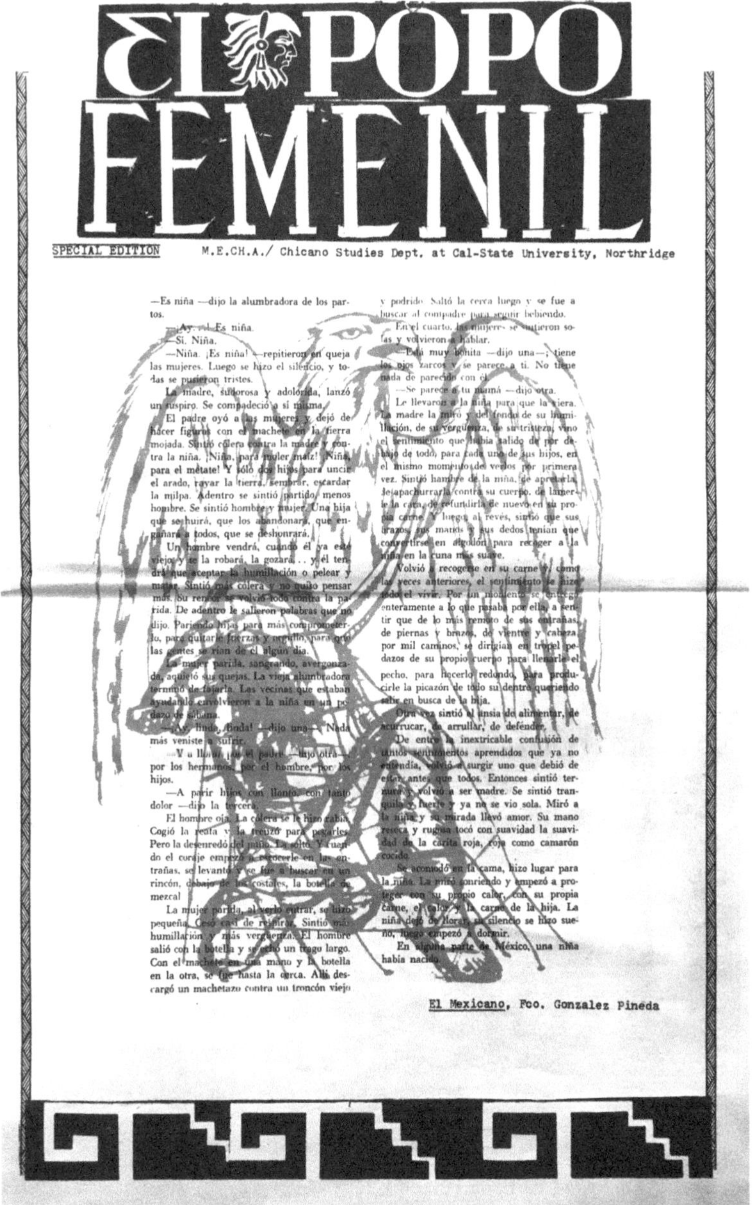

EL POPO FEMENIL

SPECIAL EDITION M.E.CH.A./ Chicano Studies Dept. at Cal-State University, Northridge

—Es niña —dijo la alumbradora de los partos.

—¡Ay...! Es niña.

—Sí. Niña.

—Niña. ¡Es niña! —repitieron en queja las mujeres. Luego se hizo el silencio, y todas se pusieron tristes.

La madre, sudorosa y adolorida, lanzó un suspiro. Se compadeció a sí misma.

El padre oyó a las mujeres y dejó de hacer figuras con el machete en la tierra mojada. Sintió cólera contra la madre y contra la niña. ¡Niña, para moler maíz! ¡Niña, para el metate! Y sólo dos hijos para uncir el arado, rayar la tierra, sembrar, escardar la milpa. Adentro se sintió partido, menos hombre. Se sintió hombre y mujer. Una hija que se huirá, que los abandonará, que engañará a todos, que se deshonrará.

Un hombre vendrá, cuando él ya esté viejo, y se la robará, la gozará... y él tendrá que aceptar la humillación o pelear y matar. Sintió más cólera y no quiso pensar más. Su rencor se volvió todo contra la parida. De adentro le salieron palabras que no dijo. Pariendo hijas para más comprometerlo, para quitarle fuerzas y orgullo, para que las gentes se rían de él algún día.

La mujer parida, sangrando, avergonzada, aquietó sus quejas. La vieja alumbradora terminó de fajarla. Las vecinas que estaban ayudándolo envolvieron a la niña en un pedazo de sábana.

—¡Ay, linda, linda! —dijo una—. Nada más veniste a sufrir.

—Y a llorar por el padre —dijo otra—, por los hermanos, por el hombre, por los hijos.

—A parir hijos con llanto, con tanto dolor —dijo la tercera.

El hombre oía. La cólera se le hizo rabia. Cogió la reata y la trenzó para pegarles. Pero la desenredó del puño. La soltó. Y cuando el coraje empezó a recocerle en las entrañas, se levantó y se fue a buscar en un rincón, debajo de los costales, la botella de mezcal.

La mujer parida, al verlo entrar, se hizo pequeña. Cesó casi de respirar. Sintió más humillación y más vergüenza. El hombre salió con la botella y se echó un trago largo. Con el machete en una mano y la botella en la otra, se fue hasta la cerca. Allí descargó un machetazo contra un troncón viejo y podrido. Saltó la cerca luego y se fue a buscar al compadre para seguir bebiendo.

En el cuarto, las mujeres se sintieron solas y volvieron a hablar.

—Está muy bonita —dijo una—; tiene los ojos zarcos y se parece a ti. No tiene nada de parecido con él.

—Se parece a tu mamá —dijo otra.

Le llevaron a la niña para que la viera. La madre la miró y del fondo de su humillación, de su vergüenza, de su tristeza, vino el sentimiento que había salido de por debajo de todo, para cada uno de sus hijos, en el mismo momento de verlos por primera vez. Sintió hambre de la niña, de apretarla, de apachurrarla contra su cuerpo, de lamerle la cara, de refundirla de nuevo en su propia carne. Y luego, al revés, sintió que sus brazos, sus manos y sus dedos tenían que convertirse en algodón para recoger a la niña en la cuna más suave.

Volvió a recogerse en su carne y, como las veces anteriores, el sentimiento se hizo todo el vivir. Por un momento se entregó enteramente a lo que pasaba por ella, a sentir que de lo más remoto de sus entrañas, de piernas y brazos, de vientre y cabeza, por mil caminos, se dirigían en tropel pedazos de su propio cuerpo para llenarle el pecho, para hacerlo redondo, para producirle la picazón de todo su dentro queriendo salir en busca de la hija.

Otra vez sintió el ansia de alimentar, de acurrucar, de arrullar, de defender.

De entre la inextricable confusión de tantos sentimientos aprendidos que ya no entendía, volvió a surgir uno que debió de estar antes que todos. Entonces sintió ternura y volvió a ser madre. Se sintió tranquila y fuerte y ya no se vio sola. Miró a la niña y su mirada llevó amor. Su mano reseca y rugosa tocó con suavidad la suavidad de la carita roja, roja como camarón cocido.

Se acomodó en la cama, hizo lugar para la niña. La miró sonriendo y empezó a proteger con su propio calor, con su propia carne, el calor y la carne de la hija. La niña dejó de llorar, su silencio se hizo sueño, luego empezó a dormir.

En alguna parte de México, una niña había nacido.

El Mexicano, Fco. Gonzalez Pineda

FIGURE 5.1. *Front page,* El Popo Femenil, *1973. Anna NietoGomez personal collection.*

MATERIALS ON
CONTEMPORARY CHICANA

1. Regeneracion P.O. Box 4157
T.A., Los Angeles, Calif. 9005
($1.00)
Volumes: I:#10- Special Chicana Issue I
II:#1 - "La Chicana--Forgotten
Woman" by Sylvia Delgado
- "Comision Feminil" by
Fransica Flores
II:#2- "Epitaph for Maria" by
Sylvia Delgado
II:#3 - Special Chicana Issue II

2. Hijas De Cuauhtemoc P.O.
Box 735, San Fernando, Calif.
91341 ($2.00)
Vol. I, #1 and 2

3. Encuentro Feminil P.O. Box
735, San Fernando, Calif.
91341 (Chicana Journal, $2.00)
Vol. I, #1

4. La Mujer En Pie De Lucha by
Dorenda Moreno; El Dorado
Publication Distributors, 2489
Mission St. Suite17, San Fran-
sisco, Calif. 94110 ($8.50)

5. Third World Women Third
World Communications, 1972;
P.O. Box 1959, San Fransisco,
California ($3.00)

6. Woman Suffrage In Mexico by
Ward M. Morton; University of
Florida Press, 1962; Gainsville
Florida ($5.00)

7. Dynamics of Mexican Nationalism By Frederick Turner;
Chapel Press ($3.95) see pgs
185-201: "Women in the Revolution of 1910"

HUMAN SEXUALITY
(recommended)

1. Birth Control Handbook, P.O.
Box 1000, Satation G, Montreal
130 Quebec (free, 25¢ mailing)

2. Our Bodies, Our Selves, Bo
Women's Health Book Collective;
Simon & Schuster, N.Y. ($2.95)

The Self-Help Clinic is going to offer a six session course on the health of women. They will show films on childbirth, tube litigation, hysterectomy, abortion and other subjects of interest to women. The series will start June 6, 7:30 p.m. at 746 S. Crenshaw. If you are interested in attending and you need a ride from the Valley call 886-5843.

FIGURE 5.2. *Back page,* El Popo Femenil, *1973. Anna NietoGomez personal collection.*

Past-future melts into present
rendering a frightened, timid
confused Chicana facing a choice.
Accept the old ways of a world passing
the silent stoic image of our mothers
and all the quiet scurrying servitude
surrounding our mistreated-scarred
men and children.
Or to bravely, aggressively demand a place
in the movement-classroom-home that
acknowledges her as a sensitive, aware,
capable, trustworthy important fighter
for freedom, equality and unity.
To emulate Dolores Huerta, who stands
up and speaks out defiantly creating a
new Chicana image.[64]

This "new Chicana image," bravely breaking the bonds of culture and tradition in the "movement-classroom-home," is subtly signified on the front page of *El Popo Femenil*. Against the backdrop of a drawing by H. Villa, a pinto (incarcerated) artist, that depicted a crouching woman cutting herself out of a net in front of an eagle symbolizing Mexican nationalism—an image borrowed from the first issue of the *Hijas de Cuauhtémoc* newspaper—the editors placed a reprinted excerpt from Mexican psychologist Francisco González Pineda's *El Mexicano: Su Dinámica Psicosocial* (1961). The excerpt recounts the birth of a girl in rural Mexico, an event that sends the patriarch of the family into an alcoholic rage. Shifting between the internal thoughts and violent actions of the patriarch, who curses his fate for having fathered a girl, and the sense of desperation that nearly overwhelms the child's mother, González Pineda's narrative paints a disturbing picture of gendered psychosocial dynamics under the Mexican patriarchal order. The juxtaposition of text and image places the two in direct conflict, suggesting that the swing of the woman's machete strikes out against not only the eagle (a stand-in for nationalism) but also the gendered family dynamics described in González Pineda's narrative. Indeed, the narrative offers a critical context for the specific nature of patriarchal oppression in Mexican nationalism—a textual gloss on the psychosocial dimensions of the net that encloses the woman in the image, keeping her crouching and submissive.

Blackwell has noted that the original image "illustrates the signifying practice of disidentification staged on the terrain of nationalism whereby its principal symbols are deployed in a manner that leaves room for alternative readings."[65] In overlaying this remediated image from *Hijas de Cuauhtémoc* with González Pineda's text (which, importantly, appears to have been duplicated directly from the book), the editors of *El Popo Femenil* engage a similar disidentificatory movida, this time directed toward Chicano studies itself, where deeply sexist texts like González Pineda's *El Mexicano* and Paz's *The Labyrinth of Solitude* were staples of the curriculum.[66] Indeed, it is notable that the Chicana voice is not present on this first page of the newspaper; instead, González Pineda's text surrounds the woman's figure even as the eagle looms over her, suggesting that together they form a net of power that she must break through. Through a chain of signification that links Mexican (patriarchal) nationalism to the Chicano studies curriculum, this striking composite image conveys an alternative reading of the field and its limitations, even as it situates the reports, essays, and poetry in *El Popo Femenil* as a collective effort to break through.

This critique of the Chicano studies curriculum is reinforced in an essay that appeared later in the newspaper, Dottie Hernandez's "Número Uno," which takes Octavio Paz to task for his exploration of Mexican (male) identity and his "attitude towards the woman, as a 'function and symbol,' as Paz puts it, which clearly eliminates her from his examination of man's solitude. If it is true that, 'woman is never herself, whether lying stretched out or standing up straight,' then to the male she doesn't have a reality of her own."[67] Like the composite image on *El Popo Femenil*'s front page, Hernandez's ironic title, "Número Uno," slyly points at the macho attitudes engendered by Paz's "examination of man's solitude," even as her critique of the deficiencies in *The Labyrinth of Solitude* articulates the need for Chicanas to develop their own curriculum. Deploying Paz's framework of the "mask" to disidentificatory ends, Hernandez states that "to analyze the Mexican woman's solitude, her thoughts and doubts concerning this reality she is subject to, her mask must be taken off."[68]

In her history of Chicanas at California State University, Northridge, published in the *Daily Sundial* in 1975, Anna notes that although *El Popo Femenil* comprised only a single issue, "it became nationally known as one of the few literary forums on the Chicana."[69] Like other anthologies of writing that became staples of the Chicana classroom in the mid-1970s, *El Popo Femenil* was envisioned as both a pedagogical and a political intervention, one that extended the learning space of the classroom to the campus and the community and thus expanded the reach of Chicana feminist thought. *Encuentro Femenil*, published a few months after *El Popo Femenil*, is a more explicitly scholarly journal (with longer articles, footnotes, and all the trappings of the genre of academic writing), and yet it draws from both the image repertoire and the content of Chicana print culture, expanding on the ideas discussed at Semana de la Mujer, including Chicanas' experiences with the welfare system, employment, and higher education, as well as the psychosocial dimensions of la familia and sexual politics. Both the title of the journal and the cover of its first issue make these linkages explicit, repurposing the H. Villa drawing once again, this time with neither the Mexican eagle nor the canonical Chicano studies text shadowing La Chicana's emergence. The varying remediations of this iconic image of a woman breaking free tell a story of the shifting challenges that Chicanas faced as they sought to nurture a collective identity and establish the historical and contemporary experiences of La Mujer as a legitimate area of inquiry. Indeed, as Anna has observed, "Chicana print culture and Chicana studies reinforced each other. They created new pedagogical, political, and historical learning. They nurtured the production of collective identity and the formation of the Chicana public cultures."[70]

Thinking about the production history of *El Popo Femenil*, I am brought back to the flowing knowledge modalities that Anna shared with me on the day of our interview in 2018, and how they are mapped across such Chicana pedagogical projects. Indeed, both Semana de la Mujer and the periodical that documented it offer stunning examples of how Chicanas mobilized the classroom to put these modalities into practice to build a body of knowledge by and for Chicanas. A "bibliography doesn't exist, so you have to build it. And then you have to see it and read it, and then you have to talk about it. Make it real. You have to touch it, incorporate it." But you also have to "interpret it, discard . . . add and search. Identify what you discard, why you discard and what you need to replace when you've discarded." And, as they did in with Semana de la Mujer, you have to

> talk about the here and now, why is this important now? If it was the present, why is it important to them in the present, in their community, in their life? You have to apply it. Or if it was about the past, how was this similar to what's going on now? How is it applicable for the here and now, you know? And ideally we look to the future. . . . But often we didn't get there. You know, often we didn't get there.[71]

Even though persistent institutional racism, sexism, and classism made "getting there" more challenging, students in Anna's classes were clearly empowered by what they were learning and doing. She notes that students in her classes evolved into committed "Chicana feminist student scholar-activists."

FIGURE 5.3. *Cover,* Encuentro Femenil, *1973. Anna NietoGomez personal collection.*

> They pioneered in building Chicana studies curriculum when it had never been done before. They proposed a new curriculum, organized feminist student organizations, and sponsored Chicana conferences. They invited Chicana community activists to speak. The students asked, "How are we oppressed?" "What are women's issues?" "What are you doing about them?" "And how can we help?" They published a newspaper about women's issues, and documented what Chicana community activists were doing about them.[72]

While there would not be another women's issue of *El Popo*, Chicanas at Northridge continued to build on the momentum of Semana de la Mujer and the publication of *El Popo Femenil*, often through applied research in Anna's classes.

In the spring of 1974, for example, Chicanas at Northridge focused their attention on making the case for Chicana classes as a requirement for Chicano studies majors in order to "address the sexism and racism encountered on campus." This effort originated in Anna's Chicana history class, when "the men and women expressed dissatisfaction with the perpetuation of negative stereotypes of Chicanas by social scientists, articles in *El Popo*, faculty, and students."[73] To respond to this persistent problem, students created a petition and visited Chicano studies classes to build support for the effort, developing "their organizing and leadership skills" in the process. They met with Chicano studies faculty to discuss the curriculum, and they "openly discussed . . . the issue of separatism of Chicanas from the Chicano Movement." Their petition, which was signed by "over 250 students and faculty," demanded nothing less than the full incorporation of La Chicana into the curriculum of Chicano studies:

> "Recognizing that the present curriculum is lacking in information regarding 51% of the Chicano population, the Chicana, and in conjunction with the California State Senate Bill 1285, which requires all social science courses to include the role and contributions of the women," the Chicanas organized a petition to propose that the [California State University, Northridge] Chicano Studies Department include in its graduation requirements for Chicano Studies majors at least two Chicana Studies classes. The petition also requested Chicano Studies faculty to study the Chicana in order to increase and expand on the role and contribution of the Chicana in their classes.[74]

By 1975 these curricular interventions had borne some fruit. The Chicano Studies Department made the Chicana contemporary issues course a requirement for graduation, and a new Chicana organization was born: Hermanas Unidas. That summer, women in this newly formed (but long in development) group would travel to Mexico City with Anna and a film crew to document the first International Women's Year conference. Many of these students would mobilize one year later on behalf of their intellectual mentor, Anna NietoGomez, as she faced what seemed like an existential battle for her own professional career, and for the nascent field of Chicana feminist studies.

## "THE END OF THE BEGINNING": CHICANA STUDIES INTERRUPTUS

It seems fitting to close this account of Chicana becoming in the 1970s with the archival trace in my mother's collection that first piqued my interest in this submerged history: *Women Struggle.* Published in 1976 by a collective that had come together to support Anna NietoGomez as she fought the negative tenure decision from the Chicano Studies Department, *Women Struggle* came to me directly from my mother's hands in 2008, a year before Linda Garcia Merchant and I initiated the Chicana por Mi Raza project. I had mentioned to my mother in passing that I wanted to share some archival objects from her collection with students in my feminist theory class in order to demonstrate that Chicanas were an active presence in the 1970s. In response to this request from her most persistent patron, my mother sent me a large-format photocopy of a newspaper that testified to this absent presence. When I first laid eyes on *Women Struggle*, it looked like any other movement newspaper: Dramatically elongated block letters marched across its masthead, demanding the reader's attention; bold woodcuts and Indigenous design motifs scattered throughout its pages illuminated poems, articles, and opinion pieces, driving home their collective message through visual strategies that drew from the familiar image vocabulary of Chicana/o struggle. But there were also strange absences and presences in *Women Struggle* that hinted at a different kind of work at play. There was no date on the masthead; no advertisements for dances, bakeries, and cleaners; and nearly all of its contributors were singularly focused on one topic: the 1976 tenure battle of Anna NietoGomez at California State University, Northridge. I would slowly come to realize—as I began to piece together the dispiriting story of Anna's tenure struggle—that what I held in my hands was not simply some long-lost Chicana newspaper, but a carefully constructed print archive documenting a threshold moment in the development of the field of Chicano studies.

In "La Chicana," an essay that Anna contributed to *Women Struggle*, she noted how over the "last seven years women involved in discussing and applying the women's question have been ostracized, isolated and ignored." Framing her tenure case as an opportunity to finally confront the gendered contradictions of the field, she stated, "It is time to evaluate this historical trend. It is time for all to study the women's question and to develop an analysis which is applicable to the Chicana and Chicano."[75] Anna's reference to the "last seven years," a time frame spanning from 1969 to 1976, pointed to an as yet unaccounted for history of Chicana studies before the publication of *This Bridge Called My Back* in 1981. In many ways, *Women Struggle* documents the transition from this early period of struggle to the development of a more robust and institutionally situated field of inquiry. Indeed, as Michael Soldatenko has noted, women who were active in this period—including Anna NietoGomez, Sonia Lopez, Enriqueta Chavez, Dorinda Moreno, Martha Cotera, Rita Sanchez, and many others—prepared the "ground for a feminist epistemology that would lead the charge against Chicano Studies in the 1980s and create the conditions for a renewed multiplicity of Chicano, Chicana, and Chicana(o) Studies."[76]

Published in 1976, at the crest of what Naomi Quiñonez has called the first wave of Chicana feminist studies, *Women Struggle* was a one-time publication distributed by the Support Anna Nieto-Gómez committee in order to bring widespread attention to her tenure battle.[77] At the time, Anna was a nationally recognized Chicana feminist thinker who had been instrumentally involved in the development of Chicano studies as a field. As an undergraduate at California State College at Long Beach, she had spearheaded the first newspaper to center Chicana voices and experiences, *Hijas de Cuauhtémoc*. She had served on the planning committee and had been a workshop coordinator for the 1969 conference at the University of California, Santa Barbara, which produced *El Plan de Santa Bárbara*, the master plan for Chicanos in higher education. And she was one of the first women to be hired, in 1971, specifically to develop and teach classes focused on La Chicana. By the mid-1970s, NietoGomez had become a leading feminist voice in the field. She and Corinne Sánchez led a curriculum workshop to develop Chicana studies and published *New Directions in Education: Estudios Femeniles de la Chicana*, a guide to teaching on La Chicana in the university setting. She was the leading force behind the first Chicana feminist journal, *Encuentro Femenil*, and a nationally sought-after public speaker on topics ranging from Mexicana/Chicana history to Chicanas in higher education (she had recently given lectures at the University of Houston and Yale University). Notwithstanding these significant professional achievements, and

# WOMEN STRUGGLE

It had to happen. Sooner or later, it was inevitable. that the question of feminism in the movement would come to a clash. Chicanos in the movement have been putting down the liberation of women as either a "white trip," a cop out, a bourgeoise trip. The liberation of women has been shoved aside. However, feminism in the Chicano movement has emerged as amost powerful movement. If understood correctly, one can clearly see that the liberation of women is in no way reactionary. It is not divisive, and least of all, it's definitely not a "white trip."

At Cal-State Northridge, the question of feminism in the Chicano movement has come to a head. Professor Anna NietoGomez a highly respected Chicana has brought the question of feminism and sexism to the doorstep of the Chicano Studies. Anna Nieto Gomez, amidst rumors, accusations, charges and hearsay, was simultaneously refused tenure and terminated as a professor of Chicano Studies.

Ana Nieto Gomez has been accused of virtually sabotaging the Chicano Studies. For the sake of unity, she is asked not to make waves. She has be been the victim of slander and character assassin-ation based on rumor. Nonetheless, a review committee of six, three students and three faculty voted to refuse Anna tenure and decided to terminate her for incompetency. In reality the decision was based not on incompetency, bu rather on slanderous rumors which attempted to discredit her character

Voted to refuse Anna tenure and decided to terminate her for incompetency. In reality, the decision was based not on incompetency, but rather on slanderous rumors which attempted to discredit her character.

COMPETENCY IS NOT THE ISSUE .

Ana Nieto-Gomez is highly regarded for her role in developing and defining Chicana feminism and exposing sexism in the Chicano Movement.

Many say that sexism is not the issue; however, the case of Ana Nieto-Gomez is a clear-cut case of sexism. She is one woman who has toured lectured, taught and developed innovative curriculum on the Chicana.

It is ironic that a woman of her qualifications is being pushed out of Chicano Studies when we are at this critical stage of ideological development. The Chicano movement is at the stage where we are defining and redefining our roles in developing consciousness and struggle. Ana Nieto Gómez provides a much-needed perspective on the exploitation of the Chicano and Chicana. The liberation of women requires an intense and critical analysis as to the nature of exploitation. Understanding the exploitation of women requires a knowledge as to the nature of racial, class and sexual oppression. Understanding these three levels of oopression can lead only to struggle against these Three levels of exploitation.This is the essence of Chicana feminism. It is the essence of the libertion of women. It is the essence of third world stuggle.

THIS IS WHAT ANA NIETO GOMEZ STANDS FOR---- THIS IS HER STRUGGLE

If Class exploitation exists, then we struggle to eradicate this exploitation If racism exists, then we combat it; if the exploitaion of women exists, then we must also combat it. The point is, that the struggle against these three forms of exploitation must be combatted simultaneously, no "after the revolution." Wherever class, racial, and sexual exploitation occur, they must be combatted. The reality of the matter is that these three forms of oppression filter into every level and sector of society because they are well-imbedded institutions. Sexism is well imbedded within the Chicano movement; however, there are those that will deny it, ignore it, or place it in the closet. Ana Nieto-Gomez has constantly argued that sexism exists not only in Chicano Studies but also in the Chicano movement as well. Sexism exists, yet it is not measured in terms of the number of women participating; rather it is measured by the level of struggle being waged. If one ignores the struggle it is guilty of sexism. Thus, if Chicano Studies, a center or oragnization ignores the women's struggle, it is guilty of sexism, regardless of the number of women participating, even if there are 90% women.

For bring up the issue of women, of sexism and of feminism, she has been slandered. She has been accused of "aiding a conspiracy to undermine and abolish Chicano Studies at Northridge." She has been accused of dividing the movement. She has been accused of creating conflict. She has been accused of hindering the development of Chicano Studies, and she has been accused of setting back the hands of the clock.

Ana Nieto-Gomez, for bringing Sexism out into the open, has been labeled a threat to Chicano Studies

We cannot support that view. We believe that she is eminently qualified to teach in the field of Chicano Studies. We believe that Anna Nieto-Gomez should be reinstated to Chicano STudies. at Northridge. This issue will have critical contemporary and historical importance in terms of how the issue of sexism in the Chicano MOvement is handled by Chicanos and Chicanas.

One Chicana summed it up best: "IF they get rid of Anna, all I learned in Chicano Studies wasn't worth shit. All that we were taught about carnalismo, about oppression, about our struggle--all this will be bullshit if we as Chicanos allow Anna to be terminated. How can we talk about oppression, of liberation and of self-determination, when we ourselves are trying to get rid of someone who has brough change and new ideas to the movement. She represents Chicanas! All this Chicano Movement, This Chicano Studies isn't worth shit if we treat Anna the way the gavachos treated us in '68."
Support The Liberat on

Support Anna Nieto-Gomez

FIGURE 5.4. *Front page,* Women Struggle, *produced by the Support Anna Nieto-Gómez committee, 1976. Anna NietoGomez personal collection.*

her national reputation, like many of her peers teaching in Chicano studies programs in the mid-1970s, NietoGomez did not hold an advanced degree. This fact—along with all-too-familiar concerns regarding the effectiveness of her teaching and whether or not her research and writing constituted "legitimate" scholarship—served as the official rationale for her tenure denial.[78]

NietoGomez was not the only movement activist who had found a home in Chicano studies only to be purged from the field as departments sought greater institutional legitimacy, but because of her foundational role in the nascent field of Chicana studies, her tenure case generated widespread attention and concern in Chicana feminist circles in California and throughout the Southwest.[79] In her examination of the controversy, Maylei Blackwell has noted that NietoGomez's dismissal from the department at Northridge, "one of the largest and most historic Departments of Chicano Studies," was "the canary in the coal mine signaling to Chicana feminista activists and writers alike the conditions in which they would have to fight in order to bring forth the vibrant field of Chicana Studies that thrives today."[80] Indeed, in "Hijas de la Malinche," her 1997 dissertation, which provides an account of the controversy, Naomi Quiñonez relates how Maria Herrera-Sobek, then a professor at Northridge, was shaken by both the institutional and the physical manifestations of this regulatory violence:

> According to Maria, the men gave Anna a hard time. "They slashed her tires, they broke her windshield . . . somebody threatened her with a gun, she was always getting nasty notes." Maria does not know if professors or students were behind the attacks. But she became disgusted with the rampant and dangerous machismo on campus and resigned. Two other Chicana professors resigned with her, in unity against the male repression. After this experience Maria became more conscious of feminist issues. "This experience made me think about feminist issues too, instead of just Chicano issues."[81]

In this sense, Anna NietoGomez's tenure battle was much more than merely another example of how the field was willing to shed its activist origins in exchange for institutional legitimacy; it served as an object lesson for the silencing of difference at a moment when Chicano studies was undergoing a disciplinary process that subjected the field, as Rodrick Ferguson notes, to the "normative ideals and protocols of state, capital, and academy."[82] In its collective defense of Anna NietoGomez and its critique of these contradictions in Chicano studies, *Women Struggle* reveals how this march toward institutionalization and disciplining was a gendered process that exiled the "women's question" to the margins of the field until its dramatic resurgence in the early 1980s. At the same time, as Herrera-Sobek's reflections on this moment of institutional regulation suggest, for many in the academy, the tenure battle brought long-standing gendered and sexual contradictions within Chicano studies to the surface, raising consciousness about the urgent need for feminist analysis within the field. Though *Women Struggle* made this case forcefully, Anna's tenure battle ended with her harassment and abrupt dismissal from the Chicano Studies Department at Northridge (despite the fact that she was entitled to a terminal year of teaching), and ultimately in her departure from academia entirely—a result that significantly undermined a deeper historical understanding of the genealogy of Chicana feminist thought, until Alma García uncovered its textual evidence with the publication of her foundational resource book, *Chicana Feminist Thought: The Basic Historical Writings*, in 1997.[83] *Women Struggle* provides vital archival evidence, in image and text, of a critical moment in the development of Chicana feminist studies, a moment that Anna NietoGomez has often described as "the end of the beginning."

Compiled by the Support Anna Nieto-Gómez committee from an array of documents—including statements of support they collected from Chicanas across the Southwest, reprinted editorials that had appeared in other newspapers, and materials from her dossier (her résumé, a list of courses she had developed, and a timeline of events that demonstrated inconsistencies in administrative processes)—*Women Struggle* offers both a counterdossier to support Anna's case and a rich compendium of Chicana (and Chicano) feminist thinking about the state of the field. Both archival object and archiving project, it hails us from the not-too-distant past, an unexpected anthology of Chicana feminist thought that documents the contradictions of Chicano studies in the mid-1970s. Like many special editions of Chicano movement newspapers, this printed remix of the counterarchive of struggle focuses on a singular case of oppression (Anna NietoGomez's tenure denial) to illustrate the larger contradictions of the system. In placing the question of gender regulation front and center, *Women Struggle* demonstrates how these contradictions were reflected and sustained in the patriarchal relations of knowledge production that had shaped Chicano studies and the broader movimiento since the late 1960s.

Featured on the first page of *Women Struggle* is a reprinted opinion piece originally written by Roberto Rodriguez for *La Gente*, a student newspaper at the University of California, Los Angeles. Rodriguez frames Anna's tenure battle as the only possible outcome of the structural silencing and punishment of feminists within the Chicano movement:

> It had to happen. Sooner or later, it was inevitable that the question of feminism in the movement would come to a clash. Chicanos in the movement have been putting down the liberation of women as either a "white trip," a cop out, a bourgeois trip. The liberation of women has been shoved aside. . . . At Cal-State Northridge, the question of feminism in the Chicano movement has come to a head. Professor Anna NietoGomez, a highly respected Chicana has brought the question of feminism and sexism to the doorstep of . . . Chicano Studies.[84]

Highlighting the broader implications of the tenure battle, the editorial insists that the underlying issue in Anna's tenure case is not competency but rather the limited definition of oppression that had shaped the Chicano movement and, by extension, Chicano studies as a discipline:

> The Chicano movement is at the stage where we are defining and redefining our roles in developing consciousness and struggle. Ana [*sic*] Nieto-Gomez provides a much-needed perspective on the exploitation of the Chicano and Chicana. The liberation of women requires an intense and critical analysis as to the nature of exploitation. Understanding the exploitation of women requires a knowledge as to the nature of racial, class, and sexual oppression. Understanding these three levels of oppression can lead only to struggle against these three levels of exploitation. This is the essence of Chicana feminism. It is the essence of the liberation of women. It is the essence of third world struggle. . . .
>
> . . . If class exploitation exists, then we struggle to eradicate this exploitation. If racism exists, then we combat it; if the exploitation of women exists, then we must also combat it. The point is, that the struggle against these three forms of exploitation must be combatted simultaneously, [not] "after the revolution." Wherever class, racial, and sexual exploitation occur they must be combatted. The reality of the matter is that these three forms of oppression filter into every level and sector of society because they are well-embedded institutions. Sexism is well-embedded within the Chicano movement: however, there are those that will deny it, ignore it, or place it in the closet.[85]

Incisively making the case for the importance of an intersectional analysis for understanding oppression, and *applying* that analysis to expose the gendered contradictions of Chicano studies as a field of knowledge, the editorial outlines how the well-embedded nature of sexism in higher education systematically marginalizes all women, from students, to faculty, to administrative staff. But for Chicanas, this structural marginalization was compounded by the particular forms of sexism they encountered within Chicano studies:

> Chicanas are the first to go and the last to be hired or granted tenure. When special criteria is used to justify a new program [e.g., hiring and even tenuring noncredentialed faculty, as had been the case at Northridge and other state institutions], it is not applied consistently to men and women in the program. Criteria is eventually standardized by the time women, as well as new faculty, are considered for retention, tenure or promotion. The goal is then to preserve the system, the program, the credentialed men and their comrades.[86]

In explicitly linking the systematic professional marginalization of Chicana feminists in Chicano studies to a process of institutionalization and incorporation of the field into the academy, Rodriguez's editorial echoes common critiques of the rise of a Chicano professional class in the waning years of the Chicano movement, but it also illuminates how the disciplinary process that established Chicano studies as a legitimate field of inquiry (with its own credentialed cadre of mostly male professionals) contributed to the marginalization of outspoken feminists who had brought questions of gendered oppression out into the open and challenged the underlying ideologies of class, gender, and race that sustained the relations of domination and subordination.[87]

*Women Struggle* also features several contributions from Anna NietoGomez, including some of her reprinted essays and an illuminating interview. For Anna, the tokenism that had characterized the nominal inclusion of women in the field in the early 1970s (at Northridge in particular) reflected the male-supremacist values of the racist institution, which sought to incorporate a vision of Chicano studies into the academy that did not disrupt its embedded heteronormative hierarchies. Indeed, in response to critics who claimed that in raising consciousness about her case as an example of sexism in Chicano studies, she had undermined the movement and played into the hands of the administration, Anna incisively observed that "as a department in the university, enforcing university rules, Chicano Studies *is* the administration."[88] Echoing this observation in a reprinted letter on behalf of "Chicanas in the Austin community," Martha Cotera points out that the decision to terminate Anna NietoGomez was a telling example of how a formerly insurgent field had become a bastion of male power and privilege, a mirrored reflection of the institution that Chicano studies had sought to transform:

> Possibly you remember the 1960s when we all so fervently worked with the establishment of Chicano Studies programs with faculties sensitive to our academic and community needs. How we advocated the promotion of Chicanos and Chicanas to faculty positions, indicating that B.A., M.A., PhD were not as important as having a person who could truly make a contribution in the field, both in theory and in practice. So our position statements cast degrees aside and helped place fledgling B.A.'s in positions never held by Chicanos. For men, fortunately, things have changed and we can boast PhDs in practically every area of concern and we can afford the luxury of demanding full credentials for academic positions. For Chicanas, this is not the case in 1976. We are in the same position as the men were in 1968. We have tragically few Chicanas in the academic field, and of these, only a handful are progressive and productive in advocating the positive development of the Chicana, and her survival in this country. . . . We consider Anna Nieto-Gomez one of these valuable resources for Chicanas in the United States. To strip Anna of her position would be destructive to her and more important, it would be demoralizing to the many Chicanas throughout the United States who have learned from her and who have been inspired to development through her lectures, coursework, research, and literary production. As a librarian, information specialist and community advocate, I can personally vouch for the contribution that Anna's research and writings have made to the community.[89]

Speaking from outside the institution, as a leading organic intellectual and community activist (her book *Profile on the Mexican American Woman* had recently been published in March of 1976), Martha Cotera highlights the relevance of Anna's scholarly work to the project of self-determination for Chicana/o communities as a whole: "We have utilized Anna's studies and the materials she has so effectively compiled and edited in Statewide educational material and public testimony, community education programs, community organization efforts and in all type of seminar activities in Texas."[90] In making this case for the impact of Anna's writing on communities far beyond the academy, Martha reminded her readers that when it was originally conceived, the purpose of Chicano studies had been not to build the professional careers of male academics but rather to "take the entire system and make it work for us."[91] Martha's focus on Anna's impact in spaces of knowledge exchange outside the academy beckoned the field to return to its insurgent roots as the "educational arm" in the struggle for Chicana/o self-determination, to produce knowledge *with* and *for* communities in struggle, to circulate that knowledge and use it as the basis for the production of new knowledge forms, new analytics, and new subjects in resistance.

Far from simply documenting one moment of regulation (neither the first nor the last) of Chicana feminists in the field, the letters, analyses, images, and timelines compiled in *Women Struggle* trace the contours of a Chicana feminist field imaginary that—as Anna NietoGomez noted in "La Chicana," one of several essays she contributed to the newspaper—was still "in various stages of development."

> However, in general, Chicana feminism is the recognition that women are oppressed as a group and are exploited as part of la Raza people. It is a direction to be responsible to *identify and act upon* the issues and needs of Chicana women. Chicana feminists are involved in understanding the nature of women's oppression in respect to such issues as childcare, reproduction, economic stability, welfare rights, forced sterilization and prostitution. The Chicana feminist is involved in research analysis in order to understand how women's oppression is related to the oppression of other groups. Finally, Chicana feminism is involved in *developing and initiating* a means to end the oppression of women and all people.[92]

Illustrating this concise description of Chicana feminism and its scholar-activist subject is a striking woodcut by Barbara Carrasco depicting a young Chicana striding forward, holding a bundled infant in one arm and a book in the other.[93] Breaking the mold of the Aztec princess, La Adelita, and the long-suffering mother, Carrasco's image draws instead on the image vocabulary of heroic male icons ubiquitous in movement newspapers, posters, and scholarly publications (including the founding document of Chicano studies, *El Plan de Santa Bárbara*, a major point of contention for Chicanas), replacing the singular male hero with a new subject: the "Chicana feminist student scholar-activist."[94] As Maylei Blackwell notes, visual archetypes such as "the pachuco, the stoic worker, or the romanticized revolutionary" in Chicano movement representational practices "came to constitute a field of subject positions" that did not include women, outside of their inscription within la familia de la raza.[95] Forging a new visual archetype for Chicana/o studies, Carrasco inscribes La Chicana as an active agent of revolutionary knowledge production within the Chicano movement, while also slyly rescripting what was at the time a dominant trope of revolutionary womanhood: the mother as guerillera. Blackwell notes how the image of a woman with a rifle slung across her back and an infant in her arms inscribed women's proper reproductive role in nationalism, locating their "revolutionary agency within motherhood."[96] By replacing the Chicana's rifle with a book, Carrasco contributes to an "iconography of the New Chicana" that "reworked the gendered nationalist constructions of the Adelita, La Revolucionaria, and other figures" to shift "nationalist representational registers" and figure "themselves as new historical subjects"—in this instance, as Chicana feminist scholars.[97]

More importantly, by retaining the baby in her iconic reimaging of the mother-as-revolutionary trope, Carrasco refuses to consign the domestic and the political—the public and the private—to mutually exclusive domains. Reflecting the scholar-activist concerns outlined by Anna NietoGomez in "La Chicana," the article paired with Carrasco's print, this key signifier of revolutionary maternity—the babe in arms—points not to the injunction to reproduce a revolutionary cadre but rather to the ways in which gendered experience informed the project of Chicana studies and its analysis of the intersection of racial, class, and gender oppression, a focus that opened up a different set of concerns for scholars contributing to the revolutionary struggle for self-determination: "childcare, reproduction, economic stability, welfare rights, forced sterilization and prostitution." Barbara Carrasco's image of the Chicana scholar fleshed the archive of Chicana writing, embodying its emergent consciousness and commitments and offering what Blackwell terms a "new apparatus of interpellation" for Chicanas. As the consequential pairing of Carrasco's image with Anna's essay suggests, such disidentificatory iconography operated hand in glove with Chicana feminist writing to "rework and resignify symbols and icons of female agency, thereby opening up new possibilities for women's participation and leadership by creating an alternative feminist apparatus of interpellation that changes the hailing mechanism of the Chicana/o subject." While such refigurations of the "revolutionary (m)Other" undoubtedly drew from—and inevitably instantiated—heteronormative visions of social reproduction (as I discuss in chapter 6 about the mujerista praxis of las mujeres de la Riva), as disidentificatory acts they also opened up a space for new signifying practices, particularly around questions of gender and sexuality.[98] It is an irony of the archive that the progressive vision of the Chicana scholar articulated in the transit between Carrasco's image and Anna NietoGomez's writing—a vision redolent with possibility for Chicano studies as a field—illustrates this moment of rupture and silencing.

Anna refers to her tenure battle as "the end of the beginning," a sly switch-up of "the beginning of the end" (the catchphrase of slow decline) that is more than just verbal play. Reversing the temporal logic of the declension narrative that characterizes many historical accounts of the movement period, Anna's formulation not only highlights the abrupt way

# LA CHICANA

By Anna Nieto Gomez

What is Sexism? Sexism is part of the Capitalist ideology which advocates male supremacist values. These values define the nature of women and men in respect to being superior or inferior. Men are defined as "naturally" stronger, more logical, and able to economically provide for others. Women are defined as "naturally" dependent, childlike, and therefore always in need of authority. Her primary functions are to secure others as a wife and a mother since her primary abilities are to conceive, procreate, and nurture. Therefore, man is defined "naturally" superior to women since man is independent and agressive, and women are dependent and passive.

**Racism**

The Psychology of Racism works in a similar manner. Racism is also a part of Capitalist ideology. These set of values support White supremacy. White supremacy measures superiority according to the color and culture of people. White people are defined more superior because they 1) are a source of authority, 2) they are wealthier, and 3) they are more aggressive. People of color, which includes both men and women, are regarded as inferior because: 1) they play subordinate roles in society, 2) they are economically dependent and constantly poor, 3) they are considered childlike and in need of authority, and are passive. It is assumed people of color are not able to determine for themselves; "their primary ability is to have sexual intercourse, and to procreate."

**Racism-Sexism**

Both the chicano and chicana experience is affected by these two ideologies. In fact both the chicano and chicana experience racist sexism. Colonized men of color are considered as inferior as women since colonized men do not have the power or authority to rule, provide economically and protect the family. Thus racist sexism considers Mexican males as either effeminate, or a "Macho," overcompensating because of his powerless position in his society.

The colonized women of color are considered more passive, dependent, and childlike than women of the superior race. Therefore white women's relationship with women of color is paternalistic and stratified.

The sexual role of the colonized women is intensified. Her skills and abilities are centered around her sexual prowess, and procreation. It is the assumption of racist sexism that the mental ability of women of color has atrophied. Thus it is justified that "those who know better" should make decisions for her. Therefore doctors decide how many children a poor Chicana may have hence continuing the practice of forced sterilization.

Since the colonized women are totally placed in a dependent state, her primary source of support hopefully will come from her children and/or husband. But this support is sporatic, since all involved are in a social-economic and political state of dependency.

**Capitalist Ideology**

All institutions in a Capitalistic society perpetuate these myths of racism and sexism. The educational institutions reinforce the division between people of different races, cultures, sex, and class, and define these divisions as natural.

In respect to sexism, educational institutions reinforce the Capitalistic ideology of male supremacy. Role models reinforce men acting, participating, initiating and creating. Verbs and adjectives describe women as apathetic, observing, receiving and preserving.

**Sexist historians omit women from their research**

Sexist historians omit the woman's question from research and analysis. Selecting only male leaders in depicting important events, reinforces the myth of women not affecting or participating in society. But more important, history minimizes the economic, social and political disabilities and assumes she was safely protected in the "stable family."

The Chicana/Mexicana is rarely depicted as participating in a struggle: during the conquest of Mexico, during the fight for independence, the reforma during the industrial revolution in either Mexico or the United States. This ommission reinforces the passive impression of women in history. Historians that assume rights were "given" to her in a paternalistic fashion. Sexual stereotypes are in literature are left without criticism or analysis. The role and impact of the Chicana in the labor movements in the United States, and the civil rights movement are excluded without too much question.

## Ana Nieto Gomez

If history excludes women, then it becomes impossible to discover the causes of the conditions of women today. An analysis of the ideologies, and the role and exploitation of women in slave, feudal, capitalistic and socialistic economies is thwarted, if data is excluded. Consequently issues such as abortion, forced sterilization, and child care remain within the emotional arena. The political economy of women and their role in reproduction, labor mainfaince and technology, and profits are excluded from understanding the nature of this oppression.

The exclusion of women from history in an effort to reinforce the sex roles is not a reflection of male egocentrism. The educational system is merely a tool to transfer an ideology, a set of values. It is a tool to sanction and explain the increased profits for the benefit the capitalist class.

Capitalists are the class of people who own all factories, equipment and resources. Capitalists employ workers, paying them a subsistance wage. The workers wage is less that the total product produced. The worker's labour becomes a commodity to be bought if a profit can be made. Whether the worker can sell his labour power is beyond his control.

Capitalists use the ideology of sexism to divide workers as they compete with each other to steal their labor. Since male supremacy dictates women stay home and men work, it does not become necessary for capitalists to share their profits and provide jobs for everyone, to both men and women. Women then represent a major part of the labor reserve pool; consequently they are usually used as scab or cheap labor.

Sexist values support that women be educated in the home, and formal education be given to men first since they will be the "bread winners." Since only a certain portion of men are employed, women are left unemployed and unskilled. Nevertheless she is still considered as temporary. Unemployment, unskilled and temporary worker status "explain" why, 1) jobs should be given to men first; 2) Unequal wages between men and women 3) exclusion from certain types of jobs.

Sexism also confuses the issues of working people. The issue against unemployment and underemployment of men and the demand for affirmative action compete with each other. Workers compete for the same jobs as opposed to demanding jobs for all. Sexism reinforces the division among male and female workers when in reality it is within their interest to unite.

As a part of the unskilled labor pool, women workers are used to threaten the mainstream worker. Low wages for women are used to control the higher but nevertheless subsistence wages of male workers. To increase profits during a depression, more women workers are brought in to the labor force as cheap labor and more men experience unemployment. Workers compete for the same few jobs as opposed to demanding jobs for all.

Racism is also used to divide workers in a like manner. White supremacy justifies a priority of employment and higher wages to white folks. Unemployment and poverty are considered to be the choice of people of color. This value system prevents workers from uniting and demanding jobs for all.

Male Supremacy creates division among men and among women. Success to the strongest justifies why men compete with each other for a few jobs. The employment rolls identify which best men won.

Male supremacy dictates that women depend on men. Therefore women must compete with other women toward developing their economic futures for better jobs, rich husbands or poor husbands. Coequently, individualism and male superiority as opposed to collective unity are within the interests of increasing profits for the capitalists.

In many places within the Chicano movement, sexism has not been considered a valid issue. In fact often times there is conflict between Chicana feminists and cultural nationalists or so-called "marxists" who do not recognize the women question.

Chicana feminism is in various stages of development. However, in general Chicana feminism is the recognition that women are oppressed as a group and are exploited as part of la Raza people. It is a direction to be responsible to identify and act upon the issues and needs of Chicana women. Chicana feminists are involved in understanding the nature of women's oppression in respect to such issues as childcare, reproduction, economic stability, welfare rights, forced sterilization and prostitution. The Chicana feminist is involved in research-analysis in order to understand how women's oppression is related to the oppression of other groups. Finally, Chicana feminism is involved in developing and initiating a means to end the oppression of women and all people.

Unfortunately a Chicana feminist is discredited by associating her with "White" women. This sexist racism implies: 1) only white women can initiate and create change, and 2) all women who speak out against sexism have the same analysis as to the cause and resolving of the issue. This is far from true. Feminist women's politics represent conservative, liberal, radical, and leftist politics. It is clear that this ignorant criticism encourages lack of support to Chicanas in their struggle for liberation. Thus an effort to integrate the issues of Chicanas with the established "legitimate" people's issues are thwarted. Ironically women are accused of dividing the movement, when their goals are to fight the effects of sexism and unite with everyone.

In organizations where cultural nationalism is extremely strong, Chicana feminists experience intense harrassment and ostracism.

Very generally, Cultural nationalism advocates group survival through group solidarity, revival of the culture and the reasseration of the pride and worth of people belonging to a particular group.

In the case of Chicano nationalism racism is identified as the issue and cause of oppression. The economic system of Capitalism is not always addressed as the focus of change.

Acknowledging a conspiracy of white supremacist to control and exploit the people, group survival is defined by preserving the language, music, folklore, folkmedicine, customs and history. In addition an effort is directed to increasing their political and social participation to all institutions in order to increase economic and educational opportunities. The base of attack to end oppression is to attack racism. Chicano representation in all socio-economic classes seems to be the goal.

The chicana feminist comes into conflict if she feels the movement is an effort to secure male priviledge for men. She cannot support male priviledge at the same time. All priviledges must be eradicated. Otherwise it would seem in her interest to fight for female priviledge. However the chicana feminist does not want to oppress, therefore she is forced to investigate beyond racism and sexism in order to understand the nature of the internal struggle within the movement. Marxist-Leninist ideology and women's history of socialist countries offer a clear analysis as to the function and division of the sex roles and of racism. However the struggle to make a clear analysis has just begun. The Chicana must apply this analysis to her conditions. If there is not sufficient data to provide a historical perspective then the struggle to develop becomes more intense.

At the same time, some cultural nationalists criticize chicanas' activities as divisive. Three priorities are constantly emphasized. Support "your" men, maintain traditional roles, and preserve the culture. This is offered as a formula for unity and success within the movement. Women are told to wait until the revolution is over before they deal with the women's question.

Many times cultural nationalism promotes paternalism. In return for services and support, people are minded to be grateful for the progress made.

Criticism and new ideas are controlled and suppressed for fear of losing existing benefits. Eventually red baiting tactics are used to preserve group unity. An appeal to the emotions, fears, prejudices and lack of information is used to rally threatened isolated group. Issues or people are discredited in associating them with something undesirable.

In respect to Chicana feminist, the credibility is reduced when they are associated with white women. They are called reactionaries and therefore a threat to the group's survival.

For example, if Chicana classes and feminism are defined as a reactionary elements in Chicano Studies, students will not take the classes and continue to remain ignorant on the women's question.

Feminists are harrassed and ridiculed as man-haters and degenerates. Many times these women become alienated from the group.

Rather than relying on emotion in order to do the right thing, a continual process of investigation research, discussion, and analysis should be a means of defining positions and action. Conflict should be seen as a struggle to develop.

In the last seven years women involved in discussing and applying the women's question have been ostracized, isolated and ignored.

It is time to evaluate this historical trend. It is time for all to study the women's question and to develop an analysis which is applicable to the Chicana and Chicano.

**Therefore if there are any criticisms in respect to this presentation, do not hold it against me. Instead, let us study the issues together — criticism can be a seed to growth.**

FIGURE 5.5. *Anna NietoGomez, "La Chicana," featuring an illustration by Barbara Carrasco,* Women Struggle, *1976. Anna NietoGomez personal collection.*

in which feminist lines of inquiry were silenced by the spectacular violence of her tenure battle but also suggests a genealogy of Chicana feminist studies that connects its moment of articulation to the birth of the field as a discipline. Indeed, the archival record of this "beginning" amply demonstrates that contrary to what some historical accounts suggest, Chicanas were critical to the formation of Chicano studies in the late 1960s and early 1970s, developing the field and even taking leadership positions in some of the most important (though still understudied) institutional efforts of the period. They too were in the trenches of academe, building Chicano studies alongside the men who would later write histories that consigned them to its discursive margins.

This was the beginning, too, of a critical consciousness born from the gendered contradictions of this institutional labor. In meetings, conferences, and classrooms, Chicanas were daily exposed to the gendered contradictions of the field's revolutionary vision for educational transformation, and they contested its heteropatriarchal orientation from the start. As Alma García, Ramón Gutiérrez, Teresa Córdova, Maylei Blackwell, and Deena González have amply demonstrated, Chicanas' experiences of contestation and contradiction in the field (and in the Chicano movement more broadly) fundamentally shaped the intersectional analytic of contemporary Chicana feminism. Less is known, however, about how this first generation of scholar-activists built the nascent field of Chicana studies through their pedagogical and scholarly praxis: the teaching, curriculum development, networking, and community-based research that was the beating heart of the field in the 1970s. These movidas produced new sitios y lenguas for Chicana knowledge production during a period when such knowledge was very hard to come by, effectively laying the critical groundwork for the emergence of Chicana feminist studies in the 1980s. But perhaps more importantly, their movidas offer us provocative examples of how subjects in opposition can move in, through, and around sites of social, political, and institutional power to create new visions of liberation. Indeed, as Roderick Ferguson points out in *The Reorder of Things*, "While the academy promises a range of conflicts—'screams in a golden ear'—that institution is also the site where critical formations might emerge, particularly ones that study and challenge the university's relationship to racial formations and other modes of difference."[99] He cites the knowledge praxis of women of color who came of age in the 1970s as providing an analytic model that helps us "imagine ways to maneuver taken-for-granted contradictions so that their economies are not constantly tilted toward identification but move in the direction of disidentification and on to more sustained embodiments of oppositionality."[100] Foundational Chicana feminist thinkers like Martha Cotera, Evey Chapa, Anna NietoGomez, Sonia Lopez, Enriqueta Chavez, Dorinda Moreno, and a host of others may have been exiled from Chicano studies in its transition from unruly counter-discipline to institutionally aligned field formation, but their archival traces remain, beckoning us to realize the futures they could only imagine.

# MUJERISTA GENEALOGIES: ENCUENTROS IN THE QUEER CHICANA ARCHIVE

***Chapter 6***

*There is an underground story of sexuality within the Chicano movement that is important to tell because it has been omitted. I hope my story contributes to undoing that erasure.*

OSA HIDALGO DE LA RIVA, "VISIONS OF UTOPIA WHILE LIVING IN OCCUPIED AZTLÁN"

*"Queering" the archive means challenging the heteronormativity of the Chicana/o archive and the whiteness of the LGBTQ archive, a process that transforms seemingly settled terrains of history, revealing them to be maps that obscure pathways and connections between movements, communities, and individuals.*

HORACIO N. ROQUE RAMÍREZ, "GAY LATINO HISTORIES / DYING TO BE REMEMBERED"

*The archive is a relation.* I am frequently reminded of this central precept in the knowledge praxis of the Chicana por Mi Raza Digital Memory Collective in my encuentros with the Chicana lesbiana filmmaker and poet Osa Hidalgo de la Riva. Perhaps it's the way she always refers to me as "cuzin," a practice she applies liberally to both friends and new acquaintances, drawing even strangers into an ever-expanding web of relation. Or maybe it's her dedication to keeping her queer matrilineal legacy alive through her films and writing, and by tending to a substantial collection of artifacts and documents that give evidence to the many ways in which the women in Osa's family modeled what she calls a "mujerista" praxis grounded in inclusivity, activism, and the will to create despite social, political, and economic challenges. Indeed, this queer matrilineal legacy is central to Osa's mujerista aesthetics and praxis, which envisions and enacts queer utopian worlds in "occupied Aztlán."

I was first introduced to Osa's mujerista praxis when I edited her contribution to the book *Chicana Movidas*, "Visions of Utopia While Living in Occupied Aztlán," which was based on a testimonio recorded by Maylei

Blackwell in 2016. In it, Osa outlined the seven elements of her mujerista moviemaking praxis:

> Number one, the Mujerista filmmaker loves herself unconditionally and often radically. She is [a] woman-identified woman whether she has experienced emotional or physical intimacy with another woman. The Alice Walker definition says, "A woman who loves herself loves other women sexually and/or nonsexually." Number two is getting the job done, willfully, using nonconventional methods, those outside of the traditional Hollywood studio system. It is the successful production and aim towards the liberation of self and others. It is focused on making access to technology by any means necessary, its ideology informs its praxis, its praxis or methodology is informed by a responsible set of personal politics, this is always in flux, changing and transforming with the changing times. Number three: Mujerista movies are educational but in a nontraditional sense, not indoctrinating or subordinating all people to a WASP patriarchal mindset and hegemony. Rather, they offer transformational experience about people, events, issues, and points of view usually not dealt with, underrepresented, and misrepresented in mainstream media. Fourth, Mujerista filmmakers are activist in nature and reclaim our stories from a women-of-color and children-of-color POV. Fifth, familia is inclusive of all peoples, ages, religions, colors, abilities, classes, genders, and sexualities. Six is teaching others and including our communities in the production process as crew members. Seven, taking risks, being outlaws to create change and transformations for healthy beings.[1]

As I read Osa's description of mujerista praxis, I could not help but see in her seven principles an uncanny echo of the protocols (also seven in number) that Linda Garcia Merchant and I had developed to guide our work with the Chicana por Mi Raza Digital Memory Collective. For us, too, unpacking our mothers' libraries—gathering their stories and documents, remaking the world through their eyes—is a gesture of radical "woman-identified" love that is animated by the fundamental belief that our stories are worth telling and preserving.[2] Like Osa's mujerista praxis, our approach to preservation is framed as a collective endeavor among familia (broadly defined), a process whereby multiple collaborators have a shared responsibility for preserving and activating Chicana memory. Thus, it too is informed by "a responsible set of personal politics" that centers relationships over the development of new digital tools, self-determination over institutional visibility and assimilation, and capacity building among a broad community over the development of expertise among a select few. Engaging an outlaw and rasquache digital praxis—"nonconventional methods," as Osa might put it—we too access "technology by any means necessary," creatively reusing existing tools and our access to university infrastructures and institutional funding to produce knowledge "towards the liberation of self and others."

Like the other moments of transformative recognition I have shared in this book, this initial encuentro with Osa's mujerista praxis seemed to suddenly thin the temporal boundaries between the present and the past, inviting me to enter the history of Chicana feminist knowledge praxis "through a different door, the door of the uncanny, the door of the fragment, the door of the shocking parallel," and to explore another territory at once familiar and strange.[3] Indeed, if this process felt like a kind of homecoming, it was also haunted by the traces of Chicana lesbian life conjured in the testimonio that Osa shared with Blackwell, which offered an "underground story of sexuality within the Chicano movement" that defamiliarized existing genealogies and historical frameworks of the movement era.[4] At once personal and collective, the underground story she tells includes the experiences of other women in her matrilineal circle: stories about her Aunt Sally (Celia de la Riva Rubio), who navigated the repressive social and political landscape of the 1940s and 1950s as a butch-identified lesbian, and Osa's mother, Lola de la Riva, who opened the Centro de Arte in her home in Long Beach, California, in the early 1970s and eventually came out as a lesbian in the 1980s. Osa recalls how as a young "out, dark-skinned lesbian," she herself navigated quite different sexual, racial, and class contradictions in the political upsurges of the 1970s, from the Chicano movement, to the women's movement, to gay liberation. In response to these contradictions, las mujeres de la Riva (Osa, her mother, and Osa's sister Liz) formed the Mextiza Colectiva in the early 1970s. Run out of the Centro de Arte, the Mextiza Colectiva organized art exhibitions and poetry readings and published the work of women of color. In 1976 they launched a bicentennial tour of Chicana lesbiana poetry across the US Southwest. It was during this period that Osa and Liz published a Chicana lesbian newsletter, *Mama Sappho*, delivering it on their motorcycles to their hometown of Stockton and distributing it by mail to the growing network of feminist and lesbian bookstores and coffee shops. In her testimonio, Osa also shares her complicated experiences at a series of transnational lesbian encuentros, bearing critical witness to the racial, class, and national tensions that threatened the solidarity efforts of global feminism in the 1980s and 1990s. Touching only obliquely on the publication of Cherríe Moraga and Gloria Anzaldúa's *This Bridge Called My Back* (1981), Osa's story reframes this foundational text in a much longer genealogy of lesbian of color writing and cultural production. In retracing these wayward paths of collective becoming (across movements, nations, and generations), Osa's testimonio provides a tantalizing narrative trace of what has been omitted from the historical imaginary of the movement years, and it charts an alternative genealogy that "transforms seemingly settled terrains of history, revealing them to be maps that obscure pathways and connections between movements, communities, and individuals."[5]

Since the early 1990s, numerous Chicana feminist scholars have challenged the silences around Chicana/Latina sexuality by uncovering and reconstructing queer genealogies and their embodied experiences through oral history, archival research, and critical analysis.[6] This body of work writes against narrative emplotments and conceptual frameworks that contribute to the marginalization and even erasure of Chicana lesbian experience in the movement years and beyond. In "Memory and Mourning: Living Oral History with Queer Latinos and Latinas in San Francisco," Horacio Roque Ramírez describes how such "narrative exclusions" in Chicano/Latino and queer historical memory reflect a central paradox of "identity-based liberation politics" in the 1960s and 1970s, which "professed racial and gender inclusion and allround liberation from all forms of oppression and exclusion" while engaging in "essentialist practices" that pitted the political interests of the "gay community" against those of the "Latino community."

> Such diametrically exclusionary conceptualizations, of course, were simply inaccurate and outright offensive for those women and men inhabiting these social markers at one and the same time: Chicana lesbians, Puerto Rican gay men, Cuban male-to-female transgender performers, and so on. In historical practice, these intersecting narrative exclusions worked their way into publications, libraries, and archives: even now (though this is slowly changing), what publications there are about gay and lesbian/queer Bay Area history and the gay and lesbian archival repositories remain generally white, and Chicano/Latino and ethnic studies historiography, libraries, and archives similarly privilege heteronormative experience and struggle."[7]

In the context of Chicano nationalism, the conceptualization of traditional culture (so central to nation building, as Frantz Fanon has shown) was intimately bound up with a heteropatriarchal vision of the Chicano family: la familia de la raza.[8] Conceived as a metonymy for the "Chicano nation," la familia de la raza was a political project that structured the gendered (and sexual) relations, leadership models, and labor of the movement.[9] As Lee Bebout has argued, this heteronormative vision of family "as the cornerstone of anticolonial and nationalist struggle reinforced the explicitly heterosexist notion that same-sex relations were a betrayal of family and culture."[10]

Mobilizing a chain of signification that equated feminism with lesbianism—as bourgeois and individualist "Anglo" elements that threatened the nation—this discourse of betrayal was often used as a regulating mechanism against feminists, particularly Chicana lesbians, who challenged patriarchal conceptualizations of la familia de la raza.[11] Indeed, Chicana feminists were frequently criticized as agringada "followers of white feminists or as lesbians" and ridiculed as unwomanly "Chicanas con pantalones" (in the words of Sonia Lopez).[12] According to Alma García, such "feminist-baiting and lesbian-baiting attacks" framed feminism "as little more than an 'anti-male' ideology" and lesbianism "as an extreme derivation of feminism," creating a discursive feedback loop in which feminism and lesbianism were viewed as "synonymous."[13] Yolanda Chávez Leyva has noted how the cultural nationalist construction of lesbianism "as a sickness we get from American women and American culture" inevitably positioned Chicana lesbians as "a threat to the community" because of their refusal to conform to the heteronormative values of "traditional" Mexican culture. This had particularly harmful effects on Chicana lesbians in the movement who "were among the most talented leaders of organizations," yet had to hide, or underplay, their sexuality at the "risk of expulsion from movement spaces," as we shall see in the case of Osa's aunt, Celia de la Riva Rubio.[14] Indeed, whether they were lesbians or not, the conflation of feminism and lesbianism as alien to Chicano culture served to control "women's sexual behavior . . . by threatening to take away their ethnic identity, by implicating them as not true Latinas."[15]

Catrióna Rueda Esquibel has argued that this "homophobic backlash" subjected *all* Chicana feminists, regardless of their sexuality, to "lesbian-baiting at both personal and professional levels," noting that both "heterosexual and lesbian Chicanas were injured in this 'purge.'"[16] Indeed, Anna NietoGomez recalls that when she was teaching at California State University, Northridge, a rumor circulated that her class was "turning people gay." She freely acknowledges that her Chicana feminist pedagogical praxis encouraged participants to be open about their identities, including their sexual identities, and to question traditional gender roles. Although some students did in fact come out in her class because they felt safe enough to do so, Anna believes that the accusation that she was "turning students gay" was a movida intended to further undermine her credibility as a Chicana scholar.[17] Such homophobic anti-feminist attacks put Chicana feminists in the unenviable position of having to challenge the conflation of feminism and lesbianism by either unconsciously or intentionally limiting the discussion of sexual politics to a distinctly heteronormative frame—what Lee Bebout has termed the "heterosexual assumption" of early Chicana feminism.[18] While the intersectional framework of Chicana feminism developed in the 1970s broke new ground with respect to its analyses of the interplay of racism, sexism, and classism, it left heterosexism largely unexamined until the 1990s.

Silences around lesbian sexuality reverberated in the institutional formations developed during the movement years, shaping the academic discourses of Chicano studies and, by extension, early Chicana feminist studies.[19] As Deena J. González has noted in her foundational essay "Speaking Secrets: Living Chicana Theory," the homophobia rampant within the Chicano movement inevitably limited the discussion of difference within Chicana feminist studies in its early years, where "some types of feminism, some types of lesbian rhetoric and analysis—especially the quiet kind—were to be abided, and others not."[20] Yvette Saavedra has shown how these dynamics played out within the National Association for Chicano Studies (NACS) in the early 1980s, when the increased visibility of Chicana feminist voices in the organization resulted in intensified homophobia (the organization changed its name to the National Association for *Chicana* and Chicano Studies, or NACCS, in 1995). Saavedra argues that the homophobic backlash within NACS resulted in a "public disassociation from queerness [that] moved the [Chicana] caucus away from the lesbian/queer imaginary and reoriented women back into line with Chicano heteronormativity. This allowed feminism to continue expanding into NACS, while decentering and subsuming the lesbian/queer feminist imaginary within it."[21] In response to this institutional erasure, Saavedra's genealogy tracks how Chicana lesbians challenged these silences within NACS, as well as the "heterocentric framings of Chicana feminism" within the Chicana caucus, in an effort to name and recuperate "the lesbian/queer feminist roots of key Chicana feminist ideologies and discourses."[22] Likewise, Catrióna Rueda Esquibel challenges silences around lesbian sexuality in Chicana feminist history in *With Her Machete in Her Hand: Reading Chicana Lesbians*, a literary genealogy that takes as its "starting point that Chicana lesbians are central to understanding Chicana/o communities, theories, and feminisms." Rejecting the traditional bifurcation of lesbian sexuality from Chicana feminism, Rueda Esquibel pushes us to think beyond an additive model of scholarship—in which lesbians are included in a genealogy that remains largely heteronormative in its orientation—and toward one that revisions the genealogy of Chicana feminist thought by surfacing its queer lineages. Her goal in imagining this new genealogy is not to "dismiss the work of heterosexual Chicanas—particularly those whose careers were ended in spite of their 'good' sexuality—but rather to point out the significance of lesbianism in these 'primal scenes' of Chicana identity."[23] Surveying a rich archive of institutional traces, oral testimony, and publications, both Saavedra and Rueda Esquibel demonstrate how Chicana lesbians were not latecomers to Chicana feminist thought, but rather were constitutive of its development, particularly in the 1980s.

Returning to Osa Hidalgo de la Riva's "underground story of sexuality" with these queer genealogical movidas in mind, I am reminded of the critical importance of oral history and embodied memory to the process of historical recuperation, particularly with respect to exploring Chicana lesbian experience prior to the 1980s. As Susy Zepeda observes in her book *Queering Mesoamerican Diasporas: Remembering Xicana Indígena Ancestries*, with few archives documenting Chicana lesbian life before the 1980s, mapping their "social and political" networks in the 1970s presents particular challenges. In her own genealogical effort to uncover the oppositional consciousness and utopian visions of Chicana/Latina lesbianas, Zepeda reorients her vision by turning to a "living archive" of queer memory, and to the guidance of historian and archivist Yolanda Retter Vargas, who was herself a participant in early lesbian political formations.[24] For Zepeda, Retter Vargas is emblematic of the "Latina lesbian gatherers and guarders of knowledge," the "archivists, scholar-activists, and artists" who "did the work of tracing and archiving unseen or unrecognizable intersectional knowledges."[25] Surfacing these intergenerational webs of relation in both its methodology and its historical recuperation, Zepeda's genealogy illuminates how the embodied archive of Chicana/Latina lesbiana memory holds reservoirs of knowledge that cannot be found in institutional collections.

Like Retter Vargas, Osa too is a Chicana lesbian gatherer and guarder of knowledge, an archivist, a scholar-activist, and an artist who has preserved a queer matrilineal archive in the face of economic precarity and health challenges. Occupying a sizable storage unit in Capitola, California, near her home in Santa Cruz, the Mujeres de la Riva Archive (as Osa has named it) offers an extraordinarily rich compendium of materials. In addition to Osa's copious writing (she began keeping journals at the age of fourteen) and videography spanning from the mid-1980s to the present day, it includes many artifacts from the women in Osa's family: a suitcase belonging to her Aunt Lucy filled with photos, letters, and personal writing documenting Mexican American life in Stockton, California, in the 1940s and 1950s; several copies of her Aunt Sally's book, *Lágrimas y Cadenas / Chains and Tears* (1994); materials related to her mother Lola de la Riva's work as an artist in the Chicano movement and her Centro de Arte; artifacts from the Mextiza Colectiva;

syllabi, course readers, and other items from her graduate work and teaching at various California institutions in the 1980s, 1990s, and 2000s; and a wealth of lesbian of color materials that document organizations, writers collectives, and cultural activities in Los Angeles, the Bay Area, and beyond.[26] Challenging "both the whiteness of queer archiving practices and the heteronormativity of Latino historiography," the Mujeres de la Riva Archive—like Osa's testimonio—offers stunning evidence of a "Chicana lesbian body politic forged at the crossroads of Chicanismo, women of color feminism, lesbian identity politics, working-class consciousness, and transnational solidarity sensibilities."[27]

In keeping with Osa's praxis of centering familia and relationality in her writing, filmmaking, and archival work, in this chapter I reconstruct a multigenerational genealogy of mujerista knowledge praxis from the traces of queer memory in the Mujeres de la Riva Archive and the personal experiences that Lola de la Riva, Osa Hidalgo de la Riva, and Liz Hidalgo de la Riva have shared in testimonios, interviews, and pláticas. Together they represent an embodied archive that surfaces "a distinct, Chicana/Mexicana lesbiana cultura . . . in the making" from the early twentieth century to the 1970s.[28] In linking this Chicana/Mexicana lesbiana cultura in the making to Osa's matrilineal family history—from the inclusive vision of familia cultivated by Osa's Grandma Angie, to her Aunt Sally's experiences as a butch-identified Chicana lesbian in the postwar years, to her mother Lola's Centro de Arte de Long Beach and the Mextiza Colectiva—I want to illuminate how these women creatively reimagined family and community, both of which have been paradoxical sites of silence and survival for Chicana lesbians "struggling to cope with what has often been a hostile, violent, racist outside environment," as spaces of queer utopian possibility.[29]

## MUJERISTA PRAXIS: A QUEER GENEALOGY

Born in Stockton, California, in 1954, Osa Hidalgo de la Riva, like many of the Chicanas in this book, came of age in the political ferment of the late 1960s, and yet she situates the development of her Chicana lesbiana consciousness within a much deeper, and distinctly matrilineal, genealogy that queers the family form. In "Visions of Utopia While Living in Occupied Aztlán," Osa foregrounds the political stakes of this queer matrilineal framing, noting that

> my aunt Sally being gay was a good role model. Then, when my mom came out much later, it was really cool, but she came out at a different

> time, like in the eighties. I learned a lot from my aunt Sally who was actively gay in the 1950s. From both of them, I get those two different languages and culturally and historically specific representations of how Chicana lesbianas were, even if it was primarily through my family. I always say my family is matrilineal because the power of the energy runs through the women or the female part of the family. With the de la Rivas, this is really strong and there is a lot of lesbian presence. I don't like the word "matriarchy" even though matriarchal is more accepted. It makes me think of a more dominant system and it reminds me of patriarchy. I use "matrilineal" because matriarchy seems like merely the opposite of patriarchy, but I am describing a completely different situation. For me, matrilineal is having the energy running through or the decision making centered within the women.[30]

This matrilineal, woman-identified legacy was central to the development of Osa's understanding of a mujerista praxis. In fact, she explicitly identifies each of the women in her family with one or more mujerista principles (inclusivity, willfulness, and activism).

Osa's mother, Lola de la Riva, and her aunt, Celia de la Riva Rubio, both of whom were active in the Chicano movement, are central figures in this queer matrilineal legacy, embodying mujerista principles like willfulness and a commitment to activism. Their mother and Osa's maternal grandmother, Angela Maria Rubio de la Riva (Grandma Angie), modeled the mujerista principle of inclusivity: an understanding of "familia that is inclusive of all peoples, ages, religions, colors, abilities, classes, genders, and sexualities."[31] Born in Villa Ocampo, Durango, in 1901, Grandma Angie migrated to the Bay Area in the 1920s, where she married Francisco Gabriel de la Riva in 1923.[32] Though she was herself a newly arrived immigrant, Grandma Angie was deeply involved in community-building efforts, teaching cooking and art classes in English and Spanish to the foreign-born through a civic organization, Mobilized Women of Berkeley.[33] Osa's grandfather Francisco also nurtured a strong sense of community among Latino immigrants in the Bay Area, organizing a literary club of "hispanoamericanos" in Berkeley that held regular poetry readings, and sponsoring tango demonstrations and dance recitals.[34] Eventually, Grandma Angie grew tired of her husband's drinking and running around and moved herself and her four children—two sons (Frank and Gabriel) and two daughters (Lucy and Celia)—to Stockton, where she purchased a large Victorian home by the train station. In Stockton, Grandma Angie continued to embody the mujerista principle of inclusivity, opening her home to tenants regardless of

FIGURE 6.1. *Studio portrait of Angela Rubio de la Riva (Grandma Angie) and her husband, Francisco Gabriel de la Riva, ca. 1930s. Osa Hidalgo de la Riva personal collection.*

their race and thus "filling a crucial community need during a time of legal segregation." Moreover, Grandma Angie loved "her daughter Celia fully," regardless of the fact that she was a butch-identified lesbian in the 1940s. "That was a radical stance in those days, especially because Celia chose to be more male-presenting in public in an era when 'cross-dressing' was illegal."[35]

Osa's mother, Lola, who was born in Stockton in 1938 after her father's return to the family, recalls that although her parents were not wealthy people (her father was a butcher, and her mother worked in canneries but later moved on to become a department store clerk), they "were much more progressive than a lot of people because . . . of the creativity going around with the different artists my father, my aunts, you know what I mean, poets and writers around us and we were performers." She notes that they were always very open to those who were, in her words, "different": "My family was real multicultural. . . . They never said look at those gays and don't go over there, because they're [gay]."[36] Because she was the last of her mother's children (five years younger than her nearest sibling, Celia), Lola had a great deal of freedom as a child, tagging along with her elder siblings when they went to dances and parties and entertaining her father and his friends on their "parandas." As a teenager Lola developed her strong organizing skills and commitment to justice, joining voter registration efforts while attending St. Mary's Catholic High School in Stockton, and later going "door to door to gain support for a petition demanding sidewalks, curbs, and gutters in their neighborhood which was eventually successful." She even participated in the "cannery strikes in Stockton, after being hired at fourteen thanks to connections via her sister Celia."[37] While Lola showed great promise early on as an artist, her formal education was cut short at age fourteen, when she met the man who would become her first husband, Louie Hidalgo, a former farmworker ten years her senior, whose family had migrated from Del Rio, Texas, to work in Stockton's agricultural industry: "Louie met me and he just kept chasing me and calling me and coming over and he wouldn't cut me loose for about a year. Then finally I got pregnant [with Osa] and I got married to him because you know my mom, in those days no one would approve."[38] Lola's marriage into a farmworker family, her sister Lucy's marriage to Ben Valverde, the cousin of United Farm Workers organizer Dolores Huerta, and her own work in the agricultural industry shaped her politics and drew las mujeres de la Riva into the struggle for farmworker rights in the 1960s.

For Osa, her mother, Lola, embodies the mujerista principle of "willfulness," of "getting the job done . . . using nonconventional methods" in "the successful production and aim towards the liberation of self and others."[39] As a young mother of three in the 1950s—Osa (b. 1954), her brother Louie (b. 1956), and Liz (b. 1958)—Lola always made sure that her children "were active community members and that their presence never curtailed her life choices, experiences, or possibilities."[40] She cultivated a domestic environment that in many ways reflected the artistic and bohemian household she grew up in, remaking her small home in Stockton into a mini cultural center filled with books, music, and art supplies. Osa recalls that her mother even knocked down a kitchen wall while her husband, Louie, was away at work, in order to expand the space to fit her artistic needs. She also used her home as a canvas for her own creative impulses, painting a mural of a lemon tree that covered the "whole kitchen wall. And there were like three little ducks or little kids, you know, there was a mama duck and the three little ducks and this big lemon tree."[41] A longtime jazz enthusiast, Lola would often organize impromptu listening parties, encouraging the children to

> [lie] down quietly on the floor in dimmed light as she played some of the latest and most progressive jazz musicians. closing our eyes softly, we were told to isolate the musical parts. "now listen to the saxophone, what do you think it is saying? now just listen to the drums. now, just listen to the clarinet," and so on, mama lola would say.[42]

Lola extended this creative circle to other children in their multiethnic and multiracial neighborhood in South Side Stockton, even setting up a recording studio in her home to support young musicians of color, one of whom was the son of longtime organizer Mattie Harrell. As she recalled to Maylei Blackwell, "Our neighbors had a whole band. They were seventeen, sixteen, fifteen years old . . . so I used to record their music for them and helped promote them." Continuing the neighborhood improvement work she had done as a high school student, Lola organized with other women in the community, including Mattie Harrell, to petition the City of Stockton for a park on the South Side. She remembers that families on the South Side "used to have to cross the street from like a major highway to go to the park. So all of us mothers from this side of the street we all had little houses and a bunch of kids. So [we] started . . . an organization and we started getting in on the talk, we went to city hall, we got petitions, we did all kinds of stuff."[43]

Lola de la Riva's willfulness was also exemplified on a more personal level. When her husband Louie's drinking and physical abuse became too much for her and her children, she did the unthinkable and walked away from the marriage after ten years. As she told Maylei Blackwell, "My husband used to kick my butt and I kept calling the cops because I didn't want to get hit anymore."[44] Though at the time Osa was unaware of the physical abuse her mother endured, she describes Lola's decision in retrospect as a kind of coming out: "She's like, you know, you're not going to hit me anymore. And I'm gonna, you know, I'll kill you. Okay, from here on out . . . this is it, you have a choice."[45] In her mid-twenties and newly single with three young children to support, Lola faced serious economic precarity: "I didn't have welfare or anything, I was on my own. I still had a house I had to pay for and a car."[46] She soon found a job that suited both her artistic sensibilities and her commitment to the community: teaching art to teenagers at Harlequin House Art Center, a sprawling compound on the South Side founded in 1959 by Maxine Lovejoy DalBen. Not unlike a contemporary maker space, Harlequin House had "over thirty rooms dedicated to studio space, art classes, framing, and other opportunities to learn and grow art practices."[47] It provided crucial training for many young artists of color in the 1960s, including the muralist Carlos Lopez, who credits DalBen with teaching him "many of the disciplines as a kid. In high school, I would do all the posters, big banners, the sets for the plays, and all that stuff."[48] Black artist Joseph Osborne also credits DalBen and Harlequin House with helping him to develop "an identity as to who I was as a creative person, as an artist."[49] Noting that his first paintings were created in art classes at Harlequin House when he was just nine years old, he praised DalBen for being "a pioneer endorsing racial equality for artists in San Joaquin County. She paved the way for people of color to have equal opportunities in the arts, as no other galleries in Stockton were open to them."[50]

For the next four years, Lola divided her time between Harlequin House, where she was employed seven months out of the year, and the local canneries, where she worked seasonally to supplement her income and pay for her children's Catholic school tuition. Her former husband, Louie, helped her with house payments; indeed, he remained supportive of Lola and the children, even after she remarried (to Anthony "Tony" Steinberg) and had twins, Laura and Timothy, in 1970. If the cannery work helped Lola pay the bills, her association with Harlequin House provided a hands-on education in the arts. In addition to teaching art classes, she also worked in the central offices, managing the exhibition space and ordering art supplies. Through her husband Louie's familial connections (his cousins were teachers in the migrant camps), Lola also developed "lesson plans for youth in the migrant camps," focusing on accessible and inexpensive art projects that parents could do with their children.[51] Though she was still in high school at the time, Osa designed a few of the covers for the bound curriculum. Lola also found time to take night school classes at Stockton Junior College, Delta College, and the University of the Pacific to further her education and develop her skills as an artist. She was eventually encouraged by DalBen and some of her art professors to exhibit her work in a one-woman show, *Color Me Wild*, at the Stockton main library (now called Cesar Chavez Central Library). According to Erendina Delgadillo and Osa Hidalgo de la Riva, "The show was intended to convey her life experiences and politics via her own acrylic paintings in service of demystifying political engagement and the voting process specifically."[52] Lola would draw upon all of these experiences when, in 1973, she launched her own art center in Long Beach: the Centro de Arte.

Lola's older sister Celia de la Riva Rubio (Aunt Sally) played an instrumental supportive role for the family during this period, especially as Osa and her sister Liz entered adolescence and began to identify as lesbians. Born in 1932, Aunt Sally was five years older than Lola, but unlike her younger sister, she had completed high school and gone on to college, earning a bachelor's degree and teaching credential in primary school education (with majors in English and history) in 1958 from San Francisco State College.[53] As a butch-identified lesbian of color in the 1950s, Celia de la Riva Rubio experienced both the pleasures of gay and lesbian nightlife in the Bay Area and also the dangers of the crackdown on queer social spaces that hit San Francisco during the postwar era.[54] She left an illuminating record of these experiences in *Lágrimas y Cadenas / Chains and Tears: Poesía y Prosa Feminista y del Ambiente / Gay Feminist Prose and Poetry*, a collection published in Morelia, Michoacán, in 1994. The essays and poems included in the volume document the social milieus and activist spaces that shaped de la Riva Rubio's lesbian feminist consciousness from the 1950s to the 1990s, providing many insights on how Chicana lesbians navigated the politics of silence and visibility in multiple movement spaces. For example, the section titled "Historia Lesbiana: 1950–1980s; In the Closet / En el Ropero" includes several poems and essays on lesbian and gay nightlife in Stockton and Oakland that significantly expand the queer social geographies explored by Nan Alamilla Boyd in *Wide-Open Town: A History of Queer San Francisco to 1965*. In one essay, de la Riva Rubio describes nightlife at the Point, "a little boat made into a bar on the West side outside of Stockton, California, situated on the edge of the [San Joaquin] river," that was a regular haunt of her gang. Conjuring the individuals, sights, and sounds of the Point, she remembers, "It was a great place because we could just be ourselves. Our kind of music, jokes, and loud laughter and plenty of beer and fun. Once in a while a fight, but not too often." She recalls meeting the bar's owners, "Annie, a big good looking blond and her chick," in San Francisco in 1954, during her first year as a student at San Francisco State, "when they owned Ann's 4-40 a Gay bar on Broadway near Finocchios."[55] De la Riva Rubio's reference to two of the most

FIGURE 6.2. *Cover (likely drawn by Lola de la Riva), Celia de la Riva Rubio,* Lágrimas y Cadenas / Chains and Tears: Poesía y Prosa Feminista y del Ambiente / Gay Feminist Prose and Poetry *(Colectivo Artístico Morelia, 1994). Osa Hidalgo de la Riva personal collection.*

well-known queer nightspots in San Francisco—Ann's 440 and Finocchio's (which, according to Alamilla Boyd, featured "gender-transgressive and racialized entertainments")—not only demonstrates that these social spaces served a diverse clientele but also expands the network of mid-century gay and lesbian nightclubs beyond urban centers like San Francisco, uncovering an underground social geography that includes working-class cities like Stockton.[56]

Notwithstanding her fond memories of gay nightlife at the Point, the Saddle (Stockton), and the Shady Lady and Chalet Club (both located in Oakland), the 1950s were also a dangerous time for butch-presenting lesbians like Celia de la Riva Rubio. Alamilla Boyd notes how in the postwar period, the lively gay and lesbian bar scene in San Francisco became a site of increased police repression: Laws were passed against same-sex couples dancing together or kissing in public, there were frequent raids on bars, and undercover police would often pose as gay men or lesbians to entrap bar patrons. As a butch-identified lesbian of color teaching at Lincoln Elementary School in Oakland's Chinatown in the late 1950s and early 1960s, Celia de la Riva Rubio was particularly vulnerable to the increased social scrutiny and police harassment that shaped lesbian society during the postwar period. As Alamilla Boyd notes, "Cold war ideologies that asserted the stability of rigidly defined gender roles and the containment of female sexuality to heterosexual marriage" projected an "uncontained or aggressive sexuality" on lesbian bodies, rendering them "a threat to the stability of heterosexual families." As women who "were not safely ensconced in families and producing children," lesbians like Celia de la Riva Rubio who outwardly challenged gendered norms ran the risk of police harassment, arrest, public humiliation, and economic vulnerability.[57]

In her preface to *Lágrimas y Cadenas*, de la Riva Rubio describes how this repressive social environment forced many "homophiles" to hide their sexuality and lead "two lives," the "so-called 'straight life'" and an undercover "gay life," with devastating consequences.

> I have had three friends that have committed suicide in the 50's and 60's with a gun. One shot herself in the mouth, the other shot herself in the stomach and the other shot herself in the heart. They had reached the breaking point because they couldn't face the paranoia caused by the tensions created by the stigma attached to homophiles, the shame it may have caused to their families and the fear of being found out by their neighbors or co-workers. This preoccupation and tension has caused needless friction with the partners of many homophiles. We must be wary every day

> of our lives, every waking minute of the day or night, how to act, what to say, where to go and with whom, how to dress, how to cut our hair, take care not to do nor say anything that may cause suspicion by the "normal people."[58]

In their Chicana por Mi Raza historia on Celia de la Riva Rubio, Erendina Delgadillo and Osa Hidalgo de la Riva argue that Aunt Sally's use of terms like "homophile" in *Lágrimas y Cadenas* was not just a linguistic throwback to an earlier time in gay and lesbian politics—when organizations like the Mattachine Society (founded in 1950) and the Daughters of Bilitis (founded in San Francisco in 1955) deployed such language in their efforts to fight social stigma. Rather, they argue, it demonstrates how Celia de la Riva Rubio "used and developed language, words, and phrases to more accurately represent her identity." Indeed, as de la Riva Rubio explains in the preface to her book, she and many of her friends preferred terms like "homophile" and "homocentric" because they signify "the love of another of the same sex" but "are not necessarily sexual in nature," unlike "homosexual," a term she does not use.[59] Rather than a deferral of lesbian sexuality, as the phrase "not necessarily sexual in nature" might suggest, Erendina Delgadillo and Osa Hidalgo de la Riva see in this positioning a refusal to reduce lesbian identity to sexuality, echoing (from the past) Osa's mujerista practitioner, a "woman-identified woman" who, in loving herself, "loves other women sexually and/or nonsexually."[60]

Although Celia de la Riva Rubio does not explicitly address her involvement with "homophile" organizations like the Daughters of Bilitis (which began as a secret society) in *Lágrimas y Cadenas*, Osa recalls that her aunt participated in lesbian events and social clubs in San Francisco "way back—and she was active—what impressed me the most . . . was how they'd have to enter these clubs soooooo secretive," using "knocks, codes, words, etc. just to enter the spaces!"[61] Liz Hidalgo de la Riva remembers that her Aunt Sally joined the Daughters of Bilitis early on, but that "she and her Hawaiian friends . . . were disgusted with the white domination of Bilitis so [they] started Hale Aikane," a short-lived organization that provided working-class lesbians of color a space to socialize.[62] Liz's recollection that her aunt, along with her Hawaiian friends, abandoned the Daughters of Bilitis raises some interesting questions about Celia de la Riva Rubio's involvement in lesbian of color communities in the 1950s, including Hale Aikane (about which very little is known), as do Osa's memories of spending time with Aunt Sally's Hawaiian friends at some of these gatherings (where she learned to play the ukulele). As intriguing as these memories are, we will likely never know the full extent of de la Riva Rubio's involvement in the formative years of the Daughters of Bilitis, because we can't ask her directly. On December 10, 2019, after retiring and moving to Morelia in the early 1990s, she "transitioned to the land of our ancestors . . . after a double mastectomy, cancer and bone-disease."[63] Nevertheless, Aunt Sally's experience with "homophile" organizing in the 1950s, inscribed tenuously in her nieces' memories, offers a provocative counterstory to a period of gay and lesbian organizing that has, more often than not, been remembered as primarily white and middle class.

Weaving together the many strands of Celia de la Riva Rubio's life as a "homophile," a "gay feminist," and a Chicana activist, *Lágrimas y Cadenas* also speaks to the silences around lesbian sexuality in the Chicano movement, healing the split produced in "diametrically exclusionary conceptualizations" of the Chicano struggle and gay liberation by centering the lived experience of a butch-identified lesbian who inhabited "these social markers at one and the same time."[64] In "Las Mujeres de la Riva," Erendina Delgadillo and Osa Hidalgo de la Riva foreground Celia de la Riva Rubio's work with Chicana/o youth in the 1960s and 1970s as "emblematic of the fourth Mujerista principle: Activism." They note that during this period, de la Riva Rubio "supported her students' protests, walkouts, and general activism," and that she was "beloved by her students (who called her 'Miss D') for creating new standards and teaching strategies that supported alternative learning styles."[65] A long-standing member of the Association of Mexican American Educators, an organization founded in 1965 to address educational inequality in California, de la Riva Rubio contributed to the development of several important social programs for Chicana/o youth in the East Bay in the 1970s, including the Aztlán Boxing Club (inspired by her father, Francisco Gabriel de la Riva, an amateur boxer who was known by the name Frankie Reeves) in 1977 and the Tiburcio Vasquez Health Center in southern Alameda County in 1971.[66]

In "An Activist and Feminist in the 1970s," an essay included in the section on Chicanas en el movimiento in *Lágrimas y Cadenas*, Celia de la Riva Rubio reflects on her thirty-five years as a teacher and counselor in the East Bay, where most of her students were working-class Latino and Black youths. During this period, she recalls, "I never hesitated to speak to any student, male or female about their sexual problems—or any problems that they may have had." Indeed, she and "a young Black teacher" were known as the "ones you could trust. We tried to give the students good counseling and advise [*sic*]. We helped in any way we could and spent many long hours after school with them."[67] Her work with students soon revealed the failures of a health system dominated by white practitioners who lacked the cultural sensitivity and linguistic competency to provide adequate services to the Raza community of Hayward. Indeed, it was a painful incident of medical racism she experienced when accompanying a young male student on a visit to the local "VD" clinic that ignited a passion for health justice in her community:

> I'll never forget the time a young bearded doctor came out after examining one of my students who was about sixteen years old. We waited three hours to see the doctor. As the young man sat leaning against me, the doctor shouted across the waiting room, "Yea, you've got it, come weekly to take the treatment with shots, and take these pills daily. And remember no sex for awhile, until you come out clean!" The young man and I walked out of the waiting room into the outer corridor while he cried quietly.[68]

Later that evening, at a hospital board meeting (she was one of two community members on the advisory board), Celia de la Riva Rubio "lit into the hospital director" and the other doctors on the board about the incident earlier that day, explaining that it was no wonder that "Raza was not utilizing the hospitals facilities, when we were treated so poorly. They preferred to go [to] the county hospital in Oakland some 40 miles away, where they were treated by many minority doctors, personnel and nurses with respect and dignity." That incident, "among many others," led Celia de la Riva Rubio and others in the community to demand that a Latino health clinic and mental health center be established to better serve their needs. Her work on this effort was considerable, involving several months of reading and taking notes on huge volumes of hospital studies, governmental reports, and building codes, lobbying the head of the county health system—an "old friend" who had been a school administrator in the school district where she had taught—and sharing her findings with "a Gringa lawyer" at the Chicano legal aid office, who agreed to help them make the case to local public health officials that "Raza clinics" were a critical need in a community that at the time was 25 percent Latina/o. In fact, Celia de la Riva Rubio emerged as a leader of this health equity struggle, earning the nickname El Terremoto (the Earthquake) because she "wasn't afraid to speak to any group, reporters, or on T.V. nor radio. I didn't give a crap whose toes I had to step on in order to bring in the much needed clinics." Eventually these organizing efforts were successful: "We were granted a Mental Health Clinic, and an outreach Health Clinic of the hospital. Facilities, such as buildings near the Chicano areas, Spanish speaking staff, secretaries, doctors and nurses."[69]

Despite the ultimate success of these advocacy efforts, Celia de la Riva Rubio admits in the essay that the only thing that "cloud[ed] the joy of helping my community, was that I could never let on that I was gay," an enforced silence that bracketed off a critical dimension of her identity. She notes that although "some people may have guessed . . . the subject was never broached. Perhaps they wanted to spare my feelings, or we were all just too damned busy to discuss who slept with whom."[70] As Erendina Delgadillo and Osa Hidalgo de la Riva observe in their historia of las mujeres de la Riva, "Like many other queer women of her generation, Aunt Sally had to strategically decide when and where" to identify as a lesbian, an imposition of silence structured by the conceptualization of homosexuality as a threat to the Chicano community. Aunt Sally's acceptance of this imposed silence about her sexuality illustrates Yolanda Chávez Leyva's observation that the community, like the family, has been a profoundly paradoxical site for Latina lesbians, in that it promises a sense of belonging and connection, "while at the same time acting as an agent of control." This "desire and need to remain within the community," she argues, raises a number of critical questions for historians of Latina lesbian experience: "What compromises have Latina lesbians made in order to remain within their communities? In what ways have Latina lesbians created forms of resistance to that silence? And how has silence allowed lesbians to maintain a place within their communities? Why was it possible, in the first place, to continue 'not talking about it'?"[71] The "gay feminist prose and poetry" in Celia de la Riva Rubio's *Lágrimas y Cadenas* answers some of these questions from the perspective of a butch-identified Chicana lesbian who endured both the state repression of "homophiles" in the postwar period and the silences that haunted her work in the community. Indeed, the explicitly lesbian poetry she included in the collection seems to offer a subtle counterstory to Celia de la Riva's accounts of her double life as a Chicana lesbian activist and feminist in the movement years.

A particularly illuminating example of this intertextual intervention can be found in two poems in the book's section on lesbian life before the 1990s, "In the Closet / En el Ropero," which follows the section on de la Riva Rubio's feminist activism in the Chicano movement. Dedicated to the lesbian poet and artist Harriette Frances, the poems "To Harriette Frances" and "To Sappho '71" were likely written the same year that de la Riva Rubio devoted so much of her time and energy to fighting for Raza health services in Hayward, as they appear to have been inspired by the publication of *Sappho '71*, Frances's collection of poetry and drawings (a selection of which was republished in *The Ladder* in 1971). In her poem "To Sappho '71," de la Riva Rubio engages directly with one particular poem, "Not Who I Am," a first-person meditation on the enforced silence around lesbian sexuality among Frances's "nine-to-five friends," who insist on a "deception" from her and want "only the / Myth of me / And not who I am." Highlighting the uncompensated affective labor of silence—which produces a "hidden self" that Frances must carry, "Heavy, from nine to five"—Frances closes the poem in the safety and comfort of her lover's "six-o-clock arms," where, in her words, "I can / Lay my self down."[72] In her response to this poem, de la Riva Rubio praises Frances for her honest depiction of the double life lesbians were forced to live in the 1960s:

> Harriet, man,
> you told it like it is,
> that's really SHOW-BIZ!
> "Not Who I Am."
> Only we understand,
> only we give a damn.
> Keep laying those
> heavy words on us.
> Keep on laying,
> and laying,
> and laying.[73]

I cannot help but read "To Sappho '71" as a subversive intertextual rejoinder to de la Riva Rubio's depressing account of the imposed silences that clouded the joy of her movement work, as she recalled in "An Activist and Feminist in the 1970s." Indeed, the essay and the poem work together in the collection, linking two movement worlds and their discourses. Through this sly intertextual narrative movida, de la Riva Rubio brings the divided parts of herself (Coyolxauhqui) back together again, "healing the split," in Anzaldúa's words, between her activist work and her sexuality.[74]

And yet, even at the height of her activism in the 1970s, Celia de la Riva Rubio's unmarried status and butch presentation were always there on the surface, waiting to be read by those who needed it most. In one of the rare archival traces of her presence in Chicano movement spaces—a prematch award ceremony for the Aztlán Boxing Club videotaped by Juan Espinoza in 1977 for the cable access show *Barrio Expressions*—"Miss Sally de la Riva" was recognized by the president of the club, Bob Guerra, as "a person [who] has done a tremendous job in the community, the schools, throughout everywhere she's been," and he presented her with a plaque adorned with a photograph of Rodolfo "Corky" Gonzales and an inscribed quote from his epic Chicano poem, *I Am Joaquin*: "Tengo que pelear y ganar esta lucha para mis hijos, y ellos deben saber de mi. Quién soy yo."[75] As she made her way up the steps to the ring, suited for the occasion in practical pants and an oversized vest, "Miss Sally de la Riva" casually ignored the outstretched hand of one of the Chicano male dignitaries and climbed forcefully through the ropes on her own. Stepping into the center of the boxing ring to receive her award, she presented viewers across the Bay Area with a Chicana feminist community leader in all of her butch splendor, stating (without words) "quién soy yo" (who I am).

In an oral history interview with me, Osa Hidalgo de la Riva reflected on the generational differences that shaped how the mujeres de la Riva lived out their Chicana lesbian sexuality: "I realized that Sally was one generation with her language and ways. Then Liz and I were another one."[76] Osa's mother, Lola de la Riva, came out later in life—in the 1980s—in the midst of an explosion of lesbian of color cultural production in which Osa and Liz played a key role. Regardless of these differences, when Osa came out in 1970 (while still in high school), some of the clandestine aspects of lesbian social life were still very much a reality in places like Stockton. In an unpublished manuscript, "Royal Eagle Bear Is Off and Running," she vividly recalls attending her "first lesbiana house party" with a friend from school, Kathy, who would later become her lover. The party was

> mainly comprised of community college dyke jocks. some femmes who were already committed, and a handful of other butches on the prowl. the radical 60's had just ended and the new decade was ours to initiate. in a strange sort of way, in retrospect, i guess not too much had changed from the house parties, somewhat clandestine in conservative *stocktone*, in repressive u.s. of a., in an otherwise patriarchal planet, we *lesbianas*, queers, dykes, gay womyn had to find a space and time to breathe, make new relationships, solidify community however dysfunctional it could have been labeled by others outside of our sensuous and hot universe.[77]

As she watched two women slow dance in front of her, Osa sat transfixed on the sofa, holding on to the guitar she had brought along "for dear queer life." Eventually the pair moved from dancing to "making out. big big big time. wow. i could nearly feel it. and they knew it, and performed their sensuality with the might of the ages"—an experience that exposed her to "a slice of reality and the gay lifestyle i knew that i wanted. i had in fact dreamt of womyn loving me for nearly a year now, nearly every single nite. lesbiana teenage wet dreams i guess."[78] She stayed with Kathy that night, sneaking back home in the early morning just in time for a school trip to the University of California, Riverside.[79] Shortly after this initiation—which, in Osa's words, "would take me to some new world that i was ready and willing to travel to"[80]—she came out to her younger sister Liz: "I was fifteen and she was eleven. Her response was, 'So what, I've been gay!'"[81]

Notwithstanding the mujerista ethos embodied in Grandma Angie's inclusive vision of familia, in Aunt Sally's gay feminist activism, and in Lola's willfulness, when Osa told her mother she was gay, her response was not quite as sanguine as Liz's had been. Lola, who had recently had twins Laura and Tim with her second husband, Tony Steinberg, took Osa straight to Aunt Sally's house in Hayward so Celia de la Riva Rubio could share her own difficult experiences as a Chicana lesbian who was forced to hide a fundamental part of her life. "Mija, if it was up to me," Aunt Sally advised, "I would not want you to be gay because it is such a hard lifestyle." Osa remembers that Aunt Sally even warned her not to "ever, ever put in writing that you are gay" (a position she clearly no longer held in 1994, when she published her gay feminist collection, *Lágrimas y Cadenas*). Notwithstanding this admonition, Osa recalls that at the end of her "scared straight" talk, Aunt Sally beckoned her in for a hug with the words, "Come here, nephew."[82] Osa moved in with her girlfriend after graduation from high school, and they set up a home in Kathy's grandmother's house in Stockton, which was unoccupied at the time. Lola soon came to accept their relationship, even dropping her baby twins off at the home Osa shared with her girlfriend for a few hours each day. Osa remembers those days with great fondness: "i would play with them, feed them, change them, clean the house before my partner came home from work at the stationery store. basically, at that point, i was practicing as a pseudo-stay-at-home mom of sorts."[83]

## WE ARE FAMILY: QUEER HOMEMAKING IN THE HEART OF AZTLÁN

In the late summer of 1972, just a few weeks before the fall semester was set to start, Osa Hidalgo de la Riva and her partner Kathy received notice of their admission (with full financial support) to California State University, Long Beach. As Osa recalls, they packed up their household in "record-breaking time" and moved to Los Angeles, where they encountered a far different lesbian scene than what they had experienced in "conservative *stocktone*."[84] Indeed, the city was in the midst of what Yolanda Retter Vargas has called a "lesbian feminist decade," when "lesbian institution-building in Los Angeles proceeded at a rapid, exuberant pace." Groups like Gay Women's Liberation (renamed Lesbian Feminists in 1971) and the Los Angeles chapter of the Daughters of Bilitis (newly radicalized by the influx of young militant women like Jeanne Córdova joining its ranks) established short-lived independent community centers like the Gay Women's Service Center (1970–1972), organized conferences like the West Coast Lesbian Conference (1971 and 1973), and published magazines and newsletters like *Lesbian Tide* (1971–1980), a publication that started as a Daughters of Bilitis newsletter edited by Jeanne Córdova.[85] A growing lesbian cultural arts scene also flourished in the city, with poetry readings and musical performances supported by new coffeehouses and bookstores. Encountering this abundance of lesbian organizing, culture, and social life, Osa meditated on the experience of living in the city:

> You can be.
> You can see all the others being. Each arm, each finger, each vein completely being.
> In the city, there are no reasons.
> The dykes, the fairies, the drag queens, the rowdy butches in holey jeans are being. Are be-ing. Being without reason. Floating. Flying high on a synthetic peace cloud.[86]

As exhilarating as this milieu of lesbian "be-ing" might have been for a young Chicana from Stockton, by the time she arrived in Los Angeles in 1972, the lesbian community was growing increasingly divided over whether or not to organize with gay men, over debates about "sexual style" (butch/femme roles), and over "the white lesbian community's indifference to racism"—issues that put a significant drag on institution building in the early 1970s.[87] As they had for her Aunt Sally a generation before, such contradictions would shape Osa's relationship to emergent lesbian feminist formations in Los Angeles, pushing her toward the development of alternative spaces for queer women of color.

Los Angeles—and California State University, Long Beach, in particular—had also been a center of Chicana/o student organizing, where in the late 1960s and early 1970s, Anna NietoGomez and Corinne Sánchez, among other Chicanas, had challenged male hierarchies in both UMAS/MEChA and Chicano studies. By the time Osa arrived on campus, however, NietoGomez had moved on to the Chicano Studies Department at California State University, Northridge, where she was focused on developing the curriculum on La Chicana. Las Hijas de Cuauhtémoc had moved off campus as well (to Hawaiian Gardens, just to the east of Long Beach), and its members were actively working on the first volume of *Encuentro Femenil* (1973). As at other colleges and universities, the high tide of Chicano student mobilizations had passed as a new generation of scholars, students, and staff focused on efforts to institutionalize Chicano studies.[88] Initially intending to study math at Long Beach State, Osa soon realized that despite a "strong stubborn streak still trying consciously to fight the power that lured [her] to play with and visit the muses often," she really liked "drawing, painting, singing, dancing, photography, poetry, playing instruments." She combined these interests with practical training, majoring in psychology, with a concentration in women's studies and industrial arts (drafting).[89]

Her mother, Lola, followed a year later—with fifteen-year-old Liz and the twins in tow—after being recruited to Long Beach State by a friend of her older brother who had become the assistant director of financial aid at the university. Eager to develop her artistic practice (and her network) in the emerging Chicano art scene in Los Angeles, Lola enrolled as a Mexican American studies and fine arts major. Recently divorced from her second husband, Tony, Lola was fortunately still on good terms with Louie, her first husband, who sold the family home in Stockton so she could purchase a property on Tenth Street, a busy commercial corridor in Long Beach. The home they purchased had once been owned by a doctor and had an additional building behind the main house that had served as his clinic. Just a few miles from Long Beach State and close to Centro de la Raza, the East Long Beach neighborhood center that offered a variety of social services and a preschool for the twins (La Escuelita), the house on Tenth would soon become a base of operations for las mujeres de la Riva, a place where they would live together and collectively pursue their educational, artistic, and political visions.

Lola launched the Centro de Arte de Long Beach from her home in 1973, transforming the large front room of the main house into an art room and opening it up to the community. Soon, the de la Riva household became an informal gathering place for young artists, poets, musicians, and activists. As Lola explained to Yolanda Retter Vargas in a 1997 interview, once she started getting involved in the flourishing Chicana/o artist and activist scene in Los Angeles, it seemed only logical for her to transform her family home into an informal community arts center: "I was the only one that had a home, everyone else [was in] transit." Moreover, as a woman in her mid-thirties, she was older than most of the artists in her milieu, and she had serious experience as a community organizer and arts administrator: "I was an elder already to them."[90] A fundraising letter for the centro (likely produced after 1976) describes how the "atmosphere" Lola nurtured in her home "was conducive to creative thinking and seemed to act as a catalyst whereby these creative individuals came together to identify their problems and sought practical solutions to them."[91] Indeed, as Lola recalled to Retter Vargas, "Everybody kept telling me, turn it into a centro, because it was like, all my money, my phone, all these people in and out my home, you see? . . . So that's how we, I ended up founding a Chicano art center called Centro de Arte." In short order, she, and the rest of the de la Riva family, converted the "little cottage out in the back" into a studio space where they could teach workshops on mask making, clay sculpture, painting, and linoleum block printing. An attached two-car garage became a gallery, and the yard between the house and the cottage was supplied with an assortment of tables and chairs so they could "do all the arts outside. We had it going."[92]

Transforming the family home into a community arts center—like Stockton's Harlequin House but on a smaller and more intimate scale—represented a natural progression in Lola's creative praxis, which had been shaped by her artistic upbringing and her experiences as a young mother in Stockton, where she had cultivated an open cultural space in her home, with books, art supplies, and recording equipment available not just to her children but to all the youths in her multiracial/multicultural neighborhood. Indeed, Osa described the establishment of the centro as the product of a "whole process of progression" that started from "the most basic . . . there's a . . . can of water and a little can of paint brushes and some stuff in a little corner there."[93] From its rasquache beginnings in 1973, to its incorporation as an independent nonprofit in 1976, to when it finally ceased operations in 1984, Lola's Centro de Arte offered a wide array of opportunities for the Long Beach community to fully experience Chicana/o art and creativity in all its forms. It had a library filled with art books collected by Lola and donated by visitors, and it offered "information and referral" services on the "state of third world art and artists." Working collectively, the mujeres de la Riva organized "third world" poetry readings (Doris Davenport, Mitsuye Yamada), musical performances (the Chicano band Tierra and the lesbian musicians Margie Adams and Vickie Allen), art exhibitions, and teatro. They taught art classes to neighborhood youths and published newsletters and poetry books, all from the family home. Osa remembers it as a time of intense creativity in Los Angeles: "I remember that feeling of a Chicano renaissance. I remember a lot of the artists painting, musicians making música, dancers, teatro, healers, lovers, writers, photographers, and so on surging with the creative spirit, doing their thing, especially at my mom's Centro de Arte. She offered her home base truly as all of our home. Mi casa es su casa."[94] Indeed, Mama Lola, as she came to be known, was "very generous with her home and familia," opening her doors at all hours for artists, academics, and organizers to exchange ideas, grab a meal, and even stay the night. Artists like Yreina Cervántez, Linda Vallejo, and Leo Limón were regular visitors, as was Anna NietoGomez, who brought copies of the *Hijas*

FIGURE 6.3. *Osa Hidalgo de la Riva, logo for Centro de Arte. The design incorporates elements of the mandala as well as Mesoamerican, Buddhist, and personal symbols. The four eldest de la Riva siblings are depicted as animal figures in the corners of the mandala. Osa Hidalgo de la Riva personal collection.*

*de Cuauhtémoc* newspaper to add to the Centro de Arte's library, and the filmmaker Sylvia Morales, whose work Osa would later explore in her University of Southern California dissertation, "Mujerista Moviemaking: Chicana Filmmakers Sylvia Morales and Lourdes Portillo."[95]

Each member of la familia de la Riva contributed in some way to the success of the Centro de Arte. Lola's son Louie, an artist who was in the military and stationed nearby, helped transform the physical space with art and murals, and he later illustrated one of Osa's poetry books, *With Poems as Guns* (published by the Mextiza Colectiva in 1978). Osa created the logo for Centro de Arte, a mandala with African, Asian, and Indigenous themes and four animal spirits at the corners representing Lola, Osa, Liz, and Louie. Lola used her expertise as a working artist and teacher to develop the art classes, and she drew upon the networks she had cultivated in Los Angeles and beyond to curate "art exhibitions of third world women." According to Lola, Osa and Liz organized "the literary part" of centro activities, which included poetry readings, writing workshops, and publication projects that centered lesbian of color experience.[96] Working together as both a familia and a colectiva, the mujeres de la Riva nurtured a cultural space in their home that, according to Osa, "crossed many boundaries."

> When we organized events like a poetry reading or a Chicano art show, we would always have family and a large mix of people. Our community crossed many boundaries. For some events, the audience would be more Chicano and straight. At others, it would be maybe more white women or lesbians of color, but we would still have a mix of family and friends coming together. At that time, I think it was important to bring everyone together. . . . What was important to me was to consciously want to read my lesbiana gay stuff to the Chicano groups, and I would read my pieces about being a dark brown woman to the white women's and gay groups, so I would always mix it up to make them feel a little uncomfortable. I felt that all those communities, identities, and sensibilities and culturas were part of me, so I didn't mind being in your face about it at that time.[97]

In her interview with Retter Vargas, Lola suggested that one reason "all these artists started coming to [her] home" was because it was the "only Latino identified, like Chicana lesbian centro, see?"[98] While Centro de Arte did not explicitly define itself as a lesbian centro in its brochures and promotional materials, it was run by woman-identified Chicanas (Lola, Osa, and Liz), most of whom were lesbians. Moreover, in addition to being a Chicano art center, Centro de Arte was also the primary base of operations for the Mextiza Colectiva, a Chicana lesbian / woman of color group that was initially organized by the mujeres de la Riva (Lola, Liz, and Osa) but eventually grew to include other woman-identified Chicanas/Latinas like Barbara Garcia, Yvette Flores, and Rosa Maria Zayas (a former Young Lord), who were also interested in developing a space where lesbians and women of color could "talk, be together, and work."[99]

It is impossible to disentangle the development of Centro de Arte from the history of the Mextiza Colectiva, as the two formations operated interchangeably from the mid- to late 1970s. In her unpublished 1983 essay "Transformation–Or–The Philosophy of El Centro de Arte: A Family Affair," Osa explains that the "nucleus" of Centro de Arte was the Mextiza

Colectiva. According to her sister Liz, the group started as an organizing project in Stockton, where they primarily worked on farmworker support and neighborhood improvement projects.[100] After the family's move to Long Beach—where they encountered a cultural milieu shaped by the political and cultural discourses of the Chicano movement, the women's movement, and gay liberation—the Mextiza Colectiva began to identify more explicitly as a lesbian and women of color group and turned increasingly to cultural production as its primary means of organizing. Forming the colectiva, Osa recalls, "allowed us to be ourselves, and since in many spaces we were discriminated against, often our work was separate. We were involved in the women's circles, and that was white and middle class. The Raza organizations were male-centric, heterosexist and sometimes we experienced homophobia from our straight Chicana sisters. The gay liberation movement was primarily white."[101] Through the Mextiza Colectiva, Osa and her sister Liz organized a number of projects at Centro de Arte from 1973 to 1978 that brought together the "communities, identities, and sensibilities and culturas" that were central to their experience as Chicana lesbians. To support these efforts, they launched Centro de Arte Press in 1973, out of "a little studio closet space, converted into our office," in the family home. Although Osa was just beginning her second year in psychology at Long Beach State and Liz was still a student at Wilson High School in Long Beach, they were determined to produce an outlet for lesbian writing on their own terms: "We were anti-publishing because publishing in our minds, at the time of the early 1970's, belonged to the patriarch. We didn't believe there would be a press that would allow us uncensored freedom of expression, and space to be ourselves." Their first publication was a "little homemade zine/rag," *Mama Sappho* (1973), which they delivered to friends and family in Stockton via motorcycle.[102] They followed *Mama Sappho* with another publication in the spring of 1974, this time with the less lesbian-coded title of *The People's Press*, a decision that appears to have been partly motivated by complaints from some of the readers of their first publication. In a letter to the editor, Charlee Spurgeon and Phyllis Moore (both of whom are listed in the same volume as members of *The People's Press* editorial team) argued that both the name *Mama Sappho* and the reference to its readers as "dear sisters" in its opening pages suggested that the publication was not for men: "We need a newspaper that will unite all 'Gay' people, not just 'Gay' women."[103]

*The People's Press* is a remarkable document in many ways. Not only is it one of the earliest publications produced by Chicana lesbians, but it also includes the work of gay and lesbian writers from Stockton, some of whom, like Liz, were still in high school. Indeed, like the poetry readings they

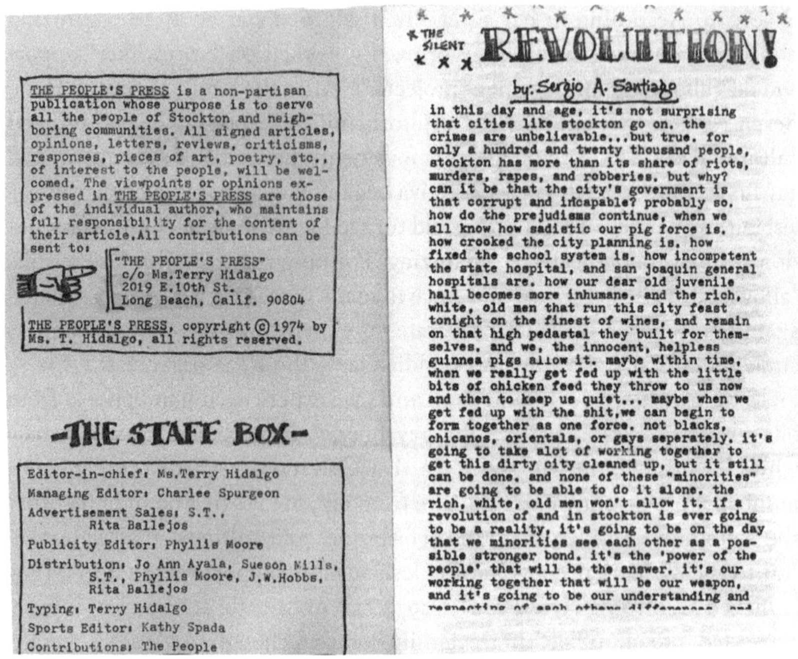

THE PEOPLE'S PRESS is a non-partisan publication whose purpose is to serve all the people of Stockton and neighboring communities. All signed articles, opinions, letters, reviews, criticisms, responses, pieces of art, poetry, etc., of interest to the people, will be welcomed. The viewpoints or opinions expressed in THE PEOPLE'S PRESS are those of the individual author, who maintains full responsibility for the content of their article. All contributions can be sent to:

"THE PEOPLE'S PRESS"
c/o Ms.Terry Hidalgo
2019 E.10th St.
Long Beach, Calif. 90804

THE PEOPLE'S PRESS, copyright © 1974 by Ms. T. Hidalgo, all rights reserved.

-THE STAFF BOX-

Editor-in-chief: Ms.Terry Hidalgo
Managing Editor: Charlee Spurgeon
Advertisement Sales: S.T., Rita Ballejos
Publicity Editor: Phyllis Moore
Distribution: Jo Ann Ayala, Sueson Mills, S.T., Phyllis Moore, J.W.Hobbs, Rita Ballejos
Typing: Terry Hidalgo
Sports Editor: Kathy Spada
Contributions: The People

THE SILENT REVOLUTION!

by: Sergio A. Santiago

in this day and age, it's not surprising that cities like stockton go on. the crimes are unbelievable...but true. for only a hundred and twenty thousand people, stockton has more than its share of riots, murders, rapes, and robberies. but why? can it be that the city's government is that corrupt and incapable? probably so. how do the prejudisms continue, when we all know how sadistic our pig force is. how crooked the city planning is. how fixed the school system is. how incompetent the state hospital, and san joaquin general hospitals are. how our dear old juvenile hall becomes more inhumane. and the rich, white, old men that run this city feast tonight on the finest of wines, and remain on that high pedastal they built for themselves. and we, the innocent, helpless guinnea pigs allow it. maybe within time, when we really get fed up with the little bits of chicken feed they throw to us now and then to keep us quiet... maybe when we get fed up with the shit, we can begin to form together as one force. not blacks, chicanos, orientals, or gays seperately. it's going to take alot of working together to get this dirty city cleaned up, but it still can be done. and none of these "minorities" are going to be able to do it alone. the rich, white, old men won't allow it. if a revolution of and in stockton is ever going to be a reality, it's going to be on the day that we minorities see each other as a possible stronger bond. it's the 'power of the people' that will be the answer. it's our working together that will be our weapon, and it's going to be our understanding and

FIGURE 6.4. *Two-page spread,* The People's Press, *produced by Mextiza Colectiva, 1973. Osa Hidalgo de la Riva personal collection.*

regularly organized at the Centro de Arte, the newsletter was a way to bridge the multiple worlds that the mujeres de la Riva traversed in the 1970s. In "Visions of Utopia While Living in Occupied Aztlán," Osa explains that "the queer situation in Stockton was so radically different than say LA, I mean it was totally the opposite. We had more of a rural situation and in LA you had an urban situation. I think that the idea was to be more inclusive of whoever wanted to be in this little gay rag."[104] Osa recalls that she and Liz would ride "motorcycles from Long Beach all the way to Stockton" to "get our articles, 'cause we didn't want to leave our friends too, you know? . . . It [was] very oppressive."[105]

The spring 1974 issue of *The People's Press* included opinion pieces, poetry that celebrated same-sex desire, reports and announcements about various gay and lesbian activities (like a women's football league) in Stockton, and advertisements for gay-friendly bars and flower shops. Several contributors called attention to issues that echoed those raised in other Chicana feminist publications during the period, including the farmworker struggle and the case of Inez García, a Latina single mother who was on trial for killing one of the men who had raped her.[106] As the author of the article pointedly observed, García's case was a matter of import to lesbians because of how prosecutors dwelled on her "background of having lived around lesbian women with an illegitimate son" in order to raise questions about "her fitness as a witness, rather than around rape as an issue."[107] Other articles focused on the political realities of Stockton. For example, in "The Silent Revolution," Sergio A. Santiago highlighted the need for unity among the multicultural community (gay and straight) of Stockton to challenge structural inequality in the city:

> Maybe when we get fed up with the shit, we can begin to form together as one force, not blacks, chicanos, orientals, or gays separately. It's going to take alot [*sic*] of working together to get this dirty city cleaned up, but it still can be done. And none of these "minorities" are going to be able to do it alone. The rich, white, old men won't allow it. If a revolution of and in stockton is ever going to be a reality, it's going to be on the day that we minorities see each other as a possible stronger bond. It's the "power of the people" that will be the answer. It's our working together that will be our weapon, and it's going to be our understanding and respecting each other's differences.[108]

Such calls for unity among many different "minority" constituencies in Stockton were a prominent feature of *The People's Press*, suggesting important regional differences between places like Los Angeles, where, according to Retter Vargas, lesbian political and social formations were increasingly moving away from the "Gay Liberation movement and the heterosexual feminist movement, and [beginning] to organize lesbian-focused centers and support groups," and Stockton, where queer and working-class communities of color faced crosscutting oppressions that pushed the question of "liberation" beyond the single issue of sexuality. As Retter Vargas notes, while "white lesbians" in Los Angeles and other urban centers had largely separated from the "gay male movement due to sexism" by the mid-1970s, lesbians of color, like the women in the Mextiza Colectiva, "found it more difficult to separate from ethnic co-gender movements and groups because of their ontological location 'at the intersection of oppressions.'"[109]

While *Mama Sappho* and *The People's Press* eventually built up a "subscription of about 250 from across California and even in other places in the Southwest," *The People's Press* appears to have ceased publication after 1975, when the Mextiza Colectiva turned to publishing projects that were more explicitly focused on lesbians and women of color.[110] This shift in focus was partly in response to the sisters' experiences at California State University,

Long Beach. Osa explains that by 1975, both she and Liz were working on their degrees in psychology and women's studies, "but the problem was that all the women's studies faculty were primarily white. We would ask, 'What about the Chicanas and the women of color?' and they said, 'If you are interested in that you have to go organize that yourself.'"[111] Like the Chicanas who had challenged an exclusively male curriculum in Chicano studies at Long Beach and elsewhere a few years earlier, the Mextiza Colectiva cultivated a "third space" (sitio) for woman-identified women (which included lesbians, women of color, and straight women) to develop their ideas and "languages" (lenguas) within an "antagonistic society" by hosting consciousness-raising meetings, workshops, and poetry readings, and by launching publication projects.[112] In 1975, the colectiva published *Women's Poetry: A Feminist Anthology of Writings and Artwork by Women from California State University at Long Beach*, a collection of works by faculty and students in women's studies, which was edited by Osa and featured a cover designed and illustrated by her mother. A year later, in 1976, they published Liz's first book of poetry, *Phoenix*, which included poetry about lesbian love and sensuality, spirituality, and politics, and a selection of poems ("A Young Person's Private Poetry") that she had produced from the ages of twelve to sixteen. In her introduction to the book, Liz explained, "Phoenix is a fire. She is an expression of myself as: Mextiza, Child, Woman, Fighter, Student, Therapist, Lover, Poet, Thug, and Spirit. PHOENIX is a picture of experience through these eyes."[113] Signaling the new direction of the Mextiza Colectiva, the book's preface described the group as "an independent collective functioning on a non-profit basis for the advancement of arte Mextiza as well as arte of all women of color," a description that shows how the colectiva's mission was aligned with that of Centro de Arte.[114] In 1976—in response to the US bicentennial—the Mextiza Colectiva organized a cross-country "Chicana lesbiana poetry tour," visiting "many women's centers, coffee houses, bookstores and battered women's shelters throughout California and the Southwest." Osa remembers that she and Liz "read our lesbiana flor y canto poetry, and that was before *This Bridge Called My Back*, so it was nice to see when *This Bridge* came out because it was like, 'Wow! This is right up our alley!'"[115] Two other books of Chicana lesbian poetry followed in 1978: Liz's *Primitive and Proud* (the title of which would inspire Osa's short film of the same name in 1992) and Osa's *With Poems as Guns*, which included detailed pen-and-ink drawings by her brother Louie.

By the late 1970s, Mextiza Colectiva's work at the Centro de Arte began to taper off. In 1977, Liz, Osa, and Rosa Maria Zayas moved to Santa Cruz, where they set up a collective home with Zayas's five children (the Branciforte House). Osa continued on at the Centro de Arte as its assistant

FIGURE 6.5. *Cover, Liz Hidalgo de la Riva,* Phoenix *(Centro de Arte Press, 1976). Osa Hidalgo de la Riva personal collection.*

director, helping her mother with the many grant applications they had to manage as a newly incorporated nonprofit and occasionally teaching classes on third world women's literature out of the centro as part of Long Beach State's continuing education program. While the Centro de Arte continued operations until 1984, the transition from a largely grassroots, family-run space to an incorporated nonprofit was difficult for Lola to manage, and it was especially challenging with her primary collaborators in the Mextiza Colectiva living 350 miles away. She nevertheless labored to establish her centro as a legitimate art center on par with other centers in Los Angeles, such as Self Help Graphics and Art (1970–) and Centro de Arte Público (1977–1981).[116] She became a Comprehensive Employment and Training Act artist in residence, mentored summer interns through the summer youth education program, and even received funding from the Long Beach Parks and Recreation Department. In 1976, she joined the board of directors for the Concilio de Arte Popular, a statewide organizational network of Chicana/o and Latina/o artists and art centers, and she even organized a three-day conference in Long Beach for the concilio, attended by "artists from all over the United States, I mean, troupes like danzantes and everything."[117] But with the promise of greater institutional visibility and legitimacy came mission creep, competition for resources, and increased oversight from a heteropatriarchal and still mostly white nonprofit system. As Osa recalled to Retter Vargas, "It was hard to see that transition from being more of a real community, [a] home-based centro [by the] freeway . . . and then having that, you know, the official stuff happening. And then at that time too, I think there was a lot of scrutiny, anyway, with these centros, period."[118]

In her 1983 essay "Transformation–Or–The Philosophy of El Centro de Arte: A Family Affair," written for a graduate seminar taught by Donna Haraway in the history of consciousness program at the University of California, Santa Cruz, Osa explains how the centro, the family, and the Mextiza Colectiva were intimately intertwined as utopian projects. The essay takes an experimental form, presenting a compendium of poetry, theoretical explication, philosophical musings, and archival documents, in an effort to "explain, unravel, paint feelings and beliefs within, of clarity and truth" regarding the centro's approach to seeding creativity in an underserved community.[119] Osa's preface—written as a "grassroots letter" to her "hermanita" Laura, who was thirteen at the time—frames the essay as an act of memory keeping rather than simply a scholarly exercise, an effort to pass down this mujerista ancestral knowledge to a younger generation: "You may, in time, come to ask . . . why was that thing called the Centro de Arte so important to your family? Why did we struggle so hard in the face of poverty to share with so many visitors and strangers? Why did your mother, brother, and sisters open their home so?" Osa's essay answers these imagined questions, offering an origin story of how

> [A] familia in the literal sense became a mergence of an extend[ed] family that led into the community that led into society, that may lead beyond

> yet. Mextiza Colectiva was the original nucleus of the group that had a common goal, interest and experience . . . the advancement of women of color. Pride is defined as the justifiable self-respect, and self-esteem is to set a high value on one self. The members of Mextiza Colectiva did this for themselves at first and then for each other in the world they were to create.[120]

Centro de Arte, the utopian space that Lola, Osa, Liz, and the other woman-identified women in the Mextiza Colectiva labored to collectively create, redefined both the home and la familia as sitios where a broad cross section of community could come together and develop new lenguas through acts of literature, art, and self-creation:

> Welfare mothers and children, young third world lesbians, older middle class wives, politicos, comadres, sisters and brothers, there were artists of all shapes and sizes and colors, there were neighbors and social prisoners of war, there were generals and nuns . . . believe the dynamics, it was powerful within such an open and warm room. Bikers, hypes, students and dreamers, they all came.[121]

Thinning the lines between family and community, private and public space, artist and nonartist, queer and straight, the Centro de Arte nurtured an inclusive vision of familia—both nuclear and extended—that not only revised the spaces and subjects of creative praxis in the Chicano movement but also rescripted nationalist conceptions of la familia de la raza.

Indeed, while Lola's Centro de Arte reflected the communitarian values of Chicano arts projects in Los Angeles and beyond, particularly the idea that everyone is an artist, it also departed from the norm in important ways. The only woman-identified Chicana-led centro in the city, it centered a third world and feminist vision of the arts rather than one focused on only the Chicano/Latino community. Moreover, through its cross-pollination with the Mextiza Colectiva (the centro's organizational nucleus), it provided a space for the articulation of a lesbian of color feminist perspective within the "Chicano renaissance." Finally, as a community arts center that was also a family home, Centro de Arte transgressed the spatial and conceptual boundaries between the public domain of art and politics and the private domain of la familia. While enlisting the "total family" in political work was a central feature of the Chicano movement, from the Raza Unida Party in Texas to the Crusade for Justice in Colorado, the queer matrilineal legacy that informed the creative praxis of Lola's Centro de Arte produced a much more inclusive vision of la familia de la raza than the discourse of "political familism" typically allowed. If, as Richard T. Rodríguez has argued, the "political familism advocated by men inevitably reproduced a Chicano communitarian paradigm in which the heterosexual male, father, and husband were placed at the center of movement discourse," then Lola de la Riva's woman-headed queer household directly challenged both private and public conceptualizations of la familia de la raza.[122] In placing women, and particularly lesbians, at the center of movement discourse, Centro de Arte and the mujeres de la Riva nurtured a queer vision of political familism that held the potential to significantly reshape the conditions and possibilities of political discourse in the 1970s, even as they set the stage for future Chicana lesbiana reconfigurations of the family. Indeed, Osa would apply the lessons she learned from this "microcosmic model of a utopia" as she moved from poetry to her mujerista moviemaking in the late 1980s.[123]

While Osa Hidalgo de la Riva has been rightly recognized for the innovative and experimental films she produced in the 1990s and 2000s, including *The Olmeca Rap* (1990), *Primitive and Proud* (1992), *Marginal Eyes: Mujeria Fantasy #1* (2005), and *Me and Mr. Mauri* (2020), much less is known about how the mujerista aesthetics and praxis that she deployed in her film work were shaped by both a queer matrilineal legacy of woman-identified women and the cultural politics of the 1970s. Indeed, her mujerista moviemaking aesthetics and praxis re-create the "home" vibe of Centro de Arte, a woman-identified matrilineal space where "familia is inclusive of all peoples, ages, religions, colors, abilities, classes, genders, and sexualities"; where "teaching others and including our communities in the production process" is seen as essential; and where "taking risks, being outlaws to create change and transformations for healthy beings" was the ultimate goal.[124]

## THE SHADOW IN THE MIRROR

It is impossible not to see in the story of the Centro de Arte and the Mextiza Colectiva a reflection of other stories of Chicana utopian imaginaries that were cut off—their radical potentialities truncated by social, political, and economic forces beyond their control. Indeed, as I was writing this chapter, it occurred to me—quite suddenly and strangely—that my mother, Martha Cotera, and Lola de la Riva were born just a few days apart, in January of 1938 (of course they are both Capricorns). And there are other striking parallels: They both came to community organizing in the 1960s, and in 1973, each launched independent, community-based projects (the Chicana Research and Learning Center and the Centro de Arte, respectively) that challenged sexist/racist/classist hierarchies of knowledge and cultural production. Both formations had mostly ceased operations by the early 1980s. These "strange affinities" inevitably raise the specter of their parallel erasures—my mother's work from histories of Chicano information science, and Lola's Centro de Arte from scholarly accounts of the Chicano arts movement in Los Angeles—a double violence that denies us the legacy of their examples.[125] When I asked Liz Hidalgo de la Riva why the Centro de Arte is not mentioned in the published scholarship on the Chicano arts movement in Los Angeles, she responded in her typical blunt fashion, stating that the directors of other centros "hated our family; they were all straight men, poverty pimps" (i.e., activists who advance themselves through grant-funded programs for underserved communities). She suggested that the informants with whom scholars had previously spoken might have intentionally written Lola, and by extension the Centro de Arte, out of their accounts of Chicano art centers. Liz's take on the erasure of woman-identified projects like the Centro de Arte highlights the importance of looking beyond the usual suspects, of seeking out and speaking to people who are not in the history books, including those who challenge the narrative exclusions of both Chicano and gay and lesbian historiography. Osa was somewhat more circumspect in her answer to this question, speculating that Lola's status as an unmarried mother, her economic precarity as a nontraditional student and working artist on public assistance, and her commitment to a grassroots vision of art and its uses (which resonates quite powerfully with Martha Cotera's understanding of information as "everything and everywhere") situated her mother as an unruly, and perhaps even unassimilable, subject in the historical imaginary of the Chicano arts movement as it evolved from insurgent roots to established institutions.

And yet, Osa's queer memory keeping—her testimonios shared with other Chicanas and women of color lesbianas (Yolanda Retter Vargas, Maylei Blackwell, Linda Garcia Merchant, and me), her persistent preservation of the archival legacy of las mujeres de la Riva, and her mujerista aesthetics and praxis—surfaces a knowledge praxis that beckons us into a dialogue with the past, reviving these utopian imaginaries, allowing their radical traces to live in our own queer visions of the future. And here a more personal resonance between our Chicanx digital praxis and Osa's mujerista praxis emerges to trouble the divide between investigator and object of analysis. For do I not also see a reflection of myself in Osa's willful attempt to keep this woman-identified matrilineal legacy alive both in her narrations of the past and in her praxis? Indeed, though Osa and I were born a decade apart, we both received an informal education in utopian possibility in our "home space," where our mothers "made sure" that we "were active community members" and that our "presence never curtailed [their] life choices, experiences, or possibilities."[126] As dutiful daughters, we flesh the archive, reviving our mothers' utopian dreams in our own precarious knowledge projects.

# CHICANA FUTURES—PAST AND PRESENT

## *Postscript*

*The here and now is a prison house. We must strive, in the face of the here and now's totalizing rendering of reality, to think and feel a then and there. Some will say that all we have are the pleasures of this moment, but we must never settle for that minimal transport; we must dream and enact new and better pleasures, other ways of being in the world, and ultimately new worlds.*

JOSÉ ESTEBAN MUÑOZ, *Cruising Utopia*

*I think you have to deal with the movements, movimientos, not just Chicano, but women's movements and gay liberation. You have to have the vision of what the better world you want would look like. You can't just criticize and say this world sucks, and this system sucks, and this racism sucks. You have to have at least a concept of what that better world would be. Imagine a better world and visualize how to make it happen. Like drawing up blueprints.*

OSA HIDALGO DE LA RIVA, "VISIONS OF UTOPIA WHILE LIVING IN OCCUPIED AZTLÁN"

I am haunted by the utopian futures that Chicanas imagined in the 1970s, the "persistent and troubling ghosts in the house" of historical memory.[1] As I hope to have demonstrated in the stories of transformative recognition that animate the explorations in this book, reading the message of this ghost requires moving beyond objectivist frameworks of inquiry that transform the radical traces of the past into objects of study (containing them in the "sepulchre" of the archive, as Achille Mbembe might put it) and embracing a relation of knowledge production in which the present and the past are in active dialogue, a space of encuentro where we can see ourselves in its blueprints for the future. In *Light in the Dark / Luz en lo Oscuro*, Gloria Anzaldúa notes that "it's not enough to denounce the culture's old account—you must provide new narratives embodying alternative potentials."[2] In *Fleshing the Archive* I offer a series of new narratives that trace these alternative potentials and the knowledge praxis through which they were articulated, not simply to bring them to greater visibility and spur more scholarly interest in the history of Chicana feminist thought (though that is a useful and necessary task) but also to imagine ourselves otherwise. Indeed, I have seen myself in the archive: in moments of transformative recognition (*reconocimiento*), when strange affinities between the present and the past make themselves suddenly evident—apparitions that point to our shared precarity, but also to a possible future, a "something to be done." As Avery Gordon has incisively observed, "This something to be done is not a return to the past but a reckoning with its repression in the present, a reckoning with that which we have lost, but never had." Thus haunting carries with it not only a will for justice (a reckoning), but also a "utopian dimension . . . encapsulated in the very first lines of Jacques Derrida's book on specters: 'Someone, you or me, comes forward and says: I would like to learn to live finally.'"[3] I dwell with these Chicana knowledge projects in *Fleshing the Archive* because in their reflection I am inspired to take up the paths not followed, to learn to live, finally.

This is a precarious time to learn to live, but as I hope to have demonstrated in this book, we have reservoirs of knowledge that provide us blueprints for survival—ways of knowing, and living, and fighting that have sustained us for generations. My focus on Chicana knowledge praxis is thus thoroughly pragmatic—a necessity, really, in these times, when the past haunts the present in ever more harrowing ways. Indeed, there are shocking parallels between the 1960s, when the Black struggle and the war in Vietnam catalyzed a global youth uprising and a host of liberation movements, and our current historical moment, which has witnessed strikingly similar contradictions coming to a head in the rise of Black Lives Matter, the war on Gaza, and the erosion of LGBTQ and women's rights, all of which demand our attention and our action. These uncanny echoes of the past in our present produce temporal slippages and, with them, moments of transformative recognition that are uncomfortable reminders of the persistence of an "oppressive reality" that, in the words of Paolo Freire, ceaselessly "absorbs those within it." But these convergences also present us with opportunities, "to no longer be prey to its force, . . . to emerge from it and turn upon it." And, as Freire notes, this "can be done only by means of the praxis: reflection and action upon the world in order to transform it."[4]

One final story of praxis from the embodied Chicana archive helps to illustrate this point: As I was finishing up the first draft of this book in the fall of 2023, I introduced a new final assignment in my course Histories of Chicana Feminisms. The class focuses on the 1960s and 1970s and draws liberally from materials in the Chicana por Mi Raza Digital Memory Collective repository, including the newspapers, magazines, and journals discussed in this book. To highlight the importance of print culture in building Chicana sitios y lenguas, I decided to help the students produce their own class magazine. As a collective project of knowledge creation, each student would contribute something—a poem, an essay, an artwork—addressing either the stories of Chicana struggle they had learned in class or their own story of becoming. I asked them to read the examples of Chicana print culture in our archive closely and to take note of the central themes, rhetorical strategies, and communities of care that supported these efforts. Because of my work on the Chicana por Mi Raza project, I understood that it was important to produce print copies of the magazine, not just for archival purposes but also so it could circulate in physical form among students, family members, and the broader community and thus become a part of their shared embodied memory. We decided to name our magazine *Tlamatini: The Knowledge Keeper*, to honor Martha Cotera (who had earlier visited the class) and to signal our belief that we are *all* producers and keepers of knowledge.

Producing our class magazine in just thirteen weeks was stressful to say the least, and chaotic at the end. Nevertheless, I was struck by how this knowledge modality, plucked directly from a long tradition of Chicana knowledge praxis, resonated with students in my class. In their final reflections on the project, they expressed their appreciation for getting the opportunity to share their work with others, not just the professor. They loved the experience of voicing their "opinions on the course materials in a way that is resonant of the past generations who did the same thing during El Movimiento." They talked about how working collaboratively on the publication nurtured a sense of community and empowerment in the classroom. One student noted that the "collective creation of the magazine in our own class" might even be an inspiration for future publications outside of class—though in closing, she struck a less utopian note: "I will be interested to see how this course moves forward as Texas lawmakers crack down on the efforts to preserve history."[5]

Indeed, in the spring of 2024, the political climate had taken a turn for the worse as a result of a coordinated attack on higher education in the Texas legislature.[6] Three senate bills were introduced in the fall 2023 legislative session. SB 16 required "all public colleges and universities to commit to an environment that promotes intellectual diversity, intellectual inquiry, and academic freedom," an innocuous-enough-sounding principle until you read the fine print. Indeed, the bill "also provides that faculty members 'may not compel or attempt to compel' a student enrolled at the institution to adopt a belief that any race, sex, or ethnicity or social, political, or religious belief is

FIGURE 7.1. *Stephanie Garcia, cover art,* Tlamatini, *no. 1 (Fall 2023). The illustration was inspired by imagery from the cover of a women of color newspaper,* Triple Jeopardy, *1972. Author's personal collection.*

inherently superior to any other race, sex, ethnicity, or belief," a stipulation understood by many to be a direct assault on ethnic, gender, and women's studies, as well as on free speech in the classroom. Apparently too far to the right for even some conservative lawmakers, SB 16 did not pass. Following this line of attack on professors' free speech was SB 18, which denied "the possibility of tenure for all university faculty in Texas who are appointed after September 1, 2023."[7] In an effort, one can only imagine, to split faculty

FIGURE 7.2. *Lorena Diosdado (art) and Alexis Martinez (title banner), cover of* Tlamatini, *no. 2 (Spring 2024). The illustration repurposes an image that appeared in multiple Chicana newspapers—a woman breaking through a net, with an eagle looming overhead—but replaces the single woman with portraits of three students from the class. Author's personal collection.*

opinion on the matter of tenure (and prevent costly lawsuits), currently tenured faculty would be allowed to retain their tenure. After numerous faculty testified to the Texas House of Representatives Higher Education Committee that the revocation of tenure would significantly affect the ability of universities to attract the most promising scholars and scientists, SB 18 was walked back.[8] Unfortunately, SB 17—popularly known as the "anti-DEI bill"—did pass, prohibiting the funding of diversity, equity, and inclusion offices; banning any "trainings on diversity, equity, inclusion, bias, oppression, gender identity, or related concepts"; and forbidding the consideration of race, gender, or ethnicity in all hiring decisions.[9] The University of Texas acted swiftly to implement SB 17, eliminating DEI offices across campus and firing over sixty staff. It also decimated the infrastructures of care on campus, defunding the Multicultural Engagement Center, which housed numerous student groups, including "Afrikan American Affairs, the Asian Desi Pacific Islander American Collective, the Latino Leadership Council, the Native American and Indigenous Collective, Queer People of Color and Allies, and Students for Equity and Diversity."[10] In a particularly cruel power play, shortly before the winter break the university announced that it was closing the Gender and Sexuality Center and that it would reopen on January 1 as the Women's Community Center. Discursively reinforcing a gender-normative framing of the center and its services, the name change implicitly stated to LGBTQ students who do not identify as women: You don't belong. In any case, this discursive violence did not last long—the university closed the Women's Community Center at the end of the spring 2024 semester.

In the face of all the turmoil and sadness that these draconian administrative measures produced—particularly among students and staff of color, many of whom had lost jobs and financial support for their groups—the start of the spring semester seemed like a dark time. With the upsurge of student protest over the decimation of Gaza (assisted by an open supply of US weaponry) and the repressive response of most major universities to rallies, marches, and encampments, students in my class began making logical connections between what we were living through in the present moment and the historical period we were studying. Many described the collective work they did on our class magazine as healing and powerful in that it gave them the opportunity to come together and analyze what was happening in their own words, to process the difficult present they found themselves in, and, as Osa Hidalgo de la Riva reminds us, to "imagine a better world and visualize how to make it happen."[11] This is what *Tlamatini* meant to them. On the last day of class, we were planning to come together as a collective to finish laying out the magazine and reflect on the semester, but it seemed as if that would be impossible. Students had called a general strike across campus, enjoining their peers to walk out in protest over a series of violent encounters with law enforcement precipitated by the university's efforts to silence and punish peaceful protesters. Of course, I told my students that I would be working on the magazine but that I didn't expect anyone to break the strike. Most of them came anyway, drawn by the urgency to get their publication finished and printed—to get their voices out there—but also by the need to collectively sort through the violence they had witnessed over the past week.

Like *Hijas de Cuauhtémoc*, *Visión*, *Imágenes de la Chicana*, *The People's Press*, and many of the other examples of print culture that my students closely studied over the course of the semester, the spring 2024 issue of *Tlamatini* spoke to the urgencies of its particular moment, but it also spoke to the past and, most importantly, the future. Indeed, we can hear the echoes of earlier voices in the introductory words of the *Tlamatini* editorial team (Brianna Chavero, Giselle Cerda, and Alyssa Soto), a startling moment of transformative recognition that illuminates the alternative potentialities released into the world when we flesh the archive. *They* should have the last word.

> Now, more than ever, it is imperative that we raise our voices, increase our awareness, and diligently work to prevent history from repeating itself. We must preserve our heritage—this is our home, and we will not lose sight of our roots! Knowing this, we fight back with our magazine because we as a people are resilient. Our ancestors paved the way for our resilience in the face of colonialism and terrorism. They fought valiantly for our rights at the height of the civil rights movement and are continuing this fight today. In the words of Martha Cotera, "We never really stopped fighting." We hold this truth to be self-evident: All people are created equal but are not treated as such. We must speak our truth, educate others, learn ourselves, and continue to do so if we want our history and heritage to be preserved. If we want our descendants to succeed, then we must succeed in our fight against the odds placed against us. This publication is our way of doing so. Our hope is that future generations will see this pathway that we created, and the struggle will continue.[12]

# ACKNOWLEDGMENTS/ AGRADACIMIENTOS

This book was made possible by the collective labor of mujeres who have struggled to create a more inclusive and just world for all of us. They have shaped its central insights and arguments in fundamental ways, especially by contributing to the archive from which I draw these stories of Chicana knowledge praxis, the Chicana por Mi Raza Digital Memory Collective. Each one of the hundreds of interviews and thousands of scanned documents they have shared with the Chicana por Mi Raza project have helped me to piece together the map of Chicana knowledge praxis that I offer in this book. Some of these mujeres have worked closely with me, guiding me as I sort through the archival landscape of their utopian dreams, fleshing the archive with their vivid stories. My mother, Martha P. Cotera, was an instrumental interlocutor as I worked to develop a deeper understanding of radical information praxis in the 1970s. She also talked me through the ways that Chicanas in the Raza Unida Party in Texas navigated distinct, and often opposed, political spaces like the National Women's Political Caucus and the Raza Unida Party. She read every chapter of the manuscript, gave me feedback, and helped me to understand how Chicanas in Texas and California worked to establish Chicana studies through distinct modalities that responded to the institutional and political realities they faced. Anna NietoGomez encouraged and advised me as I traced the early networks of Chicana scholars in California. She helped me develop a twenty-page timeline of Chicana feminist studies from the 1960s to the 1980s, read drafts of chapters, and was always willing to talk to me on the phone (sometimes for hours) when I had questions about specific events, activities, and ideas. Enriqueta Chavez and Sonia Lopez sharpened my understanding of how Chicanas at San Diego State University contributed to the fight for Chicana studies in California; their input was instrumental in helping me to see the critically important role that the Chicano Council on Higher Education played in this struggle. Osa Hidalgo de la Riva and her sister Liz walked me through the connections between their mother Lola's Centro de Arte de Long Beach and the work of the Mextiza Colectiva, an early lesbian and woman of color formation they established to amplify the experiences and perspectives of women of color. Osa was particularly generous with her time and wisdom, sharing her philosophies and experiences with me on an almost daily basis as I endeavored to understand her particular "visions of utopia." Thank you, cuzin.

This book would not have been possible without the contributions of the many students and scholars who, over the last fifteen years, have worked with the Chicana por Mi Raza Digital Memory Collective. My primary collaborator on the project, Linda Garcia Merchant, has always believed in me and in the vision of the project. In 2009, when we launched Chicana por Mi Raza, she was working nine-to-five and making documentary films on the side. She sacrificed so much in those early years, fitting her Chicana por Mi Raza work around the edges of her paid work until she made the leap to graduate school. Today, just fifteen years after we started this journey together, she has earned a PhD from the University of Nebraska (in English and digital humanities) and is the creator and first director of the Digital Humanities Core facility for digital research and scholarship at the University of Houston. Linda's intellectual and creative energy never ceases to amaze me, and I am eternally grateful that she agreed, beyond all good sense, to join me in this memory work back in 2009. She always says that I am the younger sister she never wanted. If that is true, then she is the older sister I never knew I needed. I love you, sis. I have also benefited from the support and encouragement of other collaborators on the Chicana por Mi Raza project, particularly the mujeres who worked with us on the Enriqueta Vasquez Digital History Project: Teresa Córdova, Kathy Córdova, Margie Montañez, Jaelyn deMaría, Karen Roybal, and Annette Rodríguez. Our collaboration is truly a model of how we can change the academy from within by working collectively with each other and with the communities from which our ideas emerge. I am forever grateful for what they have taught me about the ethics of grassroots knowledge production. Our partnership with Teresa Mora (head of special collections and archives at the University of California, Santa Cruz) on the Osa Hidalgo de la Riva Herstory Project was the catalyst for the final chapter in this book. Teresa did the heavy lifting as the organizer/convener of a two-week summer intensive at Santa Cruz, where a group of students learned about the work of the mujeres de la Riva and helped the Chicana por Mi Raza project scan materials from Osa's personal collection that are the basis for my analysis of her mujerista praxis. Teresa's commitment to the preservation of community memory is truly exceptional.

Of course, many cherished colleagues have provided intellectual and emotional support in the journey of this book. Since my arrival at the University of Texas in 2020, Karma Chávez has done everything in her power as chair of the Mexican American and Latino Studies Department to support my work. Her mentorship, friendship, and advocacy have nurtured this book into creation. I am also indebted to Cynthia Orozco and Marisela Chávez, who read the manuscript for the University of Texas Press and offered generative suggestions that strengthened and expanded the book in important ways. Working on *Chicana Movidas: New Narratives of Activism and Feminism in the Movement Era* with Dionne Espinoza and Maylei Blackwell was like being in an extended seminar in Chicana feminist history. Their knowledge of Chicana feminism in the 1960s and 1970s is unparalleled, and their analytical frameworks have deeply influenced my own. Maylei first introduced me to Anna NietoGomez and Keta Miranda at the 2006 MALCS (Mujeres Activas en Letras y Cambio Social) Summer Institute at the University of California, Santa Cruz, and has always been supportive of my work and generous with her knowledge. Dionne—a fellow Chicana nerd when it comes to talking about feminism in the 1970s—has been my primary sounding board for this book, sharing her knowledge and helping me to refine my ideas about the period. When it felt like the book was taking too long to finish, she would encourage me and revive my spirits with hours-long phone conversations about Chicana feminism (even though she was teaching a 4/4 and had her own book to finish). I cannot thank her enough for this support; it truly has made this a better book. Gracias, hermana.

Several institutions have also helped make this book a reality. I worked through my ideas about fleshing the archive as a Helmut Stern Fellow at the Institute for the Humanities, University of Michigan. In 2018 and 2019, my work on the book was supported by an American Council of Learned Societies research fellowship. Through their seed grant program, the US Latino Digital Humanities Center at the University of Houston has supported Chicana por Mi Raza's collaborations with several digital archiving projects, including the Enriqueta Vasquez Digital History Project and the Mujeres de la Riva Digital Herstory Project, which enabled us to digitize materials from Osa's massive personal collection. Doctoras Gabriela Baeza Ventura, Carolina Villarroel, and Lorena Gauthereau, you are the future of Latinx digital humanities! Les agradezco por su apoyo.

And where would this book be without my family? My mother—the original Chicana nerd—and her unruly library have molded my understanding of Chicana feminism and my praxis in so many ways. My father, Juan, who supported her work back in the day, even in the face of machistas who questioned his manhood for doing so, allowed her the space to pursue her tlamatini dreams. My brilliant and creative daughter, Penelope Quetzal, whose fearlessness, joy, and strength continue a matrilineal legacy of Chicana survival. And my partner, Jason—our rock—who has always nurtured a home space where we feel safe enough to pursue our dreams. In addition to his emotional and logistical support, he has been an incisive and intelligent reader of my work: reeling me in when my ideas start to wander, reminding me of what I said I wanted to do in the first place, bringing me back home. My work is a privilege enabled by this intimate infrastructure of care. I love you all.

# NOTES

## INTRODUCTION. CHICANA KNOWLEDGE PRAXIS BEFORE AND AFTER THE DIGITAL TURN

1. I am indebted to Catrióna Rueda Esquibel, whose book *With Her Machete in Her Hand* introduced me to this passage and to Sheila Ortiz Taylor's work. Catrióna Rueda Esquibel, *With Her Machete in Her Hand: Reading Chicana Lesbians* (University of Texas Press, 2006).
2. Emma Pérez developed her concept of "sitios y lenguas" over several essays published in the 1990s. In "Sexuality and Discourse: Notes from a Chicana Survivor," she offers the formulation as a shorthand to describe how Chicana lesbians built a "third space" for developing their ideas and "languages" within an "antagonistic society" (162). Later, in "Irigaray's Female Symbolic in the Making of Chicana Lesbian Sitios y Lenguas," Pérez noted that the concept was derived from the French feminist theorist Luce Irigaray to describe the "safe, decolonized spaces where Chicanas, Mexicanas, and lesbianas interact" and contribute to "a culturally specific female imaginary." She notes that within these provisional and fleeting formations (not unlike the political caucus structure employed by Chicanas to forward their interests in male-dominated spaces and white-female-dominated feminist spaces), "a distinct, Chicana/Mexicana lesbiana cultura has been in the making, even if occasionally interrupted by exhausting, invasionary discourse and politics" (90). Emma Pérez, "Sexuality and Discourse: Notes from a Chicana Survivor," in *Chicana Lesbians: The Girls Our Mothers Warned Us About*, ed. Carla Trujillo (Third Woman Press, 1991); Emma Pérez, "Irigaray's Female Symbolic in the Making of Chicana Lesbian Sitios y Lenguas (Sites and Discourses)," in *Living Chicana Theory*, ed. Carla Trujillo (Third Woman Press, 1998).
3. José Esteban Muñoz, *Cruising Utopia: The Then and There of Queer Futurity* (New York University Press, 2009), 1.
4. Michelle Caswell, Alda Allina Migoni, Noah Geraci, and Marika Cifor, "'To Be Able to Imagine Otherwise': Community Archives and the Importance of Representation," *Archives and Records* 38, no. 1 (2016): 5–26.
5. Bob Jessup, "Praxis," in *A Dictionary of Marxist Thought*, ed. Tom Bottomore, 2nd ed. (Blackwell, 1991), 435.

6. Paolo Freire, *Pedagogy of the Oppressed*, 30th anniversary ed., trans. Myra Bergman Ramos (Bloomsbury, 2014), 51.
7. In "Visions of Utopia While Living in Occupied Aztlán," Osa Hidalgo de la Riva uses the phrase "underground story" to describe her experiences as a lesbian in the Chicano movement. Osa Hidalgo de la Riva and Maylei Blackwell, "Visions of Utopia in Occupied Aztlán," in *Chicana Movidas: New Narratives of Activism and Feminism in the Movement Era*, ed. Dionne Espinoza, María Eugenia Cotera, and Maylei Blackwell (University of Texas Press, 2018), 207; Horacio N. Roque Ramírez, "Memory and Mourning: Living Oral History with Queer Latinos and Latinas in San Francisco," in *Oral History and Public Memories*, ed. Paula Hamilton and Linda Shopes (Temple University Press, 2008), 167.
8. Liliana C. González and Stacy I. Macías, "Afterword: Scanning the Chicana Lesbian Body Politic; Knowledge, Practice, Identity," *Journal of Lesbian Studies* 27, no. 4 (2023): 350.
9. Gloria Anzaldúa, "Let Us Be the Healing of the Wound: The Coyolxauhqui Imperative—La Sombra y el Sueño," in *Light in the Dark / Luz en lo Oscuro: Rewriting Identity, Spirituality, Reality*, by Gloria E. Anzaldúa, ed. AnaLouise Keating (Duke University Press, 2015), 122.

## CHAPTER 1. FLESHING THE ARCHIVE

1. For more on the Chicana por Mi Raza Digital Memory Collective, see María Eugenia Cotera, "'Invisibility Is an Unnatural Disaster': Feminist Archival Praxis After the Digital Turn," in "1970s Feminism," ed. Lisa Disch, special issue, *South Atlantic Quarterly* 114, no. 4 (2015): 781–801; María Eugenia Cotera, "Unpacking Our Mothers' Libraries: Practices of Chicana Memory Before and After the Digital Turn," in *Chicana Movidas: New Narratives of Activism and Feminism in the Movement Era*, ed. Dionne Espinoza, María Eugenia Cotera, and Maylei Blackwell (University of Texas Press, 2018); María Eugenia Cotera, "Nuestra Autohistoria: Toward a Chicana Digital Praxis," *American Quarterly* 70, no. 3 (2018): 483–504.
2. Chela Sandoval, "US Third World Feminism: The Theory and Method of Oppositional Consciousness in the Postmodern World," in Kum-Kum Bhavnani, ed., *Feminism and 'Race'* (Oxford University Press, 2000); Norma Alarcón, "The Theoretical Subject(s) of *This Bridge Called My Back* and Anglo-American Feminism," in *Criticism in the Borderlands: Studies in Chicano Literature, Culture, and Ideology*, ed. Héctor Calderón and José David Saldívar (Duke University Press, 1991); Becky Thompson, "Multiracial Feminism: Recasting the Chronology of Second Wave Feminism," *Feminist Studies* 28, no. 2 (2002): 336–360; Benita Roth, *Separate Roads to Feminism: Black, Chicana, and White Feminist Movements in America's Second Wave* (Cambridge University Press, 2004); Maylei Blackwell, *¡Chicana Power! Contested Histories of Feminism in the Chicano Movement* (University of Texas Press, 2011).

3. Blackwell, *¡Chicana Power!*, 28.
4. Alma M. García, ed., *Chicana Feminist Thought: The Basic Historical Writings* (Routledge, 1997); Ramón A. Gutiérrez, "Community, Patriarchy and Individualism: The Politics of Chicano History and the Dream of Equality," *American Quarterly* 45, no. 1 (1993): 44–72; Teresa Córdova, "Roots and Resistance: The Emergent Writings of Twenty Years of Feminist Struggle," in *Handbook of Hispanic Cultures in the United States: Sociology*, ed. Félix Padilla (Arte Público Press, 1994); Vicki L. Ruiz, *From Out of the Shadows: Mexican Women in Twentieth-Century America* (Oxford University Press, 2008); Vicki L. Ruiz, ed., *Las Obreras: Chicana Politics of Work and Family* (UCLA Chicano Studies Research Center, 2000); Dolores Delgado Bernal, "Grassroots Leadership Reconceptualized: Chicana Oral Histories and the 1968 East Los Angeles School Blowouts," *Frontiers: A Journal of Women Studies* 19, no. 2 (1998): 113–142; Yolanda Broyles-González, *El Teatro Campesino: Theater in the Chicano Movement* (University of Texas Press, 1994); Marisela R. Chávez, *Chicana Liberation: Women and Mexican American Politics in Los Angeles, 1945-1981* (University of Illinois Press, 2024); Marisela Chávez, "'We Lived and Breathed and Worked the Movement': Women in El Centro Acción Social Autónomo (CASA), 1975–1978," in Ruiz, *Las Obreras*; Dionne Espinoza, "'Revolutionary Sisters': Women's Solidarity and Collective Identification Among Chicana Brown Berets in East Los Angeles, 1967–1970," *Aztlán: A Journal of Chicano Studies* 26, no. 1 (2001): 17–58; Dionne Espinoza, "'The Partido Belongs to Those Who Will Work for It': Chicana Organizing and Leadership in the Texas Raza Unida Party, 1970–1980," *Aztlán: A Journal of Chicano Studies* 36, no. 1 (2011): 191–210; Lorena Oropeza, *¡Raza Sí! ¡Guerra No! Chicano Protest and Patriotism During the Viet Nam War Era* (University of California Press, 2005); Espinoza, Cotera, and Blackwell, *Chicana Movidas*.
5. Yolanda Retter Vargas, "Preservation of LGBT History: The ONE Archive," in *Pathways to Progress: Issues and Advances in Latino Librarianship*, ed. John L. Ayala and Salvador Güereña (Libraries Unlimited, 2011); Yolanda Chávez Leyva, "Breaking the Silence: Putting Latina Lesbian History at the Center," in *The New Lesbian Studies: Into the Twenty-First Century*, ed. Bonnie Zimmerman and Toni A. H. McNaron (Feminist Press, 1996); Deena J. González, "Speaking Secrets: Living Chicana Theory," in *Living Chicana Theory*, ed. Carla. Trujillo (Third Woman Press, 1998); Yvette J. Saavedra, "Of Chicana Lesbian Terrorists and Lesberadas: Recuperating the Lesbian/Queer Roots of Chicana Feminism, 1970–2000," *Feminist Formations* 34, no. 2 (2022): 99–124; Horacio N. Roque Ramírez, "Memory and Mourning: Living Oral History with Queer Latinos and Latinas in San Francisco," in *Oral History and Public Memories*, ed. Paula Hamilton and Linda Shopes (Temple University Press, 2008).
6. Horacio N. Roque Ramírez and Nan Alamilla Boyd, "Introduction: Close Encounters; The Body and Knowledge in Queer Oral History," in *Bodies of Evidence: The Practice of Queer Oral History*, ed. Nan Alamilla Boyd and Horacio N. Roque Ramírez (Oxford University Press, 2012), 5.

7. Enriqueta Vasquez's collected writings from *El Grito* are compiled in Lorena Oropeza and Dionne Espinoza, eds., *Enriqueta Vasquez and the Chicano Movement: Writings from "El Grito Del Norte"* (Arte Público Press, 2006).
8. I have written about the invisibilizing feedback loop in María Cotera, "'Invisibility Is an Unnatural Disaster.'" See also Antoinette Burton, ed., *Archive Stories: Facts, Fictions, and the Writing of History* (Duke University Press, 2005), 2.
9. Michael Frisch, *A Shared Authority: Essays on the Craft and Meaning of Oral and Public History* (State University of New York Press, 1990); Burton, *Archive Stories*; Alamilla Boyd and Roque Ramírez, *Bodies of Evidence*; Michel-Rolph Trouillot, *Silencing the Past: Power and the Production of History* (Beacon Press, 1995).
10. Yolanda Retter Vargas, "On the Side of Angels: Lesbian Activism in Los Angeles, 1970–1990" (PhD diss., University of New Mexico, 1999), 55.
11. Durba Ghosh, "National Narratives and the Politics of Miscegenation: Britain and India," in Burton, *Archive Stories*, 27.
12. Achille Mbembe, "The Power of the Archive and Its Limits," in *Refiguring the Archive*, ed. Carolyn Hamilton, Verne Harris, Jane Taylor, Michele Pickover, Graeme Reid, and Razia Saleh (Springer, 2002), 22.
13. Mbembe, "Power of the Archive," 22.
14. The ideas presented in the remainder of this chapter were first developed in an essay I wrote for the journal *Oral History*. See María Eugenia Cotera, "Fleshing the Archive: Reflections on Chicana Memory Practice," *Oral History* 49, no. 2 (2021): 49–56.
15. For a detailed account of this early foray into the Chicana archive, see María Cotera, "'Invisibility Is an Unnatural Disaster.'"
16. Rina Benmayor, "Testimony, Action Research, and Empowerment: Puerto Rican Women and Popular Education," in *Women's Words: The Feminist Practice of Oral History*, ed. Sherna Berger Gluck and Daphne Patai (Routledge, 1991), 170.
17. Benmayor, "Testimony, Action Research, and Empowerment," 165.
18. To date, the Chicana por Mi Raza project has curated two community exhibitions, both of which were developed in collaboration with students and the women we interviewed: *Las Rebeldes: Stories of Strength and Struggle in Southeastern Michigan* (Detroit, November 2014) and *Chicana Fotos: Nancy de los Santos* (Detroit, February 2017).
19. Sonia Olmos, "The Latina Task Force," student reflection essay written in partial fulfillment of requirements for the Summer Research Opportunity Program, University of Michigan, 2018.
20. María Cotera, "'Invisibility Is an Unnatural Disaster,'" 796.
21. Sue Anderson, Jaimee Hamilton, and Lorina L. Barker, "Yarning Up Oral History: An Indigenous Feminist Analysis," in *Beyond Women's Words: Feminisms and Practices of Oral History in the Twenty-First Century*, ed. Katrina Srigley, Stacey Zembrzycki, and Franca Iacovetta (Routledge, 2018), 170.
22. Anderson, Hamilton, and Barker, "Yarning Up Oral History," 173.

23. Anderson, Hamilton, and Barker, "Yarning Up Oral History," 174.
24. Anderson, Hamilton, and Barker, "Yarning Up Oral History," 175.
25. Rina Benmayor, "Emotion and Pedagogy: Teaching Digital Storytelling in the Millennial Classroom," in Srigley, Zembrzycki, and Iacovetta, *Beyond Women's Words*, 64–65.
26. Cindy O. Fierros and Dolores Delgado Bernal, "Vamos a Pláticar: The Contours of Pláticas as Chicana/Latina Feminist Methodology," *Chicana/Latina Studies* 15, no. 2 (2016): 98–99.
27. For more on how the Chicana por Mi Raza project draws from the long tradition of Chicana memory keeping, see María Cotera, "Unpacking Our Mothers' Libraries."
28. Olmos, "Latina Task Force."
29. Olmos, "Latina Task Force."
30. Avery Gordon, *Ghostly Matters: Haunting and the Sociological Imagination* (University of Minnesota Press, 1997), 63–64.
31. Gordon, *Ghostly Matters*, xviii.
32. Gordon, *Ghostly Matters*, 8.
33. Gordon, *Ghostly Matters*, 63–64.
34. Gordon, *Ghostly Matters*, 8.
35. Gordon, *Ghostly Matters*, 66.
36. Gordon, *Ghostly Matters*, 58.
37. Gordon, *Ghostly Matters*, 66.
38. Anna NietoGomez, "Memory Work," in the chapter "A Forum on Chicana Memory Work, Past, Present, and Future: Nuestras Autohistorias," in *Latina Histories and Cultures: Feminist Readings and Recoveries of Archival Knowledge*, ed. Montse Feu and Yolanda Padilla (Arte Público Press, 2023), 79.
39. Anderson, Hamilton, Barker, "Yarning Up Oral History," 174.
40. Ann Cvetkovich, *An Archive of Feelings: Trauma, Sexuality, and Lesbian Public Cultures* (Duke University Press, 2003), 7–8.
41. NietoGomez, "Memory Work," 78.
42. Early on in my efforts to reconstruct a coherent narrative about the birth of Chicana feminist studies, I relied on that classic infrastructure of historical meaning making: the timeline. Turning to the Chicana archive, I started with the timeline of Chicana workshops and conferences that my mother included in her *Profile on the Mexican American Woman* (1976). Shortly after I started my timeline, Anna NietoGomez sent me her own timeline. With her permission I merged the two timelines in a Google Doc that I shared with her. Soon her sidebar comments on the document morphed into changes to "my" timeline, which she discreetly distinguished through pink, orange, or blue highlighting. Our timelines had truly become one: a sprawling document that included every Chicana organization, meeting, workshop, publication, and conference, along with firsthand accounts drawn directly from Anna's unpublished memoir. For a moment I panicked—Had I somehow lost control of the critical infrastructure

for my historical narration? But I soon came to understand that the timeline we had created together was merely a textual visualization of the dialogical relations of knowledge that are introduced when we flesh the archive and give up the ghost of authority over the narrative.

43. Emma Pérez, *The Decolonial Imaginary: Writing Chicanas into History* (Indiana University Press, 1999), 6.

## CHAPTER 2. LA TLAMATINI

1. Avery Gordon, *Ghostly Matters: Haunting and the Sociological Imagination* (University of Minnesota Press, 1997), 63.
2. Stefano Harney and Fred Moten, *The Undercommons: Fugitive Planning and Black Study* (Minor Compositions, 2013), 26.
3. "La Biblioteca," *Cristal*, special issue, September 1971, 14.
4. Anna NietoGomez, "The Chicana Slideshow," March 4, 2015, unpublished manuscript shared with the author.
5. Adelaida Del Castillo has discussed the gendered dimensions of hierarchies of labor in Chicano movement organizations. She notes that while "qualitative" labor ("soft" emotional and supportive labor, focused on nurturing and relationship building) was more often than not feminized, "quantitative" labor ("hard" labor of movement building, including critical, theoretical, and analytical tasks) was seen as the domain of men. See Adelaida R. Del Castillo, "Mexican Women in Organization," in *Mexican Women in the United States: Struggles Past and Present*, ed. Magdalena Mora and Adelaida R. Del Castillo (Chicano Studies Research Center, 1980).
6. Martha Cotera, "Final Comments, May 22, 2019," unpublished manuscript shared with the author.
7. My translation; Martha's original transcription reads as follows: "El sabio: una luz, una tea, una gruesa tea que no ahuma. Un espejo horadado, un espejo agujereado por ambos lados. Suya es la tinta negra y roja, de él son los códices, de él son los códices. Él mismo es escritura y sabiduría. Es camino, guía veraz para otros. Conduce a las personas y a las cosas, es guía en los negocios humanos. El sabio verdadero es cuidadoso (como un médico) y guarda la tradición. Suya es la sabiduría transmitida, él es quien la enseña, sigue la verdad. Maestro de la verdad, no deja de amonestar. Hace sabios los rostros ajenos, hace a los otros tomar una cara (una personalidad), los hace desasarrollarla. Les abre los oídos, los ilumina. Es maestro de guías, les da su camino, de él uno depende. Pone un espejo delante de los otros, los hace cuerdos, cuidadosos; hace que en ellos aparezca una cara (una personalidad). Se fija en las cosas, regula su camino, dispone y ordena. Aplica su luz sobre el mundo. Conoce (lo que está) sobre nosotros (y), la región de los muertos. (Es hombre serio.) Cualquiera es confortado por él, es corregido, es enseñado. Gracias a él la gente humaniza su querer y recibe una estricta enseñanza. Conforta el corazón, conforta a la gente, ayuda, remedia, a

todos cura." Martha Cotera (quoting Miguel León-Portilla's translation from the original Nahuatl), email communication with the author, July 30, 2020.

8. Miguel León-Portilla, *Aztec Thought and Culture: A Study of the Ancient Nahuatl Mind*, trans. Jack Emory Davis (University of Oklahoma Press, 1963), 10–18.
9. Brenda Sendejo, "The Space in Between: Exploring the Development of Chicana Feminist Thought in Central Texas," in *Chicana Movidas: New Essays on Activism and Feminism in the Movement Era*, ed. Dionne Espinoza, María Eugenia Cotera, and Maylei Blackwell (University of Texas Press, 2018).
10. Widely recognized as "firsts" in the canon of Chicana feminist writing, *Diosa y Hembra* and *The Chicana Feminist* cemented Martha Cotera's reputation as a preeminent Chicana feminist thinker.
11. For more on the impact of the connections between the Chicano movement and the War on Poverty, see Mario T. García, "The Chicano University," in *Ghosts in the Barrio: Issues in Bilingual-Bicultural Education*, ed. Ralph (Rafa) Poblano (Leswing Press, 1973); Jaime Rafael Puente, "Juárez–Lincoln University: Alternative Higher Education in the Chicana/o Movement, 1969–1983" (master's thesis, University of Texas at Austin, 2013); Rodolfo Acuña, *The Making of Chicana/o Studies: In the Trenches of Academe* (Rutgers University Press, 2011); David Montejano, *Quixote's Soldiers: A Local History of the Chicano Movement, 1966–1981* (University of Texas Press, 2010); Juan Gómez-Quiñones and Irene Vásquez, *Making Aztlán: Ideology and Culture of the Chicana and Chicano Movement, 1966–1977* (University of New Mexico Press, 2014); Gordon K. Mantler, *Power to the Poor: Black-Brown Coalition and the Fight for Economic Justice, 1960–1974* (University of North Carolina Press, 2013).
12. See Puente, "Juárez–Lincoln University." See also Francisco García-Ayvens and Richard F. Chabrán, eds., *Biblio-Politica: Chicano Perspectives on Library Service in the United States* (Chicano Studies Library Publications Unit, University of California, Berkeley, 1984).
13. The Library Services and Construction Act of 1964 was part of the constellation of domestic programs launched by President Lyndon B. Johnson in 1964 and 1965 as part of his Great Society project. It provided federal assistance to libraries to improve their service to marginalized communities and build new library branches. For more on the Library Services and Construction Act, see Sandra Hirsch, *Information Services Today: An Introduction* (Rowman & Littlefield, 2015), 14.
14. Salvador Güereña and Edward Erazo outline many of these initiatives in their comprehensive survey of the development of library services for Latinos since the 1960s, "Latinos and Librarianship," *Library Trends* 49, no. 1 (2000): 138–181. See also Elizabeth Martinez's history, "Chicano Librarianship: On the 40th Anniversary of the Chicano Moratorium, a Leader in the Movement Remembers the Early Years in East Los Angeles County," *American Libraries*, November 2, 2010, https://americanlibrariesmagazine.org/2010/11/02/chicano-librarianship/. Firsthand accounts of these efforts can be found in library

journals from the period, including a 1970 special issue of *Wilson Library Bulletin* and the January 1973 issue of *California Librarian*, which featured a section titled "Chicano Library Service."

15. Hamer was head of the Texas collection at the University of Texas Library from 1932 to 1955, when she moved to El Paso. She was an active contributor to the Texas Folklore Society during that time, serving as treasurer for the organization from 1934 to 1951. She was librarian of the Southwest Room of the El Paso Public Library from 1955 until her retirement in 1965. See Mary Marcelle Hamer Hull, "Hamer, Elizabeth Marcelle Lively (1900–1974)," *Handbook of Texas Online*, updated February 21, 2021, https://tshaonline.org/handbook/online/articles/fhadv. Hamer's connections to other librarians, like Nettie Lee Benson at the University of Texas and Texas State Librarian Dorman Winfrey, would play a key role in Martha's professional career as a librarian. Martha Cotera, "Oral Memoirs of Martha P. Cotera," oral history conducted by Joyce Langenegger, March 3, 1973–April 6, 1973, transcript 1981, Baylor University Institute for Oral History (hereafter cited as Martha Cotera, Baylor oral history, 1973); Martha Cotera, phone interview with the author, April 22, 2019.
16. The El Paso Public Library had acquired a large collection of federal government documents as part of the Federal Depository Library Program, which made US government publications available to the public at no cost. In the early part of the twentieth century, librarian Maud Durlin Sullivan developed a nationally recognized art and Southwestern studies collection at the El Paso library, through the aid of donations and special funds. It was this extraordinarily rich collection of federal documents and Southwest archives that Martha Cotera was tasked with organizing. For a historical overview, see "El Paso Public Libraries," *Wikipedia*, https://en.wikipedia.org/wiki/El_Paso_Public_Library.
17. Martha spent four years organizing and indexing the library's collections and establishing a reading room for the public. She eventually became the department's acting director. See Martha Cotera, Baylor oral history, 1973, 14.
18. Martha Cotera, Baylor oral history, 1973, 13.
19. Martha Cotera, phone interview with the author, April 22, 2019.
20. Martha Cotera, oral history interview, University of Michigan, July 3, 2018, Martha Cotera Collection, Chicana por Mi Raza Digital Memory Collective (hereafter cited as Martha Cotera, CPMR oral history, 2018).
21. Martha Cotera, Baylor oral history, 1973, 13.
22. Martha Cotera, Baylor oral history, 1973, 13.
23. Martha Cotera, CPMR oral history, 2018.
24. The Armijo branch was opened a few years later in 1968 in a Segundo Barrio recreation center. In 1992 a building was finally constructed to house the library. Chicano library scholar Roberto Haro highlighted the work of the Armijo branch in an essay in a special issue of *California Librarian* on Chicano library service. See Roberto Haro, "Libraries on the Border," *California Librarian* 34, no. 1 (1973): 9–13. El Paso's Segundo Barrio was a primary landing site for many

immigrants fleeing the Mexican Revolution. By the 1950s, the neighborhood was characterized by residential overcrowding, substandard housing, and few city services. See W. H. Timmons, *El Paso: A Borderlands History* (Texas Western Press, 1990), 250–251.

25. Martha Cotera, CPMR oral history, 2018.
26. Martha moved to Austin in 1963, when Juan, her new husband, was admitted to the Architecture and Urban Planning Program at the University of Texas. Martha Cotera, CPMR oral history, 2018.
27. While waiting for the State Library job in Austin, Martha worked in the University of Texas archives with another of Hamer's friends, Chester V. Kielman, a "wonderful man who called himself the gay fertility God because all the women got pregnant working with him!" Martha Cotera, email communication with the author, April 23, 2019.
28. Martha Cotera, Baylor oral history, 1973, 23.
29. David Montejano, *Anglos and Mexicans in the Making of Texas, 1836–1986* (University of Texas Press, 1987).
30. Indeed, the rural invaded the urban in 1966, when a farmworker strike in Starr County launched a five-hundred-mile peregrinación from Starr County in South Texas to the State Capitol. For more on the Starr County melon strike, the 1963 electoral takeover in Crystal City, and the organizing efforts of the Mexican American Youth Organization (MAYO), see Ignacio M. García, *United We Win: The Rise and Fall of La Raza Unida Party* (University of Arizona, 1989); José Ángel Gutiérrez, *The Making of a Chicano Militant: Lessons from Cristal* (University of Wisconsin Press, 1998); and Montejano, *Quixote's Soldiers.*
31. Within the constellation of domestic programs proposed in the Johnson administration's Great Society initiative of 1964 and 1965 were federal funds to support K–12 and higher education, bilingual education, and library services to the disadvantaged. See John A. Andrew III, *Lyndon Johnson and the Great Society* (Ivan R. Dee, 1998); Marshall Kaplan and Peggy Cuciti, eds., *The Great Society and Its Legacy: Twenty Years of U.S. Social Policy* (Duke University Press, 1986); Barbara C. Jordan and Elspeth D. Rostow, eds., *The Great Society: A Twenty Year Critique* (Lyndon B. Johnson School of Public Affairs, 1986); Sidney M. Milkis and Jerome M. Mileur, eds., *The Great Society and the High Tide of Liberalism* (University of Massachusetts Press, 2005).
32. Martha Cotera, Baylor oral history, 1973, 23–24.
33. In 1963 Texas voters rejected a proposed amendment to the state constitution to repeal the poll tax, which had been in effect since 1902 and had prevented many African American and Mexican American voters from voting because of their inability to pay the tax. Just a year later, the federal government enacted the Twenty-Fourth Amendment to the US Constitution, prohibiting a poll tax from being levied in national elections. Two years later, the US Supreme Court ruled the poll tax unconstitutional in state elections. Texas amended its constitution to

repeal the poll tax in 1966. Dick Smith, "Texas and the Poll Tax," *Southwestern Social Science Quarterly* 45, no. 2 (1964): 167–173.

34. Rooted in the social analysis of left scholars like Floyd Hunter and C. Wright Mills, power structure research challenged prevailing assumptions of liberal ideology to reveal the networks of power that structurally disadvantage marginalized groups and to analyze the mechanisms by which domination is maintained. Before the advent of the internet, with its relatively free access to government documents, "most of the information needed to trace the webs of power in American society could be obtained only through extensive library and archival research, close monitoring of the press, searches of government records and documents, and interviews with knowledgeable insiders." Val Burris, "An Internet Guide to Power Structure Research," *Who Rules?*, https://pages.uoregon.edu/vburris/whorules/. For more on power structure research in the 1960s, see G. William Domhoff, *Who Rules America?* (Prentice Hall, 1967).
35. Martha Cotera, Baylor oral history, 1973, 24.
36. "Provision for White House Conference on Education," *US Congressional Record*, 83rd Congress, Second Session, May 26 1954–June 21, 1954, vol. 100, part 6, 8449.
37. SEDL serviced two regions, Texas and Louisiana, focusing on the educational achievement of Mexican American, African American, and Acadian populations. US Office of Education, Bureau of Research, "Report on Regional Educational Laboratories" (US Government Printing Office, 1968), 1.
38. In a progress report published by the US Department of Education in 1968, SEDL outlined several programmatic efforts it was pursuing to develop and demonstrate "instructional programs, materials, and activities to meet the unique needs of the Mexican American population." These included "a bilingual elementary curriculum in which Spanish is used in teaching subject-matter while the student is in the process of learning English," a migrant education program, and a "bilingual program for adult Mexican-Americans with funds obtained from the Office of Economic Opportunity." The lab also offered "inservice training opportunities" in bilingual and Spanish-immersion curricula for experienced teachers, as well as a "preservice program for college students who will teach and counsel Mexican-American children." US Office of Education, "Report on Regional Educational Laboratories," 16.
39. The Educational Research Information Clearinghouse (ERIC) program was initiated in 1966. ERIC was composed of sixteen subject clearinghouses, including the Migrant and Rural Education Clearinghouse in New Mexico (where Martha served on the board), which, along with the Bilingual Dissemination Center, concentrated on Mexican American information. According to Martha, she "participated in a consultation to set up the clearinghouses in 1966 because I was a public documents director at the state library, and this consultation in Washington DC was to determine the thesaurus for some of the specialized clearinghouses, and I believe this was in 1965–66." Martha recalls that a decade later, when she published *Profile on the Mexican American*

*Woman* (1976), she received a $1,000 grant from ERIC to do the project. Martha Cotera, email communication with the author, April 23, 2019.

40. Martha Cotera, oral history interview, 2009, Martha Cotera Collection, Chicana por Mi Raza Digital Memory Collective (hereafter cited as Martha Cotera, CPMR oral history, 2009).
41. Martha offered to set up an "information system for [SEDL], an information library, and to do their information services." Martha Cotera, Baylor oral history, 1973, 24.
42. Martha Cotera, Baylor oral history, 1973, 24.
43. According to Carlos Cantú, "between 1967 and 1970 MAYO members participated [in] and helped organize at least 39 school walkouts in Texas," bringing "to light the pervasive issues of discrimination in schools, including the lack of Mexican American teachers." See Carlos L. Cantú, "Self-Determined Education and Community Activism: A Comparative History of Navajo, Chicana/o, and Puerto Rican Institutions of Higher Education in the Era of Protest" (PhD diss., University of Houston, 2016), 141. The walkout strategy was a statewide coordinated effort developed by various chapters of MAYO. Founded in San Antonio, Texas, in 1967 by José Ángel Gutiérrez, Willie C. Velásquez, Mario Compean, Ignacio Pérez, and Juan Patlán, MAYO pursued a direct action approach to challenging Anglo hegemony in Texas, targeting three areas of need for the Chicana/o community: "economic independence, local control of education, and political strength and unity" through the formation of a political party. Within the year, MAYO had established thirty chapters across the state, including a chapter at the University of Texas at Austin. See Teresa Palomo Acosta, "Mexican American Youth Organization," *Handbook of Texas Online*, updated April 8, 2020, http://www.tshaonline.org/handbook/online/articles/wemo1. See also I. García, *United We Win*, 29; Gutiérrez, *Making of a Chicano Militant*, 119; Montejano, *Quixote's Soldiers*; Armando Navarro, *The Cristal Experiment: A Chicano Struggle for Community Control* (University of Wisconsin Press, 1998).
44. Martha Cotera, CPMR oral history, 2018. Martha's description of the institutions in which she worked as the "master's house" is a direct reference to Audre Lorde's evocative warning to white feminists in comments delivered at the Second Sex Conference, October 29, 1979, that "the master's tools will never dismantle the master's house." Lorde's commentary was later published in *This Bridge Called My Back* (1981).
45. Martha Cotera, Baylor oral history, 1973, 33.
46. Martha Cotera, Baylor oral history, 1973, 34.
47. Martha Cotera, CPMR oral history, 2018. For more on the school walkout as a direct action political strategy, see I. García, *United We Win*; Gutiérrez, *Making of a Chicano Militant*. For more on the work of TEAM in teach-ins and liberation schools, see Armando Navarro, *Mexican American Youth Organization: Avant-Garde of the Chicano Movement in Texas* (University of Texas Press, 1995).

48. In an oral history interview, Narciso Alemán, one of the founders of Colegio Jacinto Treviño, recalls how Anglo administrators would challenge demands for more Chicana/o teachers and staff by pointing out that there were few qualified teachers available. Narciso Alemán, interviewed by Sandra Enriquez and David Robles, 2015, Civil Rights in Black and Brown Oral History Project, https://crbb.tcu.edu/interviews/interview-with-narciso-aleman.
49. These issues came to a head in 1971, when a group of Chicana/o staff at SEDL, Los Chicanos del Laboratorio, staged a walkout in protest of their systematic exclusion from the top ranks. See memorandum, Los Chicanos del Laboratorio, May 28, 1971, Martha Cotera Collection, Chicana por Mi Raza Digital Memory Collective (hereafter cited as CPMR).
50. This sentiment was expressed in a letter by SEDL administrative council member J. R. Lujan that was attached to the list of grievances and demands of Los Chicanos del Laboratorio: "The premise that no well qualified individuals within the Mexican American community could be secured was then and is now a very hollow sounding one. 'Well qualified' individuals from outside this group were hard at work then and the results now are very disappointing in many areas of the programmatic effort." Memorandum, Martha Cotera Collection, CPMR.
51. Martha Cotera, Baylor oral history, 1973, 27.
52. Cantú, "Self-Determined Education and Community Activism," 122.
53. Cantú, "Self-Determined Education and Community Activism," 159.
54. Gutiérrez, *Making of a Chicano Militant*, 164–169. John Staples Shockley offers an account of the massive effort that went into TEAM's teach-in: "Commencing Monday, December 22, TEAM began tutoring more than 500 students who showed up for its first session in the city park. The first hour was devoted to a lecture on Mexican cultural history. On the second day the students split up by grade level and subjects and moved to the churches, a theater, dance halls, front porches, and private homes. Attendance throughout the holidays was reported as good, and at the end of the two weeks of instruction, the students held a rally to honor the fifty teachers from TEAM." John Staples Shockley, *Chicano Revolt in a Texas Town* (University of Notre Dame Press, 1974), 276.
55. Martha recalls that the idea of establishing an independent college emerged as early as 1966, but the process really took off during the 1968 and 1969 walkouts, when they discussed the idea in meetings across the state with walkout leaders like Aurelio Montemayor, TEAM leaders like Blandina Cardenas, academics at the University of Texas (including Américo Paredes), and members of MAYO. Martha Cotera, CPMR oral history, 2018.
56. See Gutiérrez, *Making of a Chicano Militant*; Cantú, "Self-Determined Education and Community Activism"; Puente, "Juárez–Lincoln University."
57. Andre Guerrero, "Tiempo de la Cuna," *Hojas: A Chicano Journal of Education*, 1976, 23, Martha Cotera Collection, CPMR.
58. Martha's reference to education in a "humanistic setting" draws directly from Paolo Freire's pedagogical philosophy. Freire argued that true learning

and teaching should counteract the dehumanizing racist, authoritarian, and market-oriented approach to education. In her interview with Jaime Puente, Martha notes that for the founders of the Colegio Jacinto Treviño, "Paulo Freire, of course, was the basis . . . for our approach to the human being becoming educated. And, not only to the human being, but [also] the family around him or her, the community, you know, the state . . . the nation." Jaime Puente has noted that Freirian philosophy and practice were at the core of autonomous educational projects like Colegio Jacinto Treviño, Juárez–Lincoln University, and others. Puente, "Juárez–Lincoln University," 43–45. For more on the importance of Freire to Chicana/o education projects, see H. Homero Galicia and Clementina Almaguer, *Chicano Alternative Education* (Southwest Network, 1974).

59. Martha Cotera, "Bicultural Education in a Humanistic Setting: A Position Paper," Martha Cotera Collection, CPMR; Martha Cotera, "The Library and Information Functions as Meaningful Activities in a Chicano Graduate Program: A Position Paper," Martha Cotera Collection, CPMR.
60. Puente, "Juárez–Lincoln University," 24.
61. According to a report prepared for the Chicano Mobile Institute conference in 1971 by Frank Alejandro, Paredes visited the colegio on February 11 and 20, 1971. He lectured on the "folklore of Mexico and the Southwest" and did a presentation at the public library in Mercedes, Texas. "Summary of Report," submitted to the Chicano Mobile Institute conference El Chicano y la Educación, California State College, Long Beach, 1971, Enriqueta Chavez Papers, San Diego State University.
62. Disagreements over political strategy and community engagement beset the college from the start. In these acrimonious battles, education professionals like Aurelio Montemayor, Martha Cotera, Andre Guerrero, and Leonard Mestas (the only one of the group of founders who held a doctorate) were framed as bourgeois intellectuals and referred to derisively as "the Mexican-American element" by the colegio's financial director, Narciso Alemán, who had previously worked in Denver for the Crusade for Justice. In their resignation letter, Martha and her husband, Juan, recalled a series of rancorous purges of "nonrevolutionary" elements at the colegio, and they cited a corrosive political climate that made fulfilling the colegio's mission impossible. See Juan Cotera and Martha Cotera to Guadalupe Tamez, resignation letter, March 8, 1971, Martha Cotera Collection, CPMR.
63. Individuals exiled from Colegio Jacinto Treviño did not give up their dream for an autonomous educational institution. Andre Guerrero and Leonard Mestas kept the idea alive in a new college concept, the Juárez–Lincoln Center (later University), which they established in Fort Worth, Texas, in 1971. One year later, Juárez–Lincoln moved to Austin, where it held an institutional affiliation with St. Edward's University. In 1973, Martha rejoined the effort as the director of the National Migrant Information Clearinghouse, a project that

was administered through Juárez–Lincoln. Jaime Puente's master's thesis on the university includes illuminating interviews with some of the key participants in the planning phase of Colegio Jacinto Treviño, including Andre Guerrero and Martha Cotera. Carlos Cantú's dissertation includes a chapter on Colegio Jacinto Treviño. See Puente, "Juárez–Lincoln University"; Cantú, "Self-Determined Education and Community Activism." For an interesting account of other autonomous education projects that includes interviews with their staff, see Galicia and Almaguer, *Chicano Alternative Education*. See also Joan Kalvelage, "Cinco Exemplos," *Edcentric* 4, no. 7 (1972).

64. Cantú, "Self-determined Education and Community Activism," 159.
65. Harney and Moten, *Undercommons*, 26.
66. Martha Cotera, Baylor oral history, 1973, 28.
67. Harney and Moten, *Undercommons*, 26.
68. Jack Halberstam, "The Wild Beyond: With and for the Undercommons," in Harney and Moten, *Undercommons*, 11.
69. These majorities were not electoral majorities in the strictest sense; rather, they were formed when Mexican Americans already serving on the school board and city council voted with newly elected Raza Unida Party members. For a detailed analysis of the successes and failures of MAYO's Winter Garden Project and the Raza Unida Party, see Navarro, *Cristal Experiment*.
70. Navarro, *Cristal Experiment*, 73.
71. Armando Navarro notes that the recruitment of "outsiders" to fill key administrative positions in the city and county "became a destabilizing factor in [the Raza Unida Party's] peaceful revolution." Navarro, *Cristal Experiment*, 74–75. See also Gutiérrez, *Making of a Chicano Militant*.
72. José Ángel Gutiérrez, quoted in Navarro, *Cristal Experiment*, 75.
73. José Ángel Gutiérrez claims that the Texas Education Agency encouraged teachers to boycott Crystal City schools. Gutiérrez, *Making of a Chicano Militant*.
74. Martha Cotera, CPMR oral history, 2018.
75. Martha Cotera, CPMR oral history, 2018.
76. Martha Cotera, CPMR oral history, 2018. See also Martha Cotera, Baylor oral history, 1973, 37; Navarro, *Cristal Experiment*, 231.
77. Martha Cotera, Baylor oral history, 1973, 40.
78. Martha Cotera, Baylor oral history, 1973, 38.
79. Martha P. Cotera, "Concepts of Information Services in a Chicano Context," in *Library Services to Mexican Americans: Policies, Practices and Prospects*, ed. Roberto Urzua, Martha P. Cotera, and Emma González Stupp (National Educational Laboratory, 1978), 44.
80. The fotonovela was a popular mid-twentieth-century Mexican literary form. Stefan Ruiz notes that "fotonovelas are essentially comic books illustrated with photographs instead of drawings, operating somewhere between graphic novels, films, television, and pulp novels. Developed prior to the Second

World War in Italy and France, they were originally made using film stills. They started to be produced in Latin America in the 1950s and were hugely popular in Mexico until the late 1980s, when VHS tapes of popular films and TV shows became readily available and affordable." Stefan Ruiz, "The Mexican Fotonovela: How Comic Books Illustrated with Photographs Became a Great Popular Art Form," *Aperture*, September 5, 2017, https://aperture.org/editorial/mexican-fotonovela/.

81. Martha Cotera, CPMR oral history, 2018.
82. Martha Cotera, CPMR oral history, 2009. The national Teacher Corps was a federally funded program (part of the Higher Education Act of 1965) to prepare liberal arts graduates for elementary and secondary teaching in predominantly low-income areas. In an oral history conducted in 2015, Rafael Torres discusses his work with Teacher Corps in Crystal City from 1972 to 1974. He describes the program as a "joint venture of Texas A&I–Laredo and the Crystal City Independent School District" in which students pursuing degrees in education from Texas A&I University at Laredo were trained in bilingual/bicultural education by "master teachers" working in the district. They took classes in the evenings and summers and worked on a community project. Rafael Torres, oral history interview with Sandra Enriquez, David Robles, and Max Krochmal, July 6, 2015, Civil Rights in Black and Brown Oral History Project, https://texashistory.unt.edu/ark:/67531/metapth836738/m1/.
83. See "Chicano Librarianship," special issue, *California Librarian*, January 1973; "Libraries and the Spanish Speaking," special feature, *Wilson Library Bulletin* 44, no. 7 (1970): 714–767.
84. Martha Cotera, Baylor oral history, 1973, 40.
85. Martha P. Cotera, "Library Services to Mexican Americans in Texas: A Statement," in Urzua, Cotera, and González Stupp, *Library Services to Mexican Americans*, 54.
86. Martha Cotera, "Concepts of Information Services," 41. Reading this list of the subjects cut off from the traditional library—an elite cultural space designed for white middle-class patrons—one cannot help but reflect on its resonances with Anzaldúa's conceptualization of the borderlands subject: "*los atravesados* . . . the squint-eyed, the perverse, the half-breed, the half dead," from whose vantage point, Anzaldúa argues, new epistemological orientations emerge. Gloria Anzaldúa, *Borderlands / La Frontera: The New Mestiza* (Aunt Lute, 1997), 25.
87. Martha Cotera, "Concepts of Information Services," 41.
88. Martha Cotera, "Concepts of Information Services," 47.
89. Martha Cotera, "Concepts of Information Services," 47.
90. Martha Cotera, "Concepts of Information Services," 41.
91. José Ángel Gutiérrez, interview by Martha Cotera, cited in Martha Cotera, "Chicanas and Political Familism: A Preliminary Discussion of Activist and Feminist Traditions of Mexican American Women in Texas," unpublished paper, 1991.

92. Martha Cotera, "Chicanas and Political Familism"; Maxine Baca Zinn, "Political Familism: Toward Sex Role Equality in Chicano Families," *Aztlán: International Journal of Chicano Studies Research* 6, no. 1 (1975): 13–26.
93. Questionnaire, Crystal City Public School District, 1974, 2, Martha Cotera Collection, CPMR.
94. Dionne Espinoza, "'The Partido Belongs to Those Who Will Work for It': Chicana Organizing and Leadership in the Texas Raza Unida Party, 1970–1980," *Aztlán: A Journal of Chicano Studies* 36, no. 1 (2011): 192.
95. Adelaida Del Castillo made similar observations with respect to women in Chicano student organizations and Chicano left organizations. See Del Castillo, "Mexican Women in Organization." For an analysis of how competing conceptualizations of the Chicana/o family shaped movimiento discourse, see Richard T. Rodríguez, *Next of Kin: The Family in Chicano/a Cultural Politics* (Duke University Press, 2009).
96. Martha recalls that TEAM was an exception to this early pattern of ambivalence toward Chicanas in prominent roles. She surmises that this was because the organization's volunteers were mostly teachers and parents, and they were more likely to be women. Martha Cotera, CPMR oral history, 2018.
97. Martha Cotera, CPMR oral history, 2009.
98. Martha recalls that longtime community leader María L. de Hernández was in the audience, which made the gendered contradictions exposed at the conference feel particularly acute. Martha Cotera, phone conversation with the author, May 27, 2019. For more on María L. de Hernández, see Martha P. Cotera, *Profile on the Mexican American Woman* (National Educational Laboratory, 1976); *Hearing Before the United States Commission on Civil Rights, San Antonio, Texas, December 9–14, 1968* (US Government Printing Office, 1968); María L. de Hernández, interview by Angie del Cueto Quirós, April 19, 1975, Benson Latin American Collection, University of Texas at Austin.
99. Martha Cotera, CPMR oral history, 2009.
100. Martha Cotera, CPMR oral history, 2009.
101. Martha Cotera, CPMR oral history, 2009.
102. For more on Crystal City politics in the mid-1960s, see Shockley, *Chicano Revolt in a Texas Town*; Gutiérrez, *Making of a Chicano Militant*.
103. Múzquiz was the national chair of the Raza Unida Party from 1972 to 1974. See Teresa Palomo Acosta and Ruthe Winegarten, *Las Tejanas: 300 Years of History* (University of Texas Press, 2003), 256; Gutiérrez, *Making of a Chicano Militant*.
104. Martha Cotera, "Final Comments."
105. Martha Cotera, Baylor oral history, 1973, 48–49.
106. Martha Cotera, "Chicanas and Political Familism," 13.
107. For information on two of these student leaders, Severita Lara and Diana Serna, see Gutiérrez, *Making of a Chicano Militant*. For more on Severita Lara, see José Ángel Gutiérrez, Michelle Meléndez, and Sonia Adriana Noyola, *Chicanas in Charge: Texas Women in the Public Arena* (AltaMira Press, 2007), 113–122;

Severita Lara, oral history interview by José Ángel Gutiérrez, July 18, 1996, *Tejano Voices*, https://library.uta.edu/tejanovoices/interview.php?cmasno=013; José Ángel Gutiérrez, *"We Won't Back Down": Severita Lara's Rise from Student Leader to Mayor* (Piñata Books, 2005).

108. Evey Chapa, oral history interview, February 24, 2011, Evey Chapa Collection, Chicana por Mi Raza Digital Memory Collective (hereafter cited as Evey Chapa, CPMR oral history, 2011).
109. Evey Chapa, CPMR oral history, 2011.
110. My translation; the original Spanish reads, "El propósito de esta y otras conferencias de las mujeres Pro Raza Unida es de enseñar la técnica de la política a la mujer desde la cuadra en donde vive, a su precinto y en su condado y estado." The article lists Juana Bustamante y Luera, Irma Mireles, Evey Chapa, Chelo Avila, and Martha Cotera as the conference organizers. Martha P. Cotera, "Conferencia de Mujeres por Raza Unida," *La Verdad*, September 16, 1973, 3. For a complete account of Mujeres Pro Raza Unida, see Cynthia E. Orozco, "Mujeres por la Raza," *Handbook of Texas Online*, updated February 9, 2019, http://www.tshaonline.org/handbook/online/articles/vimgh. See also Evey Chapa, "Mujeres por la Raza," in Alma M. García, *Chicana Feminist Thought: The Basic Historical Writings* (Routledge, 1997), 178–179; Espinoza, "'Partido Belongs,'" 204–205; Palomo Acosta and Winegarten, *Las Tejanas*, 235–237.
111. In her unpublished essay "Chicanas and Political Familism," Martha Cotera notes that in 1973 and 1974, Mujeres Pro Raza Unida training conferences were held throughout Texas, in San Antonio, Crystal City, Houston, Fort Worth, Austin, Kingsville, and Temple.
112. See also Linda Garcia Merchant, "Chicana Diasporic," https://chicanapormiraza.org/chicana-diasporic. Mujeres Pro Raza Unida ultimately withdrew from both the Texas Women's Political Caucus and the National Women's Political Caucus, citing the leadership's failure to support Chicanas in political races. See Orozco, "Mujeres por la Raza."
113. Martha Cotera, "Chicanas and Political Familism," 10.
114. Formerly *Chicano Times*, *Magazín* was a Chicana/o magazine published in San Antonio, Texas, in the early 1970s.
115. Martha P. Cotera, "Mexicano Feminism," *Magazín* 1, no. 9 (September 1973): 10.
116. Martha Cotera, Baylor oral history, 1973, 50.

## CHAPTER 3. TLAMATINI INFRASTRUCTURES IN THE SHADOW OF PRECARITY

1. Martha Cotera, "Final Comments, May 22, 2019," unpublished manuscript shared with the author.
2. Martha Cotera, oral history interview, University of Michigan, July 3, 2018, Martha Cotera Collection, Chicana por Mi Raza Digital Memory Collective (hereafter cited as Martha Cotera, CPMR oral history, 2018).

3. María Eugenia Cotera, "Nuestra Autohistoria: Toward a Chicana Digital Praxis," *American Quarterly* 70, no. 3 (2018): 483–504.
4. Martha Cotera, CPMR oral history, 2018.
5. Martha Cotera, CPMR oral history, 2018.
6. Jaime Rafael Puente, "Juárez–Lincoln University: Alternative Higher Education in the Chicana/o Movement, 1969–1983" (master's thesis, University of Texas at Austin, 2013), 35.
7. Puente, "Juárez–Lincoln University," 36.
8. Puente, "Juárez–Lincoln University," 6.
9. Nancy Flores, "Defying the Odds: 50 Years of CAMP at St. Edward's University in Austin, Texas," St. Edward's University, https://www.stedwards.edu/articles/featured-stories/2022/04/defying-odds.
10. Puente, "Juárez–Lincoln University," 37.
11. Puente, "Juárez–Lincoln University," 36.
12. Puente, "Juárez–Lincoln University," 47.
13. Jaime Vega et al., "National Migrant Information Clearinghouse, Juárez–Lincoln Center, Annual Report, 1972–73," report submitted to the US Department of Labor, Juárez–Lincoln Center, 1973.
14. Martha Cotera, CPMR oral history, 2018.
15. For more on how analytical biases and definitions of leadership structure such silences in the archive, see Dolores Delgado Bernal, "Grassroots Leadership Reconceptualized: Chicana Oral Histories and the 1968 East Los Angeles School Blowouts," *Frontiers: A Journal of Women Studies* 19, no. 2 (1998): 113–142; Maylei Blackwell, *¡Chicana Power! Contested Histories of Feminism in the Chicano Movement* (University of Texas Press, 2011); Dionne Espinoza, María Eugenia Cotera, and Maylei Blackwell, eds., *Chicana Movidas: New Narratives of Activism and Feminism in the Movement Era* (University of Texas Press, 2018).
16. Michel-Rolph Trouillot, *Silencing the Past: Power and the Production of History* (Beacon Press, 1995), 26.
17. I discuss Martha Cotera's work at the Crystal City library in chapter 1.
18. Martha Cotera, CPMR oral history, 2018.
19. Martha Cotera, CPMR oral history, 2018.
20. Martha Cotera, CPMR oral history, 2018.
21. Puente, "Juárez–Lincoln University," 40.
22. Vega et al., "National Migrant Information Clearinghouse," 1.
23. Vega et al., "National Migrant Information Clearinghouse," 13.
24. When Leonard Mestas and Andre Guerrero left Colegio Jacinto Treviño to start the Juárez–Lincoln Center in Fort Worth, they took a number of materials for the new library. Martha recalls that she and Guerrero built the Jacinto Treviño collection with materials they had gathered at the Southwest Educational Development Lab and from Teacher Corps: "So we had about ten boxes, and Andre also had donated his collection with Teacher Corps, where they had a lot of really good, like methodologies and things like that. So altogether, I

guess we started out with a collection of about, you know, ten to fifteen boxes of materials. And then we did have a budget to buy materials. And I made sure that we bought a lot of literary works, you know, those works that I was talking about, like some of the New Mexico [books]." Martha Cotera, CPMR oral history, 2018.

25. Vega et al., "National Migrant Information Clearinghouse," 46.
26. Puente, "Juárez–Lincoln University," 41.
27. Puente, "Juárez–Lincoln University," 50.
28. Martha Cotera, "Final Comments."
29. Puente, "Juárez–Lincoln University," 50.
30. Puente, "Juárez–Lincoln University," 49.
31. Puente, "Juárez–Lincoln University," 50–56.
32. In a telephone conversation with me on June 20, 2023, Martha recalled that Mestas "kicked the [Chicana Research and Learning Center] out of Juárez–Lincoln" in 1974, which forced the project to find a new home at the YWCA, located on Guadalupe Street across from the University of Texas. The cultural project continued for over three decades, finally resulting in the establishment of a permanent Mexican American Cultural Center in Austin. See "Emma S. Barrientos Mexican American Cultural Center," City of Austin, https://www.austintexas.gov/department/emma-s-barrientos-mexican-american-cultural-center.
33. Puente, "Juárez–Lincoln University," 51.
34. Vega et al., "National Migrant Information Clearinghouse."
35. Puente, "Juárez–Lincoln University," 53.
36. Puente, "Juárez–Lincoln University," 53. In a text communication with me on June 17, 2023, my mother clarified that while she did not write the Equal Employment Opportunity Commission report, she did "encourage women to file."
37. Puente, "Juárez–Lincoln University," 51.
38. Martha Cotera, phone interview with the author, June 12, 2023.
39. Emilio Zamora worked on curricular development at Juárez–Lincoln. He would later serve on the first advisory board for the Chicana Research and Learning Center. See Chicana Research and Learning Center (CRLC) concept paper (no byline but written by Evey Chapa and Martha Cotera), Martha Cotera Collection, Chicana por Mi Raza Digital Memory Collective (hereafter cited as CPMR).
40. Library Committee, Center for Mexican American Studies, proposal for a Chicano collection development program, July 22, 1974, Martha Cotera Collection, CPMR. For a brief history of the establishment of the Mexican American Library Program, see Maria E. Gonzalez, "Collecting Theories: Mexican American Archives at the University of Texas Benson Latin American Collection (1974–2004)," *Collections* 1, no. 1 (2004): 67–80.
41. Gonzalez, "Collecting Theories," 67–68.
42. In the late 1960s, while doing research for the Southwest Educational Development Lab, Martha discovered that the University of Texas's Foreign Language

Educational Collection (which contained many educational materials and children's books in Spanish) was going to be deaccessioned, and she worked with Nettie Lee Benson to acquire them for the Latin American Collection.

43. Santos Reyes to Martha Cotera, September 20, 1974, Martha Cotera Collection, CPMR.
44. José Cárdenas to Merle N. Boylan, Director of General Libraries, University of Texas, October 14, 1974, Martha Cotera Collection, CPMR.
45. Gonzalez, "Collecting Theories," 68–69; Margo Gutiérrez, "Mexican American Library Program Celebrates Its 25th Anniversary," *Noticias de NACCS*, February 1999.
46. Martha Cotera, "History of Library Experience," August 18, 2009, unpublished manuscript shared with the author.
47. Gonzalez, "Collecting Theories," 74.
48. Martha Cotera, "History of Library Experience."
49. Gonzalez, "Collecting Theories," 74.
50. For example, Margo Gutiérrez, who became the lead bibliographer for the Mexican American Library Program in 1989, does not mention Martha in her retrospective of the program, written on the occasion of its twenty-fifth anniversary, an omission that erases the importance of her work in the library program's early years. Gutiérrez, "Mexican American Library Program Celebrates Its 25th Anniversary."
51. Evey Chapa and Armando Gutierrez mention the exact date of the Chicana Research and Learning Center's incorporation in a paper they published in 1977. They describe it as "the first institution established in the nation which is concerned not only with providing community-oriented, social service activities but also with implementing research projects for Chicanas." Evey Chapa and Armando Gutierrez, "Chicanas in Politics: An Overview and a Case Study," in *Perspectivas en Chicano Studies I: Papers Presented at the 3rd Annual Meeting of the National Association of Chicano Social Scientists*, ed. Reynaldo Macias (Chicano Studies Center, UCLA, 1977), 148.
52. For more on the activities of Mujeres Pro Raza Unida, see chapter 2. See also Dionne Espinoza, "'The Partido Belongs to Those Who Will Work for It': Chicana Organizing and Leadership in the Texas Raza Unida Party, 1970–1980," *Aztlán: A Journal of Chicano Studies* 36, no. 1 (2011): 191–210.
53. Evey Chapa, oral history interview, February 24, 2011, Evey Chapa Collection, Chicana por Mi Raza Digital Memory Collective (hereafter cited as Evey Chapa, CPMR oral history, 2011).
54. Evey Chapa, CPMR oral history, 2011.
55. CRLC concept paper, 4.
56. Martha P. Cotera, "Concepts of Information Services in a Chicano Context," in *Library Services to Mexican Americans: Policies, Practices and Prospects*, ed. Roberto Urzua, Martha P. Cotera, and Emma González Stupp (National Educational Laboratory, 1978), 41.

57. Stefano Harney and Fred Moten, *The Undercommons: Fugitive Planning and Black Study* (Minor Compositions, 2013), 26.
58. Brenda Sendejo, "The Space in Between: Exploring the Development of Chicana Feminist Thought in Texas," in *Chicana Movidas: New Narratives of Activism and Feminism in the Movement Era*, ed. Dionne Espinoza, María Eugenia Cotera, and Maylei Blackwell (University of Texas Press, 2018).
59. The Women's Educational Equity Act of 1974 was established as an amendment (Title IV-A) to the Elementary and Secondary Education Act of 1965. Its goals were to "(1) provide educational equity for women; (2) help educational institutions comply with the law's requirements prohibiting sex discrimination in educational institutions receiving federal funds; and (3) provide educational equity for women and girls suffering multiple discrimination due to sex, race, ethnic origin, disability, or age." Through its resource center the Women's Educational Equity Act distributed "gender equity" publications and products and provided information and assistance on gender equity to educators. US Government Accountability Office, "Women's Educational Equity Act: A Review of Program Goals and Strategies Needed," December 27, 1994, https://www.govinfo.gov/content/pkg/GAOREPORTS-PEMD-95-6/html/GAOREPORTS-PEMD-95-6.htm.
60. CRLC concept paper, 4.
61. Martha P. Cotera, "Identidad," in *The Chicana Feminist* (Information Systems Development, 1977), 30. This essay was drawn from the keynote address at the Chicana Identity Conference at the University of Houston in November 1975.
62. Jack Halberstam, "The Wild Beyond: With and For the Undercommons," in Harney and Moten, *Undercommons*, 11; Martha Cotera, quoted in Sendejo, "Space in Between," 189.
63. Questionnaire, Crystal City Public School District, 1974, 2, Martha Cotera Collection, CPMR.
64. Maria Flores, a student research intern with the Chicana por Mi Raza project, discovered a copy of the concept paper in the Jesse and Juana González Papers at Michigan State University. This suggests how broadly the paper circulated through Chicana feminist networks.
65. Martha Cotera, CPMR oral history, 2018. For a history of the Educational Resources Information Center, see Delmer J. Trester, *ERIC—The First 15 Years; A History of the Educational Resources Information Center* (US Government Printing Office, 1979).
66. Martha Cotera, CPMR oral history, 2018.
67. In the late 1970s, Women's Educational Equity Act grants supported a broad variety of projects that would diversify primary, secondary, and higher education curricula, including the "development and evaluation of curricula, textbooks, and other educational materials," training programs for educators and other personnel, "research and development activities," and continuing educational activities for adult women. The funding agency disseminated these

materials through the Women's Educational Equity Act Publishing Center. US Department of Education, "Women's Educational Equity Act Program Annual Report," 1980, https://catalog.hathitrust.org/Record/002598240. The Chicana Research and Learning Center developed an array of educational resources with the help of the equity act grants, including *Multicultural Women's Sourcebook: Materials Guide for Use in Women's Studies and Bilingual/Multicultural Programs* (1981), which Martha edited with Nella Cunningham, and an assertiveness training manual for Latina girls and women, *Doña Doormat No Está Aquí*, which received a $50,000 grant but was never widely disseminated, because (as Martha predicted) the equity act's funding for publication and dissemination was discontinued in the early 1980s.

68. Martha P. Cotera, *Profile on the Mexican American Woman* (New Mexico State University, 1976).
69. Martha Cotera, CPMR oral history, 2018.
70. Martha Cotera, CPMR oral history, 2018.
71. Cordelia Candelaria, "Six Reference Works on Mexican-American Women: A Review Essay," *Frontiers* 5, no. 2 (1980): 75–80.
72. Candelaria, "Six Reference Works on Mexican-American Women," 77.
73. Martha Cotera, CPMR oral history, 2018.
74. Candelaria, "Six Reference Works on Mexican-American Women," 77.
75. Evey Chapa to Advisory Board, February 10, 2018, Martha Cotera Collection, CPMR.
76. Martha notes that the Mujeres Célebres project inspired the books *Las Tejanas: 300 Years of History* by Teresa Palomo Acosta and Ruthe Winegarten, and *Latinas in the United States: A Historical Encyclopedia* by Vicki L. Ruiz and Virginia Sánchez Korrol: "In both cases as a courtesy the respective editors consulted me before taking on their projects since Mujeres Célebres was on hold." Martha Cotera, personal communication with the author, October 3, 2024.
77. Mitsuye Yamada, "Invisibility Is an Unnatural Disaster: Reflections of an Asian American Woman," in *This Bridge Called My Back: Writings by Radical Women of Color*, ed. Cherríe Moraga and Gloria Anzaldúa, 3rd ed. (Third Woman Press, 2002).
78. Nicolás Kanellos, "REFORMA: The National Association to Promote Library Services to the Spanish-Speaking," in *The Greenwood Encyclopedia of Latino Literature*, vol. 3, ed. Nicolás Kanellos (Greenwood Press, 2008), 977.
79. Martha Cotera, email correspondence with the author, March 19, 2019.
80. Salvador Güereña and Edward Erazo, "Latinos and Librarianship," *Library Trends* 49, no. 1 (2000): 138.
81. As already noted, Martha's absence is even more glaringly noticeable in Margo Gutiérrez's retrospective account of the Mexican American Library Program. Gutiérrez, "Mexican American Library Program Celebrates Its 25th Anniversary."
82. Harney and Moten, *Undercommons*, 37–38.

83. Martha Cotera, "Caring for the Documentary Patrimony of La Raza," lecture, April 19, 2013, University of Texas at Austin.
84. In our many conversations about this event, my mother has noted dismissively that the position the library administration offered her was one she had last occupied in her very first year at the El Paso Public Library.
85. Adelaida R. Del Castillo, "Mexican Women in Organization," in *Mexican Women in the United States: Struggles Past and Present*, ed. Magdalena Mora and Adelaida R. Del Castillo (Chicano Studies Research Center, 1980).
86. María Cotera, "Nuestra Autohistoria," 499–500.
87. Sendejo, "Space in Between," 196.

## CHAPTER 4. X MARKS THE SPOT

1. Olivia Reynolds de Medina and Regina Contreras, Chicana Ad Hoc Committee of CCHE, "Notes on the Chicana Caucus of California State Colleges," March 21, 1971, Enriqueta Chavez Papers, San Diego State University, box 3, folder 24.
2. Gloria E. Anzaldúa, *Light in the Dark / Luz en lo Oscuro: Rewriting Identity, Spirituality, Reality*, ed. AnaLouise Keating (Duke University Press, 2015), 140.
3. Rodolfo Acuña, *The Making of Chicana/o Studies: In the Trenches of Academe* (Rutgers University Press, 2011).
4. Sonia Lopez, "The Role of the Chicana Within the Student Movement," in *Essays on La Mujer*, ed. Rosaura Sánchez and Rosa Martinez Cruz (Chicano Studies Center, UCLA, 1977); Adelaida R. Del Castillo, "Mexican Women in Organization," in *Mexican Women in the United States: Struggles Past and Present*, ed. Magdalena Mora and Adelaida R. Del Castillo (Chicano Studies Research Center, 1980); Cynthia Orozco, "Sexism in Chicano Studies and the Community," in *Chicana Voices: Intersections of Class, Race, and Gender*, ed. Teresa Córdova, Norma Cantú, Gilberto Cardenas, Juan Garcia, and Christine M. Sierra (University of New Mexico Press, 1993); Alma M. García, "The Development of Chicana Feminist Discourse, 1970–1980," *Gender and Society* 3, no. 2 (1989): 217–238; Maylei Blackwell, *¡Chicana Power! Contested Histories of Feminism in the Chicano Movement* (University of Texas Press, 2011); Gilberto García, "Beyond the Adelita Image: Women Scholars in the National Association for Chicano Studies, 1972–1992," *Perspectives in Mexican American Studies* 5 (1995): 35–62; Gustavo Licón, "Feminist Mobilization in MEChA: A Southern California Case Study," *Kalfou: A Journal of Comparative and Relational Ethnic Studies* 5, no. 1 (2018): 76.
5. Juan Gómez-Quiñones, *Mexican Students por la Raza: The Chicano Student Movement in Southern California, 1967–1977* (La Causa, 1978); Carlos Muñoz Jr., *Youth, Identity, Power: The Chicano Movement* (Verso, 1989); Michael Soldatenko, *Chicano Studies: The Genesis of a Discipline* (University of Arizona Press, 2009); Acuña, *Making of Chicana/o Studies*; Juan Gómez-Quiñones and Irene Vásquez,

*Making Aztlán: Ideology and Culture of the Chicana and Chicano Movement, 1966–1977* (University of New Mexico Press, 2014). Later works, like Lee Bebout's *Mythohistorical Interventions*, represent a shift toward greater attention to gender in the historical analysis of the Chicano movement. Bebout devotes two chapters to Chicanas, one of which focuses on the ways that Chicana lesbians rescripted la familia de la raza in their writing. In *Next of Kin*, Richard T. Rodríguez provides a thorough contextualization of the ways in which la familia de la raza as an ideological construct helped to consolidate male power and enforce heteronormativity within the Chicano movement. See Lee Bebout, *Mythohistorical Interventions: The Chicano Movement and Its Legacies* (University of Minnesota Press, 2011); Richard T. Rodríguez, *Next of Kin: The Family in Chicano/a Cultural Politics* (Duke University Press, 2009).

6. Dolores Delgado Bernal, "Grassroots Leadership Reconceptualized: Chicana Oral Histories and the 1968 East Los Angeles School Blowouts," *Frontiers: A Journal of Women Studies* 19, no. 2 (1998): 113.
7. Delgado Bernal, "Grassroots Leadership Reconceptualized," 124.
8. Blackwell, *¡Chicana Power!*, 44; Naomi Helena Quiñonez, "Hijas de la Malinche (Malinche's Daughters): The Development of Social Agency Among Mexican-American Women and the Emergence of First Wave Chicana Cultural Production" (PhD diss., Claremont Graduate University, 1997); Vicki L. Ruiz, *From Out of the Shadows: Mexican Women in Twentieth-Century America* (Oxford University Press, 2008); Marisela R. Chávez, "Pilgrimage to the Homeland: California Chicanas and International Women's Year, Mexico City, 1975," in *Memories and Migrations: Mapping Boricua and Chicana Histories*, ed. Vicki L. Ruiz and John R. Chávez (University of Illinois Press, 2008); Marisela R. Chávez, "'We Have a Long, Beautiful History': Chicana Feminist Trajectories and Legacies," in *No Permanent Waves: Recasting Histories of U.S. Feminism*, ed. Nancy Hewitt (Rutgers University Press, 2010); Dionne Espinoza, "'The Partido Belongs to Those Who Will Work for It': Chicana Organizing and Leadership in the Texas Raza Unida Party, 1970–1980," *Aztlán: A Journal of Chicano Studies* 36, no. 1 (2011): 191–210; Dionne Espinoza, "'Revolutionary Sisters': Women's Solidarity and Collective Identification Among Chicana Brown Berets in East Los Angeles, 1967–1970," *Aztlán: A Journal of Chicano Studies* 26, no. 1 (2001): 17–58; Becky Thompson, "Multiracial Feminism: Recasting the Chronology of Second Wave Feminism," *Feminist Studies* 28, no. 2 (2002): 336–360.
9. Blackwell, *!Chicana Power!*, 44.
10. Mexican American Youth Organization (MAYO), Mexican American Youth Association (MAYA), Mexican American Student Association (MASA), Mexican American Student Confederation (MASC), and United Mexican American Students (UMAS).
11. For a full list of conference organizers, see Chicano Coordinating Council on Higher Education (CCHE), *El Plan de Santa Bárbara: A Chicano Plan for Higher Education* (La Causa, 1971), 82–83.

12. Roberto García, a UMAS member and conference participant from the University of California, Santa Barbara, speculates that this imbalance may have been due to the nascent stage of the women's movement in the Chicano movement—several young women, though active in student organizations, were in the process of finding their own voices. Marisol Moreno, "'Of the Community, for the Community': The Chicana/o Student Movement in California's Public Higher Education, 1967–1973" (PhD diss., University of California, Santa Barbara, 2009), 206.
13. Muñoz, *Youth, Identity, Power*, 101.
14. Orozco, "Sexism in Chicano Studies."
15. The primary and secondary sources amply demonstrate that student organizations like UMAS (and post-1969 MEChA) favored male leadership, as did Chicano studies departments and programs (many of which drew their chairs and directors directly from the pool of male leaders in student organizations). As Marisol Moreno observes in her dissertation, "Despite the availability of opportunities for student participation in UMAS, duties generally reflected gendered notions of male and female spheres. Whereas men commonly dominated the public and political leadership positions of president and vice-president, women often worked behind the scenes in less recognized areas of movement mobilization. For example, a review of organizational committee notes [of UMAS at Long Beach State] reveals a disproportionate number of women involved with organizing student service activities, serving as members or as a chairperson of the counseling committee and volunteering in La Escuelita, a Head Start–type of program offering tutoring and Chicano Studies classes to young Chicana/os in nearby communities. With the exception of founding member Mary Lu Hernández, who served as UMAS vice-president in the fall semester of 1968, no other female members served as president or vice-president until the election of Anna NietoGomez in 1970." Moreno, "'Of the Community, for the Community,'" 338–339. Moreover, as Maylei Blackwell has shown in her study of Las Hijas de Cuauhtémoc, when women did take on leadership roles in student organizations, they often faced strong opposition from men, and in some cases women. Blackwell, *¡Chicana Power!* See also Lopez, "Role of the Chicana"; Del Castillo, "Mexican Women in Organization"; A. García, "Development of Chicana Feminist Discourse"; Licón, "Feminist Mobilization in MEChA."
16. Anna NietoGomez, email communication with the author, October 14, 2020.
17. Muñoz, *Youth, Identity, Power*, 101. At the Santa Barbara conference in 1969, Chicano student organizations in California agreed to unify under a single organization, MEChA (Movimiento Estudiantil Chicano de Aztlán), in order to coordinate their organizing and information exchange and to build student power across the state.
18. CCHE, *El Plan de Santa Bárbara*, 83.
19. Blackwell, *!Chicana Power!*, 64.

20. Denise A. Segura, "Challenging the Chicano Text: Toward a More Inclusive Contemporary Causa," *Signs* 26, no. 2 (2001): 543.
21. Rodolfo Gonzales, *I Am Joaquin / Yo Soy Joaquin* (El Gallo, 1967).
22. Anna NietoGomez, interview with the author, October 30, 2018, Los Angeles, California.
23. Muñoz, *Youth, Identity, Power*, 161.
24. Anna NietoGomez, "Hijas de Cuauhtémoc," May 17, 2018, unpublished essay shared with the author.
25. Elena H. García, "Chicana Consciousness: A New Perspective, a New Hope," in *La Mujer: En Pie de Lucha*, ed. Dorinda Moreno (Espina del Norte, 1973).
26. San Diego State College became San Diego State University after 1974.
27. Enriqueta Chavez, oral history interview, San Diego, California, August 1, 2013, Enriqueta Chavez Collection, Chicana por Mi Raza Digital Memory Collective (hereafter cited as Enriqueta Chavez, CPMR oral history, 2013).
28. The article notes that "one of the most important and controversial workshops that developed during the Denver Conference last March was the Chicana Workshop. The following is a statement put out by the workshop and a list of the resolutions that grew out of it." "Resolutions from the Chicana Workshop," *La Verdad* 20 (June 1970): 9.
29. Enriqueta Chavez, CPMR oral history, 2013.
30. Carlos G. Vélez Ibáñez, *Border Visions: Mexican Cultures of the Southwest United States* (University of Arizona Press, 1996). Juan Gómez-Quiñones notes that "perhaps the strongest women's effort to emerge in this early period of student activism was at San Diego." Gómez-Quiñones, *Mexican Students por la Raza*, 33. Dionne Espinoza has conducted extensive research on Las Chicanas de San Diego for a forthcoming book on Chicana feminist activism in the 1970s. Her essay "'La Raza en Canada'" documents how Chicanas in San Diego developed a third world consciousness through their participation in international meetings. Dionne Espinoza, "'La Raza en Canada': San Diego Chicana Activists, the Indochinese Women's Conference of 1971, and Third World Womanism," in *Chicana Movidas: New Narratives of Activism and Feminism in the Movement Era*, ed. Dionne Espinoza, María Eugenia Cotera, and Maylei Blackwell (University of Texas Press, 2018). See also "50th Anniversary of the Seminario de Chicanas, May 10, 2022," YouTube video, uploaded by Chicana Revolution, July 13, 2022, https://www.youtube.com/watch?v=AoYfrY7TKOI.
31. NietoGomez, "Hijas de Cuauhtémoc."
32. In *!Chicana Power!*, Maylei Blackwell offers an extensive examination of Anna NietoGomez and Las Hijas de Cuauhtémoc. See also Moreno, "'Of the Community, for the Community,'" 348–359; NietoGomez, "Hijas de Cuauhtémoc"; Benita Roth, *Separate Roads to Feminism: Black, Chicana, and White Feminist Movements in America's Second Wave* (Cambridge University Press, 2004), 135–141.
33. Gómez-Quiñones, *Mexican Students por la Raza*, 33–34.

34. Corinne J. Sanchez, "A Challenge for Colleges and Universities: Chicano Studies," *Civil Rights Digest* 3, no. 4 (1970): 36–39. Also included in this issue was an article by Ernesto Galarza and Julian Samora, "Chicano Studies: Research and Scholarly Activity," 40–42.
35. Espinoza, "'La Raza en Canada,'" 264.
36. For more on Francisca Flores, see M. Chávez, "'We Have a Long, Beautiful History,'" 77–97; Pablo Landeros, "AKA Frances: Francisca Flores and the Radical Roots of Chicana Feminism in California," in *Latina Histories and Cultures: Feminist Readings and Recoveries of Archival Knowledge*, ed. Montse Feu and Yolanda Padilla (Arte Público Press, 2023); Pablo Eduardo Landeros, "The Birth of Her Causa: The Construction, Development, and Ideology of Comision Femenil Mexicana Nacional, Inc., 1973–1993" (PhD diss., University of California, Santa Barbara, 2012); Anna NietoGomez, "Francisca Flores, and the History of the League of Mexican American Women and Its Evolution into the Comisión Femenil Mexicana Nacional, 1958–1975," in Espinoza, Cotera, and Blackwell, *Chicana Movidas*.
37. Francisca Flores, "Comision Femenil Mexicana," *Regeneración* 2, no. 4 (1975).
38. Anna NietoGomez, essay published in *Somos* (July–August 1979), reprinted in Alma M. García, *Chicana Feminist Thought: The Basic Historical Writings* (Routledge, 1997), 148–149. In an article published in *Regeneración*, Gema Matsuda notes that before the establishment of a Comisión Femenil chapter in 1971, there had been other efforts to organize women at California State Los Angeles—she mentions VELA and the Chicana Forum—but they had eventually "faded into oblivion." Gema Matsuda, "La Chicana Organizes," *Regeneración* 2, no. 4 (1975).
39. Matsuda, "La Chicana Organizes."
40. The Chicana Service Action Center also produced a monthly newsletter that became a vital resource for information on employment, education, and community issues in California (a testament to the newsletter's national importance is the fact that Martha Cotera's personal collection contains dozens of issues from the 1970s). Anna NietoGomez contributed articles on Chicana employment and educational issues to the newsletter. These articles were published, in expanded form, in the first Chicana feminist journal, *Encuentro Femenil*. For more on the Chicana Service Action Center, see Francisca Flores, "The Chicana Service Action Center," *Regeneración*, 1973, 6–7; Anna NietoGomez, essay published in *Somos* (July–August 1979), reprinted in A. García, *Chicana Feminist Thought*; M. Chávez, "'We Have a Long, Beautiful History'"; Marisela R. Chávez, *Chicana Liberation: Women and Mexican American Politics in Los Angeles, 1945–1981* (University of Illinois Press, 2024); Landeros, "Birth of Her Causa"; Sonia R. García Marisela Márquez, "The Comisión Femenil: La Voz of a Chicana Organization," *Aztlán: A Journal of Chicano Studies* 36, no. 1 (2011): 149–169; Roth, *Separate Roads to Feminism*, 141–142.
41. For more on the Third World Liberation Front and the student strikes at Berkeley and San Francisco, see Chris Carlsson, ed., *Ten Years That Shook the*

*City: San Francisco 1968–1978* (City Lights Books, 2011); Harvey Dong and Janie Chen, eds., *Power of the People Won't Stop: Legacy of the TWLF at UC Berkeley* (Eastwind Books of Berkeley, 2020).

42. Dorinda Moreno, "Margaret Cruz, the 'Little Giant': A Remembrance, 2020," unpublished essay shared with the author.
43. "La Razón Mestiza: Latina Women Begin to Speak for Themselves," *Media Report to Women*, September 1, 1975, 6; Patricia Garcia, "Concilio Mujeres," *Women's News Journal*, July 1, 1975, 5. For more on Dorinda Moreno and Concilio Mujeres, see Roth, *Separate Roads to Feminism*, 142-145.
44. Anna NietoGomez, "La Feminista," *Encuentro Femenil* 1, no. 2 (1974): 36.
45. CCHE was initially called the Chicano Coordinating Committee on Higher Education, but it was renamed the Chicano Council on Higher Education at the Santa Barbara conference. Enriqueta Chavez, "A Short Historical Sketch of CCHE," typescript, Enriqueta Chavez Papers, San Diego State University, box 9, folder 2. See also Muñoz, *Youth, Identity, Power*, 187.
46. Carlos Muñoz provides the most comprehensive account of the origins of CCHE and its role in planning the 1969 Santa Barbara conference. He notes that Rene Nuñez, who was then the director of the Educational Clearinghouse for Central Los Angeles (a federally funded program to move more Chicana/o and African American youths into college), was concerned that Mexican American youths were underserved when it came to recruitment and retention services offered by Educational Opportunity Programs in California. During this period, Nuñez was also a member of the Educational Issues Coordinating Committee, an organization at the center of community support for the Los Angeles student walkouts in 1968. Nuñez made critical connections between the racism that Mexican American youths faced in secondary education and their low numbers in colleges and universities. As Muñoz notes, "During his visits to high schools and college campuses throughout the state, [Nuñez] became convinced the problems related to student recruitment and retention and faculty hiring were similar throughout the system." Nuñez played an instrumental role in bringing together students, teachers, and professionals in higher and secondary education to address these issues through a new organization, the Chicano Coordinating Committee on Higher Education. It was under the auspices of the committee that Nuñez and others organized the Santa Barbara conference, where they formalized the organization and adopted a less wordy name, the Chicano Council on Higher Education, or CCHE. Muñoz, *Youth, Identity, Power*, 162–163. For more on the struggles over Educational Opportunity Program resources, see Ruben Salazar, "Black and Chicano Ties Worsen After Walkout in Santa Barbara," September 15, 1969, in *Border Correspondent: Selected Writings, 1955–1970*, by Ruben Salazar, ed. Mario T. García (University of California Press, 1995), 221–223.
47. Muñoz, *Youth, Identity, Power*, 163.
48. Enriqueta Chavez, CPMR oral history, 2013.

49. Anna NietoGomez, oral history interview, Long Beach, California, October 30, 2018, Chicana por Mi Raza Digital Memory Collective (hereafter cited as Anna NietoGomez, CPMR oral history, 2018); Enriqueta Chavez, CPMR oral history, 2013; Sonia Lopez, oral history interview, San Diego, California, August 6, 2013, Chicana por Mi Raza Digital Memory Collective.
50. In *¡Chicana Power!*, Maylei Blackwell notes that Chicana feminists who were also movement activists often engaged in "double-time activism." Even as they organized themselves "because their political needs were not being addressed," they also continued to carry out the "day-to-day work that keeps an organization running" (89).
51. Anna NietoGomez, CPMR oral history, 2018.
52. Enriqueta Chavez, CPMR oral history, 2013.
53. Audre Lorde, in the essays "Age, Race, Class and Sex: Women Redefining Difference" and "Learning from the '60s," has argued that monolithic visions of oppression and resistance all too often ignore differences within communities of struggle. See Audre Lorde, *Sister Outsider* (Crossing Press, 1984).
54. Though their petitions for official caucus status within the National Women's Political Caucus were denied, Chicanas nevertheless met as an informal caucus (which included Republicans, Democrats, and Raza Unida Party members). Despite not having official status, this caucus still wielded considerable power, especially when they worked in coalition with other women of color and lesbians. See Martha P. Cotera, "Mujeres Bravas: How Chicanas Shaped the Feminist Agenda at the National IWY Conference in Houston, 1977," in Espinoza, Cotera, and Blackwell, *Chicana Movidas*. See also NietoGomez, "La Feminista."
55. NietoGomez, "La Feminista."
56. E. García, "Chicana Consciousness."
57. Beyond the problem of institutional factionalism, there were other ominous developments that distracted from the formation of a statewide organization. Cuts to the state higher education budget by the conservative legislature under the leadership of Governor Ronald Reagan had specifically targeted Educational Opportunity Programs, which were seen as a main conduit for student activism. Newly established programs were being threatened and even shut down by university administrators, and attacked (sometimes violently) by conservative forces on campus. Indeed, an original plan for Fresno State College to host the follow-up to the Santa Barbara conference in June 1970 had to be scrapped because of student unrest on that campus in response to the administration's systematic undermining of its Educational Opportunity Program office and Raza studies program. See Enriqueta Chavez, "A Brief Historical Sketch of CCHE," presented by Rene Nuñez at the CCHE faculty retreat, October 28 and 29, 1971, Enriqueta Chavez Papers, San Diego State University, box 8, folder 18.
58. E. Chavez, "Brief Historical Sketch," 3.
59. E. Chavez, "Brief Historical Sketch," 3.

60. E. Chavez, "Brief Historical Sketch." See also "CCHE Conference," *La Verdad*, April 1971, news clipping, Anna NietoGomez Collection, CPMR.
61. Anna NietoGomez served a contentious year as MEChA president at California State College at Long Beach from 1970 to 1971. She recalls being frozen out of discussions and undermined by leading male members of the organization. See Blackwell, *¡Chicana Power!*, 76–81.
62. Isabel Hernandez had written a widely circulated critique of male supremacy in the Chicano movement in May of 1969, which was later republished in Dorinda Moreno's *La Mujer: En Pie de Lucha* (1973). Sonia Lopez, Henri Chavez, Anna NietoGomez, and Dorinda Moreno had all worked as counselors or recruiters with Educational Opportunity Programs. Indeed, Sonia and Henri coauthored a paper in the early 1970s on the needs of Chicana students: see Sonia Lopez and Enriqueta Chavez, "Chicanas in Higher Education," position paper, Enriqueta Chavez Papers, San Diego State University, box 8, folder 5.
63. Reynolds de Medina and Contreras, "Notes on the Chicana Caucus of California State Colleges."
64. Reynolds de Medina and Contreras, "Notes on the Chicana Caucus of California State Colleges."
65. *Hijas de Cuauhtémoc*, no. 1 (1971): 4. Notably, two of these amendments would also be put forward by the Chicano studies workshop at the San Diego CCHE conference. The resolutions from this workshop included that universities and colleges recruit Chicanas "into significant faculty and administrative positions" and that "all Chicano Studies Programs initiate and implement coursework on the Chicana." Meeting minutes, Chicano studies workshop, CCHE statewide conference, San Diego, March 20–21, 1971, Anna NietoGomez Collection, CPMR.
66. Anna NietoGomez, CPMR oral history, 2018.
67. "Chicana Studies Curriculum," March 29, 1971, Enriqueta Chavez Papers, San Diego State University, box 3, folder 24.
68. "Chicana Studies Curriculum," March 29, 1971. This claim of underrepresentation is corroborated by a national study of college faculty, conducted from 1972 to 1973, that gathered data on persons of "Mexican origin" in higher education. The study reported slightly over 1,500 faculty who identified themselves as Mexican American or Chicano. "Women accounted for less than 10 percent of this figure, in contrast to 20 percent women for all faculty." Carlos Arce, "Chicanos in Higher Education," *Integrated Education* 14, no. 3 (1976): 16–17.
69. "Chicana Studies Curriculum," March 29, 1971.
70. *Hijas de Cuauhtémoc*, no. 1 (1971).
71. In her contribution to the breakthrough 1984 anthology *Chicana Voices*, Cynthia Orozco proposes a "Plan de Santa y Bárbara" to "move forward toward our destiny as women. We will move against those forces which have denied us freedom of expression and human dignity. Due to the sexist structure of this society, to our essentially different lifestyle, and to the socio-economic functions assigned

to our community by male society—as suppliers of free labor and a dumping ground for male aggression, the female community remains exploited, impoverished, and abused." Orozco, "Sexism in Chicano Studies," 15.

72. According to Anna NietoGomez, the women at Long Beach State already had the first issue of *Hijas de Cuauhtémoc* planned when they attended the Chicana workshop in San Diego, and they were in the process of planning the regional Chicana conference in Los Angeles.
73. Flores published three special issues on women: *Regeneración* 1, no. 10 (1971); *Regeneración* 2, no. 3 (1973); *Regeneración* 2, no. 6 (1975).

## CHAPTER 5. BEYOND A HISTORY OF VIOLENCE

1. "Chicana Ad Hoc Committee," *Hijas de Cuauhtémoc*, no. 2, 1971.
2. Rosa Linda Fregoso, *The Bronze Screen: Chicana and Chicano Film Culture* (University of Minnesota Press, 2003), 14. See also Lee Bebout, *Mythohistorical Interventions: The Chicano Movement and Its Legacies* (University of Minnesota Press, 2011), 149.
3. Anna NietoGomez, oral history interview, Long Beach, California, October 30, 2018, Anna NietoGomez Collection, Chicana por Mi Raza Digital Memory Collective (hereafter cited as Anna NietoGomez, CPMR oral history, 2018); María Eugenia Cotera, "Unpacking Our Mothers' Libraries: Practices of Chicana Memory Before and After the Digital Turn," in *Chicana Movidas: New Narratives of Activism and Feminism in the Movement Era*, ed. Dionne Espinoza, María Eugenia Cotera, and Maylei Blackwell (University of Texas Press, 2018).
4. Anna NietoGomez, "Memory Work," in the chapter "A Forum on Chicana Memory Work, Past, Present, and Future: Nuestras Autohistorias," in *Latina Histories and Cultures: Feminist Readings and Recoveries of Archival Knowledge*, ed. Montse Feu and Yolanda Padilla (Arte Público Press, 2023), 79.
5. Roderick A. Ferguson, *The Reorder of Things: The University and Its Pedagogies of Minority Difference* (University of Minnesota Press, 2012), 8.
6. Anna NietoGomez, CPMR oral history, 2018.
7. See Carlos Muñoz Jr., *Youth, Identity, Power: The Chicano Movement* (Verso, 1989); Michael Soldatenko, *Chicano Studies: The Genesis of a Discipline* (University of Arizona Press, 2009); Rodolfo Acuña, *The Making of Chicana/o Studies: In the Trenches of Academe* (Rutgers University Press, 2011); Juan Gómez-Quiñones, *Mexican Students por la Raza: The Chicano Student Movement in Southern California, 1967–1977* (La Causa, 1978); Juan Gómez-Quiñones and Irene Vásquez, *Making Aztlán: Ideology and Culture of the Chicana and Chicano Movement, 1966–1977* (University of New Mexico Press, 2014).
8. For a detailed account of the 1971 Houston conference and its "faultlines," see chapter 5 in Maylei Blackwell, *¡Chicana Power! Contested Histories of Feminism in the Chicano Movement* (University of Texas Press, 2011).

9. Conference agenda, "La Mujer Latinoamericana y la Chicana: Teoría y Practica," May 12–13, 1973, Stanford University, Anna NietoGomez Collection, Chicana por Mi Raza Digital Memory Collective (hereafter cited as CPMR).
10. *Estudios Femeniles* was funded by a partnership between the University of California, Los Angeles, and Montal Educational Associates and was edited by Las Hijas de Cuauhtémoc members Corinne Sánchez (who was working at Montal at the time) and Anna NietoGomez (then an assistant professor at California State Northridge).
11. Soldatenko, *Chicano Studies*, 64.
12. Evey Chapa and Armando Gutierrez, "Chicanas in Politics: An Overview and a Case Study," in *Perspectivas en Chicano Studies I: Papers Presented at the 3rd Annual Meeting of the National Association of Chicano Social Scientists*, ed. Reynaldo Macias (Chicano Studies Center, UCLA, 1977).
13. Chapa and Gutierrez, "Chicanas in Politics," 145. Interestingly, this paper was delivered at the 1975 conference of the National Association of Chicano Social Scientists (later renamed the National Association for Chicano Studies), where Chicana scholars and activists pressured the conference organizers to hold a special session on La Chicana at the end of the conference. Soldatenko, *Chicano Studies*, 59.
14. "National List of Chicano Contacts in Higher Education," compiled by Cecilia Preciado Burciaga, Assistant to the President for Chicano Affairs, Stanford University, summer 1976, Sonia Lopez Collection, CPMR. The entries for Northridge do not include Anna NietoGomez, and the San Diego State entry shows dramatic evidence of the purge in the department.
15. Notable exceptions to this general rule are Gracia Molina de Pick (a faculty member at Mesa College), who was already a professor in 1969 when *El Plan de Santa Bárbara* was drafted, as well as a generation of women who were doctoral students in the 1970s at the following institutions (although some would not earn PhDs): Adaljiza Sosa-Riddell (University of California, Riverside, PhD earned 1971), Cordelia Candelaria (University of Notre Dame, 1976), Rosalinda Mendez González (University of California, Irvine, 1981), Carlota Cárdenas de Dwyer (State University of New York at Stony Brook, 1976), Theresa Aragon de Shepro (University of Washington, 1978), Rafaela Elizondo de Weffer (Illinois Institute of Technology, 1972), Antonia Castañeda (Stanford University, 1990), Rita Sanchez (Stanford University, no PhD), Theresa Melendez (University of California, San Diego, 1977), Teresa McKenna (University of California, Los Angeles, 1980), Beverly Sánchez-Padilla (University of New Mexico, no PhD), Erlinda Gonzales-Berry (University of New Mexico, 1978), Inés Hernández Ávila (University of Houston, 1984), Evey Chapa (University of Texas, 1981), and Marcella Trujillo (University of Minnesota, no PhD).
16. Gilberto García, "Beyond the Adelita Image: Women Scholars in the National Association for Chicano Studies, 1972–1992," *Perspectives in Mexican American Studies* 5 (1995).

17. Blackwell, introduction to *¡Chicana Power!*
18. Chicano Coordinating Council on Higher Education (CCHE), *El Plan de Santa Bárbara: A Chicano Plan for Higher Education* (La Causa, 1971), 11.
19. Agenda, Chicana study group, Enriqueta Chavez Papers, San Diego State University, box 8, folder 8.
20. Ward M. Morton, *Woman Suffrage in Mexico* (University of Florida Press, 1962).
21. San Diego State College, "1970–1971 General Catalog and Announcement of Courses," vol. 57, 1970.
22. Mexican American Lifestyles 105 syllabus, Sonia Lopez Collection, CPMR.
23. Anna NietoGomez, CPMR oral history, 2018.
24. See Sonia Lopez, "The Role of the Chicana Within the Student Movement," in *Essays on La Mujer*, ed. Rosaura Sánchez and Rosa Martinez Cruz (Chicano Studies Center, UCLA, 1977); Adelaida R. Del Castillo, "Women in Organization," in *Mexican Women in the United States: Struggles Past and Present*, ed. Magdalena Mora and Adelaida R. Del Castillo (Chicano Studies Research Center, 1980).
25. Sonia Lopez and Enriqueta Chavez, "Chicanas in Higher Education," position paper, Enriqueta Chavez Papers, San Diego State University, box 8, folder 5. Sonia describes the context in which such position papers were presented: "We would have all-day meetings and we would discuss there the direction of [where] Chicano studies was going," and "we would present position papers to our colleagues. . . . If you wanted to teach a class you often had to present a position paper articulating the need for the class." Sonia Lopez, phone conversation with the author, March 19, 2023.
26. "Women's Studies Pamphlet," Women's Studies Group, California State University, San Diego, an *Inside the Beast* publication, May 1973, Sonia Lopez Collection, CPMR.
27. Instructors for this course were Clarisa Torres, Enriqueta Chavez, Rene Lopez, and Samuel Salazar. Chicano-Chicana Course (MAS 197) syllabus, 1973, Enriqueta Chavez Papers, San Diego State University, box 8, folder 13.
28. MAS 197 syllabus, 1973.
29. Sonia Lopez, "Personal Politics in the Chicano Movement," undated position paper, 1, Sonia Lopez Collection, CPMR.
30. Lopez, "Personal Politics in the Chicano Movement," 3.
31. Anna NietoGomez, "Production of Knowledge in the Classroom and Through Student Activism," January 30, 2019, unpublished essay shared with the author.
32. Anna NietoGomez, "Hijas de Cuauhtémoc," May 17, 2018, unpublished essay shared with the author.
33. Such publication projects were a regular feature of Chicana classes across the Southwest in the 1970s. For example, in the spring of 1976, students in Inés Hernández Tovar's Chicana studies class at the University of Texas published *HEMBRA: Hermanas en Movimiento Brotando Raices de Aztlán*, a compendium of essays, poetry, and art.

34. Meeting notes, Chicana Ad Hoc Committee of CCHE, March 19–21, 1971, Enriqueta Chavez Papers, San Diego State University, box 3, folder 24. By far the largest contingent of women present at the meeting was from institutions in the San Diego area.
35. Gustavo Licón, "Feminist Mobilization in MEChA: A Southern California Case Study," *Kalfou: A Journal of Comparative and Relational Ethnic Studies* 5, no. 1 (2018): 78.
36. Acuña, *Making of Chicana/o Studies*, 153.
37. Anna NietoGomez, résumé, 1974, Anna NietoGomez Collection, CPMR.
38. Anna NietoGomez, CPMR oral history, 2018.
39. Anna NietoGomez, unpublished history since 1971 of Chicanas at California State University, Northridge, 2022, essay shared with the author (hereafter cited as unpublished history of Chicanas at CSUN).
40. Anna NietoGomez, "History of Hermanas Unidas," ca. 1975, Anna NietoGomez Collection, CPMR. See also Anna NietoGomez, "History of Chicanas at CSUN," *Daily Sundial* 29, no. 32 (1975).
41. NietoGomez, unpublished history of Chicanas at CSUN.
42. Anna NietoGomez, "Rhetoric is Non-Productive," ca. 1972, Anna NietoGomez Collection, CPMR.
43. Anna NietoGomez, "The Chicana: Perspectives for Education," *Encuentro Femenil* 1, no. 1 (1973): 59. See also Blackwell, *¡Chicana Power!*; Licón, "Feminist Mobilization in MEChA"; Muñoz, *Youth, Identity, Power*. All mention this intervention on behalf of Chicana studies, though there is some variance in the dates they ascribe to the event.
44. Licón, "Feminist Mobilization in MEChA," 85.
45. NietoGomez, "History of Hermanas Unidas." See also NietoGomez, "History of Chicanas at CSUN."
46. Anna NietoGomez, "Chicana Print Culture and Chicana Studies: A Testimony to the Development of Chicana Feminist Culture," in *Chicana Feminisms: A Critical Reader*, ed. Gabriela F. Arredondo, Aída Hurtado, Norma Klahn, Olga Nájera-Ramírez, and Patricia Zavella (Duke University Press, 2003), 90.
47. "Enfrentando la Vida," report on Semana de la Mujer, *El Popo Femenil*, 1973, 8–9, Anna NietoGomez Collection, CPMR.
48. Program, Semana de la Mujer, 1973, Anna NietoGomez Collection, CPMR.
49. In his close reading of the first issue of *El Popo*, Licón notes that "the role of men in the Chicano community and the movement was defined more vaguely and not, as with women, in a way that marked them as a distinctly gendered group. What one finds instead are images and references that indicate Chicanos should be men of action for their people and embrace machismo when they fight oppression. The experience of men is also treated as the normal and universal experience of the community." Licón, "Feminist Mobilization in MEChA," 80. See also Gustavo Licón, "'¡La Union Hace la Fuerza!' (Unity

Creates Strength): M.E.Ch.A. and Chicana/o Student Activism in California, 1967–1999" (University of Southern California, 2009), 112.

50. "Enfrentando la Vida," 8–9; NietoGomez, "History of Chicanas at CSUN," 1; "CSUN Will Place Focus on Chicanas," *Los Angeles Times*, April 20, 1973.
51. NietoGomez, "Production of Knowledge in the Classroom." Maria Diaz de Krofcheck later contributed a sample syllabus, "History of la Chicana," to the first Chicana curriculum guide, *Estudios Femeniles*, coedited by Anna NietoGomez and Corinne Sánchez.
52. NietoGomez, "Production of Knowledge in the Classroom."
53. NietoGomez, "Chicana Print Culture and Chicana Studies," 94.
54. Anna provides a detailed overview of the Semana de la Mujer events in NietoGomez, unpublished history of Chicanas at CSUN. See also "Schedule, Semana de la Mujer, April 23–27," Anna NietoGomez Collection, CPMR; "Report on Semana de la Mujer," *Barrio News Service*, Anna NietoGomez Collection, CPMR; *Daily Sundial*, April 24, 25, and 26, 1973.
55. Anna NietoGomez, CPMR oral history, 2018. See also NietoGomez, unpublished history of Chicanas at CSUN.
56. NietoGomez, unpublished history of Chicanas at CSUN.
57. Gloria Miranda, "Chicanas Take the Wrong Turn," *El Popo Femenil*, 1973, Anna NietoGomez Collection, CPMR.
58. Miranda, "Chicanas Take the Wrong Turn."
59. "Exercise in Identity," *El Popo Femenil*, 1973.
60. Blackwell, *¡Chicana Power!*, 138, 134.
61. Blackwell, *¡Chicana Power!*, 142.
62. NietoGomez, "Chicana Print Culture and Chicana Studies," 90.
63. NietoGomez, "Chicana Print Culture and Chicana Studies," 90.
64. Angelina de la Torre, "The Chicana," *El Popo Femenil*, 1973.
65. Blackwell, *¡Chicana Power!*, 120.
66. Both Paz's *The Labyrinth of Solitude* and González Pineda's *El Mexicano* were included in *El Plan de Santa Bárbara*'s bibliography, indicating their importance to the early Chicano studies curriculum. CCHE, *El Plan de Santa Bárbara*, 61–75.
67. Dottie Hernandez, "Numero Uno," *El Popo Femenil.*
68. Hernandez, "Numero Uno."
69. NietoGomez, "History of Chicanas at CSUN."
70. NietoGomez, "Chicana Print Culture and Chicana Studies," 95.
71. NietoGomez, CPMR oral history, 2018.
72. NietoGomez, unpublished history of Chicanas at CSUN.
73. NietoGomez, "History of Hermanas Unidas."
74. NietoGomez, "History of Hermanas Unidas."
75. Anna NietoGomez, "La Chicana," *Women Struggle*, 1976.
76. Soldatenko, *Chicano Studies*, 11.

77. Quiñonez identifies the first wave of Chicana scholars as those "motivated to write as a result of increased political awareness and a commitment to the cultural ideals of the Chicano movement which tied the purpose of art and culture to the struggle for socioeconomic and political change. First wave Chicana literature incorporates issues of race, class, and gender by addressing the experiences of poor and working-class Mexican and Mexican American women." Naomi Helena Quiñonez, "Hijas de la Malinche (Malinche's Daughters): The Development of Social Agency Among Mexican-American Women and the Emergence of First Wave Chicana Cultural Production" (PhD diss., Claremont Graduate University, 1997), 224.
78. For more information on this controversy, see Blackwell, *¡Chicana Power!*; Acuña, *Making of Chicana/o Studies*; Marisol Moreno, "'Of the Community, for the Community': The Chicana/o Student Movement in California's Public Higher Education, 1967–1973" (PhD diss., University of California, Santa Barbara, 2009); Soldatenko, *Chicano Studies*. Anna discusses the case in great detail in her interviews for the Chicana por Mi Raza project: Anna NietoGomez, CPMR oral histories, 2010, 2018. For more on the structural forces that continue to affect women of color in the academy, see Yolanda Flores Niemann, Gabriella Gutiérrez y Muhs, and Carmen G. González, *Presumed Incompetent II: Race, Class, Power, and Resistance of Women in Academia* (Utah State University Press, 2020).
79. By the mid-1970s, most Chicano studies departments abandoned their more radical practices, particularly around student involvement in teaching, hiring, and governance. In his account of the development of the field, Rodolfo Acuña notes that "as early as 1973, the department [at Northridge] began pressuring faculty" to acquire advanced degrees. Faculty members with master's degrees were encouraged "to matriculate into doctorate programs, and those with bachelor of arts into master's programs." Acuña, *Making of Chicana/o Studies*, 155. In a retrospective examination of the field written in 1973, Mario García observed a sense of "disenchantment" in "departments and programs—especially among students." Looking back on his experiences at San Diego State, he concluded that much of this disenchantment stemmed from the fact that the radical impulse that had founded the field had become "deflated." He noted at the time that the typical Chicano studies department "now represents a bureaucratic organization laden with incompetent and opportunistic faculty members whose sense of commitment to the students and to the Chicano Movement leaves much to be desired. This situation developed because when Chicano Studies started only a few Chicanos held the credentials (MA or PhD) to staff them. These Mexican-Americans who suddenly discovered their Chicanismo, moved directly into positions of responsibility in these programs, and while they can be as radical as possible to begin these departments and to maintain them, their radicalization goes no further; for if they make more movidas against the administration, their good salaries and the funding (in some cases quite heavy as at San Diego State)

of 'their' departments might be jeopardized—and, above all, they stand to lose their jobs." By 1974, the Mexican American Studies Program at San Diego State, García's point of reference, became a politically contested space as a result of this process of institutionalization, with students, and a significant portion of the faculty, withdrawing from the department. Mario T. García, "The Chicano University," in *Ghosts in the Barrio: Issues in Bilingual-Bicultural Education*, ed. Ralph (Rafa) Poblano (Leswing Press, 1973), 352.

80. Blackwell, *¡Chicana Power!*, 197. For more on the impact of Anna NietoGomez's tenure battle, see Quiñonez, "Hijas de la Malinche."
81. Quiñonez, "Hijas de la Malinche," 261.
82. Ferguson, *Reorder of Things*, 8.
83. Alma M. García, ed., *Chicana Feminist Thought: The Basic Historical Writings* (Routledge, 2014).
84. "It Had to Happen," *Women Struggle*, 1. While the statement bears no byline, it is reprinted word for word from an editorial that Roberto Rodriguez wrote about the case for the March 1976 issue of *La Gente* (University of California, Los Angeles). According to Anna NietoGomez, who interviewed him in the late 2000s, Rodriguez recalled attending a hostile meeting at Northridge in which she pleaded her case to the Chicano studies faculty and MEChA. Rodriguez, who attended with the artist Barbara Carrasco (a fellow student at the University of California, Los Angeles), remembers that he "realized that this was an historic meeting, because these issues had not been discussed so directly. Your [Anna's] struggle was similar to what we were doing in the Chicano movement. You confronted the issue head on. Women had not done this before. This was different from talking about women's issues at a conference. This one was a challenge to a sacred cow, Chicano studies. It was a classic confrontation between Chicana studies and Chicano studies." He further explained, "This was a battle. This was not a regular debate. It was one of rumor, slander, and innuendo. And then there was the silencing [that] Chicano studies and MEChA invoked against those who disagreed. Barbara and I were told to be quiet, to stay out of it. They said, 'Don't stick your nose where it doesn't belong. Don't air our dirty laundry.' Some people began to talk about doing something harmful." The opinion piece that Rodriguez wrote, and the cover art that Carrasco created for the March 1976 issue of *La Gente* to draw attention to Anna's case, evidently resulted in a backlash: "After the editorial, everybody was mad at us. A lot of people thought we should have let it go. Others thought that it was about time someone stepped up to discuss what was actually happening. Barbara and I were marginalized and our ideas were dismissed. Some said I took this position because Barbara Carrasco was my girlfriend." Quoted in Anna NietoGomez, introduction to "It Had to Happen," in "We Were Scholar-Activists: Selected Writings of Anna NietoGomez," manuscript in progress.
85. *Women Struggle*, 1.
86. *Women Struggle*, 2.

87. *Women Struggle*, 2.
88. "Anna NietoGomez Interview," *Women Struggle*, 4.
89. Martha P. Cotera, "A Letter from the Austin Community," *Women Struggle*, 5. Martha's observation that there were "tragically few Chicanas in the academic field" is corroborated by the previously cited list of Chicanos in higher education compiled in the summer of 1976 by Cecilia Preciado Burciaga. Out of a total of 568 faculty, only 98 were women, and slightly over half of them (51) appeared to be on the tenure track (listed as assistant, associate, or full professors). "National List of Chicano Contacts in Higher Education," Sonia Lopez Collection, CPMR.
90. *Women Struggle*, 5.
91. Martha Cotera, questionnaire, Crystal City Public School District, 1974, 2, Martha Cotera Collection, CPMR. This was the agenda outlined in *El Plan de Santa Bárbara* and exemplified in the José Vasconcelos quote that appeared in its pages: "At this moment we do not come to work for the university, but to demand that the university work for our people." CCHE, *El Plan de Santa Bárbara*, 11.
92. *Women Struggle*, 9.
93. Barbara Carrasco would also contribute the cover art to a special issue of *La Gente* (the Chicano student newspaper at the University of California, Los Angeles) that featured several editorials in support of Anna NietoGomez.
94. NietoGomez, unpublished history of Chicanas at CSUN.
95. Blackwell, *¡Chicana Power!*, 111.
96. Blackwell, *¡Chicana Power!*, 112.
97. Blackwell, *¡Chicana Power!*, 117–118.
98. Blackwell, *¡Chicana Power!*, 118.
99. Ferguson, *Reorder of Things*, 107.
100. Ferguson, *Reorder of Things*, 17.

## CHAPTER 6. MUJERISTA GENEALOGIES

1. Osa Hidalgo de la Riva and Maylei Blackwell, "Visions of Utopia While Living in Occupied Aztlán," in *Chicana Movidas: New Narratives of Activism and Feminism in the Movement Era*, ed. Dionne Espinoza, María Eugenia Cotera, and Maylei Blackwell (University of Texas Press, 2021), 222–223.
2. María Eugenia Cotera, "Unpacking Our Mothers' Libraries: Practices of Chicana Memory Before and After the Digital Turn," in Espinoza, Cotera, and Blackwell, *Chicana Movidas*, 299.
3. Avery Gordon, *Ghostly Matters: Haunting and the Sociological Imagination* (University of Minnesota Press, 1997), 66.
4. Hidalgo de la Riva and Blackwell, "Visions of Utopia," 207.
5. Horacio N. Roque Ramírez, "Memory and Mourning: Living Oral History with Queer Latinos and Latinas in San Francisco," in *Oral History and Public*

*Memories*, ed. Paula Hamilton and Linda Shopes (Temple University Press, 2008).

6. Yolanda Chávez Leyva, "Breaking the Silence: Putting Latina Lesbian History at the Center," in *The New Lesbian Studies: Into the Twenty-First Century*, ed. Bonnie Zimmerman and Toni A. H. McNaron (Feminist Press, 1996); Emma Pérez, "Speaking from the Margin: Uninvited Discourse on Sexuality and Power," in *Building with Our Hands: New Directions in Chicana Studies*, ed. Adela de la Torre and Beatríz M. Pesquera (University of California Press, 1993); Carla Trujillo, ed., *Chicana Lesbians: The Girls Our Mothers Warned Us About* (Third Woman Press, 1991); Emma Pérez, "Sexuality and Discourse: Notes from a Chicana Survivor," in Trujillo, *Chicana Lesbians*; Yvonne Yarbro-Bejarano, "Sexuality and Chicana/o Studies: Toward a Theoretical Paradigm for the Twenty-First Century," *Cultural Studies* 13, no. 2 (1999): 335–345; Catrióna Rueda Esquibel, *With Her Machete in Her Hand: Reading Chicana Lesbians* (University of Texas Press, 2006); Lee Bebout, *Mythohistorical Interventions: The Chicano Movement and Its Legacies* (University of Minnesota Press, 2011); Yvette J. Saavedra, "Of Chicana Lesbian Terrorists and Lesberadas: Recuperating the Lesbian/Queer Roots of Chicana Feminism, 1970–2000," *Feminist Formations* 34, no. 2 (2022): 99–124.
7. Roque Ramírez, "Memory and Mourning," 167.
8. Frantz Fanon, "On National Culture," in *The Wretched of the Earth*, trans. Richard Philcox (Grove Press, 2004).
9. Chávez Leyva, "Breaking the Silence"; Alma M. García, "The Development of Chicana Feminist Discourse, 1970–1980," *Gender and Society* 3, no. 2 (1989): 217–238; Maylei Blackwell, *¡Chicana Power! Contested Histories of Feminism in the Chicano Movement* (University of Texas Press, 2011); Richard T. Rodríguez, *Next of Kin: The Family in Chicano/a Cultural Politics* (Duke University Press, 2009); Bebout, *Mythohistorical Interventions*.
10. Bebout, *Mythohistorical Interventions*, 151.
11. A. García, "Development of Chicana Feminist Discourse," 217–238; Blackwell, *¡Chicana Power!*; Espinoza, Cotera, and Blackwell, *Chicana Movidas*; Rodríguez, *Next of Kin*; Bebout, *Mythohistorical Interventions*.
12. A. García, "Development of Chicana Feminist Discourse," 217–238; Sonia Lopez, "The Role of the Chicana Within the Student Movement," in *Essays on La Mujer*, ed. Rosaura Sánchez and Rosa Martinez Cruz (Chicano Studies Center, UCLA, 1977).
13. A. García, "Development of Chicana Feminist Discourse," 226. See also Bebout, *Mythohistorical Interventions*, 149–185.
14. María Eugenia Cotera, Maylei Blackwell, and Dionne Espinoza, "Introduction: Movement, Movimientos, and Movidas," in Espinoza, Cotera, and Blackwell, *Chicana Movidas*, 26–27.
15. Chávez Leyva, "Breaking the Silence," 149.
16. Rueda Esquibel, *With Her Machete in Her Hand*, 3.

17. Anna NietoGomez, phone conversation with the author, October 1, 2024.
18. Bebout, *Mythohistorical Interventions*, 151.
19. Bebout, *Mythohistorical Interventions*; Rueda Esquibel, *With Her Machete in Her Hand*; Saavedra, "Of Chicana Lesbian Terrorists and Lesberadas."
20. Deena J. González, "Speaking Secrets: Living Chicana Theory," in *Living Chicana Theory*, ed. Carla Trujillo (Third Woman Press, 1998), 49.
21. Saavedra, "Of Chicana Lesbian Terrorists and Lesberadas," 106–107. Yvette Saavedra notes that in 1990, when a lesbian caucus was formed after a series of homophobic attacks, it was "sponsored by the Chicana Caucus, of which many lesbian/queer women—whether out or closeted—were members" (111).
22. Saavedra, "Of Chicana Lesbian Terrorists and Lesberadas," 101.
23. Rueda Esquibel, *With Her Machete in Her Hand*, 3.
24. Susy J. Zepeda, *Queering Mesoamerican Diasporas: Remembering Xicana Indígena Ancestries* (University of Illinois Press, 2022), 34.
25. Zepeda, *Queering Mesoamerican Diasporas*, 112.
26. My engagement with Osa Hidalgo de la Riva's work while coediting the volume *Chicana Movidas* (ed. Espinoza, Cotera, and Blackwell) eventually led to a partnership between Osa, the Chicana por mi Raza project, and Erendina Delgadillo, a museum curator and family friend of las mujeres de la Riva. In 2021 we received a grant-in-aid from the US Latino Digital Humanities Center at the University of Houston to launch the Mujeres de la Riva Herstory Project. In this first phase of the project, Erendina and Osa scanned a selection of materials from Osa's collection to create a digital historia of las mujeres de la Riva for the Chicana por Mi Raza website: Erendina Delgadillo and Osa Hidalgo de la Riva, Las Mujeres de la Riva historia, Chicana por Mi Raza Digital Memory Collective, https://chicanapormiraza.org/content/las-mujeres-de-la-riva (hereafter cited as Delgadillo and Hidalgo de la Riva, Las Mujeres de la Riva historia, CPMR). Building on this early effort, in the summer of 2023 we partnered with Teresa Mora, head of special collections at the University of California, Santa Cruz, and John Jota Leaños, a professor of film and media, to host a summer research intensive at the university that focused on archival praxis and queer of color media. During the field school, we conducted several oral history interviews with Osa, and the students worked with her to digitize and catalog nearly a thousand items from her collection.
27. Liliana C. González and Stacy I. Macías, "Afterword: Scanning the Chicana Lesbian Body Politic; Knowledge, Practice, Identity," *Journal of Lesbian Studies* 27, no. 4 (2023): 350–351.
28. Emma Pérez, "Irigaray's Female Symbolic in the Making of Chicana Lesbian Sitios y Lenguas," in Trujillo, *Living Chicana Theory*, 90; Horacio N. Roque Ramírez, "A Living Archive of Desire: Teresita la Campesina and the Embodiment of Queer Latino Community Histories," in *Archive Stories: Facts, Fictions, and the Writing of History*, ed. Antoinette Burton (Duke University Press, 2005).
29. Chávez Leyva, "Breaking the Silence," 148.

30. Hidalgo de la Riva and Blackwell, "Visions of Utopia," 207.
31. Hidalgo de la Riva and Blackwell, "Visions of Utopia," 223.
32. Celia de la Riva Rubio, de la Riva family genealogy, Mujeres de la Riva Collection, Chicana por Mi Raza Digital Memory Collective (hereafter cited as CPMR).
33. Mobilized Women of Berkeley was established during World War I to assist in the war effort. After the war, the organization's activities shifted to more typical "Americanization" activities, including promoting "good citizenship" among "underprivileged" native-born and foreign-born communities in Berkeley through translation services, as well as classes in sewing, cooking, and civic education. For more information on Mobilized Women of Berkeley, see "Guide to the Mobilized Women of Berkeley Records, 1917–1969," collection no. BANC MSS 70/10 c, Bancroft Library, University of California, Berkeley.
34. Lola de la Riva, oral history interview, conducted by Maylei Blackwell, September 3, 2011, Mujeres de la Riva Collection, Chicana por Mi Raza Digital Memory Collective (hereafter cited as Lola de la Riva, interview by Maylei Blackwell, 2011).
35. Delgadillo and Hidalgo de la Riva, Las Mujeres de la Riva historia, CPMR.
36. Lola de la Riva, interview by Maylei Blackwell, 2011.
37. Delgadillo and Hidalgo de la Riva, Las Mujeres de la Riva historia, CPMR. In her book on the Chicano movement in Sacramento, Lorena Márquez provides a useful history of cannery worker organizing in the Central Valley, including important information on women organizers. See Lorena V. Márquez, *La Gente: Struggles for Empowerment and Community Self-Determination in Sacramento* (University of Arizona Press, 2020), 111–147.
38. Lola de la Riva, interview by Maylei Blackwell, 2011.
39. Hidalgo de la Riva and Blackwell, "Visions of Utopia," 223.
40. Delgadillo and Hidalgo de la Riva, Las Mujeres de la Riva historia, CPMR.
41. Osa Hidalgo de la Riva, oral history interview, conducted by María Eugenia Cotera, July 25, 2023, Mujeres de la Riva Collection, Chicana por Mi Raza Digital Memory Collective (hereafter cited as Osa Hidalgo de la Riva, CPMR oral history, 2023).
42. Osa Hidalgo de la Riva, "Royal Eagle Bear Is Off and Running," unpublished manuscript, Santa Cruz, California, 2015, 29, Mujeres de la Riva Collection, CPMR.
43. Lola de la Riva, interview by Maylei Blackwell, 2011.
44. Lola de la Riva, interview by Maylei Blackwell, 2011.
45. Osa Hidalgo de la Riva, CPMR oral history, 2023.
46. Lola de la Riva, interview by Maylei Blackwell, 2011.
47. Delgadillo and Hidalgo de la Riva, Las Mujeres de la Riva historia, CPMR. In her interview with Maylei Blackwell, Lola describes Harlequin House quite vividly: "They had one building downstairs that was all sorts of art supplies. The next building was print shops, and then upstairs they had classes. And then the

next building on top of the other one, they had all storage, because they used to rent art to buildings and people—if you wanted to buy something you could rent it first and see if it looked right. And then during Fridays and Saturdays she would teach little young kids from about five to ten or twelve, then after that the next class would be teenagers, and then the next class would be the adults. So she had all these classes at one time." Lola de la Riva, interview by Maylei Blackwell, 2011.

48. Clifford Oto, "Muralist Carlos Lopez Leaves Big Marks Around Stockton: Here's Where You Know His Work," *Stockton Record*, April 3, 2023, https://www.recordnet.com/story/lifestyle/2023/04/03/muralist-carlos-lopez-work-has-brightened-stockton-for-decades/70066675007/.
49. "Homage to Maxine Lovejoy DalBen," video posted to Joseph Osborne Fine Art Facebook page, 2019, https://fb.watch/t-FFr_fEbW/.
50. Joseph Osborne, "Obituary—Maxine Lovejoy DalBen, 1920–March 3, 2011," Joseph Osborne Fine Art Facebook page, September 3, 2019, https://www.facebook.com/JosephOsborneFineArt/posts/obituary-maxine-lovejoy-dalbenmy-first-paintings-age-9-56-years-ago-at-harlequin/586529028418500/.
51. Delgadillo and Hidalgo de la Riva, "Dolores 'Lola' de la Riva," Mujeres de la Riva historia, CPMR.
52. Delgadillo and Hidalgo de la Riva, "Dolores 'Lola' de la Riva," Mujeres de la Riva historia, CPMR.
53. Over the span of nearly twenty years, Celia de la Riva Rubio pursued multiple degrees in the interest of better serving the communities she cared about. She earned an adult education degree in the 1960s and a community college teaching degree in 1978. While teaching at East Bay High School in the late 1970s, she studied for her master's degree (1981) in school administration and supervision (with a concentration in political science) at California State University, Hayward, writing her thesis on *Lau v. Nichols*. A key win in the fight for bilingual/bicultural education, *Lau v. Nichols* was a 1974 US Supreme Court decision that guaranteed the right for English-language learners to attend public schools and required schools to take measures to meet their needs. In the late 1980s, de la Riva Rubio returned to California State Hayward to earn a degree in paralegal studies (1988).
54. Nan Alamilla Boyd, *Wide-Open Town: A History of Queer San Francisco to 1965* (University of California Press, 2003).
55. Celia de la Riva Rubio, *Lágrimas y Cadenas / Chains and Tears: Poesía y Prosa Feminista y del Ambiente / Gay Feminist Prose and Poetry* (Colectivo Artístico Morelia, 1994), 125.
56. According to Nan Alamilla Boyd, Ann Dee and Norma Clayton opened Ann's 440 in 1952, taking over the space once occupied by Mona's 440, San Francisco's first lesbian nightclub: "Popular with lesbians and, later, the tourist trade, Clayton managed the bar while Dee brought in entertainers like Charles

Pierce, Ray Bourbon, and, later, Johnny Mathis and Lennie Bruce." Alamilla Boyd, *Wide-Open Town*, 83.

57. Alamilla Boyd, *Wide-Open Town, 91.*
58. De la Riva Rubio, *Lágrimas y Cadenas*, 29.
59. Delgadillo and Hidalgo de la Riva, "Dolores 'Lola' de la Riva," Mujeres de la Riva historia, CPMR.
60. Hidalgo de la Riva and Blackwell, "Visions of Utopia," 222.
61. Osa Hidalgo de la Riva, personal communication with the author, August 17, 2024.
62. While Del Martin and Phyllis Lyon—two prominent advocates for lesbian and gay rights—are most often credited with founding the Daughters of Bilitis in 1955, according to Martin it was actually a young Filipina immigrant, Rosalie (Rose) Bamberger, who first envisioned the group as an informal social club where lesbians could meet each other in private homes to socialize and dance without the annoyance of "gawking tourists" or the constant threat of surveillance and arrest. When Martin, Lyon, and other white middle-class lesbians took over the leadership of the Daughters of Bilitis in 1955, a few months after its founding, they shifted the direction of the organization toward political advocacy and instituted strict rules for participation, including a dress code that alienated butch-presenting lesbians from the group. In January 1956, four of the original blue-collar founders, including Rose Bamberger and her partner, Rosemary Stepien (both of whom worked at brush-making factories), left to form their own secret lesbian groups, Quatrefoil and Hale Aikane. While little is known about these short-lived organizations—after all, they were secret societies—the name Hale Aikane, which combines the native Hawaiian words for home/lodge/family (*hale*) and same-sex relationships (*aikāne*), suggests that the divisions that led to the split within the Daughters of Bilitis were not exclusively a result of class differences, as Lyon and Martin have suggested in their writing and oral histories. Indeed, in its reference to Indigenous traditions of same-sex relationships, Hale Aikane explicitly rejected the Eurocentric queer genealogies that shaped the political imaginary of the Daughters of Bilitis, whose chosen name referenced Belgian-French poet Pierre Louÿs's collection of erotic poetry *Songs of Bilitis* (purportedly a translation of Greek poems written by a contemporary of Sappho), originally published in 1894 and republished in 1955, the same year the group was founded. For more on the Daughters of Bilitis, see Phyllis Lyon, "Lesbian Liberation Begins," *Gay and Lesbian Review / Worldwide*, November–December 2012, https://glreview.org/article/lesbian-liberation-begins/; Alamilla Boyd, *Wide-Open Town*, 169; "The Daughters of Bilitis," in *LGBTQIA+ Studies: A Resource Guide*, Library of Congress, https://guides.loc.gov/lgbtq-studies/before-stonewall/daughters-of-bilitis#s-lib-ctab-23440411–2.
63. Delgadillo and Hidalgo de la Riva, "Celia de la Riva Rubio," Mujeres de la Riva historia, CPMR.

64. Roque Ramírez. "Memory and Mourning," 167.
65. Delgadillo and Hidalgo de la Riva, "Celia de la Riva Rubio," Mujeres de la Riva Historia, CPMR.
66. The Tiburcio Vasquez medical clinic was established in 1971 by community members in the Tri-Cities region of the San Francisco Bay Area, including Tri-City Family Planning, the Brown Berets, and the Union City Health Committee. It was the first clinic in the area to provide "multicultural and linguistically appropriate" healthcare to southern Alameda County. "Our History," Tiburcio Vasquez Health Center, https://tvhc.org/history/.
67. De la Riva Rubio, *Lágrimas y Cadenas*, 105.
68. De la Riva Rubio, *Lágrimas y Cadenas*, 106.
69. De la Riva Rubio, *Lágrimas y Cadenas*, 109. One legacy of Celia de la Riva Rubio's health advocacy during this period is the previously mentioned Tiburcio Vasquez Health Center, which has been providing health services for over fifty years. "Our History," Tiburcio Vasquez Health Center, https://tvhc.org/about-us/.
70. De la Riva Rubio, *Lágrimas y Cadenas*, 109.
71. Chávez Leyva, "Breaking the Silence," 149.
72. Harriette Frances, "Selected Poems from Sappho '71," *The Ladder*, July 1971.
73. De la Riva Rubio, *Lágrimas y Cadenas*, 120.
74. Gloria Anzaldúa, *Borderlands / La Frontera: The New Mestiza* (Aunt Lute, 1997), 102.
75. "Hayward Aztlan Boxing Club: Centennial Hall 1977," two videos of the television show *Barrio Expressions*, filmed in Hayward, California, December 15, 1977, History San José collection, https://californiarevealed.org/do/e5482456-009d-4d5b-a991-d433381f6550. According to History San José, "*Barrio Expressions* was a community access television show documenting Chicanx and Latinx life in the East San Francisco Bay Area. It ran on Hayward cable television from 1976–1985. While the shows were filmed primarily in the Hayward area, they include stories from around the East Bay and San Jose. The show aired weekly, with 26 episodes per year." History San José, https://californiarevealed.org/partner/history-san-jose.
76. Osa Hidalgo de la Riva, CPMR oral history, 2023.
77. Osa Hidalgo de la Riva, "Royal Eagle Bear Is Off and Running," 152.
78. Osa Hidalgo de la Riva, "Royal Eagle Bear Is Off and Running," 154.
79. Osa was leaving early in the morning for the statewide convention of the Zonta Girls' Club, a student organization dedicated to developing leadership in young women. At the time, she was president of her high school's chapter of the "Z Club." Osa Hidalgo de la Riva, CPMR oral history, 2023.
80. Osa Hidalgo de la Riva, "Royal Eagle Bear Is Off and Running," 154.
81. Hidalgo de la Riva and Blackwell, "Visions of Utopia," 208–209.
82. Osa Hidalgo de la Riva, phone conversation with the author, September 22, 2024.
83. Osa Hidalgo de la Riva, "Royal Eagle Bear Is Off and Running," 31–32.
84. Osa Hidalgo de la Riva, "Royal Eagle Bear Is Off and Running," 32.

85. According to Yolanda Retter Vargas, the Gay Women's Service Center was established in 1970 by Del Whan of the Lesbian Feminists in a "rented . . . storefront in Echo Park on Glendale." The center, which was open for less than two years, "offered rap groups, referrals, classes, dances, pot lucks and temporary housing. The women who came to the center ranged in ages from 15–60 and included teen runaways and women in the professions." Yolanda Retter Vargas, "On the Side of Angels: Lesbian Activism in Los Angeles, 1970–1990" (PhD diss., University of New Mexico, 1999), 90.
86. Osa Hidalgo de la Riva, "Royal Eagle Bear Is Off and Running," 40–41.
87. According to Retter Vargas, these conflicts "divided lesbians, damaged organizations, reduced the coherent energy available to work on an issue, and left more than a few with 'activist [post-traumatic stress syndrome].'" Retter Vargas, "On the Side of Angels," 86.
88. Mario T. García, "The Chicano University," in *Ghosts in the Barrio: Issues in Bilingual-Bicultural Education*, ed. Ralph (Rafa) Poblano (Leswing Press, 1973), 352.
89. Though women's studies would not be launched as a degree-granting program at Long Beach State until 1975 (when it developed a minor), several classes in the emerging field were offered through the Psychology and Sociology Departments and through the Center for Women's Studies, a special program established in the spring of 1972 to help coordinate courses with a focus on women that were being taught across campus, and to work toward the establishment of an academic program. Juliane Marie Bartolotto, "An Early History of Women's Studies at California State University, Long Beach: 1968–1976" (master's thesis, California State University, Long Beach, 1996), 19–22.
90. Lola de la Riva and Osa Hidalgo de la Riva, oral history interview, conducted by Yolanda Retter Vargas, November 1, 1997, Mujeres de la Riva Collection, CPMR (hereafter cited as Lola de la Riva and Osa Hidalgo de la Riva, interview by Yolanda Retter Vargas, 1997).
91. Osa Hidalgo de la Riva, "Transformation–Or–The Philosophy of El Centro de Arte: A Family Affair," seminar paper, December 1983, University of California, Santa Cruz, 29, Mujeres de la Riva Collection, CPMR.
92. Lola de la Riva and Osa Hidalgo de la Riva, interview by Yolanda Retter Vargas, 1997.
93. Lola de la Riva and Osa Hidalgo de la Riva, interview by Yolanda Retter Vargas, 1997.
94. Hidalgo de la Riva and Blackwell, "Visions of Utopia," 212.
95. Hidalgo de la Riva and Blackwell, "Visions of Utopia," 211.
96. Lola de la Riva and Osa Hidalgo de la Riva, interview by Yolanda Retter Vargas, 1997.
97. Osa Hidalgo de la Riva, "Philosophy of El Centro de Arte," 26.
98. Lola de la Riva and Osa Hidalgo de la Riva, interview by Yolanda Retter Vargas, 1997.

99. It is important to point out that the Mextiza Colectiva was quite broad in its membership; it included white lesbians and lesbians of color, as well as woman-identified women like Yvette Flores and Lola de la Riva, who did not identify as lesbians at the time. At different times, men did work with the group, including Osa's brother Louis, who illustrated her book *With Poems as Guns*. Osa Hidalgo de la Riva, "Philosophy of El Centro de Arte," 25.
100. Liz Hidalgo de la Riva recalls that their early efforts included mobilizing support for the United Farm Workers during the lettuce boycott of 1970 to 1973 and working with neighborhood women in South Side Stockton to demand that the city make improvements to infrastructure like "sidewalks, sewers, gutters, and lights." Liz Hidalgo de la Riva, phone conversation with the author, August 17, 2024. For information on the lettuce boycott, see Lori A. Flores, "The United Farm Workers Union and the Use of the Boycott Against American Agribusiness," in *Boycotts Past and Present: From the American Revolution to the Campaign to Boycott Israel*, ed. David Feldman (Palgrave Macmillan, 2019). See also Susan Ferriss and Ricardo Sandoval, *The Fight in the Fields: Cesar Chavez and the Farmworkers Movement*, ed. Diana Hembree (Harcourt Brace, 1997).
101. Hidalgo de la Riva and Blackwell, "Visions of Utopia," 210.
102. Osa Hidalgo de la Riva, "Royal Eagle Bear Is Off and Running," 35. Unfortunately, to date, a copy of *Mama Sappho* has not been located in Osa's archive.
103. Charlee Spurgeon and Phyllis Moore, letter to the editor, *The People's Press*, 1974.
104. Hidalgo de la Riva and Blackwell, "Visions of Utopia," 210.
105. Osa Hidalgo de la Riva, CPMR oral history, 2023.
106. Inez García was a Puerto Rican–Cuban mother whose husband was incarcerated in Soledad State Prison for his connection to a bombing in Los Angeles perpetrated by Poder Cubano, an anti-Castro group. In 1971 she moved to Soledad with her son and found work in the lettuce fields, supplementing her income with welfare. On March 17, 1974, García was raped by two acquaintances of her male roommate, who threatened to kill her unless she left town. Arming herself with her son's .22 rifle, she tracked the two men down and shot and killed one of them. In her murder trial, García was represented by acclaimed civil rights attorney Charles Garry, who had defended several Black Panthers. Her case received much attention in Chicana and woman of color publications in the mid-1970s. For more on the Inez García case, see Emily L. Thuma, *All Our Trials: Prisons, Policing, and the Feminist Fight to End Violence* (University of Illinois Press, 2019), 15–54.
107. "Rape Victim: Free Inez!," *The People's Press*, ed. Osa Hidalgo de la Riva, 1974.
108. Sergio A Santiago, "The Silent Revolution," *The People's Press*, ed. Osa Hidalgo de la Riva, 1974.
109. Yolanda Retter Vargas, "Sisterhood Is Possible," in *Time It Was: American Stories from the Sixties*, ed. Karen Manners Smith and Tim Koster (Routledge, 2016), 169.
110. Hidalgo de la Riva and Blackwell, "Visions of Utopia," 210. See also Lola de la Riva and Osa Hidalgo de la Riva, interview by Yolanda Retter Vargas, 1997.

111. Hidalgo de la Riva and Blackwell, "Visions of Utopia," 211.
112. Pérez, "Sexuality and Discourse," 162.
113. Liz Hidalgo de la Riva, *Phoenix* (Centro de Arte Press, 1976).
114. Liz Hidalgo de la Riva, preface to *Phoenix*.
115. Hidalgo de la Riva and Blackwell, "Visions of Utopia," 211–212.
116. For an excellent account of the short-lived Centro de Arte Público, see Karen Mary Davalos, "Centro de Arte Público / Public Art Center," *Aztlán: A Journal of Chicano Studies* 36, no. 2 (2011): 171–178. For an overview of the Chicano arts movement in Los Angeles, see Margarita Nieto, "Across the Street: Self-Help Graphics and Chicano Art in Los Angeles," in *Across the Street: Self-Help Graphics and Chicano Art in Los Angeles*, exhibition catalog (Laguna Art Museum, 1977), 21–37; Margarita Nieto, "Le Démon des Anges: A Brief History of the Chicano-Latino Artists of Los Angeles," in *Le Démon des Anges* (Centre de Recherché pour le Développement Culturel, 1989), 218–223.
117. Lola de la Riva and Osa Hidalgo de la Riva, interview by Yolanda Retter Vargas, 1997.
118. Lola de la Riva and Osa Hidalgo de la Riva, interview by Yolanda Retter Vargas, 1997.
119. Osa Hidalgo de la Riva, "Philosophy of El Centro de Arte," 1.
120. Osa Hidalgo de la Riva, "Philosophy of El Centro de Arte," 25.
121. Osa Hidalgo de la Riva, "Philosophy of El Centro de Arte," 26.
122. Rodríguez, *Next of Kin*, 24. See also Cherríe Moraga, "Queer Aztlán: The Re-Formation of Chicano Tribe," in *The Last Generation: Prose and Poetry* (South End Press, 1993).
123. Osa Hidalgo de la Riva, table of contents, "Philosophy of El Centro de Arte," i.
124. Hidalgo de la Riva and Blackwell, "Visions of Utopia," 222–223.
125. A survey of the bibliography on the Chicano arts movement in California yields only two mentions of Lola de la Riva's Centro de Arte. The centro is listed several times in Shifra Goldman and Tomás Ybarra-Frausto's comprehensive annotated bibliography *Arte Chicano* (1985); and Lola and her centro were the focus of Chicana poet Naomi Quiñonez's 1981 article in *Caminos* magazine. See Shifra M. Goldman and Tomás Ybarra-Frausto, *Arte Chicano: A Comprehensive Annotated Bibliography of Chicano Art, 1965–1981* (Chicano Studies Library, University of California, 1985); Naomi Helena Quiñonez, "In Her Own Backyard / En Su Propio Traspatio" *Caminos* 2, no. 2 (1981): 34–36, 62.
126. Delgadillo and Hidalgo de la Riva, Mujeres de la Riva historia, CPMR.

## POSTSCRIPT. CHICANA FUTURES—PAST AND PRESENT

1. Avery Gordon, *Ghostly Matters: Haunting and the Sociological Imagination* (University of Minnesota Press, 1997), 183–184.
2. Gloria Anzaldúa, *Light in the Dark / Luz en lo Oscuro: Rewriting Identity, Spirituality, Reality*, ed. AnaLouise Keating (Duke University Press, 2015), 140.

3. Gordon, *Ghostly Matters*, 184. For the original citation, see Jacques Derrida, "Spectres of Marx," *New Left Review* 205, no. 205 (1994): xvii.
4. Paolo Freire, *Pedagogy of the Oppressed*, 30th anniversary ed., trans. Myra Bergman Ramos (Bloomsbury, 2014), 51.
5. Student reflections, Histories of Chicana Feminisms, fall 2023 and spring 2024.
6. American Federation of Teachers (AFT) and American Association of University Professors (AAUP), "Analysis of Texas SB 16, 17 and 18," 2023. See also Brant Bingamon, "The Right-Wingification of UT: Texas Targets Liberal Enemies Within One of the Top U.S. Schools," *Austin Chronicle*, November 22, 2024, https://www.austinchronicle.com/news/2024-11-22/the-right-wingification-of-ut/.
7. AFT and AAUP, "Analysis of Texas SB 16, 17 and 18."
8. Becky Fogel, "Texas House Panel Walks Back Senators' Effort to Ban Tenure at Public Universities," *KUT News*, May 9, 2023, https://www.kut.org/education/2023-05-09/texas-house-panel-walks-back-senators-effort-to-ban-tenure-at-public-universities.
9. AFT and AAUP, "Analysis of Texas SB 16, 17 and 18."
10. Lily Kepner, "What UT Lost with SB 17: American-Statesman's Guide to Changes Due to Texas' Anti-DEI Law," *Austin American-Statesman*, January 29, 2024, https://www.statesman.com/story/news/politics/state/2024/01/29/dei-ban-texas-sb17-law-meaning-guide-what-ut-public-universities-lost/72283717007/.
11. Osa Hidalgo de la Riva and Maylei Blackwell, "Visions of Utopia While Living in Occupied Aztlán," in *Chicana Movidas: New Narratives of Activism and Feminism in the Movement Era*, ed. Dionne Espinoza, María Eugenia Cotera, and Maylei Blackwell (University of Texas Press, 2021), 222.
12. Brianna Chavero, Giselle Cerda, and Alyssa Soto, introduction to *Tlamatini*, spring 2024.

# INDEX

Note: Page numbers in *italics* refer to figures.